"REGGIANE"

REGGIO EMILIA

FIGHTERS

RE.2000 *Falco* • RE.2001 *Ariete I* • RE.2002 *Ariete II*
RE.2005 *Sagittario*

LUIGINO CALIARO

THE AUTHOR

Luigino Caliaro is an acclaimed aviation photographer based in northern Italy. He has flown in the 'back seat' of many aircraft starting with an RAF Tucano in 1995. Since then he has flown numerous photo-sorties with many of the world's premier military aerobatic demonstration teams including the US Navy's Blue Angels, the Canadian Snowbirds, the Frecce Tricolori and the Red Arrows. He has photographed, air-to-air, many of the world's most advanced military jet aircraft including the F-15, F-16, F/A-18, Tornado, Mirage, MiG-29 and Harrier, and also flown a six-hour mission on board a B-1B 'Lancer'. He has visited US Navy and French aircraft carriers several times and he has made a landing and take-off in an Italian Navy Harrier from the deck of the aircraft carrier *Garibaldi*. In addition, he has flown photo-sorties with aircraft from several historical aviation collections and museums around the world.

Luigino is the author of several books on Italian aviation history and aviation photography, including the acclaimed *Savoia-Marchetti S.79 Sparviero – From Airliner and Record-Breaker to Bomber and Torpedo-Bomber 1934-1947* and in his trilogy on the Italian fighters of World War II, *Aeronautica Macchi Fighters – C.200 Saetta, C.202 Folgore, C.205 Veltro* and *FIAT Aeritalia Fighters – CR.32, CR.42 Falco, G.50 Freccia and G.55 Centauro*, all published by Crecy. He has also written numerous magazine and journal articles published in the English language in Aeroplane, FlyPast and *The Aviation Historian*.

REGGIANE Fighters
© 2025 Luigino Caliaro

First published 2025

ISBN 978-1-80035-352-7
Produced by Chevron Publishing Limited
Project Editor: Robert Forsyth
Book design: Mark Nelson

© Colour profiles: A. Brioschi
© Line artwork: A. Brioschi

The Editor wishes to thank Nick Beale and Mikael Olrog for their kind assistance during the preparation of this book.

© Crécy Publishing Ltd. 2025
Classic is an imprint of Crécy Publishing Ltd.
1a Ringway Trading Estate,
Shadowmoss Road, Manchester, M22 5LH
Visit the Crécy Publishing website at:
www.crecy.co.uk

Printed in Türkiye.

CLASSIC
An Imprint of
Crécy Publishing

MIX
Paper | Supporting responsible forestry
FSC® C176481

Contents

Preface and Author's Note
Acknowledgements
Glossary and Military Ranks

Preface

WITH this third volume dedicated to the Italian fighters of the 1930s and 1940s, it is my intention to offer a tribute, however succinct and limited by available space, to the aircraft produced by Reggiane, one of the main manufacturers of aircraft in Italy during the Second World War, which, unfairly and in some respects unjustifiably, has remained somewhat in the shadow of other well-known firms such as FIAT and AerMacchi.

In fact, despite the relatively small number of aircraft manufactured by the Reggio Emilia Officine Meccaniche Reggiane in the ten-year period following its acquisition by Caproni in 1935, it produced a successful series of single-seat fighters which had the misfortune of entering service late and in too few numbers.

Without doubt, such adverse circumstances caused a lack of understanding and support on the part of the Regia Aeronautica over the efforts of Reggiane to provide up-to-date fighter aircraft. These efforts, such as in the case of the RE.2000, included cutting-edge design and construction, the design of an aircraft with wet wings, the use of Alclad, and radiators built into wings.

Unfortunately, pressed by the war and the need to supply operationally ready aircraft urgently, Reggio Emilia Officine Meccaniche Reggiane was denied time to develop effective and practical solutions. The decision in April 1945 taken by the newly established Reggiane Management Commission, which had pushed out *Ing.* Caproni and the managerial staff of the establishment, oversaw the restructuring of the company and the final decision to abandon all aeronautical activity, thus scattering the intellectual heritage and significant experience of such an important firm to oblivion.

This was not an easy book to research, both because of the difficulty in finding a good photographic record of the period of service with the Regia Aeronautica and because of the destruction and loss of a part of the company archives and especially those of the Regia Aeronautica – in particular records covering the last year of war before the armistice. It has therefore been necessary to make good use of the considerable research carried out over the years by distinguished colleagues, and in doing so, amidst the fragmented surviving documentation with its inconsistencies, to check and cross-reference information wherever, and as much as possible to achieve an accurate account.

I hope, however, that this work will stimulate the reader's interest and I also hope that, in the near future, there will be the possibility to continue this series of publications on the aircraft and activities of the Regia Aeronautica with further studies on bombers, reconnaissance and transport aircraft.

LUIGINO CALIARO
JUNE 2025

Acknowledgements

THERE are many people I have to thank for helping me in the preparation of this work, but most of all, I extend a special thanks and my loving memory to my friend *Giorgio Apostolo*, my 'aeronautical father', who recently passed away and whose role was fundamental in the supply of documents, drawings and most of the photographs included in the book. They have been used previously by my late friend Sergio Govi in his seminal research into Reggiane and its aircraft which was published several years ago by G.A.E. (Giorgio Apostolo Editore).

From the outset of my activity into historic research, Giorgio Apostolo always helped me, advising and encouraging me as an aviation photographer and researcher, always making his immense photographic archive available to me.

This book is dedicated to Giorgio's memory.

I also give my special thanks to Giulio Cesare Valdonio, Adriano and Paolo Riatti, for their support with documents and information, and to Enrico Leproni for helping me with the chapter on the RE.2000 *Catapultabile*.

I am grateful to Paolo Waldis who provided the colour profiles and drawings of Reggiane fighters created by the late Angelo Brioschi and who, thanks to his knowledge of aircraft modelling and history, contributed the chapter dedicated to the camouflage of Reggiane fighters.

Thanks also to Mikael Olrog and Gyorgy Punka who assisted me in the preparation of the chapter on use of the RE.2000 in Sweden and Hungary respectively. My thanks also to Nick Beale for his kind assistance with information on usage of Reggiane aircraft by the Luftwaffe.

An important photographic contribution came from Mario Federighi of ASF (Archivio Storico Federighi).

ARCHIVIO STORICO FEDERIGHI

My thanks also to my friends Bruno Fochesato, Enrico Leproni, Fabrizio Sanetti, Franco Storchi, Giovanni Massimello, Loris Meneghini, Massimo Amatiello, Paolo Monti, Paolo Borgonovi, Paolo Pesaresi, Pelle Lindquist, Roberto Gentilli, Saro Finocchiaro, and to Frank McMeiken for helping me with English translation.

LUIGINO CALIARO
JUNE 2025

Photo Credits

Unless expressly indicated, the photographs in this book are taken from the Giorgio Apostolo archive (GA), via Caliaro, and also as provided by the author. The author also thanks the following for photographic material provided:

AM	fototeca Aeronautica Militare
AUSAM	Archivio Ufficio Storico Aeronautica Militare
AMAM	Archivio Museo Aeronautica Militare
ASF	Archivio Storico Federighi

Adriano and Paolo Riatti
Enrico Leproni
Fabrizio Sanetti
Federico Anselmino
Francesco Ballista
Gyorgy Punka
Giulio Cesare Valdonio
Maurizio Di Terlizzi
Mikael Olrog
Paolo Monti
Paolo Borgonovi

Pelle Lindquist
Roberto Gentilli

Author's Note

THE term Regia Aeronautica Cobelligerente is used in the text although this term has never been used officially in Italy, because until 18 June 1946 titles such as Regia Aeronautica were maintained. The 'Cobelligerente' suffix was used by the Allies, and was used in Italy by Italians after the war, very often to distinguish the activities of the Regia Aeronautica after the armistice. The author, for the sake of clarity and simplification, has used this post-war designation.

For the sake of uniformity, the initials of the Reggiane fighters have been kept in the text as they appeared in the official technical documents of the Regia Aeronautica, such as Technical Instruction Manual, that is to say with the all-capital prefix 'RE' followed by the project number.

LC
2025

Glossary

ANR	Aviazione Nazionale Repubblicana	National Republican Air Force
Aut.	Autonomo	Autonomous
B.A.	Brigata Aerea	Air Brigate
CT	Caccia Terrestri	Land-based fighter
C.T.V.	Corpo Truppe Volontarie	Volunteer Troops Corps
DGCA	Direzione Generale delle Costruzioni Aeronautiche	General Directorate of Aeronautical Construction
Gr.	Gruppo	Squadron
M.O.V.M.	Medaglia d'Oro al Valor Militare	Gold Medal for Military Valor
MM	Matricola Militare	Military Serial
R.S.I.	Repubblica Sociale Italiana	Italian Social Republic
RA	Regia Aeronautica	Italian Royal Air Force
Sq.	Squadriglia	Flight
St.	Stormo	Wing
SRAM	Servizo Riparazione Aeromobili e Motori	Aircraft and engine reparation unit

Non-Italian units

HUNGARIAN
Vadászrepülő Ezred	Fighter Wing
Vadászrepülő Század	Fighter Squadron
Vadászrepülő Osztály	Fighter Group

SWEDISH
Flottilj	Wing

Military Ranks

ABBREVIATION	ITALIAN	BRITISH	AMERICAN
Gen. SA	Generale Squadra Aerea	Air Marshall	Lieutenant General
Gen. DA	Generale Divisione Aerea	Air Vice Marshall	Major General
Gen. BA	Generale Brigata Aerea	Air Commodore	Brigadier General
Col.	Colonnello	Group Captain	Colonel
Ten.Col.	Tenente Colonnello	Wing Commander	Lieutenant Colonel
Magg.	Maggiore	Squadron Leader	Major
Cap.	Capitano	Flight Lieutenant	Captain
Ten.	Tenente	Flying Officer	1st Lieutenant
S.Ten.	Sottotenente	Pilot Officer	2nd Lieutenant
M.llo	Maresciallo	Warrant Officer	Master Sergeant
Serg.Magg.	Sergente Maggiore	Flight Sergeant	Staff Sergeant
Serg.	Sergente	Sergeant	Senior Airman
AvSc.	Aviere Scelto	Leading Aircraftman	Airman 1st Class
Av.	Aviere	Aircraftman	Airman

CHAPTER ONE

A Proud History

OFFICINE MECCANICHE ITALIANE S. A.
REGGIO EMILIA (ITALIA)

DURING the first half of the last century, Officine Meccaniche Italiane Società Anonima, also known as Officine Meccaniche Reggiane (O.M.I.), but more generally referred to by the simplified form of 'Reggiane', was a key element in the history of Italian manufacturing, and in particular in the Emilia region. Founded at the beginning of the nineteenth century and specialising in the manufacture of railway rolling stock and artillery shells, after its acquisition by the Gruppo Caproni, Reggiane became famous for the production of fighter aircraft.

The company was established in 1901 as the 'Officina Meccanica e Fonderia Ing. Romano Righi e C.' by *Ingegner* Righi and *Commendatore* Giuseppe Menada at Reggio Emilia. ln 1904 it was renamed as the 'Società Anonima Officine Meccaniche Reggiane'. This was a particularly important industrial initiative in a social and economic context for the predominantly agricultural Emilia area. It did not limit production to agricultural machinery, but rather expanded it to include the mechanical equipment and railway sectors, the firm's output including locomotives, passenger coaches and freight wagons; it expanded its operations through the acquisition of further companies, such as the Società Officine Ferroviarie Italiane Anonima in 1912, changing its company name to 'Officine Meccaniche Italiane Società Anonima'.

Above: A Reggiane advertisement from the mid-1930s highlights some of the company's products for the agricultural sector.

Above left: During the late 1920s, the production of trams was an important business line for Officine Reggiane.

Below: Between 1910 and 1937, Officine Reggiane built 160 steam locomotives, of all types, both standard and narrow gauge.

The scale of this Reggiane-built FS (*Ferrovie dello Stato*) locomotive, E428, gives an impression of mechanical power. (arch. Officine Reggiane - Sgarbi/Savi)

The FS locomotive, FS 683, was futuristic and streamlined. (arch. Officine Reggiane - Sgarbi/Savi)

An aerial view of the Reggiane works in the late 1920s. To the centre right of the photograph are the four two-storey 'Cairo' blocks with their white roofs. Their colour and relative isolation from the main works meant that they were almost a village in a 'desert', hence the name with its North African connotations. At the end of the 1930s, a third floor was added to each of the buildings (not built at the time of this photograph), which housed a total of 96 families, all numbering Reggiane employees, as well as the aviation departments and the company's after-work area.

With the outbreak of the First World War, the company commenced operations in the military sector with the production of artillery munitions, an activity requiring an extraordinary effort by the firm which, until that date, had had no prior experience in the field. Indeed, to undertake the task, Officine Meccaniche Italiane Società Anonima ordered new machinery directly from the United States and increased its number of employees from 1,200 in 1914 to almost 3,000 the following year. Production gradually expanded during the first years of the war, at its maximum level reaching more than 10,000 artillery shells produced daily by the end of 1916 by a force of 6,000 workers, 1,200 of whom were female.

In 1917 Officine Meccaniche Italiane Società Anonima entered the world of aviation thanks to an accord stipulated with the Società Aeronautica Caproni for the production of a large order for 300 tri-motor Ca.5 bombers.[1] In preparation for production, Officine Meccaniche Italiane Società Anonima built some 12,000 sq.m. of new workshops and explored the possibility of establishing an airfield adjacent to its facility for the flight-testing of the manufactured aircraft.

However, following a series of technical problems and production delays, the actual manufacture of the aircraft never took place and it was possible only to commence production and preparation of component parts. It is not known, with any certainty, if and how many aircraft were eventually constructed at Reggio Emilia prior to the end of the conflict, although certain sources state that some of the aircraft produced were lost following the destruction in a fierce thunderstorm of the workshops in which they were stored. However it has been confirmed that at least one bomber was assembled by Officine Meccaniche Italiane Società Anonima personnel at the Caproni facility.

After the war, despite numerous acquisitions of other companies aimed at diversifying production (ranging from silos and agricultural equipment to machinery for mills, bakeries and brick-making), the company went through a particularly difficult period, aggravated by the global crisis of 1929 and culminating, in 1933, with the acquisition of Reggiane by the *Istituto per la Riconstruction Industriale (I.R.I.)*, an operation which was essential in saving the company from potential failure.

The year 1935 was a turning point, as it saw the acquisition by the Gruppo Industriale Aeronautico Caproni of a majority shareholding, giving impetus to a radical transformation of the then renamed Reggiane Officine Meccaniche Italiane Società Anonima into a large military aviation complex and proving fundamental to the conditioning and direction of the company policies, while establishing the future of the industrial facility at Reggio Emilia over the successive decade.

The then *Direttore Generale* (managing director) was *Ing*. Giovanni Degola.

In a short period, and thanks to a substantial government contribution, a multi-faceted aeronautical programme was devised. This was to be achieved partly through the licence construction of the parent company's aircraft and in part by designs conceived by the Ufficio Studi e Brevetti Gruppo Caproni, constituted in 1936 at Reggio Emilia and led by *Ing*. Giovanni Pegna. The year 1936 also saw the creation of the *Motori Avio* (aircraft engine) department which produced under licence from Piaggio, the P.VII C.16 radial engine, while later, Piaggio also licensed manufacture of

[1] This was the designation given to the bomber by the *Esercito Italiano*, while Caproni designated it as the Ca.44.

GIANNI CAPRONI

BORN at Massone d'Arco in 1886, at the time an Austrian territory, GIANNI CAPRONI graduated in civil engineering from the Königlich Bayerische Technische Hochschule in Munich in 1907, gaining a further specialist qualification in electronics in the following year at the Montefiori Institute in Liège.

After some early experience in the construction of powered aircraft, in 1908 he founded the Caproni workshops at Taliedo, near Milano Linate, intended to produce biplanes. From 1911, however, he concentrated, with greater success, on the production of monoplanes. In 1914 he tested the Ca.31, a tri-motor biplane bomber which was the first multi-engine aircraft built in Italy and is considered to be the best bomber aircraft constructed in the course of the First World War. He was one of the early promoters of the use of aircraft for civilian passenger transport and in 1921 constructed the CA.60, a flying boat capable of carrying some one-hundred passengers, although this prototype was destroyed during the course of its inaugural flight. Between the wars the Caproni company assumed the scale of a true industrial group, incorporating more than twenty mechanical and aeronautical businesses which employed more than 40,000 staff, its activities expanding into the engine, factory-building, and armament sectors. From the mid-1930s, the Caproni aeronautical concern, which specialised in the construction of bomber, reconnaissance and transport aircraft, was concentrated at Taliedo (Milano) under the guidance of ingegneri Verduzio and Conflenti and at C.A.B. (Caproni Aeronautica Bergamasca) at Ponte San Pietro, near Bergamo, and directed by ingegner Pallavicino.

Despite the post-war difficulties, Caproni continued its aeronautical activities until its acquisition by the Agusta company in 1983.

Gianni Caproni, an Italian aviation pioneer and the founder of the company bearing his name, died in Roma in 1957.

Gianni Caproni sits in the fuselage of a monoplane built at Taliedo in 1911.

A Caproni Ca.32 (300 hp) at Taliedo in July 1915. On board is Giovanni 'Gianni' Caproni at left and *sottotenente* Laureati to right.

Gianni Caproni, centre with fur-lined coat, with other collaborators at the Bergamo San Pietro field headquarters of Caproni Aeronautica Bergamasca.

One of the handful of Caproni Ca.5 assembled by Reggiane workers in preparation for the commencement of production that was stopped by the end of the First World War.

The P.32 bis prototype equipped with two 815-hp Isotta Fraschini Asso XI RC.40 engines.

On 14 February 1938, a second prototype of the P.32 bis, equipped with Piaggio P.XI RC.40 engines, took flight.

This view of the Ca 405 clearly shows the sleek modifications to the front of the aircraft which had been prepared for the Istres-Damascus-Paris air race.

On 25 February 1938, during its return to the airfield at the end of the sixth test flight, the P.32 bis prototype suffered a failure in its left engine, followed by a fire. In the emergency landing, mechanics Casali and Pugi, despite severe injuries and burns, managed to escape the wreckage, while test pilot Mario Gamna tragically perished in the flames having been unable to exit the cockpit.

the C 35 and C 45 versions of the P.VII, the P.VI bis, the P.XI bis, and the P.XV. Fiat issued a licence for the production of its A.74.

During the spring of 1936 the company obtained an order to build twenty-four P.32 bis bombers, a version of the Piaggio aircraft redesigned by Reggiane on the basis of the original failed Piaggio P.32 bomber design. Compared to the original aircraft, the P.32 bis, while retaining the same wing and Isotta Fraschini Asso XI RC.40 engines, featured a new fuselage and tailplanes.

On 23 February 1937, with test pilot Mario Gamna at the controls, the Caproni Ca. 405 *Procellaria* also made its first flight. It was a newly developed version of the P.32 bis designed specifically for participation in the Istres-Damascus-Paris race scheduled for summer 1937. However, set-up delays and issues with the Isotta

Fraschini engines resulted in the decision to drop the competition.

A similar fate met the P.32 bis bomber, development of which was plagued by delays and technical problems and which led to re-engining the project using Piaggio P.XI RC40 radials. The loss of one of the two prototypes, which caused the death of test pilot Gamna, led to the reduction of the order to sixteen aircraft, but even this was eventually cancelled in 1938.

In 1937 Reggiane obtained a licence from SIAI-Marchetti to manufacture the S.79 *Sparviero* tri-motor bomber, establishing a production line in the Reggio Emilia facility the following year. This was a particularly important success, and by the end of the conflict production of the S.79 by Reggiane was second only to that undertaken by SIAI.

This opportunity, furthermore, facilitated a significant increase in the turnover of the aeronautical sector which, by 1939, accounted for 80 per cent of the industrial group's total turnover. During 1938 however, despite two years of work, the results produced by the considerable amount of design work did not live up to expectations, leading to the decision to close the Caproni Group's Patent and Study Office, reserving an advisory role for *Ing*. Pegna. Consequently, a new design office was organised under the leadership of *Ing*. Giuseppe Pambianchi, who held the official title of *Capo Ufficio Tecnico Aviazione* (Chief of the Aviation Technical Office) but who, in practice, was a general technical director, assisted by *Ing*. Fidia Piattelli.

The S.79 assembly line at Reggio Emilia.

Below: An Officine Reggiane advertisement of 1940, showing factory-fresh S.79s rolled out of the workshops.

Right: An S.79 'tri-motor' in one of the hangars built inside the Reggiane works and used for aircraft assembly. The photograph was probably taken in late September 1938.

An S.79 photographed on landing at Reggio Emilia airport after a post-production test flight. One of the assembly hangars and a control tower can clearly be seen.

GIUSEPPE PAMBIANCHI

BORN at Senigallia on 5 October 1908, Pambianchi graduated in aeronautical engineering from the *Politecnico* di Torino in 1932. For around two years he was engaged by IMAM (Industrie Meccaniche Aeronautiche Merdionali) of Napoli, where he worked on the design of the Ro.37 and Ro.41 before being recruited by Reggiane with the initial qualification of *Capo Ufficio Tecnico Aviazione* (Chief of the Aviation Technical Office) and subsequently Capo *Ufficio Progetti Aeronautici* (Chief of the Aeronautical Design Office). His work materialised with the RE.2000 and RE.2001 projects. A highly skilled technical designer, Pambianchi was, however, involved in a dispute with *Ispettore tecnico* Roberto Longhi over interference in the design process, culminating in the case of the RE.2002 wing failure, caused by unapproved modifications introduced directly by Longhi, but officially attributed to Pambianchi and resulting in the latter's dismissal. He was replaced by *Ing.* Vardanega. Having moved on to work for Caproni at Taliedo, at the end of 1943 he became *Direttore Ufficio Tecnico Progetti* (Director of the Technical Design Office) with Piaggio at Pontedera (Pisa). At the end of the war Pambianchi left Piaggio, rejoining the company in 1947 to organise a commercial network to support the sale of the Piaggio Vespa scooter. He died on 23 April 1960 at Ancona.

Ing. Giuseppe Pambianchi, head of the Ufficio Progetti Aeronautici, and responsible for the design of RE.2000 and RE.2001. (Fam. Gentili)

An RE.2000 prototype exhibited at a Milan fair in 1942.

In this arena, another important aspect must be considered, in that during the 1930s the Regia Aeronautica had pursued a policy of attempting to assign different Italian companies to different specialist sectors, which until the appearance of the AerMacchi C.200, saw fighter aircraft development conducted by an unopposed monopoly in the shape of FIAT. Probably to avoid competing with the apparent expertise and industrial and political might of the Torino-based FIAT group, in previous years the designs created by the Gruppo Caproni were exclusively focused in the bomber and transport aircraft sector. After the mid-1930s, with the requirement for the Regia Aeronautica to renew its fighter fleet, Caproni decided to engage itself in this new sector. This was probably driven by the growing success of the multi-engine bomber and transport aircraft manufactured by Savoia Marchetti, which were gradually eroding the market position established until that point by the Gruppo Caproni. However, noting a certain lack of in-house technical design capabilities, Caproni considered producing a foreign fighter design under licence.

Fundamental to the advance in quality and the advancement of Reggiane on an industrial and technical level was an educational tour of some of the most important American aeronautical companies. This took place at the end of 1937 for a delegation from the company which included *Ingegneri* Antonio Alessio, the deputy *Direttore Generale* of Reggiane, and Fidia Piattelli from the *Ufficio Progetti Aeronautici*. The tour afforded access to the new manufacturing and design techniques being introduced by American manufacturers. The tangible result of this experience on American soil was realisation of the RE.2000 design, a modern fighter, which, although appearing structurally to be a copy of the Seversky P.35, featured a completely redesigned wing and undercarriage. The aircraft achieved limited international success, although not with the Regia Aeronautica, which acquired just a limited number of examples and which preferred the FIAT G.50 and AerMacchi C.200 designs.

Over the following years, until the cessation of aeronautical activities following the destruction of the factory by Allied bombs, Reggiane designed and built another series of fighter and attack monoplanes. This was identified with the RE prefix and project numbering from 2000 to 2006, but was marked by alternating fortunes in sales with the Regia Aeronautica, evidenced by the final construction figures. Despite this situation, in some respects paradoxical, the early 1940s were a particularly prosperous period for the company, which expanded to employ more than 11,000 personnel in 1942, making Officine Meccaniche Reggiane the principal factory in the Emilia Romagna region and one of the main industries of the nation.

During this time, the company was divided into a number of production groups. The most important was undoubtedly that of *avio e motori* (aircraft and engines) which was accommodated in three large manufacturing hangars, 167 metres in length, 42 metres wide, and 18 metres high. These formed the aircraft assembly lines, to which was added another smaller building utilised by the

Aircraft were assembled close to the airport so that it would be easier to move them from the factory to test them. The proximity of the airport to the company was one of the innovations that made Reggiane a company at the forefront of aviation in Italy.

The interior of the assembly shop. In the foreground is the RE.2000 line and in the background, beyond the concrete pillars, is the S.79 assembly line. The photograph was taken in mid-December 1940.

View of the military area at Reggio Emilia airport with the three hangars built by Reggiane before the 1940-1945 war.

Advertisements from the 1940s highlight some of the products that made Reggiane famous: trains, agricultural tools, engines and aircraft.

experimental unit. Available for flight-testing was a paved runway connected to the hangars, some 1,000 metres long and 60 metres wide, together with the complete infrastructure to support flying operations, including fuel storage, a control tower, and a protected area for armament calibration.

To store the completed aircraft there were three large metal trellis construction hangars measuring 120 x 36 metres.

The aircraft and engine groups were flanked by a *ferroviaria*,[2] *agricola e di lavorazione meccaniche* (railway, agriculture and mechanical engineering) group, and by metalwork shops and administrative departments. Reggiane's significant production capacity was always a matter of concern for the Allies, who bombed the plant on several occasions, only managing to finally halt production in January 1944.

In the immediate post-war period, and under the terms of the peace conditions imposed by the Allies, the company's Management Committee took control of the company, forcing, among other things, *Ing*. Alessio to leave the management. The Committee also decided to abandon all aeronautical production – a surprising fact considering the production potential in the sector, as well as the projects being developed for the civil sector. This effectively forced Caproni to sell the company.

O.M.I. Reggiane was therefore forced to downsize and adapt its production activities in order to survive, turning mainly to the railway and agricultural mechanics sectors. A move into the automotive sector was also attempted, but to no avail.

The post-war period was also difficult because of a long series of trades union disputes, which resulted in an occupation of the factory by workers. After many years, this turned out to be the longest occupation of a factory in the history of the Italian workers' movement.

In this period of 'self-management', three R.60 farm tractors were completed which, as intended by the workers, were to represent a symbol of redemption and renewed manufacturing capacity. Their efforts were in vain and in 1951 Reggiane collapsed. Of its 11,000 employees, its fast aircraft, and the famous trains from its period of glory, nothing remained.

In 1952 there was an attempt at a recovery launched by the newly constituted Nuove Reggiane Officine Meccaniche Italiane Società per Azioni, which tried to diversify production in various sectors, resuming operations with around 700 staff.

---

[2] Railway production was the principal activity of Reggiane for decades, and between 1921 and 1946 almost 1,000 locomotives of every type were completed.

Ingegnere Antonio Alessio (left) and Roberto Longhi in front of a Hungarian RE.2000 shortly to be delivered.

ANTONIO ALESSIO

BORN in Padova in 1891, Antonio Alessio graduated in mechanical engineering from the Politecnico di Torino. After working at Ansaldo and FIAT, he was appointed to run the production facility for N.S.U. motorcycles at Heilbronn in Germany. Returning to Italy, he worked as director of FIAT's agricultural machinery factory in Modena, later moving on to work for Piaggio and subsequently at the Officine Meccaniche Reggiane, initially as Technical Director and later assuming the role of *Vice Direttore Generale*. In 1941, upon the death of Giovanni Degola following a horse-riding accident, he became *Direttore Generale* of Reggiane. After the war, he was a director of Isotta Fraschini and subsequently worked in significant roles in the racing sector of Alfa Romeo and later with a major international transport company.

TOTAL REGGIANE AIRCRAFT PRODUCTION
Aircraft Constructed under Licence

Piaggio P.32 bis: 2 aircraft
Caproni Ca.405:   2 aircraft
Savoia-Marchetti S.79:   405 aircraft (under licence from Savoia-Marchetti)

THE '2000 SERIES' FIGHTERS DESIGNED AND PRODUCED BY REGGIANE

RE.2000: 158 (of which 60 for the Swedish Air Force and 70 for the Hungarian Air Force)
RE.2001: 237 examples (including 1 Re.2001 Delta and 10 CN constructed by Caproni Predappio)
RE.2002: around 250 examples (70 constructed by Caproni at Taliedo)
RE.2003: 2 examples
RE.2005: 32 examples

Engine construction
With the acquisition of the plant by the Caproni Group, Reggiane's aviation activities commenced in 1936, including the establishment of a *Motori Avio* (aircraft engine) department. In this department, the first production work concerned the licensed construction of Piaggio P.VII and FIAT A.74 engines. After an initial slow start, with the first engine being tested in September 1936, production steadily progressed, reaching a peak of 90 engines per month produced in the following year, but declining slightly between 1938 and early 1939 as a result of delays in the allocation of new supplies and raw materials. Output totalled around 800 engines in mid-1939.

In 1940 an Engine Technical Office was set up with the task of designing its own engines, adopting the RE 101 to RE 105 designations to identify them. In reality, the engines developed in this period were reworkings of engines produced by other companies, such as the RE 104 RC.38, which was derived from the Isotta Fraschini Asso L.121 RC.40. This engine was proposed, unsuccessfully, as an alternative engine to the German Daimler-Benz DB 601 in 1941.

The only Reggiane-designed engine that was actually realised was the RE 103 RC 50, an in-line, 18-cylinder, inverted W engine with a power output of 1,500 hp, conceived in two versions for fighter and bomber aircraft. However, due to delays in development, it was only ready in 1942. Intended as a power unit for the Reggiane RE.2004, the RE 103 was abandoned in favour of the 24-cylinder Isotta Fraschini *Zeta*, having revealed serious tuning problems. In the summer of 1943, the same RE 103 engine was the basis of a design for a version optimised for high altitudes, designated RE 105, the development of which was dropped following the events of the armistice.

In the meantime, the Reggiane engine department continued the licence manufacture of Piaggio P.VII engines and the new P.XI bis until the armistice of 8 September, an event which led to the decision by the German authorities to bring a complete halt to engine development and

---

A small upturn in the company's fortunes was recorded in the 1960s and 1980s when production was diversified into the construction of plants for sugar mills and with the construction of port cranes. In 1992 the company was taken over by the Gruppo Fantuzzi, becoming Fantuzzi Reggiane, and later, in 2008, it was sold on to the American TEREX group, which relocated its operations to other sites, finally abandoning the historical home of the factory.

Brief considerations
Between 1936 and 1944, Reggiane aviation production amounted to 1,260 aircraft, including those under licence from other manufacturers, while the output of engines was also considerable. Of significance is the fact that the aircraft constructed in the greatest number was not one designed by Reggiane, but rather the Savoia Marchetti S.79 tri-motor, which was produced in 405 examples in comparison to 350 RE.2000s, 237 RE.2001s, 225 RE.2002s, and just 32 RE.2005s. These apparently limited results cannot necessarily be attributed to the company itself, as Reggiane was considered to be amongst the best of the businesses operating in the sector in Italy during the period. The production limitations resulted mainly from problems with the availability of prime materials and other resources. One example was the production of the RE.2001 which was always handicapped by the limited availability of DB 601 engines. This engine had been assigned over the preferred AerMacchi C.202, a situation which did not optimise the potential level of production offered by the firm's facilities. Even construction of the successful RE.2002 was penalised by the decision to use a relatively unreliable engine despite the aircraft's good technical and flight characteristics.

Another aspect which penalised series production was the order situation created by the Regia Aeronautica. It was almost always the case that, faced with commitments for hundreds of aircraft ordered by the *Ministero dell'Aviazione*, within a short time orders were reduced or cancelled (something which rarely occurred to those orders placed with other Italian manufacturers). The *Ministero* often cited the need to introduce technical modifications or modifications associated with revised mission requirements for the aircraft. Accordingly, this situation created difficulties for the company which, in most cases, had already committed significant sums of money to the supply of materials. Requests for modifications and variants by the Regia Aeronautica had a negative impact on production, causing slowdowns and hindrances to design and production activities as well as, of course, a consequent increase in costs.

Particularly significant in this regard was the detailed and heartfelt report addressed to the *Direzione Generale* in May 1942 by the then *Direttore Amministrativo*, *Sig.* Bellelli, who summed up the situation of the company

'Reggiane has endured notable sacrifices in its aeronautical production, and especially in that of aircraft. Production has taken place in exceptionally uneconomic conditions due to the continuous vicissitudes suffered in the progress of work. Orders initially awarded were subsequently cancelled when work had already started or cancelled with notable losses due to unutilised equipment or unnecessary work already completed or interrupted. Orders that were able to be completed proved to be economically disadvantageous due to the continual modifications introduced at the request of the responsible ministry.'

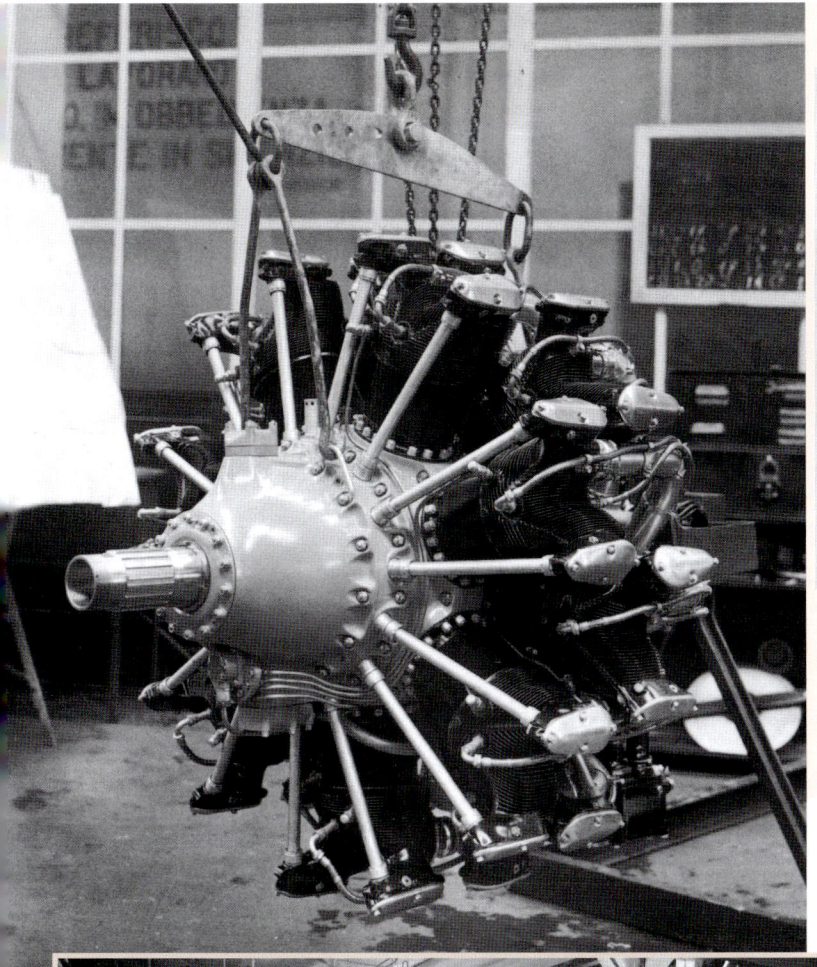

Above: Piaggio P.VII engines. It was the first P series aircraft engine produced by Rinaldo Piaggio S.p.A. based on its experience licence-producing the Gnome-Rhône 7K. Reggiane built 1,231 such engines which were used on a wide range of Italian aircraft before and during the Second World War, including the Breda 25 and 28, Caproni transport aircraft such as the Ca.133, and Ca.148, and training aircraft such as the IMAM Ro.41.

Left: A FIAT A.74 RC38 engine. A total of 1,722 engines of this type were delivered by Reggiane in the period 1936-1943. Many aircraft, including the FIAT CR.25, CR.42 and G.50, the AerMacchi C.200, the IMAM Ro.57 and Caproni Vizzola F.5 were equipped with the A.74.

Above: The engine test room with two Piaggio P.VII engines running.

Two views of the P.VII engine production lines at Reggiane.

A completed Piaggio P.XI bis engine awaiting running tests.

Three advertisements for engines built by Reggiane in 1940/1941.

production. In total, the seven active years of the *Motori Avio* department can be assessed by the delivery of 4,074 engines, divided between 1,231 Piaggio P.VIIs, 1,722 Fiat A.74s and 1,121 Piaggio P.XI bis.

The bombing of O.M.I. Reggiane

Following the German occupation of the factory after the armistice of 8 September 1943, production continued under the direct control of the General Representative of the Reich Ministry of Armaments and War Production in Italy. This continuation of activity, however, exposed Reggiane to the attention of the Allies, and the company's facilities became the target of heavy bombing raids by the Allied air forces. Despite their importance to the war effort, the Reggiane establishments possessed limited defences against Allied attacks, yet production and overhaul operations for Reggiane aircraft continued during the course of the war, even into the last months of 1943. The definitive halt in production occurred in January 1944 due to more heavy bombing raids which, besides causing the destruction of the production lines, resulted in the death of more than 260 people and injuries to another 250, as well as devastation to the Reggio Emila suburb of Santa Croce.

The first of this series of attacks, carried out on the night of 7 January 1944 by the RAF, caused at least 68 civilian casualties, but relatively little material damage to the plant due to the scattering of bombs, some of which hit the city centre and surrounding suburbs. The USAAF bombing raid on the following day, 8 January 1944, was the most destructive, and was conducted in daylight by 109 B-17 F/Gs of the 2nd, 97th, 99th and 301st Bomb Groups of the 5th Bomb Wing, escorted by 32 P-38 Lightnings of the 14th Fighter Group. The Americans dropped more than 320 tonnes of bombs over the factory, although some also struck the civilian quarters adjacent to the facility, sowing death and devastation. By the end of this tragic day there had been some 196 fatalities, the majority from the civilian population, and it was calculated that more than 1,300 bombs had been dropped on the city of Reggio Emilia in the course of the two raids. At least 350 bombs hit the large factory directly, enough to destroy the plant and its production lines, bringing output to a complete standstill.

Above: At 13.32 hrs on 8 January 1944, over 100 B-17 Flying Fortresses of the US Fifteenth Air Force dropped their bombs on Reggio Emilia and the Officine Reggiane factory. This photograph was taken from a B-17 of the 99th BG and shows a bomb falling towards the town of Reggio Emilia. The Reggiane factory is not visible due to the explosions of the bombs. (USAF)

Left and above: Two photographs taken from USAAF reconnaissance aircraft after the devastating bombing raid of 8 January 1944 over Reggio Emilia. The Reggiane factory was the main target and the factory was destroyed. (USAF)

The American bombs destroyed the factory and Reggiane's tooling, as well as a variety of aircraft under construction. Despite the military importance of Reggiane, no aerial defence was planned in the eventuality of an air attack.

CHAPTER TWO

RE.2000 *Falco*

Evolution and Production

An advertisement for the RE.2000 from 1941.

FOLLOWING the closure of the *Ufficio Studi e Brevetti* of the Gruppo Caproni in 1937, *ingegner* Pegna was employed as a personal consultant to Gianni Caproni, while *ingegner* Pambianchi took over the position of *Capo Ufficio Tecnico* (Chief of the Technical Office). With the reorganisation of the design office, it was decided to completely reassess the company's projects, which were centred principally on multi-engine aircraft and flying boats. Many of these were proving difficult to progress, so focus turned to monoplane fighter aircraft.

Fundamentally important in this context was the collaboration between Gianni Caproni and the representative of the Reggiane senior management, Roberto Guiscardo Longhi,[1] a brilliant technician who had acquired a high level of experience in new methods of metal construction thanks to his previous employment with various American companies. Roberto Longhi came into contact with Caproni during a brief stay in Italy, during which he acted as an intermediary in a dispute between Cesare Pallavicino, the chief designer at Caproni, and *colonnello* Sbernadori, the head of the DGCA in Milano. Sbernadori was known to Longhi since he had held the position of *Addetto Aeronautico Tecnico* (Technical Air Attaché) in Washington. Once Longhi was back in the USA in July 1937, Caproni commissioned him to sound out the possibility of obtaining construction licences for fighter aircraft for his company's aeronautics department.

Thanks also to the active collaboration and organisational activity of Longhi and the Italian Aeronautical Attaché, *Colonnello* Pezzani, *ingegner* Antonio Alessio, accompanied by engineer Fidia Piattelli of the Research and Projects Office, undertook a trip to the USA to visit aeronautical companies. Upon their return, they produced a detailed report highlighting the high level of industrialisation and specialisation of American industry compared to that in Italy. During the trip, the two Italian engineers, accompanied by Longhi, were able to visit the Seversky Aircraft Corporation, although their visit

was made in an unofficial capacity since at the time the American company was engaged in the construction of the P-35 fighter aircraft whose manufacture was considered secret by the American government. The subsequent report by Alessio actually mentioned this visit, even speculating the possibility of obtaining technical documents relative to the licence production of the American fighter for a sum of about *Lire* 325,000. However, it also mentioned the possibility of obtaining the necessary documents through 'other channels', probably thanks to Longhi's interest:

ROBERTO LONGHI

A 1940 portrait of Roberto Longhi.

ROBERTO LONGHI was one of the most important and controversial figures in the history of Reggiane. Born at Nembro on 21 December 1909, on completion of his technical studies he relocated to the United States where he worked with several aeronautical companies such as Waco and the Bellanca Aircraft Corporation, as well as some minor agencies, acquiring experience in technical aspects of aircraft construction. Returning to Italy in 1936 for reasons of health, he came into contact with *ingegner* Gianni Caproni, who offered him the opportunity to collaborate as a consultant for the Gruppo Caproni on his return to the United States. The knowledge he had gained in the USA proved to be significant to the company. Subsequently, a tour of numerous American companies made by ingegneri Alessio and Fidia Piattelli of Reggiane facilitated the acquisition of manufacturing drawings for the Seversky P-35 fighter, as a result of which the RE.2000 was created.

Returning to Italy in the early months of 1938, he assumed the post of *Capo Officina Sperimentale* (Chief of the Experimental Office) with Reggiane at Reggio Emilia, actively collaborating with the designers in the construction of the new fighter. In 1939 he was promoted to *Capo fabbrica Costruzioni Speciali* (Chief of the Special Construction Factory), and in 1941 also assumed the role of Ispettore tecnico (Technical Inspector). During the war Longhi oversaw the licence production of the Savoia Marchetti S.79 *Sparviero* and some FIAT and Piaggio engines. He also developed the production programme for Reggiane's own engines, culminating in the design of the experimental Reggiane RE 103 and its RE 105 derivative.

Returning to the USA after the war, he collaborated with other American companies and died on 1 December 1994 at his home in New Jersey.

[1] Roberto Longhi, despite not possessing a formal university qualification in engineering, was usually identified by the title *'ingegnere'*.

'*The well-known person* [referring probably to Longhi] *asks for the sum of USD 7,000 in Italian currency for his collaboration, half to be paid on his entry into service and half on the testing of the apparatus; he also asks for the reimbursement of his travel expenses for himself and his family... The payment of a monthly salary of Italian* Lire *5000... and a production bonus of at least* Lire *10,000 per aircraft.*'

Ingegner Alessio's report ended with some purely 'political' considerations: while the option of regularly purchasing construction licences would have allowed aircraft to be built without legal problems, equally this would have highlighted a certain inability on the part of Italian industry to propose and effect 'autarkic' construction projects. A second option – obtaining aircraft designs by 'alternative means' – as well as being decidedly less transparent, could, however remote, result in possible legal repercussions. On the other hand, it would have been possible – at least in theory – to create possible outlets for the export of aircraft.

The report also contained a description of the production methods utilised in the Seversky factory:

'*The fuselages are mounted on parallel welded tube trestles set at a convenient height on which are put into place all the components, from the engine firewall to the vertical empennage. The engine mounting is fitted to separate trestles, together with the entire frontal section of the aircraft. The wings are fitted last, the central section being directly joined to the fuselage and securely fixed to it, while the outer wing sections are dismantleable and interchangeable with others of different surfaces. This assembly line arrangement, particularly efficient for large-scale production, is all the more possible because, in reality, the Seversky company manufactures a single, basic model of which differing versions are made possible via economical conversions while retaining the*

Above and below: Assembly and fuselage production lines at Reggiane in 1940.

essential and fundamental parts of the prototype.'

The report continued with a comment on the importance of the new P-35 fighter:

'*We were speaking with Major Seversky in person, and with his design engineers and his other collaborators, and were handed photographs and confidential data on the P-35 aircraft, which, given the oversight of the factory exercised by officers of the American Army Air Force, are usually kept very secret. The Seversky aircraft is, according to some competent Americans (Ing. Carr, Director General of Glenn Martin and others), the most advanced aircraft that exists today for fighter and combat operations. A version of it, with slightly inferior characteristics to those presently with the American Army, has been*

approved for licence construction by the Russian Army, and in fact, within the Seversky workshops, there is a Russian unit... A similar licence had been approved for Britain on the eve of our departure from New York.'

Even today it is still not clear which of the two paths were selected, although objective analysis of the P-35 and especially the slightly longer EP1-106 version provided to the Swedish Air Force, reveal that the designs of the American fighter and the RE.2000 possess such similarities that they can be considered as the same aircraft. As further confirmation of this hypothesis, it is difficult to believe that, in just a few months, it would have been possible for Reggiane to design and develop, from scratch, a new fighter such as the RE.2000. Indeed, in many respects it would have been a revolutionary accomplishment considering Italian technical standards of the period, without having

The Seversky P-35 in flight. It is very evident that there was a link between this fighter and the Reggiane RE.2000. (USAF)

The first aircraft for Hungary under construction at the *Reparto Sperimentale* of the Reggiane factory in June 1940. Note the motivational inscriptions spoken by Benito Mussolini on the walls.

This page and opposite: Three photographs taken on the occasion of the first flight of the RE.2000, with Mario De Bernardi at the controls, on 24 May 1939.

had the possibility of acquiring the know-how and experience found in the technical drawings of the Seversky fighter.

Over the years that followed, further research and revelations have strengthened the belief that American technical documents came into Reggiane's possession in an extremely 'fortunate' manner thanks to Longhi's involvement.

Creation of the RE.2000

On returning from their trip to the United States and taking advantage of what they had seen and learned while visiting the various American production plants, Reggiane's designers drew up initial plans for the RE.2000 project. This was in response to a request from the Regia Aeronautica to the main Italian aircraft companies for a metal, single-engine, monoplane fighter to be introduced into service at the end of the 1930s to replace the ageing CR.32.

During the preliminary phase, Reggiane's designers adopted the Seversky design as the basis for the new fighter, reworking a number of technical aspects in order to fulfil the requirement that called specifically for a 'national' product, as well as introducing various modifications to the American fighter design.

In reality, once the American technical documentation had been obtained, *ingegner* Pambianchi began reworking the designs. He retained as much as possible of the aircraft's main elements such as the wing, with its plan forms and structural architecture, while making detailed improvements in the finish by adopting the single-sheet back wing cladding, eliminating many sheet metal joints and overlaps, and using embedded rivets to further reduce aerodynamic resistance. The fuselage, also structurally similar to that of the Seversky, was also improved in its aerodynamics, with the cockpit modified by lowering its profile and extending the canopy glazing into the hump of the fuselage behind the pilot's seat to improve rearward visibility. The instrument panel was also modified to accept instruments of Italian construction.

Having to use a domestic engine, specifically the Piaggio P.XI radial, it was also necessary to completely revise engine installation, with a slight increase in the size of the NACA by about 11 centimetres, as well as the redesign and revision of the various systems connected to it.

The most substantial modification made to the original design was the adoption of a new main landing gear, designed by ingegner Virgilio Vardanega, which, while largely tracing the original Seversky undercarriage with retraction inside wing fairings protruding below the wing, had the wheel housing flat in the wings, causing them to rotate 90° during the undercarriage extension phase. To avoid any eventual problems with the patenting of the system,[2] the rotation of the undercarriage was delayed until immediately prior to it entering the wing. The advantage of this was the ability to house the undercarriage on the outside of the main wing structure, avoiding breaking the continuity of the watertight wing box.

Construction work on the first prototype commenced in November 1938 and proceeded at a certain speed. The availability of the Piaggio P.XI RC 40 engine, developing about 1,000 hp (almost 20 per cent more than the original American R-1830), gave Reggiane's workforce high hopes of achieving good performance for the new fighter, which would assume a speed of around 550 km/h with a climb time to 5000 m of about 5 minutes and 13 seconds. The aircraft's range was also remarkable due to the fact that the integral wing tank had a capacity of approximately 640 litres of fuel.

[2] This retraction system had been patented by Boeing for the P-36.

Above: The landing gear used in almost all the Reggiane fighters was similar to that of the Seversky in concept, but it incorporated significant modifications in movement to avoid legal disputes with Boeing, the patent holder.

Above and below: The RE.2000 prototype following modifications made after the first flight. These included a spinner added to the propeller hub, while the carburettor intake manifold was lengthened (above the engine cowling) and the exhausts modified.

Reggiane was invited to present its aircraft as part of the evaluation for a new front-line fighter in 1939, in accordance with the requirements of the Regia Aeronautica's fighter upgrade programme known as the 'R Programme'. Reggiane's submission would compete against the two remaining aircraft in contention – the FIAT G.50 and the AerMacchi C.200.

Evaluation of the Reggiane fighter was undoubtedly prompted by the inspection visit, in March 1939, by Captain Engineer Pietro Noto of the *Guidonia Centro Sperimentale*. He signed a positive assessment of the activities underway at Reggiane, as well as the project being developed at Reggio Emilia.

The prototype, with the assigned *Matricola Militare* (military serial) MM408, made its first flight from the airfield at Reggio Emilia on 24 May 1939, flown by an exceptional test pilot, Mario De Bernardi, a First World War ace and winner of the

1926 edition of the Schneider Trophy. From its first flights, the RE.2000 demonstrated excellent flight characteristics and handling, achieving a speed of 541 km/h. It was afforded high praise from De Bernardi who described it in enthusiastic tones, considering it fast, agile, and safe, and, unlike the G.50 and C.200, not afflicted with autorotation problems.

After the first flight the prototype was modified with the fitment of a propeller spinner and the lengthening of the air intakes above the engine cowling.

Despite complaining about a slight delay in fitting out the aircraft in comparison with its two competitors, senior Regia Aeronautica officers were impressed by the early flights and requested Reggiane to send the prototype to Guidonia for a series of evaluation flights in mid-May 1939 with a view to a possible initial order for 300 aircraft.

After a brief period of verification trials and synchronisation of its armament at Furbara, on 18 July 1939 the prototype was sent to Guidonia, again flown by De Bernardi, where it was subjected to a cycle of official trials by test pilots from the *Centro Sperimentale*. These confirmed the aircraft's good characteristics in comparison with the fighters that were about to enter service with the Regia Aeronautica. The Reggiane machine was also assessed, with good results, against the Messerschmitt Bf 109 E, three examples of which were present at Guidonia having been sent by Germany for evaluation by the *Centro Sperimentale*. The assessment of the test pilots at Guidonia in July were quite flattering, with the aircraft demonstrating good stability (centre of gravity at 22% of the wing chord) according to American standards, but less agile than the Italian standard, requiring piloting effort. In fact, Italian aircraft designs (like French and

MARIO DE BERNARDI

MARIO DE BERNARDI was born at Venosa on 1 July 1893. In March 1916 he qualified as a military pilot and was posted to the 75ª *Squadriglia* equipped with Nieuport fighters. He was decorated with a *Medaglia di Bronzo al Valor Militare* for an attack he made against an Austrian aircraft which was forced to land in Italian territory.

He subsequently became the test pilot for Pomilio aircraft, and in May 1917 was involved in the first postal flight to connect Torino and Roma, being awarded the *Medaglia d'Argento al Valor Militare*.

After the war he served as a test pilot and technical consultant with Officine Caproni, and in 1926 won the ninth Schneider Trophy held at Hampton Roads in Virginia. In 1928, in a Macchi M.52R seaplane racer, he was the first person to exceed 500 km/h in flight, achieving 512.776 km/h. He also participated in aerobatic competitions, and in 1931 won the world aerobatic championships.

In 1933, at the controls of a Caproni Ca.111, he completed a Roma to Moscow flight, covering the 2,600 km which separated the two capitals with five passengers on board.

In his role of test pilot for Caproni he was tasked with conducting the first test flights of the Reggiane RE.2000, RE.2001, and RE.2002. In 1941 he flight-tested the Campini-Caproni C.C.2, conducting a flight from Milano to Roma.

Active in the civilian aviation sector, he designed the 'Aeroscooter', a small, light aircraft which it was hoped would offer everyone the ability to fly. It was during a flight in the Aeroscooter on 8 April 1959 that De Bernardi suffered a heart attack, but despite this he managed to land the aircraft prior to expiring. He was sixty-six years old.

For his exceptional aeronautical merit, he was also decorated with the *Medaglia d'Oro al Valor Militare*.

The well-known test pilot, Mario De Bernardi. He won the 1926 competition for the Schneider Trophy held at Hampton Roads in the US, and in 1928 was the first man to break the 500 km/h speed barrier while flying a Macchi C.52R.

Right: Mario De Bernardi in the cockpit of an RE.2000 before a test flight.

The first official photographs of the still unpainted aircraft taken on 18 July 1939 at Reggio Emilia.

Additional photographs of the still unpainted aircraft at
Reggio Emilia. The Reggiane hangars can be seen
in the background below.

The RE.2000 prototype makes a low-level pass over the airfield.

A clear view of the inner construction of an RE.2000 half-wing section on the production line, but still without its ventral skinning.

British designs) were on the limits of instability, having a balance centre point of 35% or even more), and were therefore more agile, but unsuitable for instrument flight and long trips. The same observations were made of the German aircraft which were also stable and therefore needed higher piloting efforts, which was not very agreeable to Italian pilots.

The type's speed and landing characteristics were considered to be good, while the ease of inspection, engine maintenance, the installation of some systems and pilot visibility were assessed as a little inferior in comparison with the C.200 and G.50. These were overall, however, excellent results, with the performance largely attributable to the adoption of the Clark Y wing profile, which was curved to ensure good handling in the stall, and a wing which did not suffer from any of the aerodynamic problems affecting the other two aircraft and which resulted in the dangerous phenomena of autorotation.

As far as the materials situation was concerned, a few years ago the engineer Giulio Valdonio, recalled a discussion that took place at dinner with Roberto Longhi. Longhi mentioned that during his time with Reggiane, Gianni Caproni went to Guido Donegani, head of Montecatini, whose subsidiary LLL (Lavorazioni Leghe Leggere), was the largest producer of aeronautical dural, to convince him to produce sheets, sections and nails to American standards. This was so that he could make better use of the Cleveland presses, nailers and benders that had been purchased in America by Reggiane following Alessio's trip, bringing the quality of the Reggiane workshop to levels far above usual Italian standards.

Nevertheless, it was noted that the Reggiane fighter's Piaggio P.XI engine suffered from poor reliability in comparison with the A.74 produced by FIAT, although a positive opinion was expressed about the operation of the automatic Piaggio propeller. The most important criticism levelled at the fighter by test pilots and technicians however, which also turned out to be the pretext for its rejection by the Regia Aeronautica, was its alleged excessive vulnerability in combat due to the integral tanks in the wings not being self-sealing. The Regia Aeronautica commission passed the following opinions in relation to the evaluation of the three fighters tested:

'*With regard to the MC.200, G.50 and RE.2000 aircraft, there are not sufficient elements to establish a net preference in merit in terms of the ease of series production; nevertheless, from the examinations that it has been possible to undertake at this* Centro, *it seems that the RE.2000, as opposed to the M.C.200, has been conceived with more practical criteria for series production, resulting from an accurate and detailed study of its construction with the aim of maximising the reduction of the number of individual components in the aircraft. Furthermore, this aeroplane manifests some new and interesting construction techniques such as, for example, in the attachment of the wing to the fuselage.*

'*On the other hand, given that the tank is located in the central section of the wing, and forms a part of the resistant structure, it is neither easily self-sealable nor easily repairable in the case of failure or loss. In respect of the use of national materials, the aircraft are constructed mainly from Italian-made duralumin.*'

However, the positive evaluation of the chief test pilots at the Experimental Centre, *colonnello* Angelo Tondi, *maggiore* Aldo Quarantotti and *tenente* Adriano Mantelli, were not matched in satisfaction on the part of the ministerial authorities, who did not want to accept the incorporation of tanks in the wing – at least that was the official reason. This unusual technical feature, at least unusual for Italian aircraft at the time, became the Regia Aeronautica's official pretext for rejecting the aircraft, deeming it unsuitable for an aircraft intended for military operations not to be equipped with a '*serbatoio semapizzato*' (self-sealing type tank).[3]

This view, for many reasons, was ungenerous since, as was well known, the limits of self-sealing tanks were well understood: if a projectile hit a tank full of fuel, it 'drowned' in the liquid, but if a projectile (not necessarily an incendiary), hit a half-full tank with fuel vapour present, self-sealing offered little in the way of protection. Nevertheless, some years after the war, the former *Capo di Stato Maggiore* of the Regia Aeronautica, *generale* Francesco Pricolo, stated,

The RE.2000 prototype after being painted in a camouflage scheme, prepares for a test flight before transfer from Reggio Emilia to the Guidonia *Centro Sperimentale*.

---

[3] The '*semapizzato*' was a self-sealing fuel tank formed of a supplementary duralumin structure with internal diaphragms, protected from the perforation of projectiles by a cladding known as '*semape*'. This featured special rubber sponges compressed externally by a strip of fabric. In this way, a projectile could enter the tank but the rubber assured the immediate closure of the hole.

Official photographs of the RE.2000 prototype, MM408, in front of one of the main hangars of the *Centro Sperimentale* at Guidonia. Of note are the particular colour scheme adopted of light sand/yellow patches on an original dark olive green background, and the new windscreen that replaced the former one-piece windscreen.

'In terms of fighters, another prototype existed at the Reggiane company, the RE.2000, but it had the very grave inconvenience of containing its fuel in the wings, stored in tanks. This configuration, in combat use, would have certainly resulted in disastrous consequences: it seems almost unimaginable that you would even think to conceive an aircraft for combat with this enormous defect. The designer, at my invitation, quickly agreed to build another type of reinforced wing containing self-sealing tanks, protected by a thick layer of rubber, as had already been done during the First World War.'

Nevertheless, the problem of integral tanks was easily solvable, as indeed was the case with the RE.2001. However, the pretext concealed the main motive, which was linked to the fact that compared to the C.200 and G.50, which were almost in production, the RE.2000 did not present any substantial improvements. Furthermore, the Regia Aeronautica's leaders were counting on the installation of the German DB 601 engine in the RE.2000's airframe so that it would perform better than aircraft equipped with radial engines. Strictly speaking, the Regia Aeronautica's perspective was understandable, but at the same time it

demonstrated a certain short-sightedness since, thanks to its excellent range, far greater than that of the same class fighters then in service with Regia Aeronautica, the Reggiane monoplane would have proved an excellent escort fighter for naval convoys.

Undoubtedly, the deployment of more than the few RE.2000s assigned to an experimental squadron in Sicily to be used on escort missions in the Mediterranean would have proved beneficial during the first year of the war, in view of the fact that the RE.2000's performance was more than sufficient to counter British Gladiator, Martlet and Fulmar fighters of the time.

The prototype RE.2000.

Despite this, in September 1939, the *Ministero dell'Aeronautica* advised the Emilian firm of its intention to order 200 examples of the RE.2000, although only an initial order for twelve aircraft was formalised to equip an experimental *Squadriglia*.

However, as doubts persisted over the solutions adopted and with a lack of understanding of the mission to be entrusted to the RE.2000, in April 1940 orders were reduced to a single example, which, later equipped with a Piaggio P.XIX engine, would become the prototype of the RE.2002.

This decision generated not insignificant disappointment and concern amongst the company's senior management team, in part mitigated by a request to prepare a new version of the RE.2000 equipped with the in-line DB 601 engine, a request which later resulted in the design of the RE.2001.

Meanwhile, as production of the first batch of aircraft commenced, in December 1939 Reggiane achieved significant sales success abroad, formalising a contract for 70 aircraft with Hungary, and at the same time obtaining approval from the *Ministero dell'Aeronautica* for export, since the Regia Aeronautica had by then decided not to adopt the aircraft for its front-line units. Just under a year later, in November 1940, a new export contract was signed, with 60 aircraft purchased by the Flygvapnet (the Swedish Air Force). However, at almost the same time, the order situation with the Regia Aeronautica became more complicated, as after initially cancelling the order for 12 aircraft in November 1940, it re-confirmed it and increased it to 28 aircraft, which had to be partly taken from foreign orders. For these aircraft, the *Direzione Generale delle Costruzioni Aeronautiche* (DGCA) requested substantial modifications to better adapt the fighter for certain types of mission.

Meanwhile, alongside the five aircraft in '*Intercettori*' configuration, twelve aircraft were ordered in 'G.A.' (*Grande Autonomia* – long range) configuration, one as a two-seat reconnaissance machine (which would become the RE.2003) and ten in a version that could be catapulted from ships (*Catapultabile*). The G.A. aircraft were intended to be used in *Africa Orientale Italiana* (A.O.I. – Italian East Africa) as they were equipped with oversized tanks and could be flown directly to Italian territories without the need for further stopovers, especially given the isolation of Italian Ethiopia. However, the Italian defeat in the A.O.I. in the spring of 1941 meant that this requirement was no longer needed and, as already mentioned, for this reason the fighters in production were destined to operate with an experimental squadron attached to a fighter division in Sicily, to be used for escorting naval convoys and bombers sent to Malta.

The aircraft ordered in *Catapultabile* configuration, on the other hand, were to be assigned to the Regia Marina for use as fighter and reconnaissance aircraft embarked on major units, in a way similar to the Royal Navy's Sea Hurricanes. Only eight such aircraft were built, while a further order for fifty fighters, received in

September 1941, was subsequently cancelled in December of the same year – when construction of the first of these aircraft was already under way.

The Ministry's behaviour towards Reggiane, with continuous orders and requests for modifications and variants followed by cancellation of orders caused the company so many problems that on several occasions the management expressed its displeasure with the Regia Aeronautica leadership. In a report dated 1942, the management explained how it was forced to make huge investments which were promptly nullified by the lack of promised orders or their sudden cancellation:

> '*As a consequence of these cancellations and reductions we have suffered heavy damage derived from lost profits from our orders and the loss of licence rights… The losses, the missing profits and the expenses on non-offsetable equipment reached a sum of more than* Lire *68 million, which is not reflected, we believe, in the balance sheets of any company that has intended, as in our case, to make an effective contribution to the strengthening of our industrial war effort… The liabilities occurred by Reggiane exceed, to date,* Lire *80 million.*'

These were not insignificant figures and the report also pointed out that as a result of the sudden, limited orders for RE.2000s, Reggiane was forced to equip and modify new aircraft (*Catapultabili*) and delay deliveries to Sweden and Hungary,

> '*The diversion of these aircraft have had harmful repercussions on the delivery programmes already established with Hungary and Sweden, programmes already suffering badly from the difficulties emerging in the provision of materials.*'

Production and variants

Prototypes excluded, some 158 series production RE.2000 fighters were effectively completed, 130 of which were provided to the air forces of Hungary and Sweden.

- **1 prototype RE 2000** MM408 (later assigned the serial MM5074)
- **2 prototype RE 2000** *Catapultabile* MM471-MM485 (catapult-launched)
- **5 RE 2000 I Series '*versione Normale o Intercettore*'** (standard or interceptor variants) MM5068-5072. The aircraft in this configuration, very similar to that of the prototype, had the air intake on top of the engine cowling lowered to improve the pilot's forward visibility and modifications to the engine cowling access panels to improve accessibility. These aircraft, moreover, retained the rear glazing in the fuselage fairing to improve visibility in the rear sector. Five aircraft were delivered, three of which were subsequently converted to the *Grande Autonomia* (G.A. – long-range) variant.

The RE.2000, MM5069, belonging to the first series of five interceptors built and then modified in July 1941 as the G.A. (Grande Autonomia) variant. The photograph bears De Bernardi's dedication to the other Reggiane test pilot, Silvio Casarotto.

Below: Title page of the RE.2000 parts manual valid for the fighter variants.

Another image of MM5069 at Reggio Emilia airport. In the background is the RE.2000 V401, the first of a series of 70 examples destined for Hungary.

A Reggiane RE.2000 *Catapultabile* positioned on a naval catapult aboard an Italian warship.

One of the first Reggiane 2000s destined for export seen undergoing an engine test at Reggio Emilia. The aircraft belongs to the *'Serie* 1' and seems to have already been prepared for Hungary, as evidenced from the distinctive Hungarian Air Force marking under the wing and on the fin and rudder.

- **12 RE 2000 II** *Serie 'versione Grande Autonomia (G.A.)'* (long-range variants) MM8059-8070. This variant was created to further extend the radius of action of the fighter, adding two new 170-litre tanks in the fuselage, positioned behind the cockpit, which provided the aircraft with a range of around 1,850 km at a speed of 430 km/h. The engine was replaced with the more reliable Piaggio P.IX bis R.C.40, and further detailed modifications included changes to the fairing of the cockpit, with the disappearance of the rear window, new radio apparatus, and the ability to carry two Nardi sub-munition dispensers under the fuselage together with hard points on the wings for 80/100-kg bombs. In total, twelve aircraft were constructed.

- **8 (9) RE.2000 III** *Serie 'versione Catapultabile'* (catapult-launched) MM8281 to MM8288. This variant was also fitted with the more reliable Piaggio P.IX bis R.C.40 engine, and was characterised by the lack of rear glazing, similar to the G.A. version, with the headrest incorporated into the pilot's seat back, new on-board systems and radio apparatus as well as,

naturally, special structural reinforcements and external hard points positioned under the wings and on the fuselage sides, known as '*aggrappi*' (holds) for catapult launch from ships.

The original order was for ten aircraft, but in fact only eight were completed. A ninth aircraft should be added to this total, in reality the first to be modified and utilised for the launch trials in May 1942, which was assigned the serial MM8281. It was later re-used as the first production aircraft. This aircraft was drawn from the batch originally ordered by Hungary and was in an *Intercettore* variant modified to a *Catapultabile* version, albeit retaining the glazing in the fuselage cladding.

- **70 RE.2000 I** *Serie 'versione Normale or Intercettore'* **serials V-401-V470** supplied to the Magyar Kiraly Legiero (Hungarian Air Force). The fighters were identical to those of the first series under construction for the Regia Aeronautica. It should be noted that Hungary was also awarded a licence to construct the fighter, issued to the MAVAG company, which built 192 examples.

- **60 RE.2000 I** *Serie 'versione Normale or Intercettore'* **serials 2301-2360** supplied to the Flygvapnet (Swedish Air Force). These aircraft, similar to those of the first series in production for the Regia Aeronautica, incorporated some small detail modifications, such as a rear-view mirror mounted on the windshield and a supplementary strut in the rear glazed section of the canopy.

The Flygvapnet J.20 2312 in the colours of F 10. The aircraft was decommissioned in July 1945.

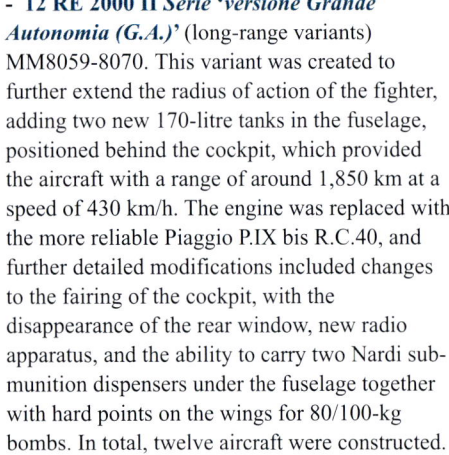

The cover page of the last edition (1942) of the official *Manuale di Manutenzione e istruzione* for the 'single-place pursuit' aircraft, the Falco I, powered by a Piaggio P. XI RC 40 engine.

Technical aspects

The fuselage of the second prototype RE.2000 under assembly, late August 1939.

View inside the RE.2000's circular fuselage. Note the control rods and the compressed air cylinder at right.

The first prototype windscreen was formed from a single piece of plexiglass.

After the first test flights, the curved, one-piece windscreen was replaced by another framed design.

The Reggiane RE.2000, also known by the common name 'Falco' (Hawk), was a cantilever, low-wing, single-engine, single-seat monoplane. The metal monocoque fuselage was circular in section. The cockpit was fitted with a canopy that slid to the rear and was capable of being jettisoned in flight. The windscreen was fitted with reinforced glass plate.

The wing shape was semi-elliptical with an asymmetric variable profile decreasing towards its extremities and was formed by five spars connected by ribs. It was divided into five parts, including in its centre section the fuel tanks, contained in the same wet structure, while in the two lateral sections were the main undercarriage bays. Then came the two outer sections with the aileron hinges and the two wingtip pieces.

The split flaps were mechanically controlled and extended from one aileron to the other, also continuing under the fuselage. The ailerons were located near the wingtips and were of fabric clad metal construction. The metal cantilever tailplanes had their moving surfaces clad in fabric.

Continues on page 41

A good view of the upper part of the RE.2000 wing.

Below: Two views of the interior structures of the outer wing and central wing section of the RE.2000 which was built as a 'wet wing'.

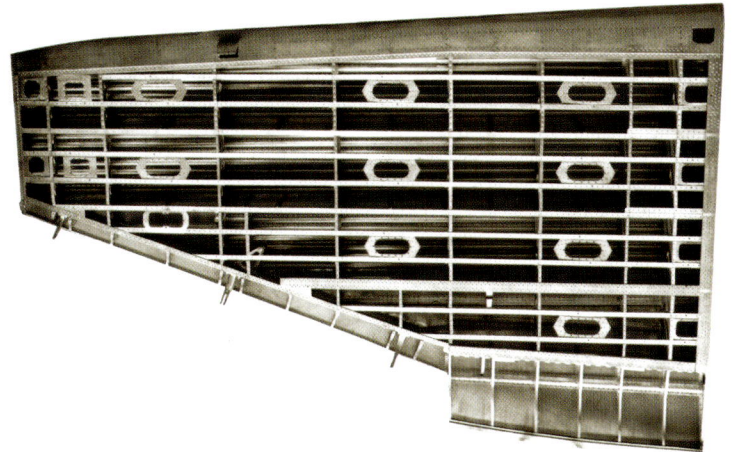

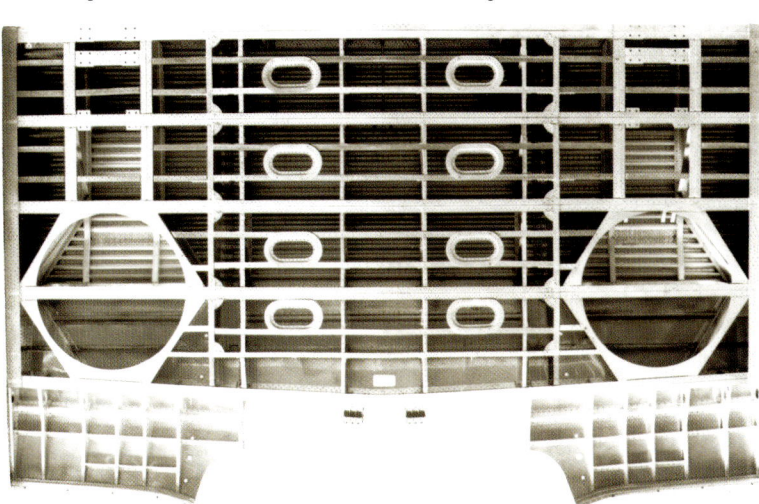

Above: Hungarian *Hejas* under assembly. The design and build of the central wing section – one of three which went to form the whole wing – can be seen here.

Despite not being of the best quality, the photograph shows the lower part of the RE.2000 with flaps and tail surfaces.

Left: Clear view of the central flaps.

THE UNUSUAL REGGIANE UNDERCARRIAGE

The RE.2000, in common with the RE.2001 and RE.2002, had an electro-mechanical undercarriage. It had a retractable landing gear consisting of a single oleo-pneumatic unit capable of taking side loads and bending, while the fore and aft loads were borne by drag struts.

The struts were attached to forged type fittings in the wing and were provided with manual and mechanical retraction. The retraction process saw the legs rotating rearwards while simultaneously rotating on their own axis so that the wheels, once the landing gear had retracted, lay flat and backwards inside the wells provided in the centre section, while their legs with their fairings adhered to the centre section in the direction of flight.

The undercarriage retraction mechanism was electrically operated with an emergency manual control. The mechanical transmission, effected by means of torque tubes, was the same in both cases.

The tailwheel was retractable simultaneously with the landing gear, while on the RE.2001 and RE.2002, the fixed tailwheel was steerable.

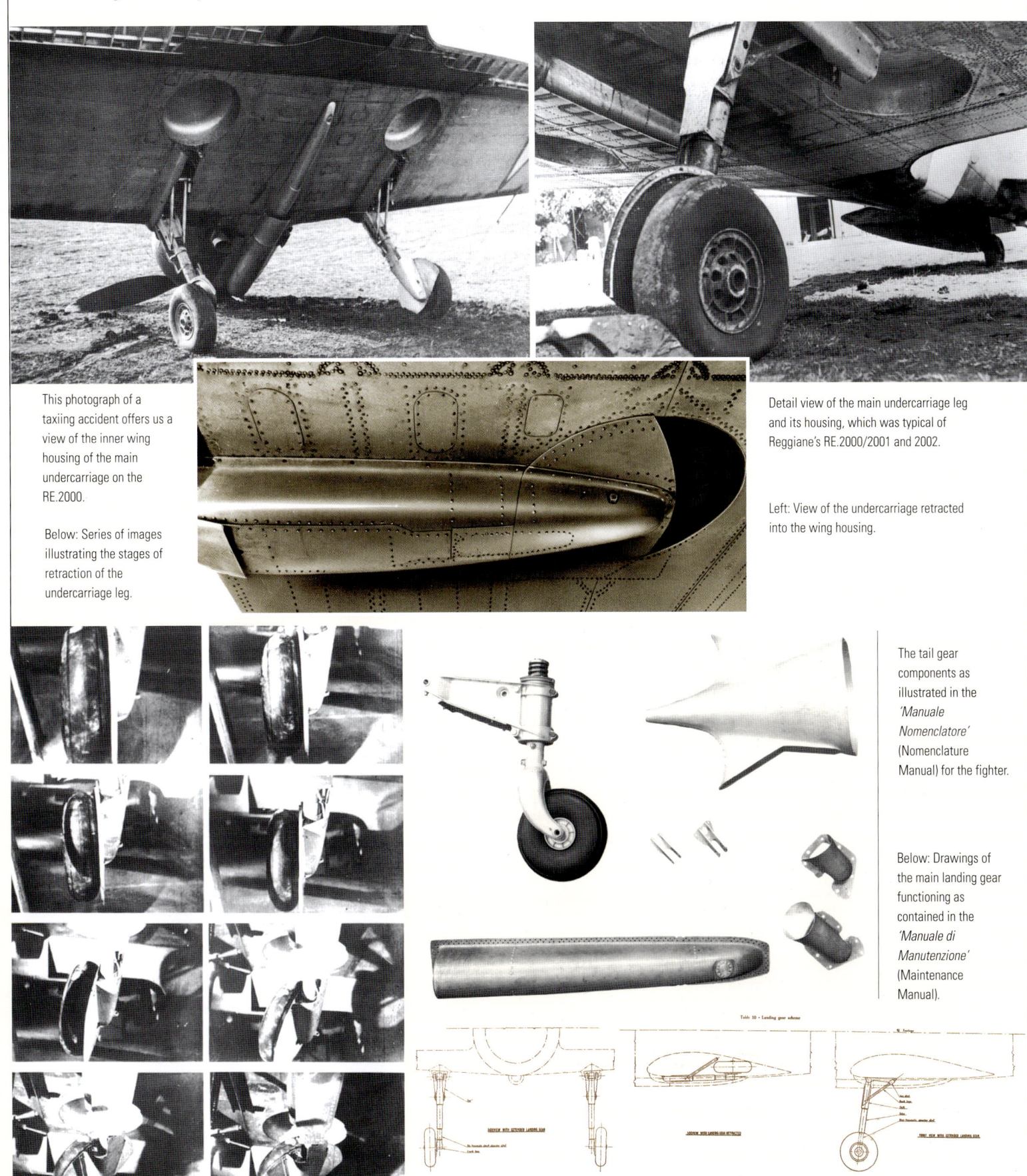

This photograph of a taxiing accident offers us a view of the inner wing housing of the main undercarriage on the RE.2000.

Below: Series of images illustrating the stages of retraction of the undercarriage leg.

Detail view of the main undercarriage leg and its housing, which was typical of Reggiane's RE.2000/2001 and 2002.

Left: View of the undercarriage retracted into the wing housing.

The tail gear components as illustrated in the 'Manuale Nomenclatore' (Nomenclature Manual) for the fighter.

Below: Drawings of the main landing gear functioning as contained in the 'Manuale di Manutenzione' (Maintenance Manual).

An RE.2000 fuselage with a freshly mounted Piaggio engine.

Right: The Piaggio P. XI bis engine on display at the Museo dell'Aeronautica Militare at Vigna di Valle.

Piaggio P.XI / P.XI bis engine

In 1934 Rinaldo Piaggio S.p.A commenced construction of the 610 hp P.XI RC radial twin-row, air-cooled, 14-cylinder engine which derived directly from the French Gnome-Rhône 14K Mistral Major for which the Italian company had obtained a manufacturing licence.

In 1938 the P.XI RC 40 version appeared, fitted with a reducer and compressor, and capable of developing 1,000 hp at an altitude of 4,000 m.

The performance of the P.XI bis did not differ from that of the preceding P.XI, but the new version included modifications to improve its reliability – the real Achilles heel of this engine.

Piaggio P.XI RC40 technical details
- Normal power at sea level with 2,200 rpm at a supply pressure of 860 mm Hg: 870 CV
- Normal power at standard altitude (4,000 m) at 2,000 rpm at a supply pressure of 860 mm Hg: 870 CV: 1000 CV
- Standard rpm: 2,200 rpm
- Standard altitude: 4,000 m

- Supply pressure: 960 mm Hg (ratio 1 : 1,61)
- Propeller control: de-multiplied
- Number of cylinders: 14
- Bore: 146 mm
- Stroke: 165 mm
- Single cylinder volume: 2,762 ltr
- Total cylinder volume: 38,600 ltr
- Volumetric compression ratio: 6:1
- Engine dry weight, complete with standard accessories: kg 655 + 1%
- Carburettor: Piaggio T 2 100
- Carburettor feed: one Romec pump
- Magnetos: Marelli MF 14
- Number of magnetos: 2
- Number of plugs: two per cylinder
- Lubrications system: pressure
- Overall dimensions: external diameter 132.8 mm, total length (without propeller boss and generator) 170 cm

Left: Official photographs of the 1000-hp Piaggio P. XI bis RC 40 engine. The P. XI was a licensed version of the French Gnome-Rhône *Mistral Major* 14K.

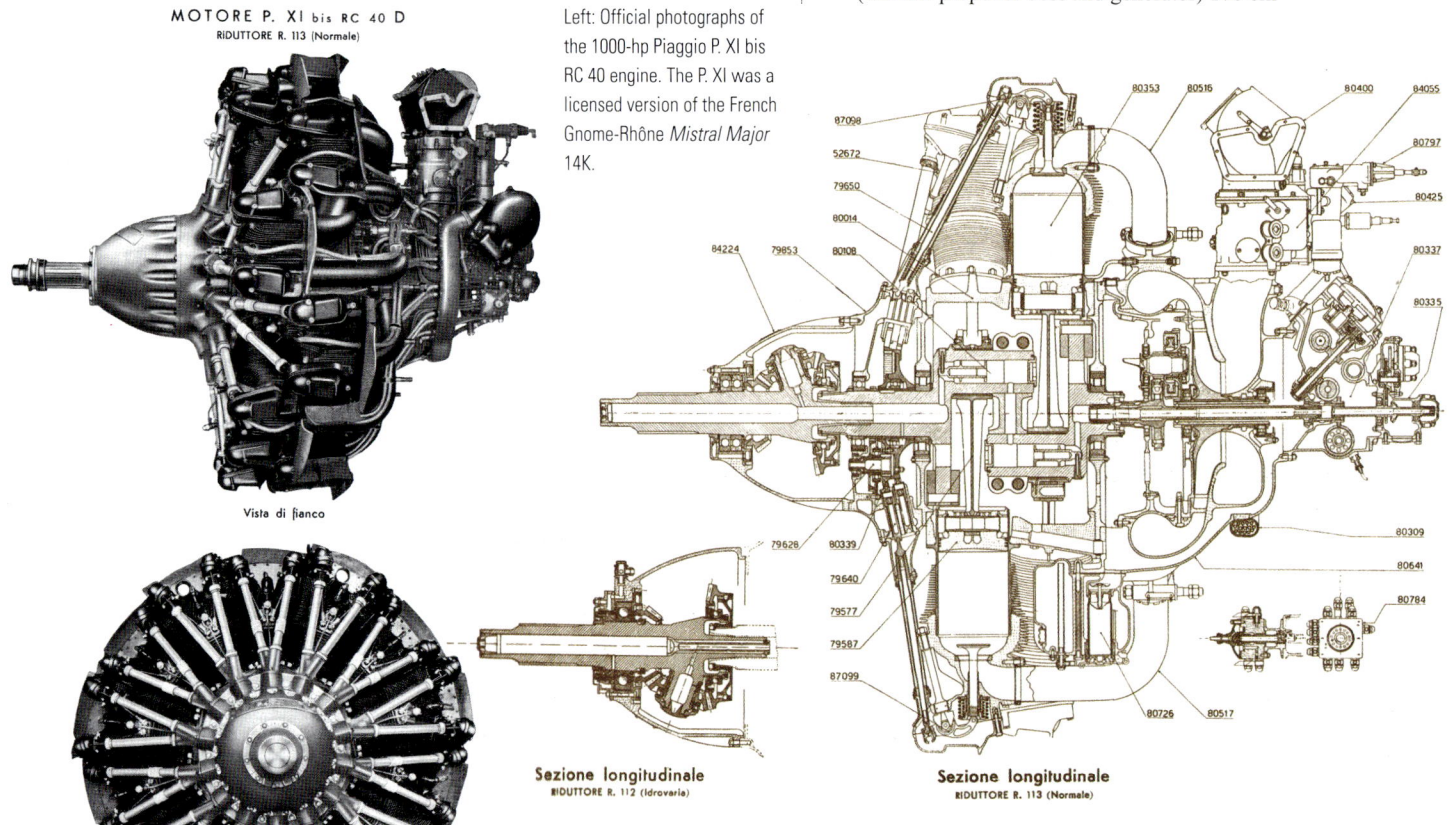

MOTORE P. XI bis RC 40 D
RIDUTTORE R. 113 (Normale)

Vista di fianco

Sezione longitudinale
RIDUTTORE R. 112 (Idrovaria)

Sezione longitudinale
RIDUTTORE R. 113 (Normale)

Longitudinal section drawing of the Piaggio P XI RC 40.

RE.2000 Technical Data *

Length	11.00 m
Height	3.20 m
Wing area	20.40 sq.m.
Wingspan	7,990 m
Empty weight	2,090 kg
Total weight	2,850 kg
Engine	Piaggio P.XI RC, 1,000 hp
Maximum speed	460 km/h
Minimum speed	115 km/h
Range	1,300 km
Climb to 2,000 m	2' 46"
Climb to 4,000 m	5' 52"
Climb to 6,000 m	7' 45"
Ceiling	10,500 m
Take-off run	168 m
Landing run	55 m

* Data taken from Reggiane RE.2000 *Catalogo Nomenclatore I* Serie*, 1942

The cockpit and instruments of the RE.2000 prototype. Also visible are the reflector gunsight and the framework of the open canopy.

The pilot's instrument panel in a production RE.2000. Note the pendulum foot pedals attached to the underside of the panel which were different to those used on the other Reggiane fighters, which had a more standard pedal footboard hinged to the floor.

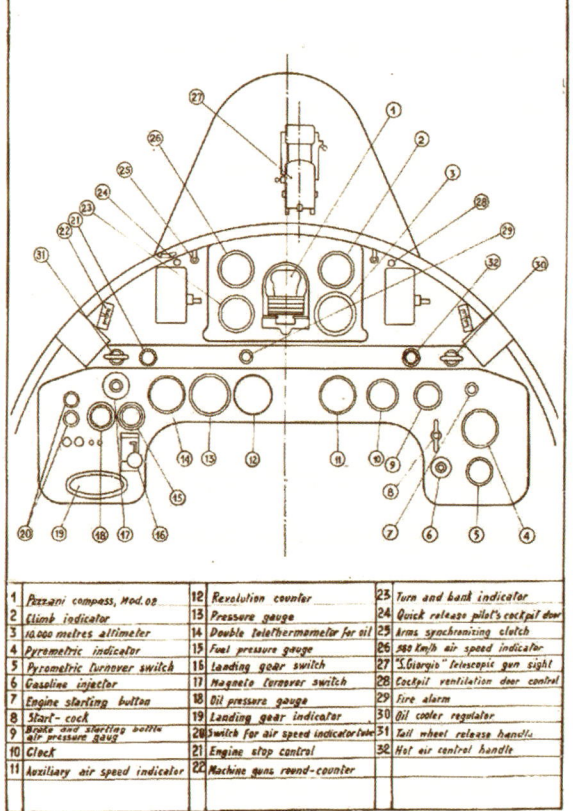

Table 26 - Front view of pilot's seat with instrument panel

1	Pizzani compass, Mod.02	12	Revolution counter	23	Turn and bank indicator
2	Climb indicator	13	Pressure gauge	24	Quick release pilot's cockpit door
3	10.000 metres altimeter	14	Double telethermometer for oil	25	Arms synchronizing clutch
4	Pyrometric indicator	15	Fuel pressure gauge	26	580 Km/h air speed indicator
5	Pyrometric turnover switch	16	Landing gear switch	27	"S.Giorgio" telescopic gun sight
6	Gasoline injector	17	Magneto turnover switch	28	Cockpit ventilation door control
7	Engine starting button	18	Oil pressure gauge	29	Fire alarm
8	Start-cock	19	Landing gear indicator	30	Oil cooler regulator
9	Brake and starting bottle air pressure gauge	20	Switch for air speed indicator/clock	31	Tail wheel release handle
10	Clock	21	Engine stop control	32	Hot air control handle
11	Auxiliary air speed indicator	22	Machine guns round-counter		

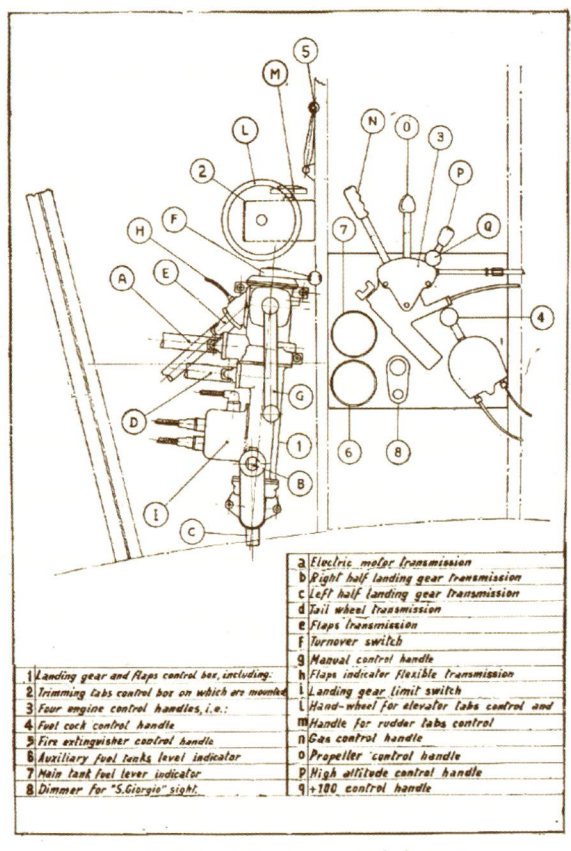

Table 27 - Left sideview of pilot's seat

a	Electric motor transmission
b	Right half landing gear transmission
c	Left half landing gear transmission
d	Tail wheel transmission
e	Flaps transmission
f	Turnover switch
g	Manual control handle
h	Flaps indicator flexible transmission
i	Landing gear limit switch
l	Hand-wheel for elevator tabs control and
m	Handle for rudder tabs control
n	Gas control handle
o	Propeller control handle
p	High altitude control handle
q	+100 control handle

1	Landing gear and flaps control box, including:
2	Trimming tabs control box on which are mounted
3	Four engine control handles, i.e.:
4	Fuel cock control handle
5	Fire extinguisher control handle
6	Auxiliary fuel tanks level indicator
7	Main tank fuel lever indicator
8	Dimmer for "S.Giorgio" sight.

Layout of RE.2000 cockpit instrumentation and left side as taken from technical manuals.

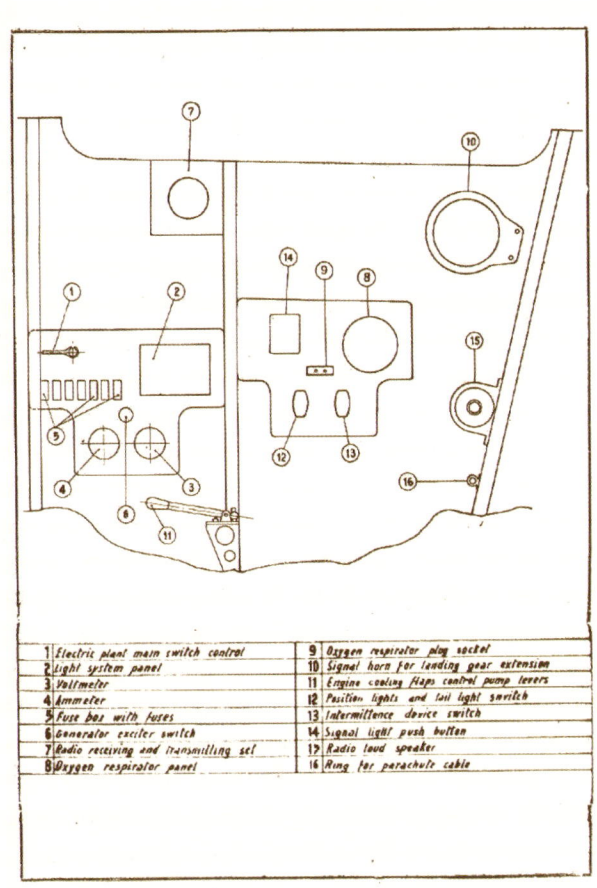

1	Electric plant main switch control	9	Oxygen respirator plug socket
2	Light system panel	10	Signal horn for landing gear extension
3	Voltmeter	11	Engine cooling flaps control pump levers
4	Ammeter	12	Position lights and tail light switch
5	Fuse box with fuses	13	Intermittence device switch
6	Generator exciter switch	14	Signal light push button
7	Radio receiving and transmitting set	17	Radio loud speaker
8	Oxygen respirator panel	16	Ring for parachute cable

Right side of the cockpit as taken from technical manuals.

The pilot's seat in the RE.2000 *Catapultabile* with incorporated headrest.

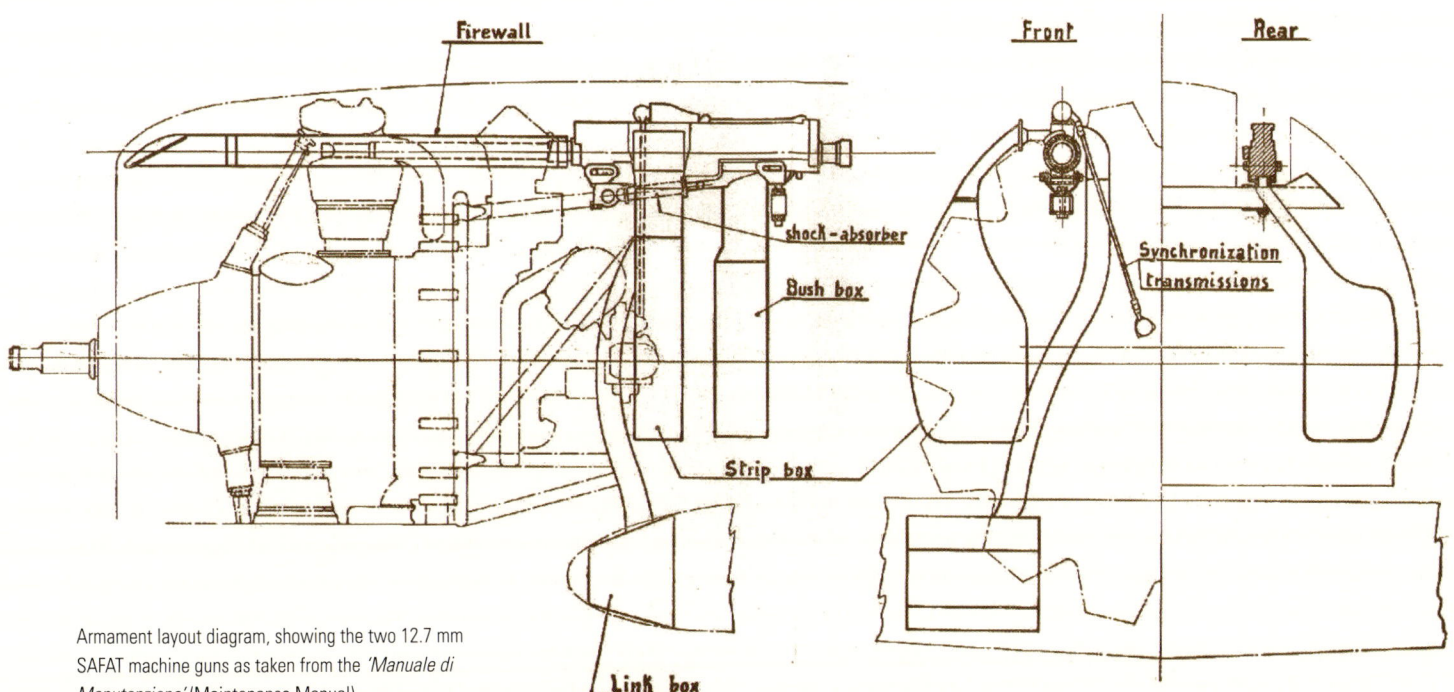

Armament layout diagram, showing the two 12.7 mm SAFAT machine guns as taken from the *'Manuale di Manutenzione'* (Maintenance Manual).

Table 23 - Machine guns installation diagram

The engine used to power the RE.2000 was the 14-cylinder, air-cooled Piaggio P.XI R.C. 40, providing 1,000 hp at the normal operating altitude of 4,000 m. The propeller was a three-bladed metal Piaggio P.1001 with a diameter of 3.40 m. It was a constant speed, variable pitch propeller controlled electromagnetically by the pilot in flight. During the course of the production run, and also as a feature of some variants of the fighter, the engine was upgraded to the P.XI bis version, which introduced modification that slightly improved its functional reliability.

The lubrication oil was contained in a tank mounted in the engine frame and had capacity of 25 litres, while a secondary tank of 20 litres was also connected. The *Grande Autonomia* version of the fighter had a main 40-litre tank.

The RE.2000 *Grande Autonomia* and the *Catapultabile* versions were equipped with the more reliable Piaggio P.XI bis R.C.40 engine, also providing 1,000 hp.

Above: View of the open panel allowing access to the machine gun ammunition boxes. This RE.2000 served with 74ª *Squadriglia* at Comiso.

View of the launch catapult attachment points on the underside of the aircraft.

AVVERTENZE IMPORTANTISSIME

1) LE ARMI DEBBONO ESSERE SINCRONIZZATE AL BORDO D'USCITA DELLE PALE DELL'ELICA *(vedi figura)*

   P₁ P₂ P₃ Punti di fase

2) NELLA MESSA A PUNTO DELLA SCATOLA DI SINCRONIZZAZIONE LA CORSA RESIDUA DEL PUNTA- LINO OLTRE LO SCATTO, MISURATA CON L'APPOSITA SONDA, DEVE ESSERE COMPRESA TRA 4 E 6/DI m/m ⁄₁₀

3) NON SI DEVE MAI SPARARE CON IL MOTORE AL DISOTTO DI 1000 GIRI AL 1'

The information plate on machine gun synchronisation. Armourers were instructed that, 'Weapons must be synchronised with the trailing edges of the propellers (see diagram).'

As mentioned, the fuel was contained in two tanks located in the wet wing structure, with the main tank on the rear wing holding 450 litres while the forward tank contained 190 litres. The *Grande Autonomia* version possessed two further 170-litre tanks positioned in the fuselage to the rear of the pilot, these bringing the potential total fuel load in this version to 980 litres and providing the aircraft with an endurance of between three or four hours, depending on the payload carried.

Engine start was achieved through compressed air at 18 atmospheres contained in a specific tank. The aircraft was further equipped with a Silma type anti-fire system controlled by the pilot. The electrical system was fed by a 24 V accumulator battery with a 300 W dynamo mounted on the engine and which was fitted with a regulator used to recharge the battery. The only receiver mode radio system fitted was the A.R.C.1.

The fighter's armament was formed of two standard Italian Breda SAFAT 12.7 mm machine guns synchronised to fire through the propeller disc, with a normal ammunition supply of 300 rounds per gun.

Positioned beneath the fuselage was also a ventral hard point to which could be attached a Nardi bomb rack/munitions dispenser, with four containers each carrying twenty-four 2-kg bomblets. The bomb release was actioned by the pilot with a pneumatic control. Some fighters were also equipped with underwing racks on which could be transported 80/100-kg bombs.

The catapult version differed from the normal RE.2000 by the installation of launch equipment systems for operations off ships, with attachment points which emerged from the fuselage above the wing trailing edge, and catapult attaching point below the aircraft.

REGGIANE CANOPIES

The two versions of the RE.2000 canopy fairing. At left, the earlier fenestrated fairing as used in prototypes and the first production series aircraft to be built. At right, the later version without fenestration.

The various prototypes and production aircraft built by Reggiane featured a variety of canopy types. The RE.2000 was fitted with a canopy that slid to the rear, mounted on ball bearings on lateral gliders on the fuselage cladding. The prototype featured a windshield formed from a single piece of curved plexiglass, while in the subsequent aircraft the windshield was strengthened by a longitudinal brace in its upper part. The canopy could be locked in a closed or semi-closed position by spring latches connected to a lever that fitted into the notches of the guide rails, and featured a handle that could rapidly jettison the canopy in the event of an emergency. At the front, the sliding canopy was fitted with two spring latches connected to a control lever located internally to the pilot's left on the front edge of the hatch, which was used to lock and unlock the canopy.

On the prototypes the moving part was formed by a single curved sheet of glass, while in those aircraft operated by the Regia Aeronautica and on exported machines, a cross-bracing reinforcement strut was introduced. In all the RE.2000s manufactured for export and those of the first series delivered to the Regia Aeronautica, the rear fairing of the cockpit was composed of transparent panels to improve the pilot's visibility, but in the twenty aircraft of the *Catapultabile* and *Grande Autonomia* versions these were replaced by a closed fairing.

A completely different canopy was adopted on the RE.2001, formed by a frame that folded laterally to the right, dividing into two sections at the time of opening through means of a longitudinal hinge. Mounted in the upper part of the canopy were four transparent plexiglass panels, while each side of the moving parts featured two shatter-proof windows, the rear one being fixed while the forward part could be opened by sliding it backwards. A subsequent modification saw the addition of a cable attached to the headrest plate which held the door in place on opening and stopped it tipping completely over and onto the fuselage. The canopy opening mechanism was positioned in the two lower parts of the door and comprised two handles which could be opened from the outside with keys.

The RE.2002 prototype, MM454, having been prepared from a RE.2000 airframe, featured the canopy and rear fairings of the type used on the export and early production RE.2000s. In production-model RE.2002s, however, a new canopy was introduced, formed by a single principal mainframe opening to the right with three transparent plexiglass panels mounted in its upper part. In the sides of the framework two shatter-proof glazed panels were mounted, the rear panel fixed and the forward openable. This canopy also featured an attached cable to hold it in place when opened. Rapid canopy release was performed by moving two levers located in the middle section of the lower hatch upwards. The armoured windshield featured armoured glass.

The canopy of the RE.2005 was very similar to the RE.2002 canopy. The prototypes featured three transparent panels in the upper section of the canopy, these being reduced to two in the production aircraft. The pilot's seat was also lowered by around 19 cm.

The RE.2000 production canopy with the rear-sliding canopy.

The RE.2001 cockpit canopy opened on the right side and featured a folding panel.

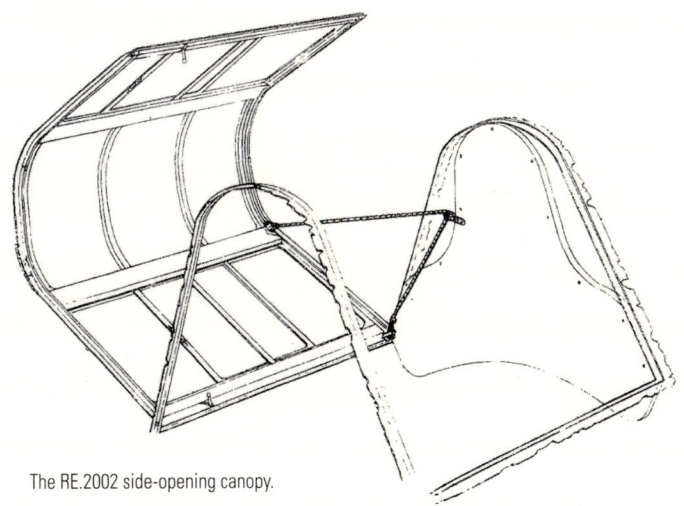

The RE.2002 side-opening canopy.

Continues next page

Reggiane Canopies (cont/d)

Above and top right: The RE.2002 prototype with the first type of sliding canopy. It was abandoned in favour of a side-opening canopy. Right: Female workers on the production line for RE.2002 canopies.

Below: Evolutionary scheme of the RE.2005 canopy. The development of canopy design, as seen on the prototype MM494, the modified version MM495, and the Serie 'Zero'.

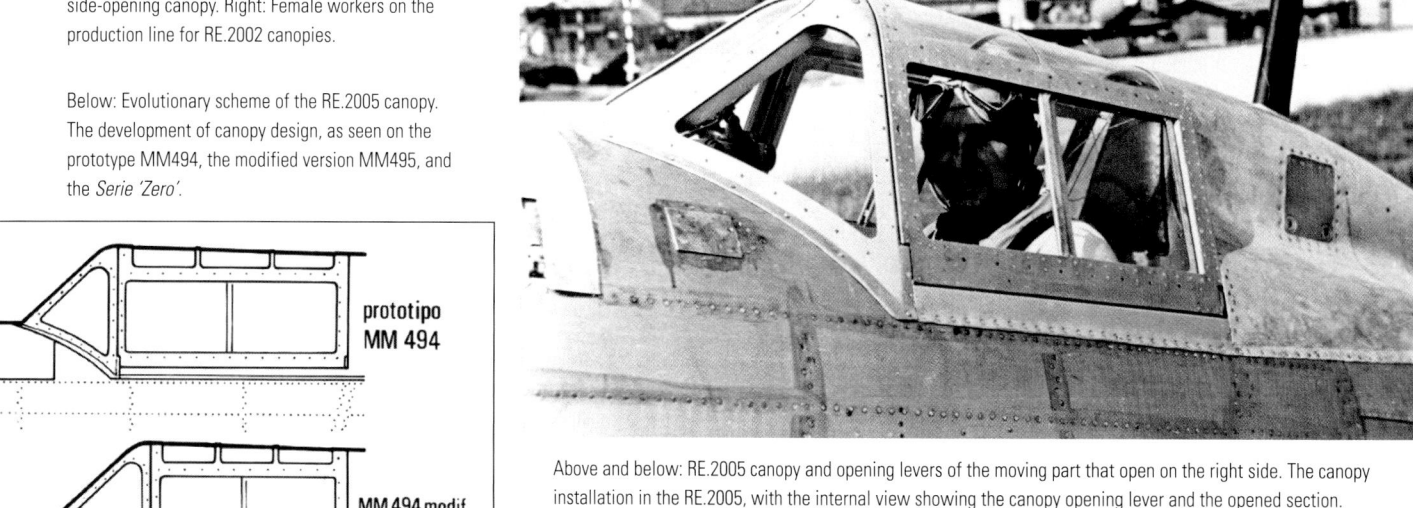

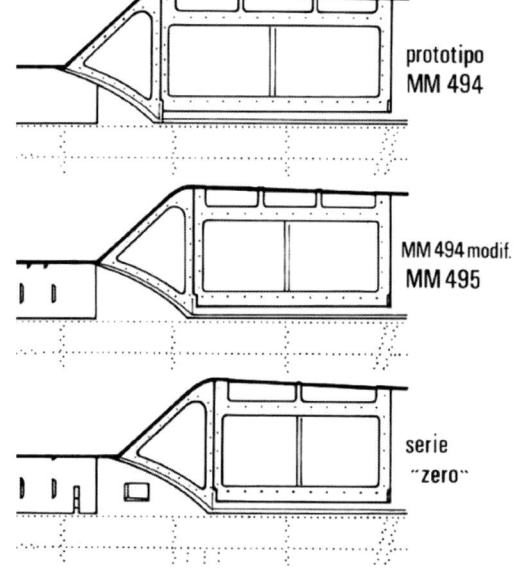

prototipo
MM 494

MM 494 modif.
MM 495

serie
"zero"

Above and below: RE.2005 canopy and opening levers of the moving part that open on the right side. The canopy installation in the RE.2005, with the internal view showing the canopy opening lever and the opened section.

In service with the Regia Aeronautica

HAVING identified a requirement to deploy fighter aircraft with greater endurance than the G.50 and C.200 in order to escort convoys and bombers between Italy and North Africa, *Superaereo*[4] decided to place an order with Reggiane for a small batch of five RE.2000s which would be assigned to a small unit known as the *Sezione Sperimentale* (Experimental Section) based in Sicilia. Diverted directly from those originally assigned to foreign orders, the aircraft belonged to the Iª *serie 'Intercettori'* (interceptors) and were characterised by canopy glazing which extended to the rear of the cockpit. They received *Matricole Militari* from MM5068 to MM5072. These aircraft were subsequently joined by the prototype MM408 which had been refurbished and reallocated as MM5074.

Towards the end of March 1941, the *Sezione Sperimentale* was initially assigned to the 156° *Gruppo* CT based at Catania and led by *capitano* Pietro Calistri, but shortly after, following the disbanding of the *Gruppo*, on 8 April 1941 it was incorporated into the 74ª *Squadriglia* of the 23° *Gruppo Autonomo* CT, based at Comiso with a staff of eight pilots, four of whom were officers.

Continuing under the command of *capitano* Calistri, the *Sezione Sperimentale* was reorganised and reinforced with some new pilots from the *Gruppo*. A period of training on the new aircraft was complicated by technical problems which culminated in the loss of MM5074 (the former prototype) on 19 April, when the aircraft crashed in unknown circumstances during a training flight, with the loss of *tenente pilota* De Angelis.

This page: RE.2000 Iª Serie *'Intercettori'* assigned to the *Sezione sperimentale* in Sicilia which was initially under the control of the 156° *Gruppo* CT.

---

[4] *Superaereo* was the name given to the General Staff of the Regia Aeronautica during the Second World War; it became operational on 1 June 1940 and depended directly on the Italian Supreme Command.

Continues on page 48

Above: An RE.2000 assigned to 74ª *Squadriglia* of 23° *Gruppo* at Trapani. Note the covers in place to protect the mainwheel tyres from the sun.

Right: An RE.2000 formerly of the *Sezione Sperimentale* assigned to 74ª *Squadriglia* of the 23° *Gruppo* Autonomo CT, before a mission in sun-filled skies at Comiso.

Above and right: An RE.2000 of the newly formed 377ª *Squadriglia*. Note the black-coloured engine cowling and the wheel covers bearing the *Squadriglia's* number.

A Reggiane RE.2000 of 377ª *Squadriglia* at Palermo-Boccadifalco in March 1942. The standard factory finish of this type included a three-tone scheme, while the black cowling denotes the aircraft was assigned to the first *Sezione* of the *Squadriglia*.

A Reggiane promotional postcard of the RE.2000 published in 1940.

landing in MM5068. This concluded with the aircraft overturning, but without fire and fateful consequences for its pilot.

On 1 August 1941 *Comando Aereo della Sicilia* disbanded the *Sezione Sperimentale* and this led to the forming of the 377ª *Squadriglia* with a staff of twelve pilots and 26 mechanics. Once again, this new unit reported to the 23° *Gruppo Autonomo CT* under *maggiore* Tito Falconi and was deployed to Trapani Milo airfield.

The new unit took charge of twelve RE.2000s of the IIIª *Serie* G.A., to which standard three of the former Iª *Serie* aircraft (MM5069, 5071 and 5072) were converted. The early period of its existence was decidedly difficult for the new unit, with low aircraft availability. The low point was reached on 9 August, when just one aircraft was serviceable, in part due to the return to the manufacturer of some aircraft for technical modifications. In this period the fighters were also modified with underwing racks, each capable of carrying a payload of around 100 kg, their prospective task being the conduct of attacks against airfields on Malta.

Operating from Trapani Milo and Comiso airfields in the second half of 1941, the RE.2000s were engaged in flying escort for naval convoys and interdiction patrols over the Mediterranean between Sicily and North Africa, as the range of the Reggiane meant that it was the only aircraft capable of successfully conducting such operations. On 27 September 1941, while engaged in a long-range reconnaissance mission extending

Despite this tragic event, Calistri managed to complete a first operational mission on 20 April 1941, providing protection to some seaplanes engaged in a rescue mission.

After subjecting the aircraft to a series of modifications and the installation of the Piaggio P.IX bis engine, which was more reliable than the previous powerplant, the *Sezione Sperimentale* continued its training with the new aircraft over the following months. Pilots complained about numerous technical problems, particularly involving the Piaggio engine, with two accidents occurring on 7 and 9 July. The first and most severe of these saw the destruction of MM5070 when its tailwheel broke on landing, causing the aircraft to bounce and overturn. The fighter caught fire and was burnt out, but the pilot, *tenente* Moruzzi, survived with minor injuries. The second incident involved *tenente* Solaroli, who suffered an engine failure and performed an emergency

Outdoor maintenance for an RE.2000 from 377ª *Squadriglia* which appears to have been parked in a stone-walled revetment.

Capitano Solaroli poses alongside one of the first RE.2000 '*Intercettori*' of the *Sezione Sperimentale*.

almost to the Tunisian coast, *tenente* Solaroli spotted a British naval formation which was subsequently attacked by Italian torpedo bombers.

Malta, however, proved to be a constant threat and the Italian commanders continually pressed for permission to mount attacks against the 'fortress' island and its airfields with any available aircraft. The 377ª *Squadriglia* was also tasked with attacking the island's infrastructure, although these orders created a difficult situation, as confirmed post-war by Solaroli:

'*Returning to Trapani after a brief period of leave, having collected a new RE.2000 from Reggio Emilia, I unexpectedly found myself promoted to commandant of the squadriglia. I found out the reason why in the mess. Capitano Calistri had devised a surprise operation, aimed at disrupting and strafing Malta, according to a sensible tactic that promised success at least equal to the risk.*

But his proposal was completely revised by Comando Aereo della Sicilia, resulting in enormous risks and no chance of success, so he had refused to lead the mission.

'*I can still picture capitano Calistri, his olive face, black hair and eyes, slow and measured movements, describing without anger or emphasis, advanced manoeuvres, or defensive and offensive tactics. He was always calm in giving orders, or reprimanding or praising staff. All through the night I considered my duties as new unit commander, and whether I was right to accept the post, despite having little option.*

'*The following morning the commander outlined to me the operation which I would have to command. Crazy! It meant departing from the airfield at Comiso (the closest to Malta) at night, climbing up and approaching the island from the east at 2,000 metres, then diving to release munitions onto the airfield at Mikabba and strafing it, where it seemed many bombers had just arrived, and then retiring to the west or north, confronting the anti-aircraft barrage both inbound and outbound in a delicate aircraft and one without flame dampers, which meant that, at night, the flames from the exhaust could be seen from a great distance. Moreover, none of our senior commanders had even considered that none of us had ever flown at night, not even in a simple tourist aircraft!*

RE.2000 of 377ª *Squadriglia* photographed while operating from the airfield at Comiso.

'*But orders are orders. In the afternoon I left for Comiso with* tenente *Pausi and* marescialli *Albani and Carmello; a transport aircraft simultaneously brought our mechanics and our armament.*'

After an initial operation, attempted on the night of 14 November, against Malta was aborted due to inclement weather – probably providentially considering the pilots' lack of experience in night flying – the following day, 15 November, a first offensive action was conducted over Malta, albeit not before having reconsidered the methodology of the operation. Four RE.2000s departed from Comiso at 0520, flown by *tenente* Solaroli, *sergente maggiore* Albani, *tenente* Pausi (from the 75ª *Squadriglia*) and *maresciallo* Carmello. The latter, however, was forced to return to Comiso with engine problems. The specific details of the mission were recalled with great clarity by *tenente* Solaroli:

'*A day of tension, of anxiety, with nothing to do and the sky permanently overcast. I woke again at three in the morning; the weather had improved, flat clouds and the crescent moon reflecting in the white clouds that rode across the sky. Everything was ready. At four I received the order to depart. I went with my wingman to the end of the airfield where there was a red signal light. Take-off direction was indicated by some green lights arrayed vertically ten metres apart, and at the end of the runway there was another red one. Take-off. All good, undercarriage up, and I slightly closed cowling flaps, and brought up the enormous wing flaps. Albani quickly reached me and we set off in formation, just like in daylight: he could see me clearly, as I could see him, illuminated by the flames from my engine.*

'*I looked down: everything was black as ink, and all I saw were the flames of the other pair which had taken off after us. My instruments, illuminated by phosphorous, were all working well, and only the compass, which was not phosphorescent, had to be illuminated by a pocket light.*

'*We climbed slowly over the airfield: we were heavy, 180 kg of bombs and a full load of fuel. At 4,000 metres I turned sharply south; my vision had become accustomed to the night, and I saw the division between land and sea and the whiteness of the surf against the coast around the lighthouse at Capo Scaramia which was due to be illuminated in an hour to indicate the direction of the airfield. One hundred kilometres of sea separated us from our objective: 15-20 minutes ... an enormous amount of time!* '*Ahead and a little below us was an ocean of white clouds, while the little moon and myriads of stars were above us in a clear sky. I headed east, then made a wide turn and returned to where I presumed Malta was.*

'*It seemed as though there was nothing to be achieved other than return home and wait for dawn. While I was pondering this problem, through a gap in the clouds I noticed a red light. It was Malta. I dived down from 4,000 metres, silent, engine at minimum, cowling flaps closed; Albani followed me on my right. That red light was in my gunsight and was rapidly approaching, when suddenly a searchlight and the runway lighting came on. We found ourselves on the exact landing path into Mikabba: they must have mistaken us for British bombers returning from an operation. Luck was with us.*

'*We descended to almost ground level and spread out. I saw a flash on my right: it was the first*

searchlight that had fixed on Albani's aircraft, and I could clearly see the cluster of incendiaries falling from his belly. I released my bomb load simultaneously and opened fire with my machine guns. Now all the searchlights were on us; the quick passage from complete darkness to the light of the searchlights completely blinded me. By a miracle I avoided a steeple or a tower as I finished firing and headed off towards a cloud ahead and slightly above me. I had an artificial horizon, and I hoped to be able to navigate with that and the gyroscopic directional. A false hope! As I entered cloud, the horizon and directional went completely out of phase. I had never trained in instrument navigation or blind-flying, and had evidently made too abrupt a pull-up, and now I had to base my flying on instinct and logic alone. I heard the engine lose rpm; the aircraft must have been vertical, so I manoeuvred to level out, hearing the engine which was not picking up, and thought I was in a dive, so I pulled gently up, still blind. For the second time I felt like I was hanging in the air with an engine that had almost stopped, so I had to get upside down, and I manoeuvred to exit the spin. I was in a bad place, with an engine that was losing power, so I decided to bail out, as there was nothing left to do.*

'*I had to still be over the island. Seconds passed, but they seemed like centuries. I tried to jettison the cockpit canopy, but in the dark I could not locate the emergency handle. I entered a spin for a third time and manoeuvred to escape. This time I came out of the clouds, but I was almost inverted: 'above' me was the port of Valletta. I levelled out and headed off towards the sea, followed by searchlights and anti-aircraft fire, but I kept on going – straight. By a miracle, nothing had hit me. I was out of their range and drew a breath.*

'*All seemed to be going well, but I could no longer find the pocket lamp, which must have been blown away together with my oxygen mask, which had literally been torn from its helmet attachments and tube. I couldn't see either the compass or clock, neither of which were illuminated. Somehow, I had to go north, and remembering my training at the Accademia, I looked for the North Star. Fixing it exactly on my nose I headed for Sicilia. It was, however, impossible to calculate the time: minutes seemed like hours. After a century I saw land, but no lights were lit. The land was giving reflections off water, it seemed to be a marsh: between Capo Passero and Capo Scaramia. Instead, it should have been very dry.*

'*I kept the land on my left: if I was over Sicilia I must at a certain point find Augusta, Catania or Etna; however, if I was over the gulf of Taranto, I would see the coast and then turn from north to east. After a certain period (I had no sense of minutes or tens of minutes), I saw a dense black cloud dead ahead. I decided to reverse my course and wait for dawn, heading for where the weather* was clear with the idea of later attempting an emergency belly-landing on a beach. I found a promontory, which, from its shape, had to be Capo Passero, but it was strangely bordered by lagoons, so I turned west and finally saw the Capo Scaramia light illuminated. I was safe.

'*Dawn began to break, and a few minutes later I was over Comiso airfield, and I made ready to land. I saw two RE.2000s on the ground. With minimal light, and without airfield beacons or airfield lighting, I made a perfect landing and taxied to my blast shelter.*

'*The mechanics surrounded me, telling me that* tenente *Pausi had landed just a few minutes previously, and that* maresciallo *Carmello had been forced to return a few minutes after departure with engine problems. As the exceptional pilot that he was, he had made a perfect landing in the dark.* Maresciallo *Albani was missing.*

'*I climbed out, chatting with Carmello and the ground crew, but after a few steps I had to sit down on the wet grass because my legs, after the emotions of three hours with stressed nerves, would no longer support me.*

'*It seemed that during our absence a huge storm had broken out which had flooded the entire area of the capes, which was why I had not been able to recognise them. I met up with* tenente *Pausi in the mess, where the first thing I did was gulp down a nice hot coffee laced with cognac and then, between one mouthful and another, listened to Pausi's report, only to be interrupted by the roar of an RE.2000 that was making a beeline for the control tower. Thank God, it was Albani. So, we had all returned!*

'*Pausi, in his colourful Veneto accent, described to us his adventure with a British nightfighter, probably a two-seat Boulton Paul with a four-gun turret,[5] and which even before his arrival over the island had plastered him with hits. With the bright flames from his engine, he made a highly visible target, while all he saw of his adversary were streams of tracers. He had been able to disengage twice with a sharp inversion, but had to dump his bombs into the sea and take himself back home. Albani, however, had disengaged and departed southbound over the island at low level and, with a wide turn, had made a much-delayed return. I communicated the results to the* Comando di Squadra *at Palermo, who seemed enthusiastic about them!*

'*Some days later,* colonnello *Falconi accompanied me to the* Comando Squadra *as it seemed that they wanted the operation to be repeated. From information supplied by a German bomber squadron that operated from a nearby airfield, we learned that the enemy forces on Malta had set up a barrier of barrage balloons at a height of 200-300 metres. Perhaps our operation had had unexpected results, but*

with the balloons in place it would be impossible to repeat it.'

On the day after the mission six of the seven serviceable aircraft were transferred from Trapani to Comiso with the intention of conducting further attacks on Malta. In command of the detachment was *tenente colonnello* Falconi, accompanied by *tenenti* Solaroli and Pausi, *sottotenente* Bisio, *sergente maggiore* Albani and *sergente* Mocchiuti.

On 19 November, Falconi, Solaroli, Pausi and Albani departed at 0530 to attack Hal Far airfield, on which they dropped 352 incendiaries. The violent reaction of the anti-aircraft artillery caused no damage to the Italian fighters, and Falconi managed to evade an attack by a British fighter. The four Reggianes returned to Comiso at 0715 without any problems. Solaroli recalled the operation:

'*Two days later we were back at Comiso, and three hours before dawn we left in the following pairs: Falconi with Carmello, me with Albani. Clear in my mind were the tactics that we would use to have any possibility of escape and to allow the famous Bollettino to report that Malta had been bombed.*

'*I climbed to 7,000 metres to the east of Malta. The moonless night was fairly clear with a myriad of stars. I dived at full power with my wingman heading west, crossing the island at 1,500 metres, and released my munitions roughly over Mikabba airfield. Once again luck was with us. The searchlights and anti-aircraft*

batteries, taken by surprise, were activated after our pass. I departed at sea level to some 20 kilometres west of Gozo, and then we climbed back to 4,000 metres. This time everything worked well. I managed to illuminate the compass and clock, heading for Capo Passero where, cruising slowly, we waited for the dawn to land.

'*Tenente colonnello* Falconi *and* maresciallo *Carmello never managed to reach Malta: they were intercepted by nightfighters and, with great difficulty, managed to disengage themselves and return. Certainly, the operation would never be repeated, as it would waste pilots and aircraft on absurd and idiotic actions. The* Comando Squadra *was not of the same opinion: it was essential that Malta had to be disturbed at night at all costs.*'

Over the following days routine operations continued, such as liaison flights to other airfields, convoy escort missions, and patrols searching for enemy shipping, none of which resulted in any significant results. On 27 and 28 November 1941, some aircraft were tasked to patrol the airspace over Trapani Milo airfield on the occasion of the visit of His Majesty Vittorio Emanuele III, the King of Italy.

On 4 December two RE.2000s, flown by *tenente* Solaroli and *sergente maggiore* Albani, departed from Comiso at 2300 for a nocturnal cluster-bomb attack on Hal Far airfield. Despite difficult flying and violent anti-aircraft reaction, the two pilots returned undamaged to Comiso at 0050 having dropped 176 sub-munitions. *Tenente* Solaroli again recalled this mission:

Trapani Milo airfield: on 28 November 1941, His Majesty Vittorio Emanuele III King of Italy reviewed the Regia Aeronautica units in Sicilia. The RE.2000s assured the air defence of the region.

[5] Pausi is describing a Boulton Paul Defiant.

Continues on page 54

Two RE.2000s of 377ª *Squadriglia* photographed while operating from the airfield at Comiso. Note the different styles of individual aircraft numbers used after formation of the unit. '18' does not carry unit insigna, but the regular '*fascio*' insignia used on Regia Aeronautica aircraft (see the author's companion volumes on Macchi and FIAT Fighters).

A rare photograph of an RE.2000 prepared for a night bombing mission over Malta. Note the pilot's parachute lying on the port wing and the 50-kg bombs on the ground.

From left, *sergente* Capatti and *maresciallo* Carmello stand in front of an RE.2000 armed with the Nardi 'spezzoniera' (bomb rack) fitted beneath the central fuselage.

The 377ª *Squadriglia Autonoma* CT fighters operated for short periods from the advanced airfield on the island of Pantelleria.

'With a full moon, I left at midnight without any airfield lighting or beacon. It was a magnificent night – some white clouds, thousands of stars, and a very low temperature. I slowly gained height; I had two 100-kg bombs under the wings. Everything on board was functioning, and I checked the instruments frequently. Experience would have warned me immediately if the needle of one of the instruments was out of place. I controlled the engine cylinder head temperature with the cowling flaps in accordance with the decreasing outside air temperature. After thirty minutes I had reached 8,000 metres, so I set course for Malta. As I crossed the outer ring of Malta's defences, the heavy calibre anti-aircraft batteries thundered into life. I could easily see the first shots; they were small white or black clouds, but they were fairly inaccurate, much lower, and off the right. I flew decisively over the island. It was a magnificent spectacle; it seemed to be like Venezia on the night of the Redeemer: there were white, green and red flashes. It was dangerous to think of them as benign, because, on the contrary, they were quite dangerous, as they were the tracers from the 20 mm and 47 mm anti-aircraft guns. I managed to avoid them with continuous turns, variations in engine control, dives, and climbs. The time passed slowly. I entered and left the island, always pursued by the anti-aircraft fire.

'I was inexplicably calm and continued this harassment operation for an hour. The British must have been furious, as they continued their pointless firing. Having turned on their searchlights during many of my passes, the beams of light attempting vainly to highlight me, they now started firing with the assistance of radar direction. I could see no lights on the ground, only the flashes from the cannon and guns, but the moon made the outline of the coastline highly visible, and I could easily identify the port of Valletta where, having completed the time period I had been assigned to stay in place, from a dive I released two bombs at 300 metres.

'I then sped towards home, diving at 500 km/h, recognising Capo Scaramia where I fired the recognition rocket of the day and, lowering the undercarriage and flaps, prepared to land. I was just about to touch down when a searchlight lit me up,and I was dazzled by its reflections from the wings, which were shiny and wet from the humidity, and I only just managed not to lose control.

'But this operation had gone well. There were no others, as a few days later the entire unit (the 23° Gruppo CT, to which Solaroli was assigned) was transferred to Africa to protect a convoy of warships transporting fuel for our troops to stop the second British advance at Agedabia.'[6]

Over the following few days, pairs of aircraft conducted interdiction missions near Capo Bon without any significant results, while similarly uneventful were two convoy escort flights performed on 7 December off the island of Ustica by four-aircraft and two-aircraft formations, throughout the day.

On 11 December, with the transfer of the 23° *Gruppo Autonomo* CT to North Africa, *capitano* Calistri officially handed over command of the 377ª *Squadriglia* to *tenente* Giuseppe David. The average operational serviceability of the unit during this period was eight or nine aircraft per day. On 19 December 1941, following precise orders from the *Comando di Sicilia*, the *Squadriglia* was transferred to Chinisia airfield, although some aircraft still operated from Trapani airport and some deployed to Reggio Calabria for convoy escort, although operations were limited. In 1941 the combat record of the 377ª *Squadriglia* amounted to 88 flights, totalling 250 operational flying hours, while non-operational flying amounted to 349 flights, totalling 280 flying hours.

On 30 December, following an order from the *Comando di Sicilia*, the *Squadriglia* left the control of the 23° *Gruppo* CT and was reorganised as 377ª *Squadriglia Autonoma* CT, reporting directly to the *Comando Caccia di Sicilia* (Sicilian Fighter Command). The main base of the unit was Trapani Milo airfield, as at the time, Chinisia was not operational. Eleven pilots were on strength, six officers and five NCOs, commanded by *tenente* David, but there were only six RE.2000s combat

---

[6] The interviews with *tenente* Solaroli featured in this chapter were generously provided by *ing.* Giovanni Massimello.

RE.2000 of the renamed 377ª *Squadriglia Autonoma* CT seen while operating from Palermo Boccadifalco. Note the mobile starting carts (above).

ready. Despite a small number of aircraft, the unit performed the usual convoy escort mission and patrols, often operating from the advanced airfield on the island of Pantelleria. During this period more accidents occurred which further limited the number of available fighters.

On 26 January 1942 *tenente* Martini, paired with a C.200 of the 7° *Gruppo* CT, conducted a convoy escort mission north of the Verkenna Islands in the afternoon. At the end of the mission, bad weather did not allow the three Italian fighters to land on Pantelleria, forcing the pilots, because of the lesser range of the AerMacchi fighter, to land near the racecourse at Kassar Said in Tunisia, where the Reggiane overturned on landing but without injuring the pilot. On 14 February another Reggiane was damaged during a deployment of seven aircraft to Comiso, when it nosed over on the muddy surface of the airfield there.

Another two Reggiane fighters were damaged the following day when the aircraft flown by *sottotenente* Ruggeri and *sergente maggiore* Brini, returning from an interdiction mission south of Calafrana (Malta), were involved in two separate incidents following engine faults. In the first event *sergente maggiore* Brini was forced to make an emergency landing near Murro di Porco

(Siracusa), resulting in a roll-over, while *sottotenente* Ruggeri, although managing to reach the outer limits of Comiso airfield, struck an obstacle on landing and the aircraft was subsequently out of use.

Ruggeri was also involved in an accident while landing at Comiso on 12 February in RE.2000, MM5069, one of the last remaining Iª *Serie* aircraft in use. The aircraft was destroyed after it collided on the ground with a Luftwaffe Bf 109 F. On 21 February another RE.2000 was damaged on returning from a patrol over the port of Messina when it came down on muddy terrain, the result being, inevitably, locked wheels and a nose-over.

An order from the *Comando di Sicilia* on 21 March 1942 transferred the unit to Palermo

Boccadifalco airfield and changed its designation to the 377ª *Squadriglia Autonoma Intercettori*, as well as adding some CR.42 biplanes to its inventory.

On 12 April 1942 *sottotenente* Pederzoli Wisdor was killed when he dived inexplicably into the ground near Arenella (Palermo) during a flight to test his radio and to provide training for the DICAT[7] forces.

A few days later, on 18 April, another tragedy struck the unit. During an inspection visit by *generale* Silvio Scaroni, commander of the *Aeronautica della Sicilia*, some aircraft were ordered to scramble in a readiness demonstration. *Tenente* Ruggeri, serving with the 377ª *Squadriglia Autonoma Intercettori*, took off in an AerMacchi

---

[7] Anti-aircraft defence.

Capitano Marcolin Luciano, posted as commander of 377ª *Squadriglia Autonoma* CT on 23 May 1942.

C.200 of the *Reparto Volo Comando Caccia*, but soon after lift-off suffered engine problems and was killed in an unsuccessful attempt to return to the airfield.

In the meantime, the fleet of Reggianes was reducing, a result of their worn-out condition and the chronic shortage of spare parts, to the point that in mid- April 1942 there were only four available aircraft. Despite this, the pilots maintained maximum effort, and on many occasions were scrambled to intercept British reconnaissance aircraft which, even if never caught, were always driven away, impeding the completion of their mission. By May 1942 the fleet of the 377ª *Squadriglia Autonoma Intercettori* comprised three RE.2000s, eight CR.42s (used principally for nightfighter operations), and a single AerMacchi C.200.

On 23 May 1942 *capitano* Luciano Marcolini assumed command of the unit, which in the month of June was involved in a deployment to the airfield on Pantelleria to participate in two of the most important air-sea battles conducted in the central Mediterranean, known to the Allies as Operation Harpoon and Operation Pedestal.

In this period the few available Reggianes of 377ª *Squadriglia Autonoma Intercettori* conducted numerous protection and escort missions on behalf of the 7ª *Divisione Navale,* which in June was engaged against the passage of enemy convoys during Operation Harpoon – which was intended to ferry in reinforcements to Malta.

During the first mission of the day on 15 June, commencing at dawn, Reggianes piloted by *capitano* Marcolini and *sergente maggiore* Aldo Sgubbi intercepted some British aircraft. Marcolini managed to engage one of them and reported having effectively machine-gunned the enemy aircraft. In the course of the fourth mission of the day, Marcolini and Sgubbi again intercepted a Bristol Blenheim, and after a brief combat, the British twin-engine bomber was claimed as shot down by the two Italian pilots.[8]

In total, between September 1941 and March 1942 the RE.2000s of the 377ª *Squadriglia Autonoma Intercettori* performed 170 combat missions for a total of more than 400 flying hours, while in the final period, up to September 1942, the activity of the Reggiane fighters was merged with those of the *Squadriglia's* other aircraft, which totalled 332 combat missions for around 600 flying hours.

RE.2000 combat missions continued until 16 September 1942, when the last remaining monoplanes, by then almost not fit for combat operations, were withdrawn from service and sent to Officine Reggiane for overhaul and conversion into the naval variant. It seems that a few aircraft were transferred for training purposes to the 1° *Nucleo Addestramento Intercettori* at Treviso, although their actual flying activity was, in reality, almost non-existent until the announcement of the armistice on 8 September 1943 – after which the story of the Reggiane RE.2000 in the colours of the Regia Aeronautica came to an end.

RE.2000 Cat. (*Catapultabile* - Catapultable)

Despite interest in aircraft carriers within the Regia Marina, Italy entered the Second World War not only without a carrier but without any projects for the use of ship-mounted aircraft. Following the battle of Punta Stilo, known also as 'The Battle of Calabria', which saw poor tactical cooperation with Regia Aeronautica aircraft and the successful incursion conducted by British torpedo aircraft on the port of Taranto on the night of 11 November 1940, the Regia Marina was deprived of half of its battleships and seriously reconsidered the use of shipboard aircraft. The Taranto action also revealed the strategic error made by the Italian military leadership in not proceeding with the acquisition of aircraft carriers at the end of the 1930s.

At the end of the first year of war, the head of *Supermarina* (the Naval General Staff) began to display firm interest in carriers and in the development of a fighter aircraft capable of being catapult-launched from battleships, to supplement or replace the IMAM RO.43 seaplane, a slow-embarked reconnaissance biplane that was totally incapable of protecting itself against hostile air action. The new aircraft would need to possess good manoeuvrability, enabling it to defend Italian

Promotional poster for the RE.2000 produced by Reggiane in 1940.

---

[8] This information is recorded in the 377ª *Squadriglia Autonoma* operational diary. Nevertheless, it seems that this loss was not admitted on the British side.

Catapulta Gagnotto – The Gagnotto catapult

The catapult installed in the principal warships of the Regia Marina was manufactured by the Officine Meccaniche Bargiacchi factory based at La Spezia and designed by *ingegnere del Genio Navale* (Naval Engineer) Luigi Gagnotto.

The launching system comprised a 21-metre-long steel framework with a single launch rail positioned on a rotating base at the prow of the vessel. This was electrically rotated to a maximum of 42° either side of the direction of travel. At full power, corresponding to a maximum pressure of 80 kg/cm², the trolley to which the aircraft was attached – weighing up to a maximum of 5,000 kg – was moved at a speed of 36 m/sec (corresponding to around 130 km/h) along the length of the rail to almost the very end, when the aircraft was detached from the trolley in a final braking section 2.5 metres in length.

Launching of the aircraft was initiated through a piston system powered by compressed air, developing the necessary thrust required to catapult the aircraft away from the ship at a speed sufficient to enable it to generate lift. In the course of the launch the aircraft and its pilot would be subjected to accelerations of around 3 g.

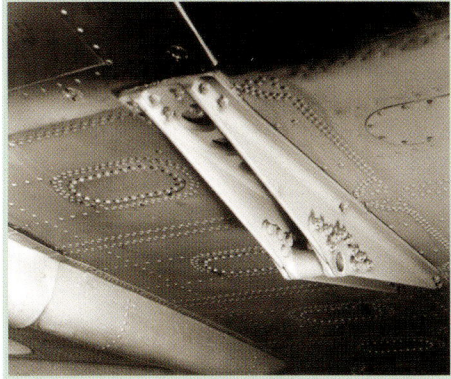

Above and below: Fuselage attachment points for lateral support which secured the RE.2000 Catapultabile to the launch framework and a wing attachment point for the catapult.

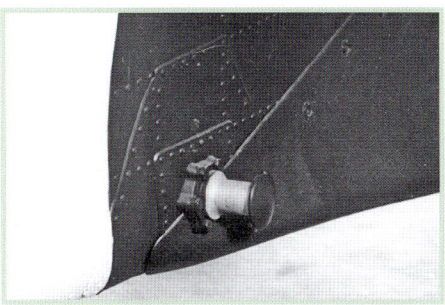

Below: The emblem applied to the rudder of the RE.2000 Cat. is said to have originated during the period the aircraft was commissioned at Tenere. Reiner, in conversation with technicians, mentioned that he was thinking about the possibility of ditching: '*I wish it was like a goose.*' The phrase was taken up by a specialist from the Regia Aeronautica who was then working for Reggiane, who immediately painted a small black duck on the aircraft as a 'lucky charm'.

An RE.2000 *Catapultabile* taking off from the battleship *Vittorio Veneto*. The aircraft is marked with a red '6' and lacks its sliding canopy but it appears to have additional padding behind the pilot's head. Strangely, no markings are painted under the wings, while the *fascio littorio* appears on the engine cowling.

warships against attack by torpedo-carrying aircraft. At the end of its mission the fighter, thanks to its prospective endurance, would be able to fly to the nearest friendly airfield in the combat area or, in some cases, would be abandoned by its pilot who would parachute to safety close to friendly shipping.

Following an initial evaluation of the ubiquitous CR.42, preparation of a series of suitably modified Reggiane RE.2000 fighters was proposed for operations off larger warships using pre-installed catapults. Despite the fact that this aircraft had been excluded from the competition for a new monoplane fighter for the Regia Aeronautica, because of its excellent range and overall good flight performance, the RE.2000 was considered the ideal aircraft to undertake such

Above and below: The fighter launch trolley developed for catapult use from Italian warships. The hook release system had a particularly difficult development, causing considerable delay to the programme.

Left and above: An RE.2000 *Catapultabile* on the launch trolley aboard the *Marina Militare* battleship *Vittorio Veneto* during trials.

operations, especially since its design could quickly be adapted to accept the modifications necessary to support its launch by the Gagnotto-Bargiacchi catapult as used on major Regia Marina battleships.

In order to use the RE.2000 for this particular mission, the fighter was installed with special catapult attachments known as *aggrappi* (launching clutches) formed of four large metal grips used to anchor the aircraft to the catapult trolley during its take-off run. Two forward grips were located on the underside of the wing and two protruded from the fuselage sides, just behind the trailing edge.

These *aggrappi* were then attached to moveable hooks installed on the uprights of the launch trolley. The trolley would be firmly attached to the launching rail, while the aircraft's engine was set at maximum rpm during the entire length of the catapult run. This was the most critical point of the launch, with everything depending on the correct functioning of the release mechanism to ensure that the aircraft was safely

catapulted. In view of the speed that had to be reached to enable the aircraft to become airborne, the slowing of the trolley at the end of the catapult run and the release of the attachment clamps meant that there had to be perfect synchronisation.

This problem of timing emerged during the first launch trials, when the retaining hooks of the grips, which were not perfectly synchronised,

interfered with the lower structure of the tailplanes, resulting in damage to the aircraft. This created a considerable delay in the programme and certification of the fighter at a very critical time for the Regia Marina when the availability of a defence aircraft on board large vessels was considered essential. The situation was further exacerbated by the tragic loss of *capitano* Fabbri

Below and opposite page top: RE.2000, MM8281, in which *tenente* Reiner visited his former colleagues from the 4° *Stormo* CT who operated from Gorizia airfield. (Asso4Stormo)

GIULIO REINER

Tenente Giulio Reiner (above) seen at centre (below). To the right side is *ingegner* Vardanega who supervised the catapult trials.

BORN at Como on 12 April 1915, GIULIO REINER enlisted in the Regia Aeronautica in July 1936 as a *Sottotenente di complemento* (short service commission second lieutenant) after completing his pre-military pilot training at the Aeroclub di Como, from where he transferred to the *Scuola Militare Idrovolanti* (Military Seaplane School) at Como and the *Scuola Centrale di Pilotaggio Idrovolanti* at Portorose. Initially assigned to the 199ª *Squadriglia Bombardamento Marittimo* at Brindisi, equipped with the SIAI Marchetti S.55, in the same year he was admitted to the *Accademia Aeronautica* to become a member of the 'Rex' course. On obtaining his nomination as *Sottotenente in Servizio Permanente Effettivo* (a full commission), he was posted to the 73ª *Squadriglia* of the IX° *Gruppo*, 4° *Stormo* C.T. at Gorizia. From the outbreak of the war he served with this unit throughout its operational service in North Africa. Returning to Italy in June 1941, his piloting abilities resulted in his detachment to the *Centro Sperimentale* at Guidonia to undertake flight-testing for the Reggiane RE.2000 *Catapultabile* and after concluding that work, on 14 July 1942, he returned to the 73ª *Squadriglia* in North Africa, becoming its commander on 16 July with the rank of *Tenente*. Following repatriation to Italy with his unit in January 1943 and further promotion based on the merits of his war service to the rank of *Capitano* on 12 January, he participated in the defence of mainland Italian territory and later fought in Sicilia between June and July of that year. After 8 September 1943, together with all the 4° *Stormo* and his 73ª *Squadriglia*, Reiner joined the co-belligerent Regia Aeronautica and participated in various operations over the Balkan theatres. On 27 March 1944, he was tasked with organising the *Nucleo Recuperi del Materiale Aeronautico* (Aviation Equipment Recovery Unit) in Sicilia, and on 6 June 1944, he assumed command of the *Presidio Regionale* of Eastern Sicilia.

On 29 January 1948 he was posted back to the 4° *Stormo* and detached to Napoli to undertake flight-testing of P-51Ds emerging from repair or maintenance at the associated *Squadra Riparazione Aeromobili e Motori* of the 4°*Stormo* and those from the 5° *Reparto Tecnico Aeromobili*. He also oversaw the training of the *Stormo*'s pilots in individual and formation aerobatics. Benefitting from the post-war displacement laws, which sanctioned the redundancy of staff considered excess to military requirements, on 26 June 1949 he transferred to the *Servizio Ausiliario* (Auxiliary Service), and for several years undertook the role of flying instructor at the Aeroclub di Como. He also worked as an engineer at a vehicle distributor in Varese. He died at Beregazzo con Figliaro (Como) on 6 March 2003.

on 21 May 1941. Fabbri had been assigned to conduct the flight trials but lost his life in the first ready RE.2000 *Catapultabile* (MM471) during its transfer flight from the Reggiane factory to Taranto. Caught in a violent storm over the Apennines, the aircraft crashed on the mountainous terrain near Costa San Savino (Gubbio). Then the second prototype, MM485, was badly damaged during the transfer of the aircraft onto the catapult. In order to proceed with the flight trials, it was necessary to convert another aircraft, destined for export and drawn from the Reggiane production lines.

Following the loss of *capitano* Fabbri, *tenente* Giulio Reiner was selected to carry out the flight tests, albeit not before pilots of the calibre of Agello, De Bernardi and Colombo of SAI had declined the opportunity to conduct the trial launches.

After trials had once again encountered problems with the launch system, on 25 July 1941 tests were conducted with further modified launch parameters and it seemed that, apparently, all worked well. However once the mock-up aircraft had been recovered, it was noted that once again the left-hand stabiliser had been severely damaged by the forward attachment grip, as a result of the grip's insufficient speed of retraction from the mounting that attached it to the launch trolley. Further testing into retraction speeds were conducted on 2 August 1941, these still obtaining negative results, this time due to the supports becoming deformed by the hard stop made by the trolley at the end of the catapult launch rail. A subsequent attempt on 5 August with reinforced trolley legs similarly failed due to the strengthening being insufficient, and only on 12 August was it finally possible to obtain a positive test outcome, this achieved after yet further modifications and adjustments to the grip retraction speed.

Further tests were conducted on 25 September and 5 October 1941, but after a new report submitted by Reiner, which caused doubts over the functioning of the launch system, the Ministerial Commission charged with overseeing the tests decided to suspend work and send the launch trolley to the naval *Arsenale* (shipyard) at Spezia. Here *capitano* Taddei, responsible for the trolley design, undertook a complete rebuild of the trolley, taking into consideration all the experience gained over the course of the failed launches. It was believed that the failures in the numerous launch attempts were attributable to the less than perfect design and development of the launch trolley, resulting from the urgency of its preparation and the pressures emanating from senior military officials.

Having revised the trolley design and undertaken launches with mock-ups that provided encouraging results, the 14 March 1942 was fixed as the date for the first live launch with a pilot on board. Following some delays caused by minor technical issues, the first launch was rescheduled, but it was also decided carry it out on the seaplane-launching catapult installed on the RN *Miraglia*.[9]

The RN *Miraglia*, used for the first real catapult trials. The *Miraglia* had the earlier catapult, fixed aft, replaced in 1935 by a similar 35°-pivoting device on each side. (arch. E. Bagnasco)

Regia Nave *Giuseppe Miraglia*

Initially, the RN *Giuseppe Miraglia*, (commonly known as RN *Miraglia*), was ordered as a postal delivery ship for the *Ferrovie dello Stato* (Italian State Railway) with the name *Città di Messina*. However, after her launch on 20 December 1923, she was incorporated into the Regia Marina as a seaplane support ship, providing logistical support to the air component assigned to the Italian fleet's battleships and cruisers. Conversion into what was effectively a floating air base began on 24 January 1925 and during the conquest of Abyssinia in 1935 and 1936, the vessel served as an aircraft transport for East Africa. She was equipped with two hangars and, including those on deck, could carry around twenty aircraft, depending on the model. She had the same assignment during the Spanish Civil War, operating in 1935 and 1936. Unharmed during the Allied raid on Taranto, on the night of 11-12 November 1940, the ship was later used profitably for subsequent actions in the Mediterranean.

Two *Gagnotto* model catapults were installed to launch aircraft from the ship. She was also capable of operating with seaplanes that were recovered by lifting them from the sea by using a revolving crane that extended nine metres outboard at the centreline of each side opening on the hangar beams.

Following the armistice, the aircraft carrier *Miraglia* departed Venice, surrendered to the Royal Navy and anchored in Saint Paul Bay, Malta. After the war, the ship was used to repatriate Italian prisoners from camps in Egypt and Algeria, and civilians from Libya and the Dodecanese Islands.

She was later taken to the Taranto *Arsenale* to be used as a barracks ship for torpedo crews and later as a workshop ship.

The vessel was decommissioned on 15 July 1950 for subsequent scrapping.

Preceded by a pair of positive mock-up launches, finally, on 9 May 1942, the RE.2000, MM8281, with *tenente* Giulio Reiner at the controls, was successfully launched from the deck of the RN *Miraglia* in front of *Ammiraglio* (Admiral) Angelo Jachino, Commander in Chief of the Regia Marina.

Reiner recalled those moments sometime later: '*The launch conditions were established: detachment speed 48 metres per second, obtained* by combining the 32.5 m/sec of the catapult with the 15.5 m/sec of the relative wind. The technicians informed me that the catapult launch would result in an acceleration of 3.5 g, and I asked them whether the aircraft would support it (it was not in fact designed to tolerate a stress value greater than 3 g). All went well, except that I remember that I was practically blinded by a film of grease on my goggles which occurred at the most critical moment as I pushed the stick forward to increase

[9] RN is an abbreviation for Regia Nave ('Royal Ship').

my airspeed. As I came off the catapult, the aircraft was on the edge of a stall.'

After the fighter had left the catapult trolley, those witnessing the event were filled with trepidation as the fighter disappeared below their line of sight for some moments (Reiner said that he was slightly distracted during the launch by his attempt to remove his grease-filmed goggles). There was a collective sigh of relief when the aircraft was seen in flight. Reiner then went on to perform a series of spectacular aerobatics which were observed enthusiastically by the sailors and officers aboard the vessel.

Over the following days, further positive launches were performed, with no technical issues recorded. In the course of these trials, conducted with slightly varying parameters, an ideal launch velocity of 41 metres/second was identified, with a flap setting of 15°. During the launch the pilot was subjected to an acceleration of around 3 g.

At the end of this test cycle, *tenente* Reiner prepared a report on his assessment of the flying qualities experienced in the RE.2000:

Flying qualities: In normal and aerobatic flight, the aircraft is very pleasing as it lacks any essential defects and is, above all, easy to fly in all manoeuvres. It is very 'kind' to pilots, and undoubtedly within the capabilities of all pilots. In the dive, the machine is slow to gain speed because of its frontal profile.

Detachment manoeuvre: It is easy, and the best condition is achieved by setting the flaps at 10°. There is a slight tendency to yaw to the right which is easily correctable. The speed on the ASI at detachment is 150/160 km/h (the test was conducted only with a full load of fuel and the on-board machine guns, but excluding the radio system and ammunition, and the hooks necessary for the catapult system).

Landing manoeuvre: This is also simple, with the flaps fully down and with an approach speed of 180 km/h which at the point of contact with the ground reduces to 150/130 km/h).

Visibility: When taxiing, visibility is very poor. In flight it is also poor in a longitudinal sense, where the dynamic air intake for the engine

This page and following: An excellent photographic sequence of the launch trials of the RE.2000 *Catapultabile* under the command of *tenente* Reiner from the RN *Miraglia* near the Gulf of Taranto, which was crowned by the first successful launch on 9 May 1942. Other launches were carried out over the following days, again all crowned by success. (P.Monti)

located above the cowling makes this inconvenience even more serious. Visibility to the rear is fair, but is hindered by the reinforcing strut in the rear canopy. The most important drawback occurs during hard manoeuvring, as with relatively fierce acceleration come irregularities in engine function (reductions in rpm probably due to flooding of the carburettor caused by the faulty functioning of the float chamber plug). This potential handicap should be taken into consideration, especially during the launch phase, when, by necessity, there is acceleration of around 3 g.

Total weight of the aeroplane: *The empty weight of the prototype is 2,059 kg. As series production aircraft become heavier, and when the fittings for catapult operations are added, a higher empty weight of at least 2,200 kg is predicted.*

Speed*: the predicted speed for detachment of the trolley with the above quoted weight is 150/160 km/h, equivalent to 41,6644.44 m/sec. The maximum speed in flight with a payload of 779 kg at a constant 2,380 rpm with maximum boost pressure can be assessed as around 390/400 km/h at sea level; at 2,000 metres – 430/445 km/h; at 5,500 metres – 490/505 km/h, this latter height being that at which the maximum speed was recorded.*

Endurance: *With the tank completely full of fuel and taking into account all the other flight factors (altitude, propeller pitch, boost pressure etc.), the maximum operational range can be considered to be around 1,000 km or around 2 hours and 40 minutes flight time.*

Consumption: *In the cruise, consumption is around 0.45/0.46 kg/km; in the climb, around 1.11/1.16 kg/km. Hourly consumption is approximately 172/175 kg of fuel (considering that the last 20-30 litres remaining in the tank are not utilised). Oil consumption, considering the maximum endurance, is around 8/10 kg.*

Practical service ceiling: *The aircraft can reach around 11,200/11,300 metres altitude.*

CONCLUSION: *Once the carburettor faults have been eliminated, catapulting the RE.2000 (future variations aside) requires a catapult capable of launching a mass of around 3,000 kg at a minimum speed of 44 m/sec while maintaining an average predictable acceleration not greater than 2.7/2.8 g. (Acceleration could be increased if specific training was provided, but which, however, for operations, would be best if kept as low as possible). Since there is no catapult capable of these tests available, and having used the one that is most suitable, it is an indispensable condition for the launch that the vessel should be moving, so that at the moment of launch the aircraft can benefit from a speed of 35/45 km/h in a longitudinal sense that is opposite to the traction of the propeller.*

Guidonia, 18 June 1942.

Despite the fact that, even with the considerable delay to the programme, launch trials had been completed successfully, actual operations of the aircraft off warships proved to be limited and quite complex. The aircraft had to be delivered by road for embarkation from the nearest airfield, installed on a dedicated railway-type trailer fitted with a special framework that allowed the aircraft to be held with its wing angled low down in the direction of travel and the fuselage inclined at 45°.

Moreover, the fighter was positioned on the trailer with its propeller and tailplane mobile surfaces dismantled, and was subsequently towed to the embarkation point on the dockside from where it was transferred to the ship on a barge, positioned alongside, and then lifted onto the catapult by a hoist.

Operational use of the RE.2000 was also limited by the fact that the aircraft could be used only for one sortie launched from a warship, and

This page and opposite: This sequence of photographs illustrates the method used for boarding ships during the RE.2000 catapult launch trials. The aircraft, with its undercarriage extended and propeller removed, was transported on a special trolley pulled by a truck to a barge for loading on board ship.

also prior to any gun being fired by the vessel. This problem was exacerbated by the post-mission recovery process, as the pilot had to return to the closest airfield, relegating the use of the fighter to ships sailing within the boundaries of maximum aircraft endurance. Alternatively, there was the risk of the loss of the fighter in the case of a recovery on the high seas when the pilot would be forced to leave the aircraft by parachute in proximity to friendly naval units, as occurred with RAF Sea Hurricanes of the Merchant Ship Fighter Unit.

The aircraft was, moreover, initially selected for embarked operations off the new aircraft carrier *Aquila*, at the time under completion at Genova, and to this end Reggiane received an order for fifty fighters in catapult configuration, although this order was subsequently cancelled towards the end of 1942 in favour of an equivalent number of navalised RE.2001s.

In service with the Regia Marina

Following the execution of the trials, of the ten aircraft in the first small batch of fighters acquired, only eight were delivered, with *Matricole Militare* assigned from MM8281 to MM8288. These aircraft were assigned to the battleships RN *Vittorio Veneto*, RN *Littorio* and RN *Roma*, the only battleships of the Regia Marina capable of embarking and operating catapult-launched fighters. The aircraft were assigned to the newly-formed 1ª *Squadriglia* FF.NN.BB. *(Forze Navali da Battaglia)*. This unit, initially operating from a base at Grottaglie airfield near Taranto, home base of the *Regia Marina Squadra Navale*, was placed under the command of *capitano* Donato Tondi, who had replaced *tenente* Reiner for the continuation of the operational development of the new aircraft and the training of its new pilots.

Capitano Donato Tondi who continued Reiner's work, later becoming the first commander of the 1ª *Squadriglia* FF.NN.BB. *(Forze Navali da Battaglia)*.

Following a movement of the *Squadra Navale's* base to Napoli, and subsequently to La Spezia, in April 1943 the 1ª *Squadriglia* FF.NN.BB

The RE.2000 *Catapultabile* MM8285 was involved in a minor accident while taxiing at Grottaglie.

The wreckage of RE.2000, MM8288, piloted by *sottotenente* Morelli, which crashed on 10 September 1942 on the edge of the runway at Grottaglie following a training flight after fuel flow problems. Fortunately, the pilot escaped with minor injuries.

Below: Another minor accident while landing RE.2000, MM8284, at Grottaglie.

was re-formed into the 1° *Gruppo di Riserva Aerea delle* FF.NN.BB., comprising three *squadriglie*. The first two were equipped with the RE.2000 operating from Sarzana and Grottaglie airfields, while the third *Squadriglia*, equipped with Ro.43 seaplanes, operated from La Spezia.

The operations of the RE.2000 *Catapultabili* were limited, influenced by the low activity of Italian warships prior to the armistice, and it seems that the aircraft were never involved in combat operations, restricting their activity to some patrol flights along the Italian coast, almost always operating from their home airfields.

The sole mission conducted from a battleship was an armed reconnaissance flown on 23 August 1943, when RE.2000, MM8064, piloted by *tenente* Parrozzani, was sent off the *Vittorio Veneto*. At the end of the mission the aircraft landed at Sarzana.

On the date of the armistice, four RE.2000 catapult fighters were still in service, two operating

An RE.2000 *Catapultabile* ready to launch from the stern catapult of one of the battleships of the *Marina Militare*.

The battleships that embarked RE.2000s were the RN *Roma*, RN *Vittorio Veneto* and RN *Littorio* (later *Italia*). In addition to a fighter, the ships could take on board one or two IMAM RO.43 reconnaissance hydroplanes.

from land bases and the other two embarked on the battleships *Roma* and *Italia*.[10] The following day, 9 September 1943, in compliance with the terms of the armistice, the ships of the Italian fleet sailed from the port of La Spezia and set course for Malta. Two RE.2000s were embarked on the *Vittorio Veneto*, while the other two battleships, RN *Roma* and R.N *Italia*, sailed with a single RE.2000 as, at that time, they had been operating with one RE.2000 and an IMAM Ro.43 reconnaissance biplane.

Paradoxically, the only occasion in which an RE.2000 was catapulted on a mission of the kind for which it was intended, was during the Italian fleet's cruise to Malta. The attack on the Italian warships resulted in the sinking of the battleship *Roma* and the consequent loss of its embarked RE.2000 – MM8283.

Following the loss of *ammiraglio* Bergamini in the sinking of the *Roma*, *ammiraglio di divisione* Romeo Oliva, who was sailing on the cruiser *Eugenio di Savoia* and was the most senior officer amongst the admirals in the naval formation, ordered the battleships *Vittorio Veneto* and *Italia* to catapult their fighters to escort the naval units and offer protection against potential further German attacks. The *Vittorio Veneto* successfully catapulted RE.2000, MM8284, 'Red 4', while the aircraft on the *Italia* could not be deployed due to damage to its launch trolley caused by the explosion of a rocket bomb which had struck the ship.[11] Towards 1900 hrs this fighter, by now unusable, was catapulted into the sea without a pilot. Worthy of note is the fact that this latter aircraft was none other than the first RE.2000 modified to catapult-launch configuration, used by *tenente* Reiner for the launch trials from the *Miraglia* in May 1942.

On reaching the limits of its endurance, flown by *tenente pilota* Guido Parrozzani, the Reggiane launched from the *Vittorio Veneto* was directed to land at Ajaccio in Corsica, but was destroyed in a landing accident in the darkness following a collision with an anti-aircraft artillery piece positioned at the side of the runway. The pilot was injured.

For this reason, only the second RE.2000 remaining on the *Vittorio Veneto*, MM8287, arrived with the ship in Malta. This aircraft was returned to Italy and offloaded at the port of

The battleship RM *Roma* in Trieste sailing in its first camouflage scheme. (Marina Militare)

The sinking of the battleship *Roma*

The battleship *Roma*, launched on 9 June 1940 and the pride of the Regia Marina, was sunk on the afternoon of 9 September 1943 off the island of Asinara by an attack conducted by a formation of Dornier Do 217 K twin-engine bombers from the Luftwaffe's *Kampfgeschwader* 100, armed with the Ruhrstahl SD 1400 *Fritz* X guided bombs. Two bombs struck the warship: the first passed through the hull and exploded under the water, opening a flaw which resulted in the flooding of the boiler rooms and the stern engine room, while the propellers at the far stern became jammed, reducing the speed of the battleship from 22 to 16 knots.

A few minutes later, at 1552, the ship made a 60° turn to port, but was hit by a second bomb, which struck the post side adjacent to the armoured tower which housed the Admiral's and Ship's commander's stations. The weapon penetrated the deck between the armoured tower and turret No.2 (three 381 mm guns) and the systems for the left forward 152 mm gun turret. The impact was devastating, causing the explosion of the magazines while simultaneously opening a wide vent. Water flooded into the engine rooms, and the engines stopped. The explosion of the armoured tower instantly killed *ammiraglio* Bergamini, the commander of the Regia Marina's battle fleet and its *Stato Maggiore*, the commander of the battleship *Adone Del Cima*, and a good part of the crew. Less than half an hour after being struck, the *Roma* capsized and split into two sections, taking to the depths of the Tirreno Sea 1,393 sailors of the almost 1,900 who comprised the crew. It should be noted that not all sources agree about the numbers of sailors embarked on the ship.

A rare photograph of the RE.2000 and the Ro.43 embarked on the RN *Roma* days before it sank. (Marina Militare)

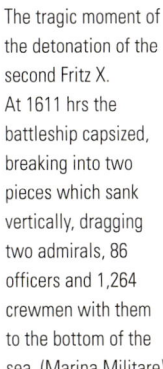

The tragic moment of the detonation of the second Fritz X. At 1611 hrs the battleship capsized, breaking into two pieces which sank vertically, dragging two admirals, 86 officers and 1,264 crewmen with them to the bottom of the sea. (Marina Militare)

Above: A pristine German PC 1400 '*Fritz X*' glide-bomb resting on its timber delivery cradle.
The photograph shows the bomb's cruciform tail unit with struts, spoilers and control surfaces.
The interior of the bomb encased by the tail unit housed the venturi tubes and roll control gyroscope.
The connection points for the flare unit are also visible. Two of these bombs hit the RN *Roma* and caused such devastating explosions that they led to the sinking of the mighty battleship.

This rare photograph shows RE.2000, MM.8287, embarked on the battleship *Vittorio Veneto* at anchor in Malta after the handover of the Italian fleet following the armistice. (M.Amatiello)

[10] On 30 July 1943 the battleship RN *Littorio* was renamed as RN *Italia*, after the fall of Fascism on 25 July.
[11] The ship was attacked also by a Dornier Do 217 which twice hit it with Ruhrstahl SD 1400 X glide-bombs. One bomb fell on the castle and the other narrowly missed the stern, causing some damage.

An RE.2000 undergoing static catapult tests. The catapult grab under the tail is just visible. Strangely, 'V.458', which was destined for Hungary, was used for these tests. In the list of aircraft assigned to Hungary, it appears that V.458 was delivered somewhat late.

familiarisation flights, ferrying it to Grottaglie on 14 July for the first launch tests from the *Vittorio Veneto*. In reality, however, following technical problems with the launching system during the launching of mock-ups, the first positive test occurred only on 9 May 1942 when the aircraft was fired from the catapult installed on the RN *Miraglia* in the Gulf of Taranto. The aircraft was lost on 9 September 1943 after the battleship *Italia*, sailing with the remainder of the Italian fleet towards Malta, was struck by a German *Fritz* X guided bomb. The weapon caused damage to the structure of the warship and the aircraft, no longer flyable, was catapulted empty into the sea.

The second RE.2000 *Catapultabile* identified with the serial MM8281 was constructed in March 1942 and, like other aircraft of *Serie* III, did not feature the rear fuselage glazing. After being transferred to Grottaglie, it was embarked on the *Vittorio Veneto* and was eventually lost on 16 April 1943 after being launched to conduct an escort and patrol mission in support of a naval formation. Finding himself running short of fuel while attempting to return to Sarzana, the pilot, *maresciallo* Guerrieri, was forced into performing an emergency ditching at sea in the gulf of La Spezia.[13]

Augusta, from where it was subsequently recovered by Italian personnel and operated at the start of 1944 by *maggiore* Giulio Reiner, who subsequently converted the aircraft to two-seat configuration.

Confusion over serial MM8281

Over the years, the attribution to two RE.2000s with the same *Matricola Militare*, MM8281, has generated not a little confusion in the determination of the exact histories of the two aircraft.

The first RE.2000 *Catapultabile* to fly as MM8281 was an RE.2000 *Intercettore* built for the Hungarian order and requisitioned by the Regia Aeronautica for modification to catapult configuration in April 1941. The aircraft was construction number c/n. 324, and had originally been allocated for the Swedish order, as evidenced by the reinforcement struts on the sliding part of the canopy. It was subsequently diverted to Hungary and assigned serial V.458,[12] being then requisitioned by the Regia Aeronautica. Using this aircraft, *tenente* Reiner conducted a series of

---

The title photo above shows the heading to a particularly interesting wartime document, kindly provided by the late Giorgio Apostolo, signed by *Ing.* Vardanega of Reggiane and pilot Guido Reiner, relating to the trials involving RE.2000 Cat. MM8281 conducted in May 1942 on board the RN *Miraglia*. The English translation is below.

Report on the catapult trials with the Re. 2000 conducted on the *Regia Nave Miraglia*

ON 4 and 5 [May 1942] on board the RN *MIRAGLIA* the first launch trials were conducted using a wooden mock-up structure (not an aircraft), all with satisfactory results, and on the basis of these it was decided to embark the aircraft onto the ship.

The transport of the aircraft, its positioning onto the launch trolley, engine tests, and the detachment of the bolts took place on the 6th and 7th, all with satisfactory results. The Commission was notified that the first catapult trial had been fixed for 9 May.

First catapult test, 9 May, 13.30 hours
The aircraft's load condition was as follows:

Empty weight	2,205 kg
Fuel	260 kg (165 litres forward tank, 200 litres rear tank)
Oil	30 kg
Pilot and parachute	85 kg
Overall weight	2,580 kg

The resulting catapult speed was assessed at 48 m/sec, obtained with 32.5 m catapult velocity (acceleration 3.1 g) and 15:5 relative wind velocity (ship + wind). The deflectors[14] should be closed.

A few moments prior to the launch it was noticed that the resulting velocity achievable would be 46 m/sec, it being impossible to obtain the intended speed from the ship, and the commander immediately suggested to the pilot that the launch should be conducted with 3.4 g acceleration instead of 3.1 in order to obtain a catapult velocity of 35 m/sec.

The undersigned believes that in consideration of the lower weight of the aircraft in comparison with the normal load, even at 3.4 g, the maximum stress on the grips should not be exceeded, with which the pilot agrees.

The launch occurred at 13.30 hours.

The catapult velocity proved to be 49.5 m/sec, obtained with 35.5 m/sec from the catapult and a relative wind velocity of 14 m/sec.

The outcome was regular. The aircraft's lift on detachment from the catapult was excellent, without any noticeable loss of height. The behaviour of the engine and propeller (keyed into the fixed test point at 2,050-2,100 rpm) was good.

After landing, an accurate inspection of the condition of the aircraft demonstrated that the condition of the grips and the wing in connection with their attachments was normal.

During the surface transport from Grottaglie to Taranto for the second launch, the undersigned noticed that the forward grips displayed traces of wear in their rear part. On checking these traces when the aircraft is positioned on the launch trolley, it was noticed that these are, undoubtedly, produced by the crossbars of the retention hooks on the front legs. Given the lack of corresponding signs on the stringers (recently repainted), it is reasonable to assume that these marks were produced during the preceding mounting and dismounting of the aircraft on the launch trolley. In any case, the crossbars are removed and placed in a position so as to leave the grips free.

A bolt release test was conducted, and the 13th [May] has been fixed for the second catapult test.

---

[12] Subsequently, Reggiane constructed a second V.458, which was delivered to Hungary towards the end of 1941.
[13] Recovered from the sea off Punta Mesco near Portovenere in 2013, today its remains are displayed in the *Museo Aeronautica Militare* at Vigna di Valle.
[14] NACA flaps.

Second catapult test, 13 May, 11.30 hrs

The second test was conducted with maximum load, divided as follows:

Empty weight	2,205 kg
Fuel	460 kg (both tanks full)
Oil	40 kg
Weapons	64 kg
Ammunition	66 kg
Pilot and parachute	85 kg
Ballast	70 kg (in place of radios and other kit)
Oxygen bottle	10 kg
Overall weight	3,000 kg

The catapult velocity was fixed at 48 m/sec, obtained through a 32 m/sec catapult speed (acceleration 3.1 g.) with 16 m/sec relative wind (ship + wind).

The launch was conducted at 11.30 hrs in the forecast conditions.

The deflectors were closed. On exiting the catapult, a small jet of oil hit the pilot in the face, forcing him to remove his goggles. During this operation the machine assumed a nose-up attitude, but this was quickly brought under control by the pilot who set the aircraft into a shallow dive, after which the flight continued normally. Apart from this incident, the outcome of the catapult launch was normal.

Engine and propeller behaviour were normal, while the aircraft's lift, on exiting the catapult, was good, and without any loss of height.

Examination of the aircraft shortly after landing revealed that the jet of oil produced at the moment of catapulting was caused by a leak occurring in the tank adjacent to the carburettor which, in turn, was caused by the continual shocks suffered during road transport to the space between the aforementioned tank and the fuel itself, given the narrow space (1/2 mm) between the two. Oil leaking from another hole created in part of the tank accumulated in the machine guns, subsequently being projected internally during catapulting.

With the tank replaced, the date for the third trial launch was set for 18 May. In consideration of the results of the first two trials, it was agreed to establish a programme of six trial launches: three with decreasing velocity by two metres in two metres with deflectors closed, and three with a constant velocity of 42 m/sec and with the external deflectors progressively opened by 5°.

The pilot, taking account of the difficult and dangerous conditions of the road transport, which continues to be conducted with ad-hoc equipment given that the planned dedicated transport trailer has yet to arrive, decided to undertake the next launch at a speed of 44 m/sec rather than 46 m/sec.

Third catapult test, 18 May, 11.30 hours

The test took place at 11.30 hours. The catapult velocity, instead of the intended 44 m/sec, was actually 42 m/sec due to windspeed reduction, which actually resulted in a rushed launch signal even before the pilot had lowered his hand in an 'all ready' sign. Despite this, the launch was normal and the aircraft still demonstrated good lift, albeit suffering from a noticeable decrease in speed.

In view of the outcome of this latest launch, and also to conclude the trial with the minimum number of road journeys, the pilot decided to perform the fourth launch with 41 m/sec velocity and deflectors open at 10° (7 cm maximum opening). The test was scheduled for 20 May.

Fourth catapult test, 20 May, 10.30 hours

The test was performed at 10.30 hours.

The aircraft, just after detaching from the catapult, immediately changed attitude and lost height. The pilot allowed this movement while controlling the aircraft, which in the meantime had descended to two metres above the sea, and then resumed normal flight. A check of the launch velocity revealed that instead of being 41 m/sec it had actually been 38.5 m/sec, resulting from a launch velocity of 27.5 m (the average of the last three recordings measured by two different sets of equipment as 27 m/sec for one, 28 m/sec in the other (with 2.44 g acceleration) and +10 m/sec of relative wind (ship + wind).

The pilot considers that this catapult velocity is on the extreme limit of sustaining flight with an all-up weight of 3,000 kg. Also that a launch conducted in these conditions would be extremely dangerous, even as it was conducted with a low acceleration value (2.44 g), a factor which permitted the immediate perception of the aircraft's lift situation just after it exited the catapult. To conclude the trials it

was decided to conduct a final launch in safe conditions, with the pilot electing to fly it at 41 m/sec launch velocity and with the deflectors open at 15°.

Fifth catapult test, 23 May, 12.50 hrs

The resulting velocity was 41 m/sec as predicted, obtained by 32 m/sec catapult velocity (acceleration 3.2 g) and 9 m/sec relative wind. The trial was conducted successfully without any loss of height to the aircraft.

Conclusions

The pilot considers that the lower limit of catapult speed for an RE.2000 with a full load of 3,000 kg flown by average pilots should be set at a value of 42 m/sec, obtained by a launch acceleration not greater than 3 g.

This has been determined by the conduct of launch tests at speeds decreasing from 48 m/sec, 44 m/sec, 43 m/sec, and 42 m/sec.

In respect of the deflectors, their use is advisable, also as during routine training the pilot will be required to check the position of the 'Flettners' so that they are sufficient to neutralise the descending influence they exert and so as to be able to reset the 'Flettners'[15] position at the moment of a launch with the deflectors open. During the training trials on the launch ship with 43 m/sec velocity, a launch can be made with the external deflectors open at 10° and at 42 m/sec velocity with the external deflectors open at 15°. As a consequence, the internal deflectors remain closed. The aircraft should be accurately set up as follows:

1 – The propeller must be set as to deliver 2,050/2,100 rpm in the fixed point test at full power.
2 – The connections between the control column and ailerons must not present the slightest play so that the response of the latter is of maximum sensitivity.
3 – The radio equipment should have a safety fastening to the rear to ensure that if it breaks away from its fittings because of the launch, it is not thrown into the tail.
4 – The oil tanks should be protected from eventual shocks against the fuel system by a rubber cap or a further elastic part placed on the other closest parts of the fuel system.
5 – The pilot's seat should be fitted with supplementary fastenings, comprising two bolts securing the base of the two rear guide rails.
6 – The sliding canopy of the pilot's cockpit should be fitted with a steel cable with a handle, located to enable it to be used to pull the canopy shut after launch is complete, during which it is prudent to leave it slightly ajar.
7 – The forward grips should have the hub positioned forward in order to create a 5 mm flat support of the retaining bolt along the entire length of the hub.

It would be convenient to install two supporting foot-stops inside the cockpit for the pilot.

The oil tubing must be carefully checked from time to time, and care should be taken not to excessively lubricate the weapons in order to avoid spray of lubricant (the use of goggles is essential during launch).

Ten. Guido Reiner
Ing. Virgilio Vardanega
Taranto, 24 May 1942

TARANTO 24 maggio 1942 XX

---

[15] Flettner trim tabs.

Foreign Operators: Hungary and Sweden

IF, in Italy, the RE.2000 attracted no interest on the part of the Regia Aeronautica, paradoxically things were very different abroad. Reggiane, convinced of the quality of the aircraft and considering the interest that it was arousing amongst some European air forces, developed numerous contacts which eventually came to fruition on 27 December 1939 with an order from the Hungarian Air Force for seventy aircraft, plus spare parts, and the grant of a licence to manufacture the fighter.

Prior to the formalisation of the contract with Hungary, a British commission, comprising Lord Hardwick and Colonel H. Thornton, toured Italy to visit several aircraft manufacturers. They gained a positive impression of Reggiane and in particular its RE.2000. In somewhat surprising circumstances, considering the delicate international situation, in December 1939 British test pilots Gray and Bennett travelled to Reggiane, where they were offered the opportunity to flight-test the RE.2000. They returned home with very positive impressions of the aircraft. During the following month news arrived at Reggiane from Britain confirming a potential order for 300 aircraft, but unfortunately the message coincided with a degeneration in the international political situation. With the ensuing outbreak of war in Europe, the contract, which it had been intended would conclude in early April 1940, was never finalised due to its being vetoed by the Italian Government. Reggiane even attempted to bypass the embargo by transferring the aircraft through a Portuguese branch of the company, but Italy's entry into the war on 10 June 1940 brought an end to the negotiations.

However, war did not bring an end to attempts to sell the fighter, and between 1940 and 1941 both Switzerland and Spain expressed interest in the acquisition of fifty aircraft each, while Finland had initiated negotiations for the purchase of 100 aircraft. Yugoslavia, moreover, besides pursuing an order for fifty fighters, expressed the intention of acquiring a licence to manufacture the aircraft. Nevertheless, the Italian Government blocked the sale for both political and industrial reasons, not wanting to deprive itself of prime materials indispensable for the national war effort.

A very different outcome was achieved from negotiations with the Swedish Government as, on 28 November 1940, a contract was signed for the acquisition of sixty RE.2000. An important aspect of the contract was the fact that payment would, in part, include the supply of prime materials essential for Italian industry, in particular chromo-nickel, of which Italy suffered a severe shortage.

In service with the Magyar Királyi Honvéd Légierő, Hungary *By Gyorgi Punka*

As previously mentioned, on 27 December 1939 a contract was agreed between Reggiane and the General Staff of the Magyar Királyi Honvéd

The RE.2000 V.440 crashed on the tarmac at Reggiane due to a clumsy manoeuvre.

A landing accident on 24 February 1941 at Reggio befell the Hungarian V.446 at the end of a test flight.

Heja coded V457 is assembled in Hungary after arriving in the country by rail.

A Hungarian RE.2000 ready for delivery, parked at Reggio Emilia.

Légierő (Royal Hungarian Air Force) for the supply of seventy RE.2000 interceptor variants at a price of 1,150,000 *lire* per aircraft, including their Piaggio P.XI engines, armament, and full instrumentation, with the exception of a radio system. The terms of the contract required the completion of deliveries by July 1940, the supply of a consistent stock of spare parts, but also the payment for every aircraft delivered by air from Italy of a sum equivalent to 32,000 *lire*. Another of the clauses in the contract specified an eventual potential supplementary supply of aircraft without engines at a price of 860,000 *lire* each. Once again, as an element of this

sale, part of the payment would be satisfied by an equivalent supply of grain.

In March 1940, a Hungarian delegation, led by the son of the Regent of Hungary, *Hadnagy* (Lieutenant) *István* Horthy, visited Italy to complete the final arrangements, which also included the issue to the Hungarians of a licence to produce the fighter. This was placed with the MAVAG (Magyar Királyi Állami Vas-, Acél- és Gépgyárak) company in Budapest. During the same month, the first five Hungarian pilots arrived in Italy for training, these being followed by another group in the summer of the same year.

The Hungarians assigned the fighter the local designation *Héja* I (Falcon), and they were assigned individual serial numbers applied to their fuselage, running from 'V.401' to 'V.470'.[16] The first aircraft, V.401, was delivered by air from Reggio Emilia by test pilot Mario De Bernardi in May 1940, to be used for pilot training and flight evaluation. It was during one of these training flights that a pilot undergoing conversion, used to flying in fixed-undercarriage aircraft such as the CR.32 and 42, suffered a landing accident on 7 June 1940 when he 'gently' set the aircraft down on the grass runway after forgetting to lower the undercarriage.

Despite that, deliveries of the aircraft had been scheduled to commence in July 1940. However, production delays created by the fact that the aircraft intended for Hungary had been diverted to the Regia Aeronautica, a shortage of prime materials needed for their construction, activities connected with the fine-tuning of completed aircraft, and minor accidents during flight-testing, resulted in a very bad delivery situation. As a result, only seven aircraft had been delivered by December 1940. The numbers of aircraft delivered rose slightly in the early months of 1941, and by July, 48 fighters were flying in Hungary. Nevertheless, the completion of the order only occurred in the spring of 1942. A total of just fifteen fighters were sent dismantled to Hungary by rail freight, being reassembled at Debrecen airfield with assistance from Reggiane engineers, while the balance of the aircraft had been delivered by air, flown by both Italian and Hungarian pilots.

The combat debut of the first Italian-built *Héjas* occurred in August 1941, when the first unit of what would be seven, the *Kísérleti Vadászrepülő Század* (Experimental Fighter Squadron), commenced operations on the Russian Front, operating principally in the bomber escort role. The first mission was conducted on 11 August 1941, when five *Héja* Is escorted Caproni Ca.135 bombers engaged in a raid near Nikolajev. During this first mission the *Héja* I of *Hadnagy* Lasztoczy failed to return, while over the following months further *Héja* Is were lost in flying accidents caused by navigation errors or mechanical failures affecting their engines. On 27 August, the *Héjas* shot down three I-16s without loss. In October the unit returned home. In the same period the *Héja* Is in service were fitted with a new radio and batteries, and armour protection was fitted for their pilots, albeit that these modifications were performed without authorisation from Reggiane. The more than 140-kg increase in aircraft weight, the 25-mm thick seat and head armour (alone weighing almost 127 kg, and concentrated mainly in the rear section of the aircraft), compromised the correct balancing of the aircraft, displacing the centre of gravity and creating a variety of problems. These included frequent tailwheel failures and a tendency to spin, a phenomenon never previously experienced in the original fighter, and which impacted on the aircraft's handling and flying qualities.

It was the modifications to the aircraft that contributed to the grave accident that occurred on

An RE.2000 of the 1/1 Fighter Squadron with 'Wasp' markings at Szolnok. In engagements with Russian fighters, the *Héja* acquitted itself well, only one machine being lost through enemy action.

20 August 1942 – an incident which resulted in the death of the aforementioned *Főhadnagy* (2nd Lieutenant) *István* Horthy, eldest son of the Regent of Hungary and possibly his successor. Horthy arrived with the 1/1. '*Dongó*' (Wasp) *vadászrepülő század* on the Russian Front on 2 July 1942. The squadron operated with nine Re.2000s from Ilovskoye airfield. On 30 July, another fighter squadron arrived, the 2/1 '*Keresztespók*' (Spider), also with nine aircraft. Combat missions began on 6 July with an escort for Ca.135 bombers. On 6 August, the *Héjas* reported their first victories, a LaGG-3 and an Il-2 destroyed over Uryv.

Up to 20 August the Hungarian fighters shot down seven aircraft. On that day two *Héjas* belonging to the 1./1 *Vadász Osztály* had taken off from Ilovskoye airfield to escort some reconnaissance aircraft. *Főhadnagy* Horthy, flying RE.2000 V.421, was making a left-hand turn at around 300 metres above the ground when his aircraft suddenly entered a spin and crashed, leaving him no possibility of escape. Horthy, who had acquired only limited experience in the

The wreckage of István Horthy's crashed aircraft on 20 August 1942. Accidental losses were rather numerous, for despite the RE.2000's good manoeuvrability and general lack of problems, the *Heja* was rather nose-heavy at low speeds and was inclined to be tricky in the final stages of landing approach. (Fortepan)

Reggiane, having totalled just 75 flying hours on the type by the fateful day, was probably concentrating on maintaining his position with the slower reconnaissance aircraft, and initiated a turn at too low an altitude and at too low an airspeed, resulting in a wing stall, a flat spin, and the fatal crash. There were rumours about possible sabotage by the Germans, since it was well known that *Főhadnagy* Horthy had Anglophile sympathies, but the inquest decided that the aircraft had crashed in a flying accident.

Having returned to Hungary for a brief period in October 1941, in early 1942 the Italian fighters returned to action in Russia with two fighter squadrons placed under the control of the

[16] The letter V was an abbreviation of '*Vadasz*', the Hungarian term for "fighter".

Above: The *Héja* V.450 is repositioned across the grass by manpower after a minor taxiing accident, probably at Szolnok.

Below: A line-up of RE.2000 *Héja* I Serie belonging to the 1st Fighter Group, a unit already equipped with Italian Fiat CR.32s. From June 1941, the time of the start of operations against the Soviet Air Force, the Hungarian RE.2000s also received new national insignia, in compliance with the German regulations on the standardisation of recognition markings.

Right: In 1942 the Hungarian Air Force operated two squadrons of the Independent Fighter Group, 2nd Air Force Brigade, equipped with RE.2000s on the Russian Front. The first Italian-built *Héjas* were tested in combat in June 1941 when six aircraft were sent to Russia. The unit flew bomber escort and ground-strafing missions, but because of the relative lack of opposition there were few aerial engagements.

Autonomous Fighter Wing of the 2nd Air Brigade. In clashes with the Russian fighters, the *Héja* Is demonstrated their prowess, with only one combat loss being recorded. Commencing in October 1942, the *Héja* Is were gradually withdrawn to Hungary and by December only one squadron remained on the front line in Russia. It is believed that by the end of the year, while flying the Italian fighters, the Hungarian pilots had achieved at least

Most of the MÁVAG-built machines served with advanced training schools, although it appears that many were thrown back into combat in the face of the Red Army's final, victorious onslaught of 1944. This MÁVAG *Héja* II was damaged after an air battle on 13 April 1944. (Fortepan)

A Hungarian-built *Héja* II. Despite the poor photograph, the smaller diameter of the WM14 engine is discernible, as is the resulting bulge of the two 12.7 mm guns. The Hungarian engine was lighter than the original Piaggio, and it also slightly increased the overall length of the fighter, but it did provide an improvement in forward visibility for the pilot.

twelve air combat victories against the loss of just two aircraft. Following the deterioration of the military situation in early January 1943, the last Italian-built fighters in Russian territory were destroyed on the ground by their Hungarian operators to prevent them from falling into enemy hands. In the same period, the Hungarian fighter force commenced its re-equipment programme onto the German Bf 109 G fighter and as a consequence the surviving *Héja* Is were passed on to territorial defence units and advanced flying schools.

Héja II – licence-built Reggiane fighters

As mentioned above, a particularly relevant part of the contract for the supply of RE.2000s to Hungary was the grant of a licence for its manufacture. It is believed that the Magyar Királyi Honvéd Légierő ordered 230 *Héja* IIs, as the serial numbers traced ran from 'V.471' to 'V.500' for the first thirty aircraft, with two further batches with assigned serials from 'V.501' to 'V.600' and 'V.605' to 'V.704'. However, only 191 seem to have been completed. These aircraft, identified as *Héja* IIs so as to distinguish them from those provided directly by Reggiane, incorporated some significant modifications. Firstly, the aircraft manufactured by MAVAG in Hungary were fitted with the WM K/14 B engine, which was actually the 985-hp Gnôme-Rhone K.14 built under licence by the Manfred Weiss S.A. company of Budapest. Also incorporated was a three-bladed Hamilton Standard propeller with a slightly increased diameter than those installed on Italian-built aircraft, intended to overcome the problems encountered with the malfunctioning of the original electric propeller controls.[17]

The installation of these engines and the associated balance and centre of gravity issues resulted in a slight increase in the length of the aircraft of around 40 cm in comparison with the *Héja* I, as well as a modest increase in speed. The Hungarian engine, furthermore, being slightly less bulky than the Piaggio, permitted a tighter cowling and an air intake which had smaller dimensions

and a different length, thus improving pilot visibility. The Breda SAFAT machine guns were also replaced by the locally produced Danuvia Gebauer M.40 12.7 mm calibre weapon.

Further modifications included the adoption of a FuG 16Z radio produced in Hungary, new armour for the pilot and, albeit not in all the aircraft, the removal of the glazed section of the rear part of the cockpit. Another substantial difference from the Italian-built fighter was the adoption of self-sealing tanks, these containing less fuel. Aside from a reduction in endurance, the lower quantity of fuel compensated for the greater weight of the modifications introduced. Again, the start of production was affected by significant delays in the preparation of the assembly lines and in the deliveries of the Hamilton Standard propellers, to the point that the first *Héja* II modified with the WM.14B engine flew on 18 May 1942. The first Hungarian series production aircraft flew in October of that year, while the first deliveries to operational units occurred almost simultaneously with the arrival of the first Bf 109 Gs, these also manufactured under licence by MAVAG at its Gyor facility. It would be the entry into service of this more capable German fighter that led to a reduction in priority assigned to *Héja* II production, with slow-downs and temporary suspensions in assembly, to the point that in the following year 130 aircraft were delivered, with the sixty remaining fighters completed in 1944.

Although their performance was slightly superior to the version of the fighter produced in Italy, at the time of their entry into service in 1943 the *Héja* IIs were decidedly outclassed, and the majority of them were issued to training units. Just a few aircraft were assigned to air defence units, with whom they protected airfields in Hungary. There is a report of an isolated encounter with the USAAF on 13 April 1944, when some *Héja* IIs unsuccessfully attempted an attack on American bombers. In an attempt to 'revitalise' the aircraft, there was also a plan, subsequently abandoned, to utilise *Héjas* in the dive-bomber/ground-attack roles, and to this end two aircraft were modified

with wing pylons for the carriage of 250-kg bombs and electrically controlled dive brakes, another type of airscrew and modified engine cooling. However, with the conclusion of hostilities, the fighters were withdrawn from front-line service, although some of the Reggianes continued to fly for some years, serving as advanced trainers.

In service with Flygvapnet, Sweden
By Mikael Olrog

At the outbreak of World War II, Sweden's air defence was limited, formed only by 55 Gloster Gladiators (designated as the J 8 in the Flygvapnet) stationed with the F 8 wing in Barkarby to protect Stockholm. Recognizing this deficiency, Sweden ordered 120 Seversky EP-106 fighters (J 9) to replace the outdated Gladiators. However, in mid-1940, the US imposed an export embargo, cancelling the contract for the 60 Seversky EP-106 that had not yet been delivered, as well as an additional contract for 84 Vultee 48C Vanguard (J 10). With no access to aircraft from Germany, Britain, France, or The Netherlands, Sweden turned to Italy, which was willing to sell aircraft in exchange for raw materials and money.

Sweden had initially placed an order for 12 Fiat CR.42 fighters to be delivered to Finland as aid in the fight against the Soviet invasion. When the Winter War ended in March 1940, Finland asked for money instead of the twelve Fiat fighters. Sweden agreed to transfer money to Finland and accept the fighters, while ordering 60 additional Fiats, designated J 11, which were delivered to the F 9 wing based at Save, outside Göteborg.

To equip with new fighters, the F 10 wing, which was tasked with protecting Malmö, *Överste* (Colonel) Nils Söderberg, head of the *Flygvapnets*

---

[17] It seems that some Reggiane-built RE.2000s were also subsequently re-engined with the Hungarian engine.

The first flight of s/n 2320 was carried out by test pilot Caracciolo on 26 January 1942, but ended with a forced landing due to engine trouble. The aircraft resumed flights on 11 April 1942 with test pilot Agello at the controls.

The Swedish Air Force operated the RE.2000 from 1941 to 1945. Designated the J 20 in Flygvapnet service, the aircraft were flown by the F 10 fighter wing based at Ängelholm.

Materialavdelning (the Air Force's Department for Materiel) travelled to the Reggiane factory in December 1940 to evaluate the RE.2000 *Falco* I fighter, for which Sweden had received an offer of 60 aircraft. Söderberg confirmed the excellent flying qualities of the *Falco* I, but highlighted as well was the unfortunate construction with the centre section of the wing also serving as a main fuel tank. This presented a risk if hit by enemy fire or if a belly-landing had to be carried out.

The negotiations were not easy and would also include the possibility for Italian companies to purchase specified volumes of raw materials and products such as steel, sheet metal, nickel, aluminium, mica for spark plugs, rubber, copper and tin. In addition to this, more raw materials were included in the agreement to compensate for what would be consumed when building the aircraft. Included in the contract signed on 28 November 1940 were 60 RE.2000 *Falco* I,

(assigned Swedish serials 2301 to 2360), powered by Piaggio XI bis RC 40D engines of 1,000 hp. Twenty spare engines and propellers were also ordered, as well as 10,000 spark plugs and 1.7 million cartridges for the Italian machine guns. These included 500 tracers, 500 incendiary, 500 armour penetrating and 200 standard bullets. The total contract value was 4,408,000 USD for 60 aircraft, 569,000 USD for the additional engines and spare parts and 771,000 USD for ammunition.

The contract stipulated that the last twenty aircraft were to be delivered with additional fuel and oil to increase range. Two technical solutions were evaluated for this purpose: either fitting extra tanks in the fuselage or in the wings. It was decided to opt for tanks in the outer wings. This would have increased the fuel volume by 320 litres in addition to the original 630 litres and 25 litres of oil in and over the former 40-litre oil tank.

Some minor technical requirements were included in the contract: a rearview mirror was mounted on the roof of the windscreen, the inversion of the handling of the engine controls (since the common operation in Sweden was in the opposite direction) and the additional fitting of seat armour to protect the pilot. It was also agreed that the aircraft were to be delivered in standard Italian camouflage, with Swedish national markings and

The two J 20s seen here served with F 10 in 1943.

A pilot climbs on to the wing of a J 20 of F 10 Wing, 1 Division, of the Flygvapnet at Ängelholm in 1942.

Above and left: The only fighter in Swedish service capable of intercepting the latest European and American types, the J 20 was given the delicate task of forcing down intruding aircraft from the belligerent nations which violated Swedish neutrality. (P.Lindquist)

serials applied. Large aircraft numbers would be applied upon arrival in Sweden, together with appropriate Squadron emblems. During 1944, a decision was made to replace the numbers with equally large letters. This was implemented at the beginning of 1945 on the J 20, thus it was used only for a very short period of time.

The production and delivery of the sixty RE.2000 to Sweden proved challenging and as eventful as the aircraft's service in the Flygvapnet. With orders for the Fiat CR.42, the Caproni CA.313 and the RE.2000, it was decided to dispatch a delegation from Sweden to the contracted factories in Italy to monitor production

quality, perform acceptance flights, handle all the practical questions that always arise during production, and most importantly, ensure that the agreed delivery schedules were kept. The team for the RE.2000 agreement would include a manager, four control engineers, a weapons expert, a radio expert and a test

Several USAAF bombers were intercepted after entering Sweden during their return flights from missions over Germany, and escorted by the aircraft of F 10 to Bulltofta airfield. Similarly, many Luftwaffe aircraft of all types were intercepted throughout the war. The photograph shows an RE.2000 escorting an American B-17 as it lands on 11 April 1944.

A line-up of Swedish *Falcos*. Just visible, under the rear part of the cockpit, is the cable outlet for the radio system which had been modified from its original form.

pilot to undertake test flights, as well as some administrative staff.

The Swedish delegation overseeing production arrived in Italy in March 1941. However, Reggiane was already producing seventy RE.2000s for Hungary, and thus the Swedish order became delayed. A shortage of landing gear parts and a general shortage of raw material further disrupted production. Additional complications arose from a factory accident on 14 March which killed Reggiane's test pilot, *tenente colonnello* Pietro Scapinelli, during a test flight with an RE.2001 the day prior to the planned first flight of the first Swedish RE.2000. This tragic fatality was followed a few days later by the death of Reggiane's managing director, Giovanni Degola, who suffered a fatal horse-riding accident.

The first two Swedish aircraft (nos. 2301, 2302) were completed in March 1941, but their test flights revealed speed and rate of climb deficiencies. Factory testing and records were found to be unreliable, further frustrating the Swedish inspectors. By April 1941, the first two aircraft were shipped to Sweden by rail. Around

this time, eight aircraft allocated originally to Sweden were reassigned to Hungary by the Italian Government, forcing Sweden to renegotiate replacements and further delaying deliveries.

By June 1941, the first four aircraft (nos. 2301–2304) were ready, but two had damage to their undersides, possibly due to belly-landings or sabotage. Despite lengthy discussions, Sweden refused acceptance until the damage was properly repaired. The transportation of aircraft to Sweden also faced issues as the Caproni Ca.313 reconnaissance aircraft built and delivered at the same time were flown to Sweden and the idea was to make the transfer flights together, facilitating navigation. However only two aircraft, nos. 2303 and 2304, were delivered by air on 18 September 1941, with the remaining RE.2000 delivered by train.

Once in service, the RE.2000 (designated J 20) generated mixed reviews. Pilots appreciated its speed and manoeuvrability, but mechanics found it difficult to maintain due to poor access panels and inferior production quality. Common issues included engine reliability problems, structural weaknesses, cockpit discomfort (later, seats were modified to be adjustable), and canopy detachment at high speeds.

Sweden also considered buying engineless RE.2000s and mounting the 1,065-hp STWC-3

Pratt & Whitney engine that Sweden had successfully copied and set into production without a licence. This version would have been known as the J 20 B. Reggiane also put a possible deal for the RE.2001 fitted with the DB 601 engine on the table, but ultimately nothing came out of either option, which was probably best for all parties concerned.

Operations with F 10 wing in Sweden

The first two aircraft (nos. 2301 and 2302) were delivered to *Försökscentralen* (FC), the experimental and development unit that oversaw evaluation and production of maintenance and operational procedures, manuals and instructional guides. It was decided to make aircraft 2302 available to SAAB early on, which was designing the engine installation for the SAAB B 17 C dive-bomber, the sub-version that was fitted with the same Piaggio engine as the J 20. Two aircraft (2303 and 2304) arrived at F 10 Bulltofta in late September 1941. Initially, pilots who had previous experience of flying the J 9 Seversky fighter were permitted to fly the *Falco* I. The latter was around 30 km/h faster than the J 9 which was appreciated by the pilots; however a written report in November 1941 highlighted the fact that the *Falco* I was difficult to service since it lacked access panels and that the seating was very uncomfortable. Later the seat would be rebuilt by the unit to enable it to be adjusted by the pilot. The first accident occurred as early as 13 January 1942 when *Löjtnant* (Lieutenant) Olof Roland crashed and was killed at Bulltofta airfield in no.2303 after suffering engine problems after take-off. The cause was water in the fuel which created ice plugs in the fuel line. A second crash occurred sometime later, on 24 March 1942, with the *Försökscentralen* when test pilot *Löjtnant* Mörne induced a spin as part of a test programme. Prior to take-off, the aircraft had been fitted with new seat armour and a radio with batteries in the aft fuselage, thus shifting the balance of the aircraft.

A formation of J 20s in flight over southern Sweden. The yellow flashes on the fuselage identified the aircraft as being with 2 Squadron.

Left: The Swedish order for 60 RE.2000s placed in November 1940 was attractive to the Italian Government since a good proportion of the 18,700,000 Sw.Kr. price was paid in chrome-nickel metal – vital for the hungry Italian industry.

Mörne failed to exit the spin and left the aircraft successfully at 1,000 metres, landing by parachute.

Deliveries of assembled aircraft to the second squadron of F 10 wing were begun from March 1942, thus finally replacing the obsolete and worn-out J 8 Gladiators. On 28 May, the unit suffered a loss when the canopy of 2306 detached during a dive, hitting the pilot in the head and leading to a fatal crash. The third squadron began to receive their J 20 fighters during the summer of 1942, while the first squadron did not convert to the J 20 until autumn 1942. F 10 wing was fully converted by the beginning of 1943, which would prove quite timely with the increase in Allied air raids on Germany. The flight characteristics and performance of the *Falco* I was appreciated by the pilots, but the mechanics still disliked the aircraft

due to the challenges in servicing and a lack of quality in the production of the aircraft and the engines. The engines were especially plagued by malfunctions and broken parts, likely the effect of production quality issues, and also the lack of raw materials to create the proper alloys. To improve serviceability, four mechanics from Reggiane were brought to Sweden and they stayed over a year. Obviously, there was a language barrier between the Italian and Swedish technicians, but it proved useful that they were there.

Located in the south of Sweden, close to Denmark and the Baltic Sea, the F 10 wing often encountered Luftwaffe fighters and other types when patrolling Swedish territory and waters. Several aircraft from the Flygvapnet were shot down by German fighters, but only one J 20

appears to have been lost. This occurred very late in the war, on 3 April 1945, when a Dornier Do 24 flying boat appeared over Swedish territorial waters. Two J 20 were ordered to scramble, but one malfunctioned and aborted, while the other (2331) successfully took off. *Furir* Erik Nordlund flew east and apparently detected the Do 24. Few details are known, but Nordlund radioed that he was hit by fire from the Dornier and that he was trying to return to land. A minute later, at 1228, he radioed that he could not land and that he was about to leave the aircraft, but the aircraft exploded at 800-1000 metres, likely caused by the fuel in the centre fuselage tank.

The second aircraft took off eventually and succeeded in turning away the Dornier. German authorities later acknowledged responsibility for what had happened. With the war coming to an end and deliveries of the new JVSS J 22 fighter also reaching the F 10 wing, the last neutrality protection operation with the J 20 was concluded on 3 May, when the third squadron handed over the responsibility to the second squadron which, by that time had been refitted with the indigenously developed J 22 fighter. Discussion had been underway to replace the J 20 with the F 10 from 1944 in the hope of securing fighters

The Swedish J 20s were characterised by the application of large, individual numbers on engine cowlings and rudders. From 1944 the numbers on the tail were replaced by letters. (P.Lindquist)

Below: RE.2000 No. 31, was the only *Falco* to be shot down during the entire war; while on an intercept mission it fell victim to the gunner of a German Do 24 on 5 April 1945.

Below: The J 20 had a long career with the Flygvapnet as it was only in late 1944 that the first deliveries of the Swedish-designed and built FFVS 22 (J 22) fighter came on stream which began the progressive withdrawal of the Reggiane from service with F 10.

from England or the US. The Spitfire, P-47 and P-51 were test-flown in England, but eventually the P-51 was selected and delivered to Sweden. However, it was decided to not re-equip F 10 wing with the Mustang since it was thought that it would be unsuitable to use an American aircraft to turn away American bombers, and so the J 22 was considered preferable for this. The last operational flight with the J 20 was made on 20 July 1945 as a target for anti-aircraft training. A final loss occurred when 2351 was to be flown on 7 August

1945 from *Försökscentralen* to F 6 wing at Karlsborg where it was to serve as a practice target, but it suffered fuel pump malfunction and the pilot had to make a belly-landing in a field en route, with substantial damage to the aircraft.

Of the 60 aircraft delivered, 26 were lost for various reasons, with nine pilots killed. This is obviously an extremely high attrition rate which, to some extent, can be attributed to quality issues in production, the design of the fuel tank in the centre of the wing, the substitute of raw materials

used in production, and also to the fact that the Flygvapnet used the aircraft more extensively and for a longer period than it had been constructed for. Average flight time was around 200 hours per aircraft, over a period of three years, while in Italy the aircraft was regarded as a more 'expendable' piece of equipment, with a much shorter life expectancy. Despite its shortcomings it proved to be an important cornerstone in Sweden's neutrality protection and it successfully guided several damaged USAAF bombers to a safe haven.

After the Armistice and post-war usage

At the time of the armistice there were no remaining RE.2000s. In early 1944 a 'recovery team' detached to the Augusta area notified *capitano* Giulio Reiner, at the time commander of the *Presidio Regionale di Sicilia*, about the presence of an RE.2000, apparently in good condition, albeit incomplete, in a hangar at the Augusta seaplane base. Following verification, it was discovered that the aircraft was the RE.2000 *Catapultabile*, MM8287, the aircraft that had been embarked on the *Vittorio Veneto* which was sent to Malta with the rest of the Italian fleet on 9 September 1943. The fuselage and the central wing section were complete with undercarriage and catapult attachments, the rear fairings were on the canopy, and a red '5' had been painted on a white fuselage band. However, the aircraft was missing its engine, a large part of its instrumentation and also its battery, tailwheel, and the tailplanes. The wings were present, but not attached. *Capitano* Reiner, who was very familiar with the aircraft, issued an order to return it to flying condition, intending to use it as a training aircraft and for rapid communication duties.

Having transported the fighter to Catania airfield and benefitting from the fact that, in the meantime, six still-crated Piaggio P.XI bis engines had been discovered abandoned, a team of engineers set to work rebuilding the aircraft to flying condition, fitting tailplanes from an RE.2001 and the tailwheel from an AerMacchi C.202. On 8 July 1944, *capitano* Reiner flew the

This photograph, taken in Catania in 1948, provides a good view of the modification made to the single-seater to create a second seat for a passenger, using an AerMacchi C.202 canopy.

The RE.2000 two-seater in Catania after application of a silver colour scheme. *Capitano* Reiner was the pilot who flew it and decided to convert it into a two-seater.

This photograph, taken in Catania in 1948, provides a good view of the modification made to the single-seater to create a second seat for a passenger, using an AerMacchi C.202 canopy.

rebuilt fighter, which had been repainted in the classic Regia Aeronautica colour scheme of olive-green upper surfaces, with new tricolour roundels applied. Post-war and in order to carry a passenger, *capitano* Reiner decided to convert it into a two-seater, similar to the unlucky RE.2003 which he had tested at Reggio Emilia a few years earlier. The two-seater modification, relatively simple to undertake, but from a technical aspect 'unofficial', saw the installation of a second seat and the modification of the canopy. After the modification, the aircraft was painted overall in an aluminium colour and was flown again at the end of March 1948, after Reiner was reassigned to the 4° *Stormo Caccia*. As a consequence of this posting, the only pilot qualified to fly the aircraft had gone, and another pilot under training on the type, *capitano* Cremona, had previously lost his life in a flying accident in another aircraft. For this reason, with no pilot qualified, the RE.2000 was retired and subsequently dismantled and stored. The fuselage has survived to this day, and is conserved in the storage facility of the Museo Caproni waiting for better times.

Right: With the transfer of *capitano* Reiner and the death in a flying accident of the other pilot who was qualified to fly it, *tenente* Cremona, the aircraft was abandoned and never flew again.

CHAPTER THREE

RE.2001 *Ariete* I

Evolution and Production

THE development of the Reggiane RE.2001 originated simultaneously with the rejection of the RE.2000 by the Regia Aeronautica and the availability, in the summer of 1939, of the German 1,175-hp Daimler-Benz DB 601A-1 liquid-cooled engine, for which Alfa Romeo had acquired a manufacturing licence. In June 1939, the prototype of the RE.2000 *Falco* was undergoing evaluation with the Regia Aeronautica, which, in view of the generally favourable impression it had of the *Falco*, proposed to Reggiane that the company re-engine it with the German in-line engine in the belief that as a replacement for the Piaggio P.XI radial, it would offer an appreciable increase in performance.

Thus, on 20 July 1939, Reggiane was ordered to fit out a prototype. In order to effect speed of completion, the company decided to modify the cellular centre section of the second example built of the RE.2000, maintaining the RE.2000's wet wing and retractable wheel layout.

The design of the new aircraft was identified as the RE.2001 and the name *Falco* II (Hawk II)

assigned, which was later replaced by *Ariete* *(Aries)*. In this regard, however, it must be stressed that the aircraft's name was rarely used to identify it during operations.

From a technical viewpoint, the new fighter did not offer particularly radical modifications, with the forward section of the RE.2000 fuselage adapted to accept the installation of the Daimler-Benz engine, thus creating a streamlined and aerodynamic frontal area, and with weight being redistributed in compensation for the greater length of the engine. As mentioned, the wing of the first prototype to be completed was the same as that of the RE.2000, comprising five longerons with integral fuel tanks and the engine cooling radiators positioned under the outer wing sections and semi-contained within the thickness of the wing. This configuration quickly proved to be ineffective and the radiators were repositioned to sit freely under the wing. However, aside from not resolving the cooling problems, this also had a negative impact on the aircraft's aerodynamics, limiting its top speed.

Following the construction of a wooden mock-up, Reggiane received an order from the *Ministero*

December 1939: the wooden fuselage mock-up of the RE.2001 fitted with a German-built DB 601 engine.

dell'Aeronautica to prepare a second prototype, fitted with separate fuel tanks in order to obviate the unhappy experience of the integral tanks in the wing of the RE.2000.

Meanwhile, in mid-June 1940, the first prototype, MM409, was completed and undertook its first test flights between 22 and 24 June, (the date is uncertain) with test pilot, Mario De Bernardi, at the controls. The new aircraft had a decidedly streamlined form compared to its predecessor but, similar to the early RE.2000 series, it was characterised by the use of a rear windowed canopy. The planned armament still consisted of two 12.7 mm machine guns above the engine. Following the initial test flights, development of the aircraft was assigned to *tenente* colonnello Pietro Scapinelli, who conducted seventeen flights between 25 July and 28 August prior to the RE.2001 being transferred to the *Centro Sperimentale* of the Regia Aeronautica at Guidonia in September 1940 for military evaluation trials.

Prior to the transfer of the prototype to the Regia Aeronautica's *Centro Sperimentale*, some

Above: The RE.2001 prototype photographed during assembly at the Reggiane *Reparto Sperimentale*.

Right, below and following pages: The first RE.2001 prototype, MM409, ready for its first flight at Reggio Emilia airport in late June 1940, when it was piloted by Mario De Bernardi.

external modifications were made to the engine cowling and the oil radiator, while additional cooling vents were added to facilitate engine cooling. The trials conducted at *Centro Sperimentale* in Guidonia had a positive outcome, especially with regard to speed, with the aircraft reaching more than 560 km/h at 5,500 metres altitude. During these flight tests, however, the aircraft's speed proved unattainable for mass-produced fighters, probably due to the fact that the prototype had an original, German-built DB 601 engine and not an engine built in Italy. The latter engine, built using inferior metal materials, could not fully replicate the performance of the original German engine.

In light of the positive test results, the *Ministero dell'Aeronautica*, requested further substantial

modifications to the prototype, which were also to be applied to the commissioned second prototype. These included the adoption of a three-longeron wing with self-sealing fuel tank (known in Italy as *semapizzati*), a retractable tailwheel and the installation of two Breda-SAFAT 7.7 mm guns with 600 rounds per gun in the wings, in addition to the two Breda-SAFAT 12.7 mm calibre machine guns in the frontal position. Modifications to the first prototype were completed in November 1940, while the second modified prototype, identified by the official serial MM408,[1] was first flown by Scapinelli on 18 December 1940.

The second prototype differed externally from the first prototype by some minor changes to the engine cowling, but mainly through the abolition of the rear windowed canopy.

Against a demand to accelerate the start of production, but with their assembly lines not fully ready, on 31 October 1940 the Reggiane management elected to build an initial batch of ten RE.2001s using the company's own *Reparto Sperimentale* (experimental unit). These aircraft were the so-called 'Serie Zero' with the serials MM8071 to 8080 assigned. At the same time, Reggiane received an initial order from Regia Aeronautica for 200 aircraft, while further orders for a total of 400 aircraft were also issued to Breda and to the Caproni factories at Taliedo and Predappio. All these aircraft were required to incorporate the modifications introduced into the two prototypes, including the fixed tailwheel. As previously stated, the engine selected was the Alfa Romeo RA 1000 RC.41 *Monsone* –

[1] Bizarrely, this was the same serial number as that of the first R.E.2000 prototype. This is probably an interpretation error, as authoritative sources state that the exact *Matricola Militare* was MM468.

Continues on page 91

"REGGIANE"

2001 ARIETE I

RE.2001, MM409, painted in a dark green scheme just before leaving the Reggiane factory for Guidonia in August 1940 to perform its first military test flight.

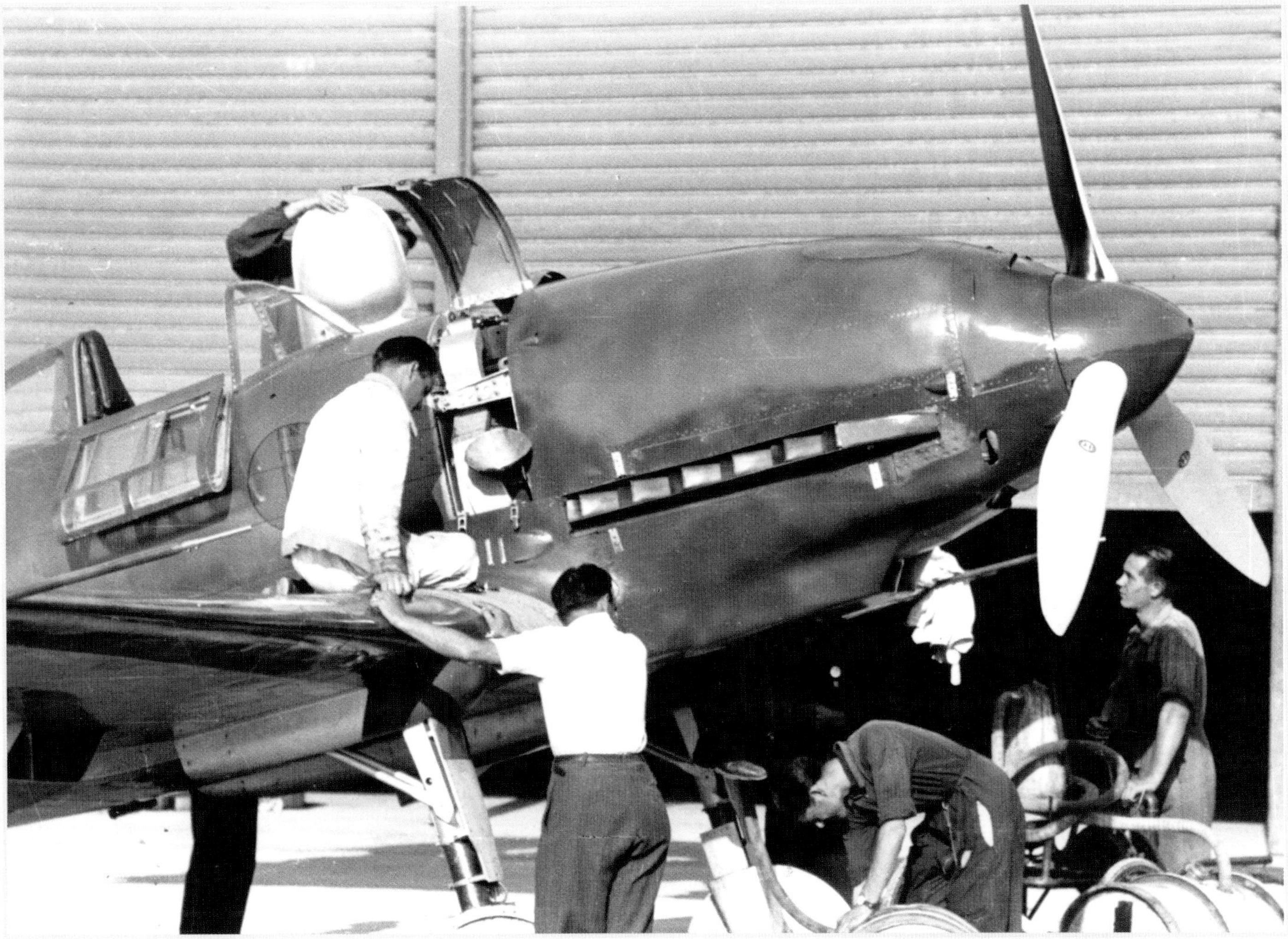

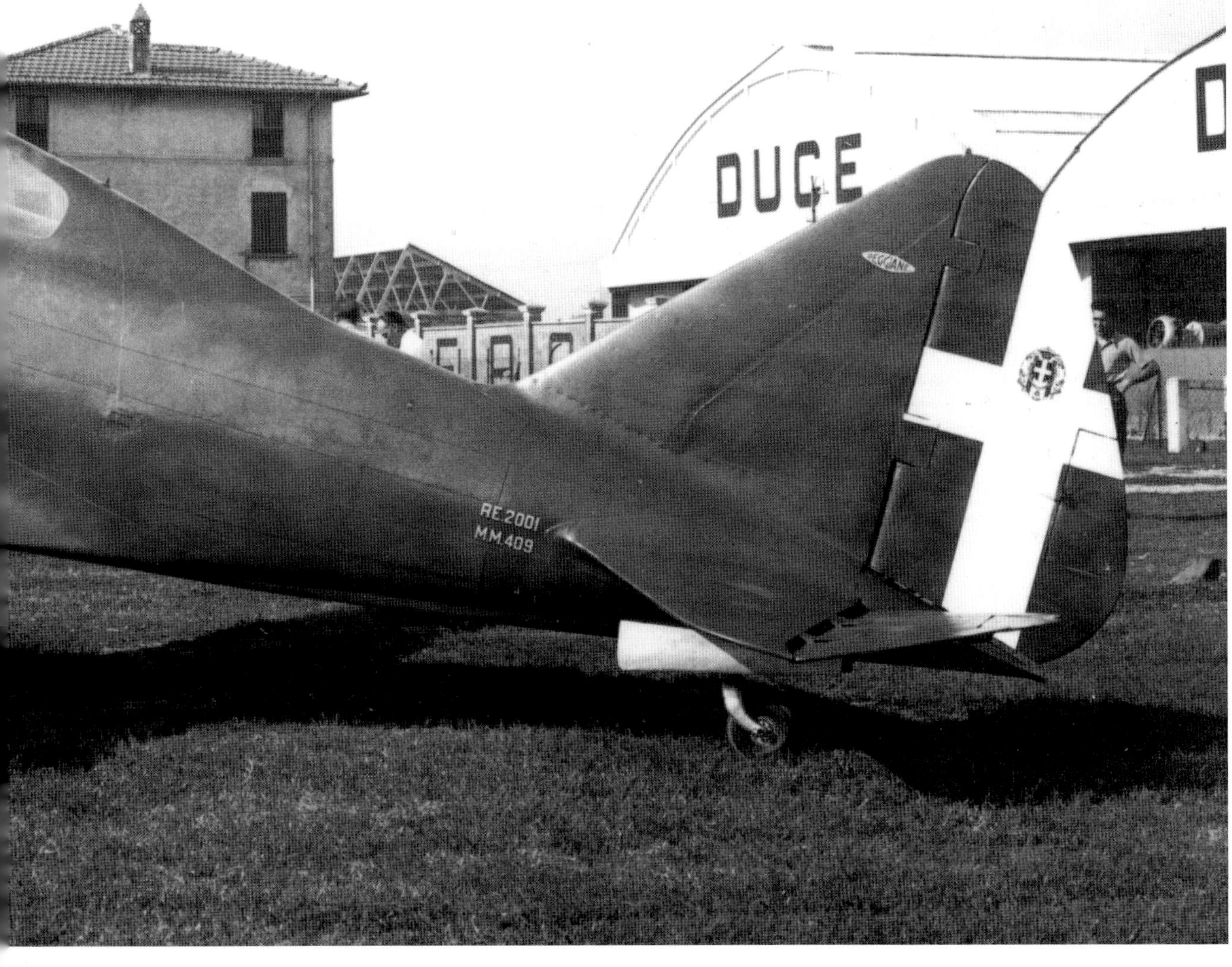
DUCE
RE.2001
M.M.409

RE.2001, MM409, just before leaving the Reggiane factory for Guidonia in August 1940 to perform its first military test flight.

The prototype, MM408, suffered a taxiing accident due to the muddy surface of the airfield in January 1941.

An official photograph, dated 14 March 1941, of the second RE.2001 prototype. The background has been censored. A few hours after it was taken, Pietro Scapinelli flew it on its last, tragic flight.

The seventh pre-production RE.2001, MM08077, at Guidonia during military evaluation at the *Centro Sperimentale* during the spring of 1941.

PIETRO SCAPINELLI'S FATAL ACCIDENT

IN the afternoon of 14 March 1941, *tenente colonnello* PIETRO SCAPINELLI took off from Reggio Emilia in the second prototype of the Reggiane RE.2001, MM408, for a customary flight test. The flight continued without event and ended with numerous manoeuvres over the airfield.

Turning onto his final approach to the grass runway, Scapinelli found himself overshooting and applied power to regain height and to circle to make another attempt. However, the engine failed to respond to Scapinelli's inputs because of a propeller pitch control problem (the variable pitch control was managed electrically by an actuator which was still in its experimental phase) and the pilot, having passed over the airfield and crossed the river Rodano to its east, attempted a wheels-up landing in a field. The manoeuvre was initially a success, but as the aircraft slid at speed along the field, the pilot was unable to stop it running into trees. In the violent collision, the fuselage became detached from the wings. Scapinelli was gravely injured when his head struck the control column as his harness had not been sufficiently tightened. Although quickly rescued, he died soon after arriving in hospital, having never recovered consciousness. He was 37 years of age.

Test pilot Pietro Scapinelli aboard one of the first RE.2000s. He replaced test pilot Mario De Bernardi.

Above: This photograph, taken on 24 February 1941, is one of the last taken of Pietro Scapinelli, seen here landing with the second RE.2001 prototype, MM408 (the aircraft he was later to lose his life in a month later). Visible in the foreground is a Hungarian RE.2000 which crashed at the end of a test flight.

Two photographs of the accident that claimed the life of Pietro Scapinelli on 14 March 1940. Visible are the two trees that held back the wings, separating the fuselage of MM408 from the wings, fatally injuring the pilot when his head struck the control column due to his harness not being sufficently tightened.

PIETRO SCAPINELLI

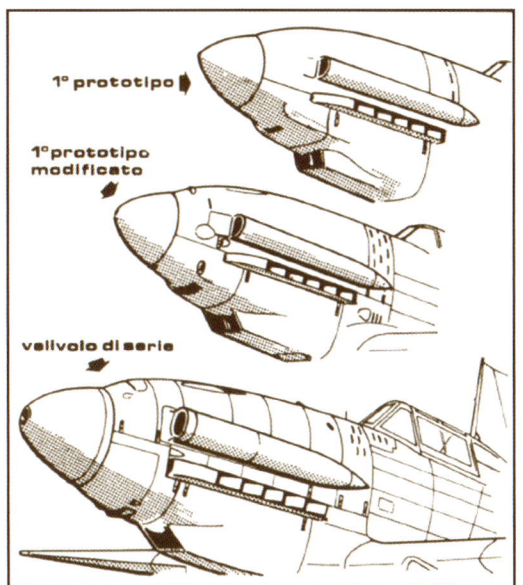

1° prototipo

1° prototipo modificato

velivolo di serie

The different types of engine cowlings used in early prototypes and series aircraft.

the Daimler-Benz DB 601 produced under licence in Italy.

So far, it seemed as if the RE.2001 had a bright future, more so than the RE.2000, but the reality would prove to be very different. The problems started with the tragic loss of the greatly respected test pilot Pietro Scapinelli on 14 March 1941, who died in a flying accident involving an RE.2001, due to technical failure. This ominous event was followed by further technical problems and consequently delays to the start of the first production batch.

The production delays were due to various causes, including Reggiane's workforce, much of which had been hired en masse at various stages to meet the needs of the war. Though the workers were relatively skilled, they had no experience in the aviation sector. To this problem, which the company tried to solve by setting up an in-house technical school, was added the equally serious scarcity of Alfa Romeo engine supplies, the low production rate of which was slowed even further by a shortage of raw materials. Inevitably, this led to delays in the completion of aircraft with an accumulation of ready-made airframes parked outside the factory awaiting propellers. As if these problems were not enough, the performance of the production RE.2001s proved to be inferior to expectations and the *Ministero dell'Aeronautica* preferred prioritising the production and deliveries of the Alfa Romeo engine to the AerMacchi C.202. Confirmation of this situation is provided by the fact that the first batch of 100 Alfa Romeo engines provided to Reggiane was delivered over a period of almost one year, this set against Reggiane's production potential that was much greater.

Supply problems with Alfa Romeo engines were also at the root of the failure of the possible negotiation to export around 100 fighters to Sweden. The Swedes, who were very interested in the aircraft, also considered the possibility of buying the fighters without engines, but even this hypothesis was not followed up.

The RE.2001's production problems were related to the management of orders by the *Ministero dell'Aeronautica* which, from the end of 1941, began requesting a series of modifications to the aircraft from Reggiane in order to adapt it to different types of mission, thus leading to the waste of limited resources and energy. It was no coincidence that the Ministry asked Reggiane to split the first 100 aircraft ordered into relatively small variant batches. Hence, in December 1941, Reggiane was asked to break the order into two groups of 50 aircraft each, the first one consisting of RE.2001 fighter versions and the other of RE.2001 for the O.R. (*Organizzazione Roma*) for on-board use on the planned Italian aircraft carrier that was under conversion from the transatlantic passenger liner SS *Roma*. Subsequently, in May 1942, a new request saw the order split into 47 fighter variants; 39 examples of the RE.2001CB (*Caccia bombardiere*) with a ventral attachment for a 250-kg bomb; 2 *lightened* aircraft for ground catapult tests, and 12 aircraft equipped with an arresting hook for carrier operations. In June 1942, the *Ministero dell'Aeronautica* submitted a new order for another 30 RE.2001 fighters, followed in August by another order for 100 aircraft, 50 of them of O.R. versions and 50 RE.2001GV ground-attack variants, an order that was subsequently converted into RE.2001CNs for nightfighter operations.

In the early months of 1943 Reggiane received another two orders for sixty RE.2001s, but these could not be fulfilled as the armistice announced on 8 September 1943 brought fighter production to an end.

The total number of RE.2001s built is thought to be 237, though this figure varies when individual variants figures are taken into account.

– 2 prototypes – MM408 (or MM468)/MM409
– 10 'Serie Zero' – MM08071-08080
– 1 prototype with an IF Delta engine (MM 9920) converted by Caproni di Taliedo
– 100 aircraft – MM7209-7308, sub-divided into 47 fighters, 39 CB fighter-bombers, 2 lightened aircraft (pre-series versions of the OR) and 12 OR

Another photograph of the seventh pre-production RE.2001, MM08077, at Guidonia in 1941.

One of the RE.2001 prototypes makes a low-level pass over Reggio Emilia airfield. In the background are the company's large hangars.

RE.2001s lined up in front of the hangars in the testing area, awaiting completion and acceptance flights.

The RE.2001 MM08072 was the second fighter in the 'Serie Zero' of ten aircraft built by Reggiane at the factory *Reparto Sperimentale* pending completion of the assembly line in the main factory.

least 87 aircraft, since those planned as nightfighters were deprived of their wing guns and used as day fighters as well. Alongside the fighter variant, the **RE.2001CB** (*cacciabombardiere* – fighter-bomber) was developed and optimised for the ground-attack role. The modifications included a ventral attachment point beneath the fuselage which was used to distance a bomb from the propeller disc at the moment of release: this attachment could carry a bomb of up to 250 kg. Some aircraft were also fitted with underwing racks capable of carrying small calibre bombs. Even for these aircraft, which were among the first series of 100 aircraft of the initial order, it is not possible to determine how many were actually built or used by the Regia Aeronautica, since during the course of the war, RE.2001 fighters had bomb attachment points fitted.

The **RE.2001CN** (*caccia notturna*) was a nightfighter variant developed to incorporate specific modifications such as the adoption of flame-dampers, an overall black colour scheme,

– 30 aircraft – MM 9921-99250, as standard fighters (some subsequently converted into CN nightfighters)
– 50 '*Serie VI*' aircraft – MM 90751-90800, nightfighter versions
– 50 aircraft – MM 90000-90049, CN nightfighter versions. Of these only 34 were built prior to the halt of production following the armistice, of which 25 were actually flight-tested
– 10 aircraft – MM6547-6556, CN nightfighter versions, built by Caproni-Predappio

Production variants

As recorded in the previous chapter, although a relatively limited number of RE.2001 were built, several variants were available.

The first variant was the standard fighter version, identified by the basic designation **RE.2001**. It was armed with two 12.7 mm fuselage-mounted machine guns and two 7.7 mm guns in the wings. It is not clear as to exactly how many were built, but it is believed to have been at

Some RE.2001s in front of one of the assembly hangars at Reggio Emilia, ready to be delivered to a Regia Aeronautica front-line unit.

FILMING *PRIMO VOLO* (FIRST FLIGHT)

Below: Test pilot Caracciolo with members of the *Istituto Nazionale LUCE* during filming of the short promotional film *Primo Volo*.

N MARCH 1943, a delegation from the *Istituto Nazionale LUCE* arrived in Reggio Emilia to shoot a short promotional film of about 15 minutes intended to illustrate the birth of a fighter aircraft starting from the drawing board, through all stages of construction and flight tests. The fighter chosen was the RE.2001, which was in production at the time, and all the stages of production were filmed for the documentary, up to the long-awaited 'First Flight'. The director of the documentary was Vittorio Gallo, and the filming was quite innovative and creative, as a camera was mounted on an aircraft, while other impressive sequences were filmed from a twin-engine aircraft. The documentary ended with some operational images of RE.2001 of the 2° and 22° *Gruppo Aut. CT* filmed over San Pietro di Caltagirone airport.

RE.2001, MM90755, during preparation for take-off. At the controls (below) is test pilot Caracciolo, who piloted the aircraft for the film *Primo Volo* (First Flight).

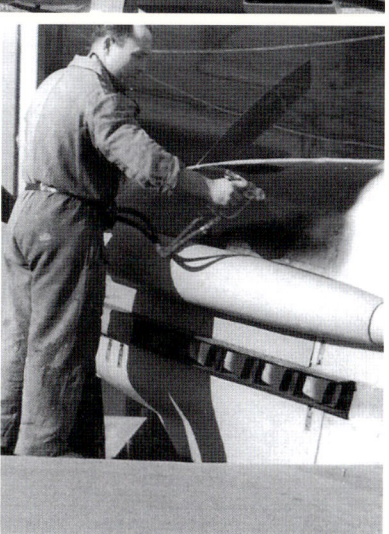

A line-up of RE.2001CBs with bombs fitted. This variant had a different bomb release system to the RE.2001GV, consisting of a special 'fork' that moved the bomb away from the propeller when it was released from the aircraft.

aircraft was placed with Reggiane. Despite these orders, it is believed that only 94 CN variants were officially built (30 from *Serie* III, 34 from *Serie* IV, ten recovered from an order issued in 1941 to Caproni at Predappio and 20 from *Serie* II) before the announcement of the armistice of 8 September 1943 brought an end to all work.

The **RE.2001 *fotografico*** (photographic*)* was a reconnaissance variant equipped with cameras or film cameras on the wing leading edge housed in two external fairings. The term '*fotografico*' was not official but was used to distinguish it from the other variants since the aircraft were, to all intents and purposes, externally modified from fighter variants on the production lines. The exact number of such modified aircraft is not known. To be noted also is that the photo modification was not directly undertaken on the Reggiane factory production line.

RE 2001GV The letters 'GV' denote the initials of the second names of *tenente* Aldo Galimberti and *tenente* Riccardo Vaccari, and although this should not be considered an official variant, it merits inclusion because it involved the modification of three CB machines by mounting a

and the replacement of the two wing-mounted machine guns with two 20 mm MG 151 cannon mounted under the wing in two gondolas with sixty rounds each. However, not all examples of the CN featured this armament because of the shortage in supply of the cannon and some machines were delivered with standard fighter armament fitted.

Thirty aircraft in this version were ordered in June 1942 as *Serie* III, followed by another fifty as *Serie* IV three months later. Subsequently, between March and April 1943, an order for another 120

Few aircraft were built or modified as photo-reconnaissance versions using a Robot type camera which was contained in a special fairing fitted to the leading edge of each wing. Little information is available about operational employment in this regard.

Above and below: This in-flight photograph of an RE.2001, still in a natural metal finish, shows clearly the two pods in the leading edge of each wing for holding camera equipment.

RE.2001CN (Caccia Notturna) equipped with underwing 20 mm cannon, during an engine test run. The aircraft is painted with an all-over black scheme.

Top right, right and below: The RE.2001CB variant during tests at Guidonia in late March 1943, using a liquid oxygen bomb. The trials did not produce any viable operational results.

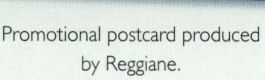

Promotional postcard produced by Reggiane.

reinforced ventral bomb attachment capable of carrying the 630-kg 630PD anti-shipping bomb (PD = *perforante-dirompente* – armour-piercing) with an explosive charge of 120 kg, derived from the 381 mm projectile used by the Regia Marina. After the variant's sole operational sortie, conducted on 12 August 1942, which demonstrated the feasibility of the weapon, trials were abandoned, and the aircraft were converted for photo-reconnaissance duties.

After the experience with the 650-kg armour-piercing bombs, in March 1943, at Furbara, a special liquid-air bomb was loaded beneath an RE.2001. The results of this experiment, however, are unknown.

RE.2001S: A number of Co-belligerent Air Force examples were converted to this standard in 1944 with the adoption of an additional ventral tank; in this case the suffix 'S' indicated use as an escort fighter.

Also worthy of mention are the studies for a project identified by the designation **RE.2001H** which envisaged the modification of a fighter to an anti-tank role, with wing bomb racks in addition to two 20 mm cannon as present in the nightfighter version. The project was not followed up, however,

as the armistice of 8 September put an end to any development work.

In addition to the above-mentioned variants, which differed in only a few details from the basic fighter variant, some versions that required significant structural modifications should be mentioned.

RE.2001 bis This variant was designed by Reggiane in late 1940, with the intention of improving the fighter's speed. The main modification featured a new wing, without weapons, and housing the engine cooling radiators which were completely recessed in it, with an opening on the leading edge and exit on the back and under the wing in order to eliminate the aerodynamic resistance of the radiators positioned under the wings. The aircraft's drag coefficient was lowered, resulting in an increase in speed. Thus modified, the aircraft, belonging to the *Serie Zero*, was only later assigned as MM538. It was flown by Francesco Agello in 1941. Despite having recorded a speed 50-60 km/h higher than the standard configuration, touching 600 km/h at an altitude of 6,000 m, inexplicably it did not go into series production, and was later converted to production standard.

Later, the aircraft was reconverted to a standard RE.2001 fighter and delivered to the Regia Aeronautica.

RE.2001OR (*Organisation Roma* – named after the organisation in charge of building Italian aircraft carriers). Fifty examples of this embarked version were ordered, destined for the units that were to be embarked on the aircraft carriers *Aquila*

and *Sparviero* (the first of which was in an advanced stage of construction in Genoa). In reality, only 12 examples were built, which differed from the production aircraft for embarked use, with structural reinforcements, catapult attachments and arresting hooks. Appropriate hooks on the fuselage and wings would have allowed the aircraft to be suspended from the ceiling of the hangar. It was also planned that it could drop a 640 kg bomb or a 450 mm torpedo. The first evaluations were carried out beginning in the summer of 1942, on the mock flight deck, on which cables similar to those in use on aircraft carriers had been set up transversely.

Fifty examples of this embarked version of the fighter were ordered, destined to be operated by the units which were to be embarked on the carriers

Aquila and *Sparviero* (the first of which was in an advanced stage of fitting out at Genova). However, the considerable delays in the planned completion of the first carrier resulted in the cancellation of the associated fighter programme, and the small number of RE.2001OR which had been built were converted as standard fighters and distributed to fighter units.

In addition to the OR version were two 'lightened' RE.2001s intended for catapult tests in anticipation of use on *Aquila* and *Sparviero*, and so called because they were without all armour and non-essential systems. The first tests with the catapult and arresting hook were carried out by test pilot, Piero De Prato, at Reggio Emilia with the

two prototypes. On 16 January 1943, manoeuvrability tests were carried out with a third prototype built by Reggiane (MM 7260), the aircraft's centre of gravity having been shifted backwards due to the addition of the arresting hook. The tests continued until 12 February 1943, after which the aircraft were transferred to Perugia S.Egidio for the next phase of testing. In 1942, this airfield, although far from the sea, had been designated as a testing ground for the installations intended for the new carrier. Lacking a training ship and having necessarily to postpone the first landing tests until the completion of the *Aquila*, the technical departments of the Air Force and Navy had decided to simulate, on land, the flight

Three photographs of the only RE.2001 bis built, a version modified with an internally mounted wing radiator.

conditions from a ship's deck, reproducing the 'runways' of the aircraft carrier with the same braking, catapulting, lighting and guidance systems. At the beginning of 1943, the runway with braking system was therefore set up and hooking and braking tests were concluded satisfactorily over the course of a few days. The tests were performed with the support of German personnel, as well as a Luftwaffe Arado Ar 96 and Ju 87 E which were intended to carry out landing trials and comparison tests. At the conclusion of these tests, there was a positive opinion of the RE.2001OR, although some defects were highlighted in the braking hook, the shape of which was not considered to be good, in addition to its excessively small dimensions and general weakness. However, once the suggested modifications had been made, the entire apparatus was deemed to be more than acceptable. The RE.2001 was preferred to the RE.2000, and it was not disposed to folding wings since it was planned to save space by attaching the aircraft to the ceiling of the aircraft carrier hangars with special harnesses.

The deterioration in Italy's military situation and the delays in preparing the aircraft carriers led the 160° *Gruppo*, to which the aircraft were initially assigned, to redeploy to Decimomannu.

The armistice put an end to the *Organisation Roma* and then came the order of 15 October 1943 which ordered the immediate dissolution of the

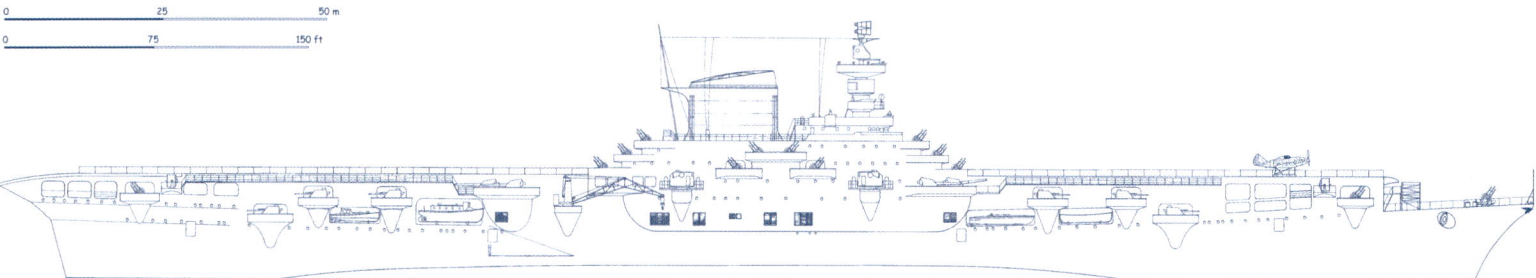

L'Aquila was an aircraft carrier designed by the Regia Marina during the Second World War, and created by reusing and modifying the hull of the transatlantic liner Roma. L'Aquila was the first Italian aircraft carrier to be built, but it never entered active service.

A sad view of aircraft carrier L'Aquila moored at La Spezia after the war and shortly before its demolition.

An example of the RE.2001OR (Organizzazione Roma) variant fitted with an arrester hook and tested at Perugia in early 1943.

These models show the proposed method of parking and storing the RE.2001 under the flight deck of the planned Italian carrier L'Aquila.

Detail of the arrangement of the arrester hook on an RE.2001OR during testing or construction.

Marinavia (Higher Command of the Navy Aviation) and of the 160° *Gruppo*, which had nevertheless managed to save some of the aircraft and personnel but the wealth of naval experience accumulated in the previous two years was dispersed.

Structurally similar to the RE.2001OR, was the sole example of the **RE.2001G,** a torpedo attack variant with potential to be embarked. MM9921 was appropriately modified and featured special ventral attachments capable of supporting a small torpedo to be used by fast aircraft, generally known as the '*silurotto*'. The aircraft had a taller tailwheel intended to ensure that the torpedo tailplane was unable to make contact with the ground. The aircraft retained its armament of four machine guns, and after completion in June 1943, it was sent to the *Nucleo Addestramento*

Aerosiluranti at Gorizia for evaluation. Subsequently, the armistice halted any further development.

To make up for the slow supply of Alfa Romeo engines, the Regia Aeronautica commissioned Caproni Taliedo to build a prototype fitted with the Isotta Fraschini[2] Delta IV RC.16-48 inverted-V twelve-cylinder, air-cooled engine, capable of 840 hp (626 kW) at 5,300 m.

This new aircraft was known as **RE.2001 Delta** and despite being aware of the lower powered engine, the *Ministero dell'Aeronautica* and Caproni were confident that the weight reduction obtained would allow performance comparable to that of the standard RE.2001 (Reggiane was not so optimistic).

The RE.2001 Delta prototype was assembled in the summer of 1942 at the Caproni factory in

Taliedo and assigned as MM9920. For its construction an RE.2001 airframe was used, modified in the front section to mount the Isotta Fraschini engine.

Expectations were such that on 8 September, Caproni proposed an option for 100 or so aircraft, despite the fact that the aircraft had not yet flown. This happened on 12 September 1942, with Caproni test pilot, Giovanni Berretta, at the controls. Already, during initial flights, results showed that the speed was slightly lower than that of the RE.2001. Berretta reached a speed of about 520 km/h. This was considered acceptable given the limited engine power and despite the aircraft's overall weight reduction of over 220 kg.

In November, the prototype was transferred to Guidonia where numerous flights were made by test pilots at the *Centro Sperimentale*. On the one hand, they appreciated the aircraft's qualities, but they also confirmed that its speed performance was not particularly good. Over the course of the flights, conducted by several pilots in addition to Berretta, the aircraft never exceeded a speed of 500 km/h, and only in one flight did it reach 495 km/h at an altitude of 4,500 m. There were complaints of engine overheating problems which forced the test flights to be suspended on more than one occasion.

A serious engine problem on 27 January 1943 saw the end of the programme, when Berretta was performing a climb test. The breaking of a connecting rod caused the engine crankcase to burst, affecting the fuel lines, and the engine caught fire, forcing the pilot to jump out with his parachute.

---

[2] Isotta Fraschini was another company within the Gruppo Caproni.

Continues on page 103

The RE.2001, MM 9921, with lengthened tail section for the fitting of a torpedo under the fuselage.

Another photograph of the RE.2001, MM 9921, with lengthened tail section for the fitting of a torpedo under the fuselage. Note extended tailwheel.

The sole example of the RE.2001 *Delta*, MM99205. This aircraft was lost in a crash on 27 January 1943. Apart from its powerplant and altered nose contours, the RE.2001 *Delta* was similar to the standard V12 powered version.

The RE.2001 *Delta*, MM9920, under testing at Guidonia. The aircraft was an unsuccessful attempt to solve the availability problem of the DB 601 engine by replacing it with an Isotta Fraschini engine.

Below: The RE.2001 *Delta* together with other aircraft built by the Caproni group. With the two pilots seen here is believed to be designer Luigi Pambianchi.

Above: Views of the modification of the forward area of RE.2001 *Delta*. To accommodate the air-cooled, 12-cylinder, inverted-V Isotta Fraschini Delta engine, the front part of the aircraft was fitted with an intake mounted below the spinner.

Two in-flight photographs of the RE.2001CN prototype, MM90760, unpainted but with two cannon pods fitted.

The RE.2001CN variant with underwing gun pods. Each gun was armed with 60 rounds.

Close-up showing the installation of an underwing gun pod for 20 mm cannon.

RE.2001CN with flame dampers and ventral pods, but lacking the wing cannon. The low availability of these weapons caused delays to the programme and the accumulation of incomplete aircraft awaiting fitment.

Technical aspects

Mock-up of the RE.2001 fuselage structure.

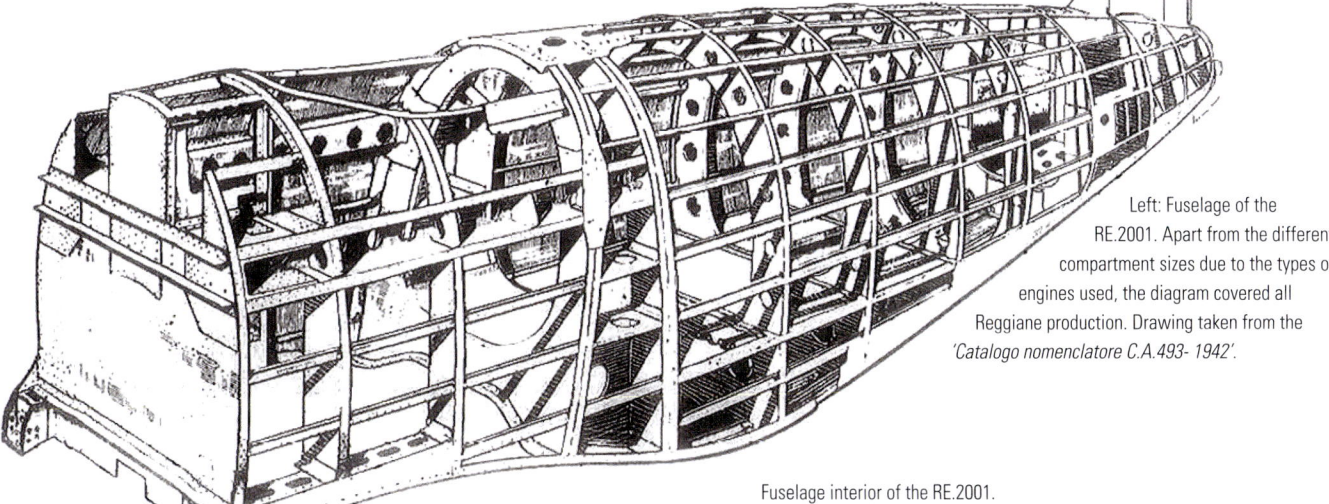

Left: Fuselage of the RE.2001. Apart from the different compartment sizes due to the types of engines used, the diagram covered all Reggiane production. Drawing taken from the *'Catalogo nomenclatore C.A.493- 1942'*.

Fuselage interior of the RE.2001.

The Reggiane RE.2001 *Ariete* I was a low-wing, single-engine, monoplane fighter. The fuselage was built in duralumin with a shell structure consisting of 13 sheet metal frames and plating, stiffened by stringers with a cockpit enclosed by a canopy that could be opened sideways and fitted with sliding windows. The windscreen, as with the following RE.2002 and 2005 types, incorporated 50-mm thick armoured glass. The wing was elliptical in planform with a biconvex asymmetric profile which decreased towards its extremities. The monocoque wing structure was all-duralumin and formed of spars connected by ribs, its upper cladding reinforced with corrugated sheet metal and its undersides by stringers.

The wing was divided into five essential sections:

– a central section with a three-spar structure containing, at its centre, two fuel tanks, with the lateral sections housing the main undercarriage bays

– two outer wings with attachments for ailerons and the hinges for the flaps on the trailing edge, with space for the partial housing of the water radiator. The aileron structure was duralumin and the cladding was fabric. The left aileron was fitted with a trim tab adjustable on the ground.

The flaps were operated either mechanically or electrically, and were all-metal, extending the entire wing length from wingtip to wingtip, passing under the fuselage, and were divided into four sections, two attached to the central section, and one to each outer wing section.

The tailplanes were cantilever structures and comprised a fixed stabiliser with the elevator and a fin with attached rudder. The stabiliser was formed of two separate halves, with a two-spar structure clad in duralumin, fixed to the fuselage by attachments corresponding to the spars. The vertical tail was similarly formed of two

The underside of the centre section of the RE.2001 wing with the fuel tank housing clearly visible.

RE.2001 wings under assembly.

Starboard lower wing underside under assembly. The radiator compartment is visible.

The upper part of the central section of the wing, which also acted as the cockpit floor.

1401

RE.2001 tailplanes. The structure was similar to that of other Reggiane fighters.

Tail structure of the RE.2001 from the *'Catalogo nomenclatore* C.A.493- 1942'.

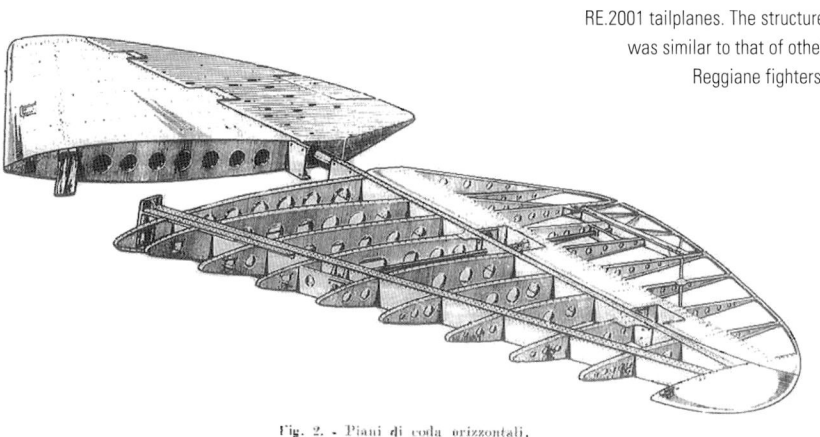

Fig. 2. - Piani di coda orizzontali.

independent parts and was a duralumin structure clad in fabric. Both elevator and rudder featured trim tabs adjustable in flight.

The retractable main undercarriage was similar to that of the RE.2000 with the wheels being housed flat within the thickness of the central wing section, with their legs being protected by dedicated fairings.

The undercarriage retraction controls were electrical with a secondary, back-up, mechanical lever system. Correct undercarriage operation was displayed to the pilot on an electro-mechanical panel. The wheel brakes were actioned by compressed air fed by the on-board pneumatic system. On production aircraft, the tailwheel was fixed and fitted with FAST oleo-pneumatic shock absorbers.

The pilot's flying controls consisted of the stick and pedals, the former engaging with the

ailerons and stabiliser through rigid dural tube controls, while rudder inputs were actioned by dual flexible metal cables. The movement of the trim tabs on the rudder and stabilisers was controlled by the pilot through a flywheel for the vertical tab and a crank for the horizontal, coupled into the same box, the commands being transmitted by flexible cables to the appropriate surfaces.

The pilot's seat was made of armoured steel with housing for the parachute and attachments for the harness. It was adjustable horizontally and vertically, oleo-dynamically.

In production versions of the RE.2001, the engine installed was the Alfa Romeo RA 1000 RC.41 *Monsone* V12, a licence-produced copy of the Daimler-Benz DB 601. The engine was capable of developing an output of 1,175 hp on take-off and 1,050 hp at 2,400 rpm, at a height of 4,100 m. The propeller, also manufactured by Alfa

Romeo, was the RA.1000 three-blade, constant speed, variable pitch, clockwise-rotating R.A.1000 of all-metal construction with a diameter of 3.10 m.

Engine power was controlled by a throttle, on the grip of which was mounted a button which enabled the lever to be moved further to the rear, enabling the insertion of the +100 boost. The normal starter was electric, while the safety starter was hand-cranked. The fuel system comprised three tanks, two of which were installed in bays in the central wing section, the other being in the upper fuselage, mounted behind the pilot's seat. The forward wing tank had a capacity of 280 litres, the rear tank 200 litres, and the fuselage tank could hold 77 litres. All the tanks were '*semapizzati*' (self-sealing), while the rear wing tank and the fuselage tank were connected by a flexible tube. Fuel was to be no less than 87 octane.

Continues on page 117

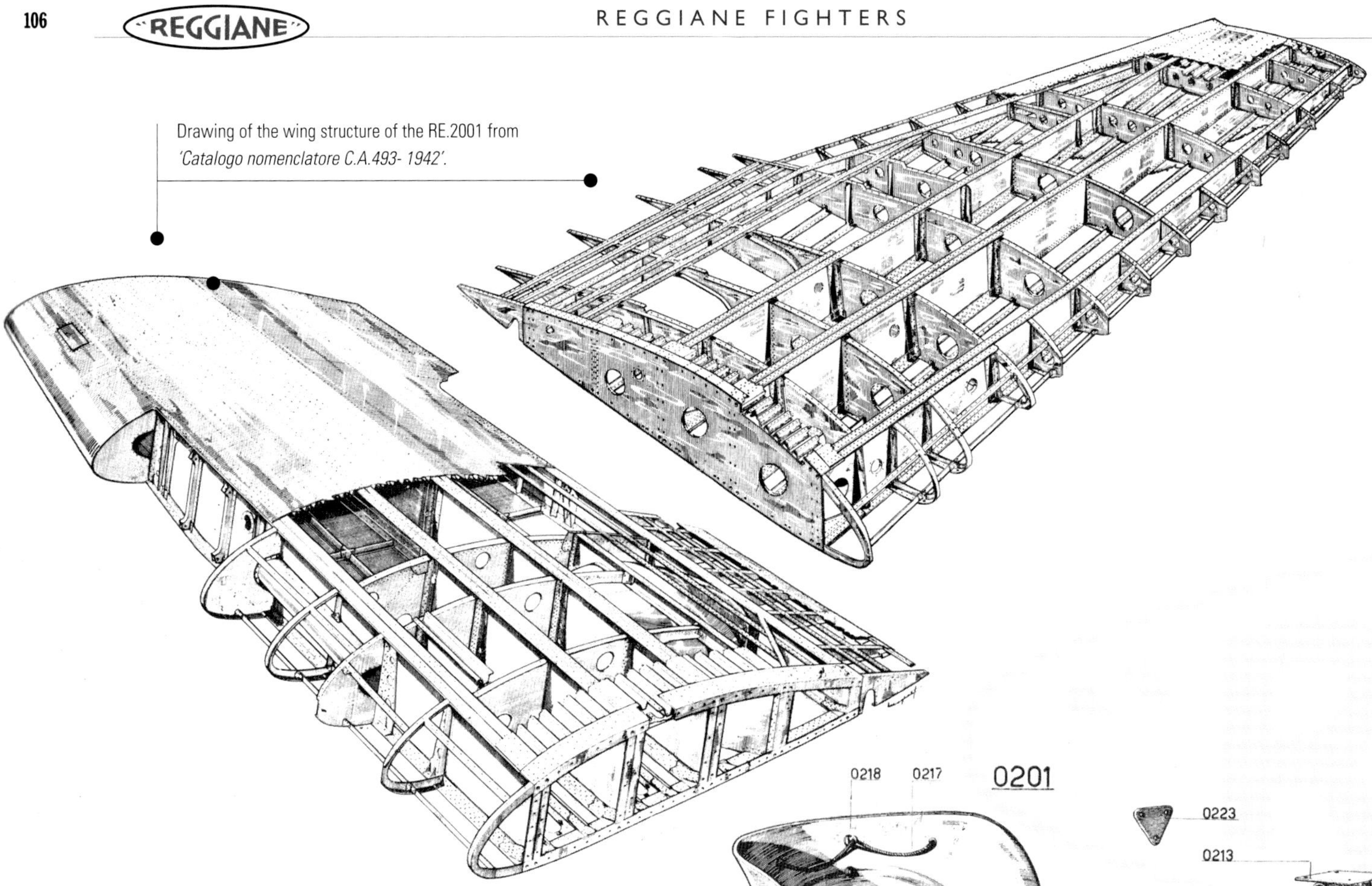

Drawing of the wing structure of the RE.2001 from *'Catalogo nomenclatore C.A.493- 1942'.*

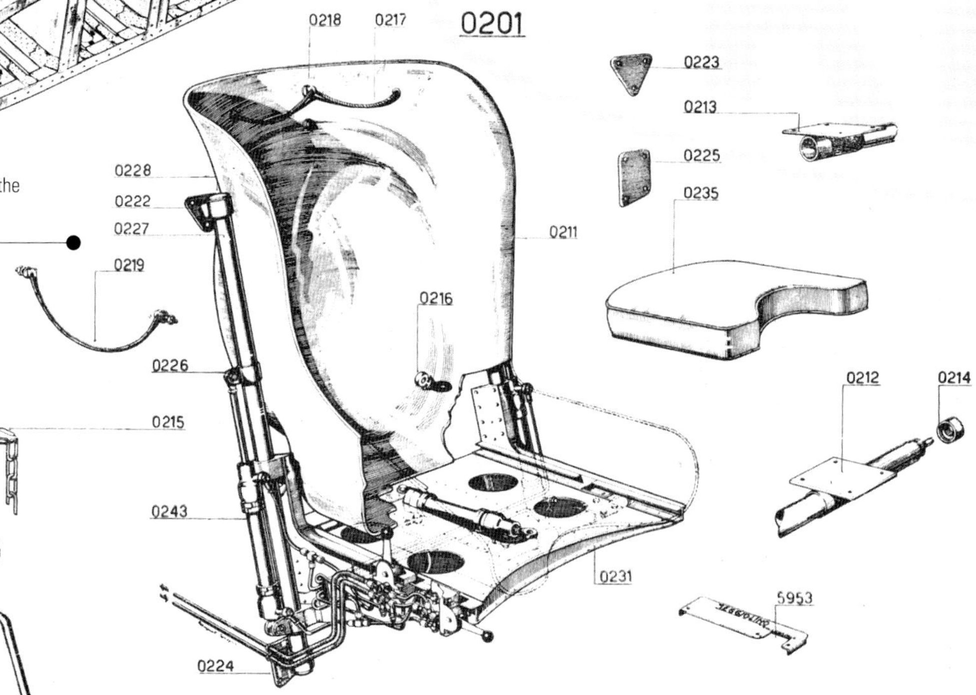

The pilot's seat and main parts in the RE.2001 from the *'Catalogo nomenclatore C.A.493- 1942'.*

0218　0217　**0201**

0223
0213
0225
0235
0211
0216

0228
0222
0227
0219
0226
0215
0243
0231
0212　0214
5953
0224

0172　**0171**

0152　**0158**　0160　**0151**　**016 7**

0153　0159

0165　0166

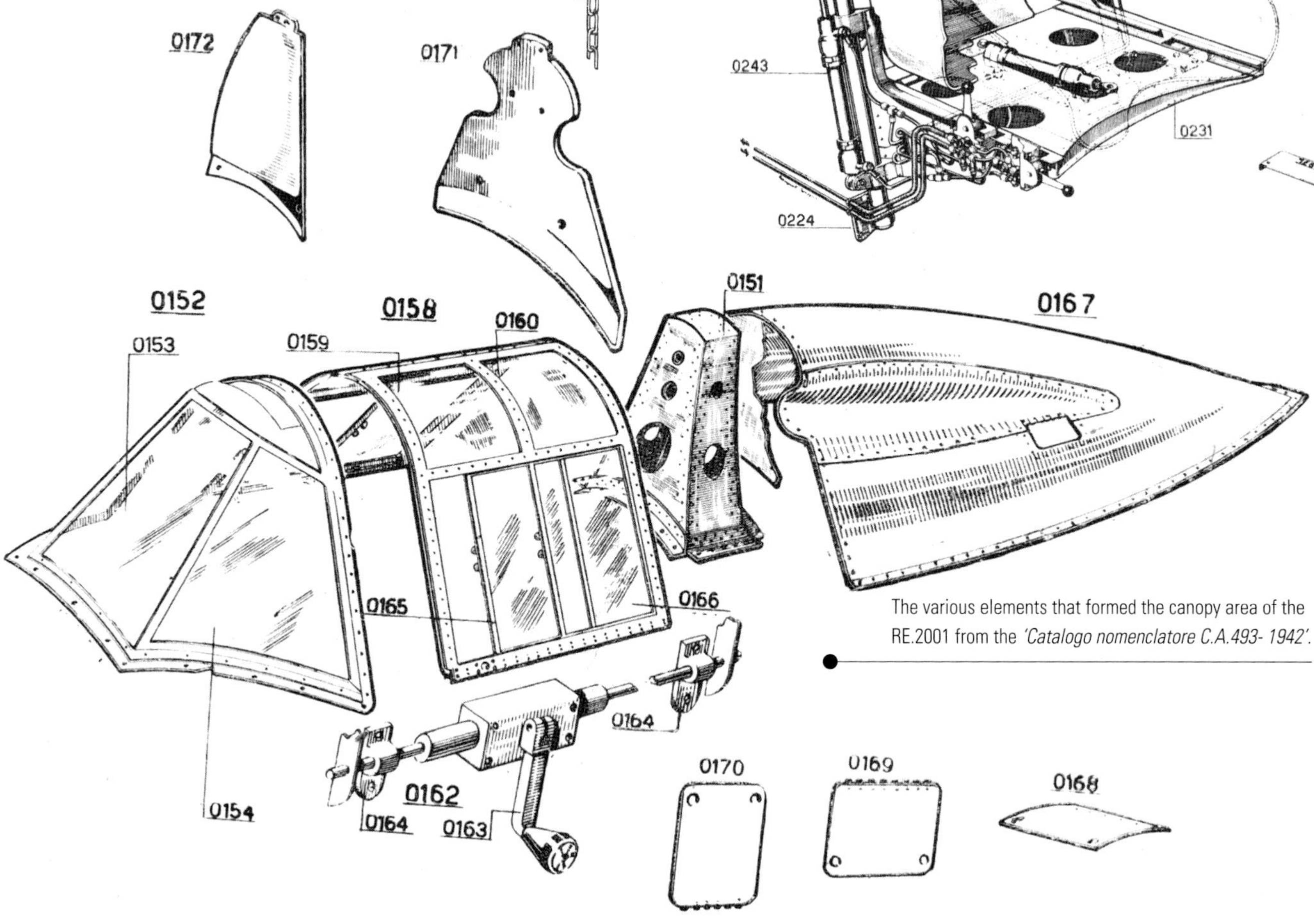

The various elements that formed the canopy area of the RE.2001 from the *'Catalogo nomenclatore C.A.493- 1942'.*

0154　**0162**　0164　0163　0164

0170　0169　0168

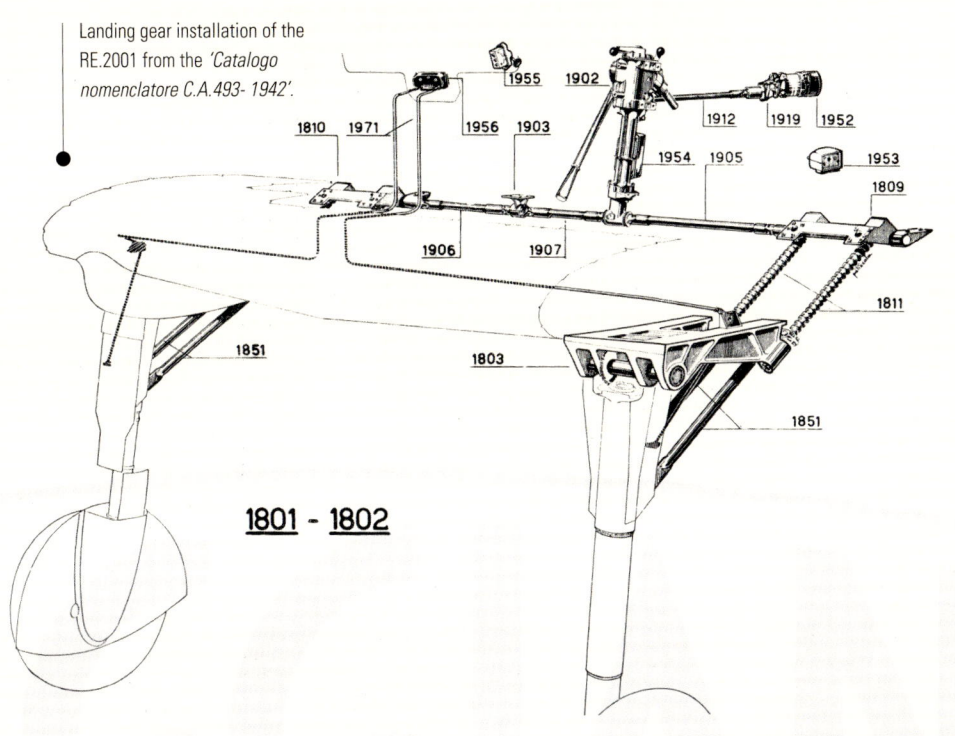

Landing gear installation of the RE.2001 from the *'Catalogo nomenclatore C.A.493- 1942'*.

1955 1902 1912 1919 1952
1810 1971 1956 1903 1954 1905 1953
1809
1906 1907
1811
1851 1803 1851
1851

1801 - 1802

The mishap that occurred to this RE.2001 allows an excellent view of the wing underside with radiators and undercarriage housings.

Arrangement of the two 12.7 mm Breda SAFAT machine guns from the *'Catalogo nomenclatore C.A.493- 1942'*.

6207 6206 6242 6202 6204 6203
6371
6201/A
6233
6201
6212
6243
6244
6222
6240
6259
6241
6237

6210

6205 6391
6272

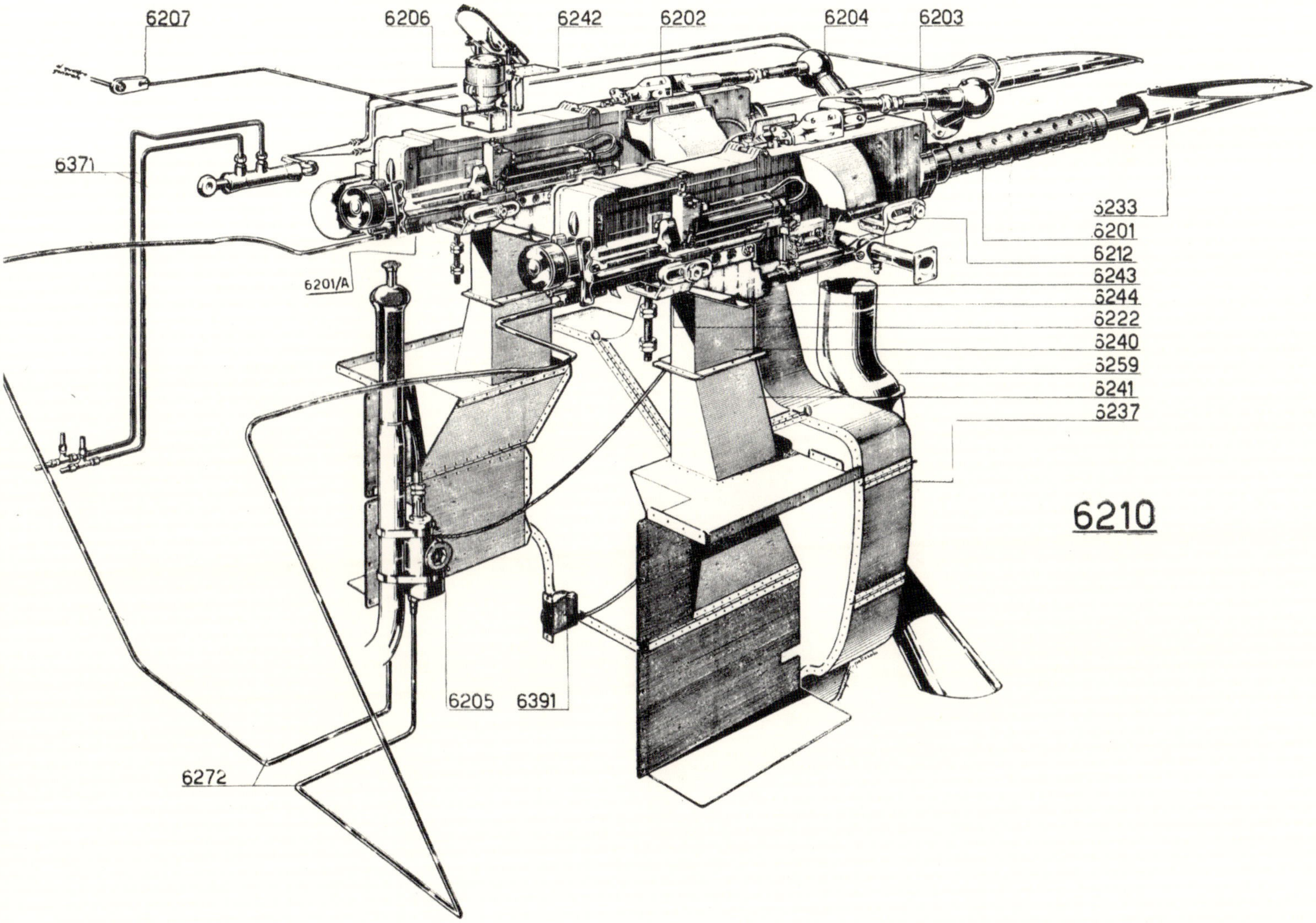

The RE.2001 central control column with the armament firing button. *'Sicura'* denotes the gun trigger safety position.

View of the RE.2001 instrument panel, gunsight and rudder pedals.

The wing centre section with the pedal rests and controls attached.

Drawing from the *'Catalogo nomenclatore C.A.493-1942'* showing installation of the Alfa Romeo RA 1000 RC 41 engine.

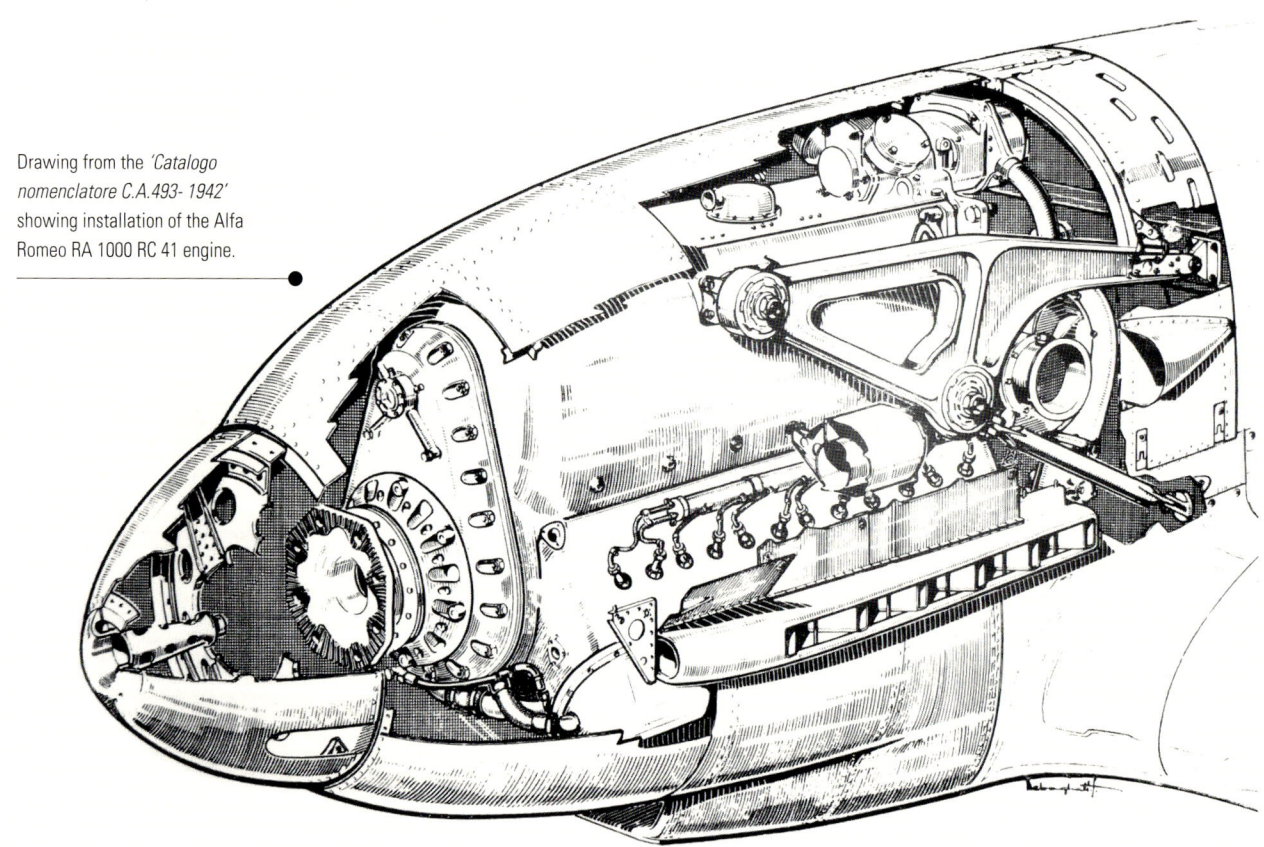

This page and following: A selection of images showing the installation of the Alfa Romeo RA 1000 RC 41 engine.

E SEVERAMENTE
VIETATO FUMARE

RE 2001 - Tavola N. 1

SISTEMAZIONI INTERNE
(vista di fianco)

LEGGENDA:

1 - Barra comando
2 - Pedaliera
3 - Comando alette di compensazione sul timone di profondità
4 - Leva comando carrello e ipersostentatori
5 - Commutatore comando elettrico e a mano carrello e ipersostentatori
6 - Motorino elettrico comando carrello
7 - Motorino elettrico comando ipersostentatori
9 - Avviatore acustico carrello
10 - Cruscotto oscillante strumenti di volo
11 - Cruscotto strumenti motore e vari
12 - Cruscotto ausiliario
13 - Manette comando gas ed elica
14 - Commutatore comando elettrico e a mano, ipersostentatori
14 - Serbatoio anteriore benzina in ala
15 - Serbatoio posteriore benzina in ala
16 - Serbatoio benzina in fusoliera
17 - Carico del serbatoio benzina in fusoliera e posteriore in ala
18 - Carico del serbatoio anteriore in ala
19 - Scarichi serbatoi benzina
20 - Gruppo filtri e rubinetti benzina
21 - Rubinetti riserva
22 - Valvola di non ritorno
23 - Iniettore benzina avviamento
24 - Serbatoio olio
25 - Radiatore olio
26 - Valvola corto circuito olio
27 - Tappo riempimento sotto pressione olio
28 - Tappo di carico olio
29 - Tappo di scarico olio
30 - Serbatoio acqua
31 - Radiatori acqua
32 - Valvola sfiato acqua
34 - Avviatore elettrico
35 - Presa a strappo cuffia e laringofono
36 - Batteria accumulatori
38 - Quadretto luce
39 - Fanalino di coda
42 - Apparati ricevente e trasmittente
43 - Modulatore
44 - Servoltore impianto R. T.
45 - Quadretto comandi apparati R. T.

46 - Mitraglie in fusoliera cal.
47 - Sincronizzazione
48 - Scatola porta nastro
54 - Collimatore di puntamento
55 - Mirino a visuale libera
56 - Serbatoio impianto idraulico
57 - Bombola aria compressa
58 - Compressorino aria
59 - Deviatore freni
60 - Bombola ossigeno
61 - Inalatore ossigeno
63 - Attacchi per sollevamento braga
64 - Nicchia per sollevamento vecchio con martinetto
65 - Foro per sollevamento apparecchio con tubo
66 - Attacco per ancoraggio ap
70 - Pompa elettrica benzina

RE 2001 - Tavola N. 2

SISTEMAZIONI INTERNE
(vista in pianta)

LEGGENDA:

1 - Barra comando
2 - Pedaliera
3 - Comando alette di compensazione sul timone di profondità e direzione
4 - Leva comando carrello e ipersostentatori
5 - Commutatore comando elettrico e a mano e ipersostentatori
6 - Motorino elettrico comando carrello
7 - Motorino elettrico comando ipersostentatori
9 - Cruscotto oscillante strumenti in volo
10 - Cruscotto strumenti motore e vari
11 - Cruscotto ausiliario
12 - Manette gas ed elica
13 - Commutatore comando elettrico e a mano ipersostentatori
14 - Serbatoio anteriore benzina in ala
15 - Serbatoio posteriore benzina in ala
16 - Serbatoio benzina in fusoliera
17 - Carico del serbatoio benzina in fusoliera e posteriore in ala
30 - Serbatoio acqua
31 - Radiatori acqua
32 - Valvola sfiato acqua
34 - Avviatore elettrico
36 - Batteria accumulatori
37 - Quadro generale impianto elettrico
38 - Quadretto luce
39 - Fanalino di coda
40 - Fanalino di via
41 - Tubo Pitot
42 - Apparati ricevente e trasmittente
43 - Modulatore
44 - Survoltore impianto R. T.
46 - Mitraglie in fusoliera cal. 12,7
48 - Scatola porta nastro
49 - Scatola porta bossoli
50 - Convogliatore di scarico maglioni
51 - Mitraglia in ala 7,7
52 - Scatola porta nastri
53 - Convogliatore di scarico maglioni
56 - Serbatoio impianto idraulico
57 - Bombola aria compressa
58 - Compressorino aria
59 - Deviatore freni
60 - Bombola ossigeno
62 - Thermos
65 - Foro per sollevamento apparecchio con tubo

Right and opposite page:
Performance Tables of RE.2001.

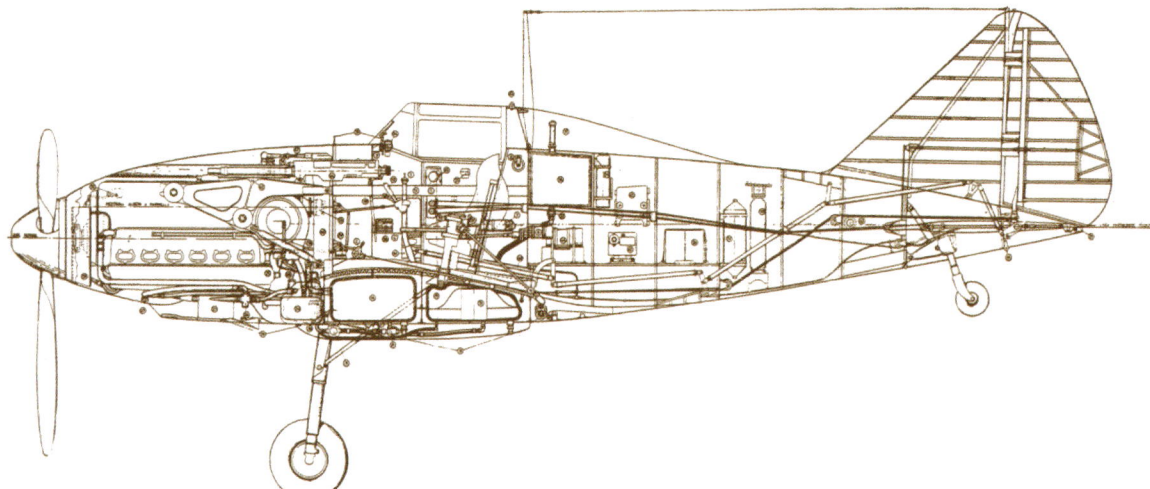

SEGRETO

TABELLA
DI PRESTAZIONE PRATICA

— o —

AEROPLANO DA CACCIA

RE. 2001

Motore "R. A. 1000 „ R. C. 44 I. a. ("D. B. 601 Aa„)

Elica epicicloidale Alfa-Romeo

Provvisoria

CARATTERISTICHE GENERALI

Velivolo	Apertura alare m. 11,00 — Lunghezza m. 8,20 — Altezza m. 3,12 — Superficie portante m.² 20,12 ; carico superficiale max. kg./m.² 163 — Diametro elica m. 3,10 — Coeffic. robustezza cellula 14,25. (P.T. 2950 kg.)

Motore "R.A. 1000" R.C. 44 I.a. ("D.B. 601 A a")

Potenza omologata C.V. 1100 a quota 4400 m. Giri 2400/1'; Press. alim. 1,35 kg./cm.²

Condiz. di volo	Giri/1'	Pressione kg./cm.²	Limite tempo	
Distacco norm.	2400	1,3 ÷ 1,35	1'	Questi dati di prestazione del motore sono prescritti per quote comprese fra 0 e 6000 m.
Distacco eccez.	2400	1,4 ÷ 1,45	1'	
Salita normale	2200	1,2 ÷ 1,23	Senza limite	Sopra i 6000 m. sono consentiti senza limite di tempo 2400 giri/1' e pieno gas —
Salita spinta	2400	1,2 ÷ 1,23	10'	
Salita eccez.	2400	1,3 ÷ 1,35	5'	
Velocità max.	2400	1,3 ÷ 1,35	5'	
Picchiata	Fino a 2800/1'		10"	

Armamento — Nº 2 Mitragliatrici calibro 12,7 in caccia con tiro sincronizzato attraverso il disco dell'elica. — Dotazione nº 400 cartucce per arma. — Nº 2 Mitragliatrici calibro 7,7 alari. — Dotazione nº 500 cartucce per arma.

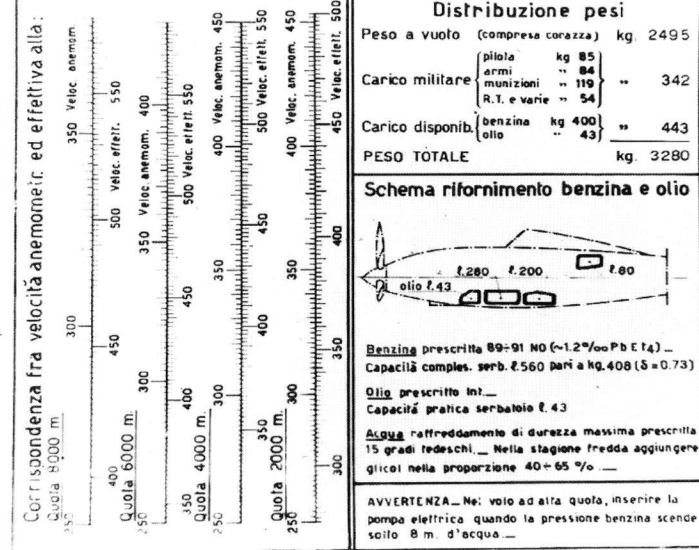

Corrispondenza fra velocità anemometr. ed effettiva alla: Quota 8000 m. — Quota 6000 m. — Quota 4000 m. — Quota 2000 m. — Quota km 0

Distribuzione pesi

Peso a vuoto (compresa corazza)			kg. 2495
Carico militare	pilota kg. 85 — armi " 84 — munizioni " 119 — R.T. e varie " 54	"	342
Carico disponib.	benzina kg. 400 — olio " 43	"	443
PESO TOTALE			kg. 3280

Schema rifornimento benzina e olio

ℓ.280 ℓ.200 ℓ.80 — olio ℓ.43

Benzina prescritta 89÷91 NO (~1.2%oPb E ℓ4) — Capacità comples. serb. ℓ.560 pari a kg.408 (δ=0.73)

Olio prescritto Int. — Capacità pratica serbatoio ℓ. 43

Acqua raffreddamento di durezza massima prescritta 15 gradi tedeschi. — Nella stagione fredda aggiungere glicol nella proporzione 40÷65 % —

AVVERTENZA — Nel volo ad alta quota, inserire la pompa elettrica quando la pressione benzina scende sotto 8 m. d'acqua.

Percorsi e tempi in volo orizzont. e corrispond. velocità

Velocità km./h effett./anem.	ℓ. 300 km.	Tempo	ℓ. 200 km.	Tempo	ℓ. 100 km.	Tempo	ℓ. 50 km.	Tempo
420/399	390	56'	250	36'	115	16'	45	7'
375/357	495	1ʰ 19'	320	51'	145	23'	60	9'
290/276	560	1ʰ 56'	360	1ʰ 15'	165	34'	65	14'
440/395	405	55'	260	35'	120	16'	50	7'
390/354	500	1ʰ 17'	325	50'	145	22'	60	9'
305/276	570	1ʰ 51'	365	1ʰ 12'	165	33'	65	13'
480/392	445	56'	290	36'	130	16'	55	7'
420/343	515	1ʰ 14'	335	47'	150	21'	60	9'
335/276	565	1ʰ 40'	365	1ʰ 06'	165	30'	65	12'
460/337	475	1ʰ 02'	310	40'	140	18'	55	7'
410/301	515	1ʰ 15'	335	48'	150	22'	60	9'
375/275	580	1ʰ 32'	375	1ʰ —	170	27'	70	11'
440/288	495	1ʰ 08'	320	43'	145	20'	60	8'
410/268	515	1ʰ 15'	330	49'	150	22'	60	9'

in volo orizzontale, temperatura olio, all'entrata motore : normale 60° ÷ 75°, massima transitoria 80° — all'uscita motore : normale 90° ÷ 100°, massima transitoria 100° ÷ 110°

Corrispondenza fra pressione in mm. Hg e pressione in kg./cm.²

Salita — Discesa

Press. kg./cm² (mm.Hg)	Giri/1' costanti	Velocità indicata km./h	Consum. benzina litri	km. percorsi orizzont.	Tempi	km. percorsi orizzont.	Tempi	Quote a.t. m.
1,15 (845)	2200	280	20	—	—	—	—	Bassa quota (~1000)
1,15 (845)	2200	280	30	15	3'30"	15	2'30"	2000
1,15 (845)	2200	270	45	35	7'	25	5'	4000
0,9 (662) 1 (735)	2200 2400	260	60	60	11'	40	8'	6000
0,80 (588)	2400	250	85	100	18'	60	12'	8000

Temperature massime consentite dell'acqua all'uscita dal motore — Quota km 0

(*) Sopra i 6000 m. — (**) Compresa benzina necessaria per messa in moto. — (***) Le quote riportate corrispondono praticamente a quelle altimetriche con clima medio invernale ; in aria estiva corrispond. a quote altimetr. inferiori di circa 400 m

Volo orizzontale — Percorsi e tempi totali (compresa salita)

REGIME	GIRI	Pressione alimentazione kg./cm² (mm. Hg)	Consum. orario ℓ/h	Velocità km./h effett./anem.	Carico normale Benzina ℓ.480 km.	Tempo	Max. autonomia Benzina ℓ.560 km.	Tempo
Croc. veloce	2200	1,15 / (845)	290	420/399	590	1ʰ 27'	715	1ʰ 42'
Crociera	1800	1,00 / (735)	205	375/357	765	2ʰ 03'	905	2ʰ 25'
Croc. attesa	1410	0,85 / (625)	140	290/276	870	3ʰ —	1040	3ʰ 35'
Croc. veloce	2200	1,15 / (845)	295	440/395	625	1ʰ 27'	740	1ʰ 42'
Crociera	1800	1,00 / (735)	210	390/354	775	2ʰ —	920	2ʰ 22'
Croc. attesa	1470	0,83 / (610)	145	305/276	875	2ʰ 35'	1040	3ʰ 25'
Croc. veloce	2200	1,15 / (845)	290	480/392	685	1ʰ 28'	810	1ʰ 44'
Crociera	1800	1,00 / (735)	220	420/343	790	1ʰ 55'	935	2ʰ 15'
Croc. attesa	1620	0,83 / (610)	160	335/276	860	2ʰ 35'	1020	3ʰ 03'
Croc. veloce	2400	1,00 / (735)	260	460/337	730	1ʰ 38'	865	1ʰ 56'
Crociera	2000	0,85 / (625)	215	410/301	785	1ʰ 57'	930	2ʰ 18'
Croc. attesa	1800	0,80 / (588)	175	375/275	875	2ʰ 22'	1040	2ʰ 47'
Croc. veloce	2400	0,80 / (588)	240	440/288	750	1ʰ 47'	890	2ʰ 06'
Crociera	2000	0,75 / (550)	215	410/268	775	1ʰ 57'	925	2ʰ 19'

Le autonomie calcolate prevedono una rimanenza teorica di benzina pari a ℓ.15+5% della benzina caricata. — Alla quota di 5000÷6000 m. a pieno regime il consumo massimo è di 350 ℓ/h. —

A selection of images showing the installation of the Alfa Romeo RA 1000 RC 41 engine.

Right and opposite page: Arrangement of the two nose-mounted 12.7 mm SAFAT machine guns.

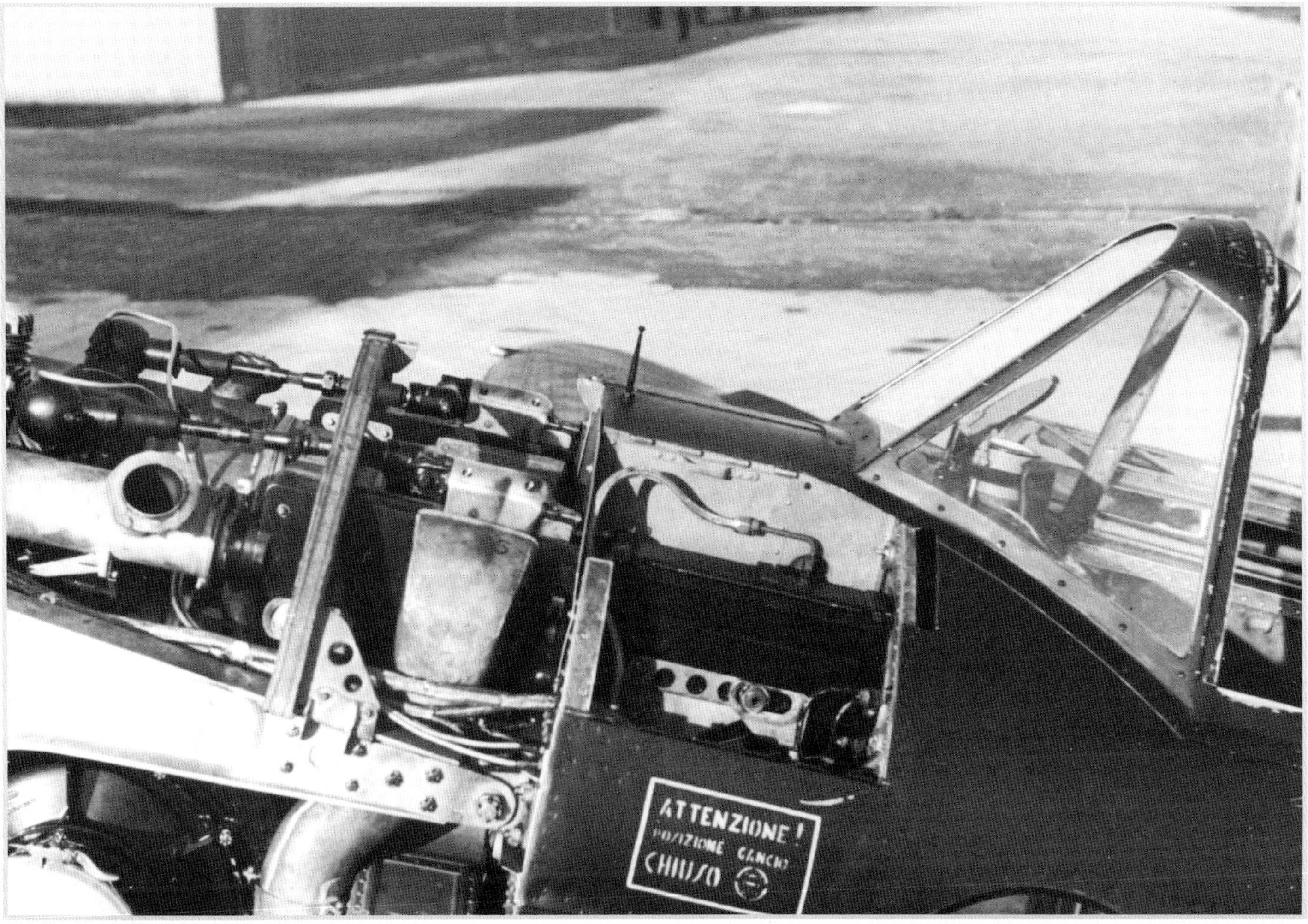
ATTENZIONE!
POSIZIONE GANCIO
CHIUSO

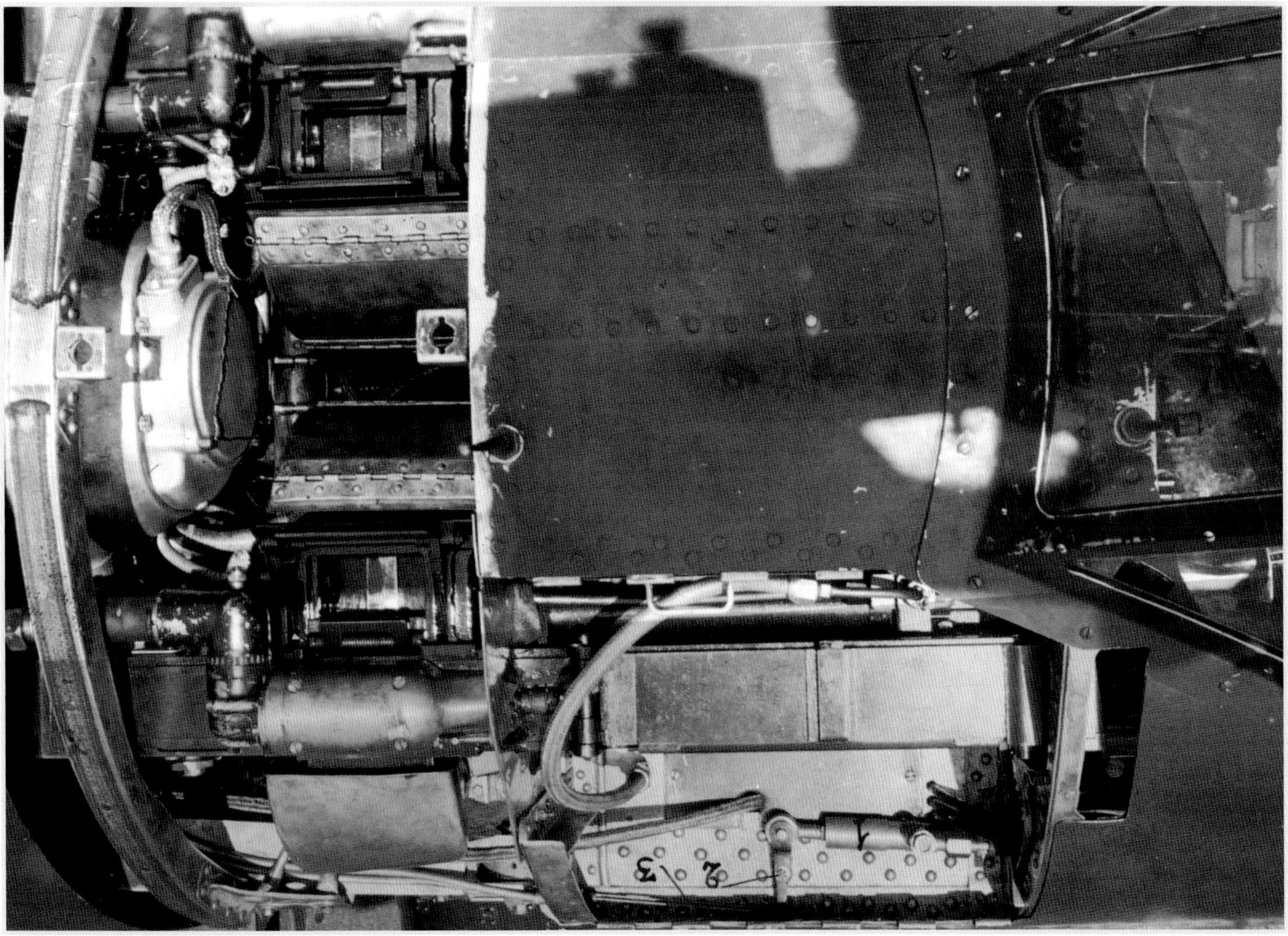
1
2
3

An armourer loads one of the
ammunition boxes for the two nose-
mounted 12.7 mm SAFAT machine guns.

This photograph shows clearly the original folding side
panel on the canopy of the RE.2001.

The central rack for attachment of the 630-kg bomb
for the RE.2001GV.

The compartment for the wing-mounted 7.7 mm SAFAT machine gun.

RE.2001 Technical Data *

Length	11.00 m
Height	3.15 m
Wing span	8,360 m
Wing area	20.40 sq.m.
Empty weight	2,460 kg
Total weight	3,240 kg
Engine	Alfa Romeo RA 1000 RC41 1,050 hp
Maximum speed	563 km/h
Minimum speed	130 km/h
Range	1,100 km
Climb to 1,000 m	41"
Climb to 3,000 m	2'19"
Climb to 6,000 m	5'43"
Ceiling	10,800 m
Take-off run	168 m
Landing run	255 m

* Data taken from Reggiane RE.2001 *Catalogo Nomenclatore* C.A.493, 1942

The engine cooling circuit had a water tank with a nominal capacity of 18 litres, located in front of the engine and radiators, and positioned in the rear ventral part of the wings. A pipe connected the water tank to the engine, while two other lateral connections located at the front of the engine, each communicating with the tank, collected the heated water and conveyed it directly to the radiators. The oil tank was installed at the front of the central plane. Its capacity was 30 litres. The circuit, comprised entirely of hoses, was cooled by a partitionable radiator located under the engine. There was also a fire extinguisher system of the Silma C.0.4 type and the pilot had an O.M.I. oxygen system with two cylinders of 3 litres each installed in the cabin on the right side.

The aircraft was equipped with a radio receiver and a transmitter system powered by the on-board battery. The equipment was positioned in the fuselage to the rear of the pilot.

The aircraft's electrical system was powered by the current supplied by four 12 Volt Tudor batteries which fed the general switchboard equipped with voltmeter, ammeter, main switch and fuses, installed in the pilot's cabin. A Marelli 1,200 Watt dynamo, mounted on the engine and equipped with a voltage regulator, recharged the batteries. A special plug socket was installed on the outer side of the fuselage for ground charging.

The principal armament comprised two Breda SAFAT 12.7 mm machine guns, synchronised to fire through the propeller disc and re-armed pneumatically, and two Breda SAFAT 7.7 mm machine guns housed in the wings, firing outside the propeller disc. There was a magazine of 350 rounds for each of the 12.7 mm guns and 600 rounds each for the 7.7 mm guns. Depending on the variant, the aircraft could be equipped with supports for the attachment of bombs weighing up to 250 kg or supplementary fuel tanks. For aiming, the pilot could utilise a San Giorgio type C '*a Tuffo*' gunsight and free-mounted ring and bead sight.

Operational service with the Regia Aeronautica

The first pre-series aircraft – or *Serie Zero* – were delivered on 16 September 1941 to the 150ª *Squadriglia* of the 2° *Gruppo Aut. CT*, commanded by *tenente colonnello* Giuseppe Baylon and at the time based at Ravenna airfield. The *Gruppo* also controlled two other *squadriglie*, the 152ª and 358ª, which started conversion onto the new fighter a few weeks later.

The impressions gained by the pilots regarding their new aircraft were very positive, as evidenced by *maresciallo* Jellici of the 150ª *Squadriglia*.

'*On 17 September 1941, I took off. I liked this aircraft at first sight and in the air even more so; I was really at ease. It was an excellent fighter for manoeuvrability and patrols and, at that time, also for speed. After a few months, together with* capitano *Tullio De Prato and* maresciallo *Olindo Simionato, we organised aerobatic flights that were very successful, and*

The RE.2001, MM08077, at Guidonia where it was used for several tests, including that of the propeller drive, throttle control and dive tests with 250-kg bombs in the Furbara area.

An RE.2001 of the 150ª *Squadriglia*. The 2° *Gruppo Aut.* CT was the main Regia Aeronautica unit to use the Reggiane fighter.

RE.2001 of the 358ª *Squadriglia* of the 2° *Gruppo Aut.* CT ready for transfer to Sicily. It was not until 4 May 1942 that the entire group completed its deployment to San Pietro Caltagirone airfield.

Below: The 152ª *Squadriglia* was the second *Squadriglia* of the 2° *Gruppo Aut.* CT to commence transition onto the RE.2001, operating from Ravenna and Reggio Emilia. (P.Monti)

Another 152ª *Squadriglia* RE.2001 of the second *Squadriglia* of the 2° *Gruppo Aut.* CT. (P.Monti)

Left: An RE.2001 with a rare personal insignia, inscribed around the unit insignia. The name '*Pierino*' was perhaps that of a pilot of the 2° *Gruppo Aut.* CT.

Pilots of 2° *Gruppo Aut.* CT, identifiable from left as *tenente* Bartolozzi, *capitani* Fassi, Larese, Celentano, *tenente colonnello* Aldo Quarantotti, commander of the unit, and *capitano* Seganti.

San Pietro Caltagirone, summer 1942. These RE.2001s of the 2° *Gruppo Aut.* CT are about to set off on a new mission over Malta.

we were enthusiastic about the ease with which this aircraft could be controlled, perhaps even more so than the CR.32 because it had a more powerful engine. I threw it into all the attitudes and it never wanted to go into a spin. To do this, you had to force it, but as soon as you let go of the controls, it would immediately get back on the flight line. The armament was good too, two 7.7 mm machine guns in the wings and two 12.7 mm guns in the nose, synchronised with the propeller, with very effective interspersed fire: armour piercing, tracer, incendiary and explosive, which made RAF pilots envy us a lot.'

To complete training on the new fighter, part of the unit was transferred to Gorizia, from where it operated until the end of the year, when the 2° *Gruppo Aut.* CT received an order to relocate to Roma Ciampino for a period of preparation preceding an operational deployment to Sicilia in support of operations against the island of Malta, and in particular flying escort missions to protect Axis bombers.

On 5 February the *Gruppo* underwent a change of command, with *tenente colonnello* Aldo Quarantotti replacing Baylon, and by the end of April the unit boasted a fleet of thirty-five aircraft. After a somewhat lengthy training and preparation phase, on 3 May 1942, the 2° *Gruppo Aut.* CT was

RE.2001s of 2° *Gruppo Aut.* CT at dispersal in what appear to be earth blast shelters, lined with wooden panels, at San Pietro di Caltagirone airfield, *Squadriglia Autonoma* CT on 23 May 1942.

Below: Reggianes of 2° *Gruppo Aut.* CT at San Pietro Caltagirone in Sicilia in the summer of 1942.

transferred to San Pietro di Caltagirone airfield in the province of Catania.

The first mission over Malta, a free fighter sweep, was conducted on 10 May 1942 by some twenty fighters, but achieved no results. Very different was the outcome of the second mission on the same day, conducted by ten RE.2001s together with twenty AerMacchi C.202s of the 4° *Stormo* CT, tasked with escorting five CANT Z.1007 bis bombers attacking a military installation near La Valletta. On this occasion the Italian fighters were met by RAF Spitfires which, at the end of the clash, had shot down one trimotor and a C.202. However, the Italians claimed three Spitfires and a Beaufighter as destroyed, together with two Spitfires damaged.

After another air combat the following day, with no appreciable results, on 12 May 1942 there was an encounter with nine Spitfires. This time fifteen RE.2001s together with C.200s were escorting three Savoia-Marchetti SM.84s. Again, on this occasion the British fighters managed to engage the Italian bombers, shooting down one and damaging another, but the 2° *Gruppo Aut.* CT pilots claimed the destruction of two Spitfires by *sergente* Paolo Marchio who, in turn, was obliged to perform an emergency landing near Noto, emerging with serious injuries.

Further victories were claimed by Italian pilots over the following days during seaplane escort operations and fighter sweep missions. On 19 May, thirteen RE.2001s were assigned as escort to

CANT Z.1007 bis bombers heading for Malta. In a clash with RAF fighters, which managed to

Tenente Larese describes an air combat over Malta to pilots Rovina and Metellini, September 1942.

The emblem of the 2° *Gruppo Aut.* CT was often painted on the tail of the unit's RE.2001s. *Sergente* maggiore Dringoli was the creator of the emblem.

The 2° *Gruppo Aut.* CT Emblem

The 2° *Gruppo Aut.* CT, the first unit to fly the RE.2001, adopted an emblem designed by *sergente maggiore* Dringoli, featuring a chick marching in Roman-style and carrying a rifle. The emblem was painted onto a white shield and worn on the fin of the unit's aircraft.

Metal uniform insignia of the 2° *Gruppo Aut.*
(P.Monti)

impede the bombers' attack, the Italian pilots claimed one Spitfire and one Beaufighter destroyed, together with five Spitfires damaged.

Two more Spitfires were claimed as destroyed on 23 May, and a couple of days later, on the 25th, five 2° *Gruppo* CT pilots flying as escorts for SM.84 bombers each claimed the destruction of a fighter at the end of a hard-fought clash. The air battles continued and between 26 May and 2 June, the Reggiane fighters' efforts cost the RAF eight aircraft (five destroyed and three damaged) for the price of the loss, on 26 May, of *capitano* Sterzi, who fell over Malta, as well as damage to three Italian aircraft.

Tenente Giacomo Metellini related his impressions of the initial phase of combat operations over Malta:

'*We commenced operations against Malta with two types of mission: direct escort to bomber aircraft, which consisted of flying alongside them, providing close protection against enemy attacks, and free fighter sweep operations, where we flew directly over the island in an attempt to engage British aircraft in combat. In both these cases we flew as a Squadriglia or as a* Gruppo*; once reaching the island we had to deal with the Spitfire Mk Vs flying from their Maltese bases, and so we quickly adopted mobile tactics in order not to give the enemy the opportunity to attack us from the rear. Unfortunately, even doing this, we did not always manage to come off best, and the principal reason for this was down to the fact that the British, thanks to their radar, were fully aware of our movements from the time we left Sicilia, while we had to wait until our single transmitter informed us of what it had managed to understand from intercepted British communications. The direct escort missions, therefore, were very risky: the British, having a timely alert of our arrival, took off and climbed*

to altitude, far higher than us, and there they would lie in wait. With the sun at their backs, they would dive headlong towards us, each of them selecting an individual target and making a single pass, machine-gunning the unfortunate victim who sometimes would not even have time to realise that he was under fire.

'*For us it was difficult to oppose this type of attack because, when we spotted the British, they had usually completed their initial attack dive and were rapidly disappearing, exploiting all the speed acquired during the dive. The notion of following them was out of the question, given that, because of their post-dive speed, they were far faster and, besides, we would have had to abandon providing the escort to the bombers we were tasked with defending.*

'*To try to intercept the Spitfires before they dived on us, we were often provided with an indirect escort, formed by AerMacchi C.202s from Gela, who flew high up above us. The Germans, however, never really wanted to perform this role with their Messerschmitt Bf 109s because, they said, we could be easily confused with the Spitfires, as the elliptical planform of their wing was very similar to that of our Reggianes. Nevertheless, when the Macchis were engaged in other operations we missed their high-level protection and had to look out for ourselves. Out of necessity, we used our experience to develop a new tactic and, instead of remaining alongside the aircraft we were escorting, we began to fly around them, enveloping them in a formation, similar to a sphere. Not leaving any area uncovered, we were thus able to prevent the enemy from making a surprise attack. This tactic of extreme manoeuvrability proved to be very effective because, by occupying the attention of the*

enemy fighters, it gave the bombers the chance to complete their mission and return to base.

'*Returning to the escort mission, if, at first, surprise played in favour of our adversaries, once we were engaged in combat, we managed to defend ourselves well and, in the air combat in which we engaged, we managed to achieve some positive results, thanks to the abilities of our pilots and the aerodynamic characteristics of the RE.2001. In fighter sweeps and direct escort missions, therefore, we were continually manoeuvring: in pairs, if we were in a large group, but nearly always isolated, given the shortage of serviceable aircraft. What is certain, is that if the Reggiane had possessed a more powerful engine, and perhaps had increased armament, we would often have been capable of beating our adversaries. Instead, the inferiority of our aircraft was the cause of many losses among the members of the* Gruppo*: many pilots whose aircraft had been hit, or who had been wounded, were forced to bail out over the stretch of sea which separated us from Malta. Few of them succeeded in their attempts in reaching Sicilia, as the 80 kilometres of sea that separated the two islands was too much to cross in a damaged single-engine aircraft. Also worth remembering again was the inferiority of our RE.2001 in terms of both engine and armament; it was not even advisable to enter into a direct engagement with the Spitfires, from which it was difficult to escape once they got on your tail. Nevertheless, the better manoeuvrability of our 2001s allowed us to pull much tighter turns – tighter than the British could fly, which allowed us to get out of trouble on more than several occasions.*

'*The dogfights did not last very long – at the most a few minutes – because our endurance was limited and so, once we had reached the island, we had little fuel available for any potential clash and for our return to Sicilia. At a certain point we had to try to disengage, and on the return leg we were frequently followed by the British who, thanks to their proximity to their bases, possessed greater endurance and could exploit the situation for longer.'*[3]

At the end of the first month of operations the balance sheet for the 2° *Gruppo Aut*. CT was, to all accounts, positive. Set against the loss in combat of *capitano* Sterzi, to which was added that of *sergente* Marchio, who died of injuries sustained in the emergency landing of 12 May, and that of *tenente* Cazzolli, who was taken prisoner after bailing out over Malta, some 30 aerial victories had been claimed against RAF aircraft.[4] At the start of June, the unit possessed thirty-two fighters, of which twenty-one were combat ready.

However, 6 June 1942 would be recorded as one of the most inauspicious days for the 2° *Gruppo Aut*. CT, with the loss of four pilots in

Tenente Giacomo Metellini of 2° *Gruppo Aut*. CT in Sicilia in 1942.

Due to its position in the centre of the Strait of Sicily, Pantelleria airfield was often used by Italian units engaged in missions against Malta or as a staging point for transfers to North Africa.

A mechanic from 150ª *Squadriglia* proudly displays his unit's emblem.

Maintenance work on the fighters of the 2° *Gruppo Aut*. CT at San Pietro Caltagirone. Note the unit's emblem on the fin of the aircraft in the foreground.

---

[3] Taken from *Un pilota racconta* by Giacomo Metellini, self-published in 2007.
[4] Readers should be mindful of the difference between victories *claimed* and victories *confirmed*.

The RE.2001 of *sergente maggiore* Giovanni Dringoli of 358ª *Squadriglia*, 2° *Gruppo* CT after a belly-landing on return from a mission over Malta.

Below: A pilot of 358ª *Squadriglia* stands close to his aircraft, ready to fly another bomber escort sortie, while an S.79 bomber returns from a mission over Malta in early 1942.

three missions. During the unit's first mission the Reggiane pilots, on one of their endless bomber escorts to Malta, after engaging British fighters in combat, claimed the destruction of a pair of Spitfires, but also recorded the loss of *sottotenente* Venturini who, with a damaged aircraft, was seen to descend towards the sea in order to attempt a probable ditching. On returning to Sicilia at the end of the mission, RE.2001, MM7216, flown by *sergente* Dringoli was also forced into making a belly-landing near Comiso after suffering severe damage.

Maresciallo Jellici, who participated in the action, recalled the encounter with the RAF which concluded with him achieving an aerial victory:

'*Just after departing the island on the return route, I saw to my left two fighters in full combat. I had a good look around to make sure that there were no other enemy aircraft in the area. I then waggled my wings to alert the* Comandante*, then asked with hand signals – because the radio was not functioning – if I could go to help our comrade who was in a bad position with the British fighter. Having obtained permission, I turned sharply to starboard to join the combat area. I aimed at the British fighter which, at that moment, had begun a climb to gain on our comrade. At around 300 metres, I fired a first burst ahead of its nose to force it to abandon its prey, but without any results. Consequently, I approached closed in and fired a second burst. I immediately realised that I had hit the pilot, perhaps even with the first burst. An instant later I had to break away so as not to collide with the enemy aircraft, given that it had pulled up, out of control, and subsequently fell in a spin into the sea to the east of Malta. Immediately I rejoined the* Comandante *who had watched my attack from a distance and had witnessed the shoot-down of the British aircraft.*'

A few Italian pilots, having refuelled, took off again to try to identify the location where Venturini had gone down, in the hope that he had managed to bail out or possibly made an emergency ditching. The eleven airborne Reggianes were subsequently intercepted by an RAF formation. At the end of the ensuing dogfight, the RE.2001 of *capitano* De Merich had been shot down, while the British suffered the loss of a Beaufighter. On the same day, a subsequent mission to escort a CANT Z.506 seaplane saw another clash which resulted in the loss of two RE.2001s over the sea, piloted by *sergenti* Baraldi and Germinian, both of whom were killed.

On 10 June, after another dogfight in Maltese skies, the RE.2001, MM7215, flown by *sergente* Dringoli sank at sea after an emergency landing following engine damage. The pilot, probably injured in the action, disappeared into the sea with his aircraft.

On 14 June, fifteen RE.2001s, together with some C.202s, were tasked with escorting fourteen S.79 torpedo-bombers planning to attack the British ships of the Malta supply convoy sailing from Gibraltar as 'Operation Harpoon' (known to

the Italians as the '*Battaglia di Mezzo Giugno*'). While the trimotors launched their attacks, the Italian fighters were bounced by Sea Hurricanes airborne from the British carriers which were sailing with the convoy as protection. The air battle concluded with the Italians claiming eleven Sea Hurricanes destroyed against the loss of one Reggiane, its pilot managing to escape by parachute. Several other Italian fighters were seriously damaged, amongst which was the aircraft of *maresciallo* Simionato who was forced to make an emergency landing over Tunisia.

The clash with the Sea Hurricanes once again highlighted the air combat characteristics of the Reggiane 2001 which proved to be robust and able to withstand considerable damage. In terms of overall performance, when compared to the Spitfire Mk V, the Reggiane was slightly inferior, unless engaging in combat at medium to low altitudes. However it proved to be universally superior to the Hawker Hurricane. As confirmed on several occasions by the pilots, it did not suffer from the seemingly inferior armament of the six/eight 7.7 mm guns which proved to be less effective than the SAFAT 12.7, especially when the

Tenente Gasperoni, mid-1942.

latter employed high-explosive ammunition.

On the day after the encounter with the Sea Hurricanes, on 15 June 1942, the fighters of the 2° *Gruppo Aut.* CT were deployed temporarily to the airfield on the island of Pantelleria to support operations in the closing stages of the aero-naval battle, flying escort missions on behalf of Italian torpedo-bombers. While engaged in escorting Italian ships, nine RE.2001s intercepted British torpedo-bombers (Swordfish or Albacore biplanes) which were about to launch an attack on the Italian vessels. The unequal fight was a clear victory for the Italian aircraft, with four of the biplanes shot down together with a Beaufighter which was leading the torpedo formation. *Capitano* Salvatore Teja shot down one of the torpedo-attack biplanes and recalled:

'*I fired all my ammunition against five British aircraft, and only one of them managed to approach our ships of the* Divisione Navale *and release its torpedo, which passed a few metres across the bow of the cruiser* Montecuccoli, *which avoided it thanks to a timely and skilful swerve. I had run out of ammunition, so I landed at Pantelleria to give the alarm, departing soon after in another aircraft, looking for the fifth British bomber which, having released its torpedo, was heading east (towards Malta). With me was* tenente *Gasperoni. Not far from Pantelleria I spotted the British pilot on the sea in a dinghy. The aircraft, which had probably been hit earlier, had not managed to reach Malta.*'

After some days of reorganisation, on 23 June

1942 eighteen RE.2001s provided an escort for SM.84s conducting a bombing raid on Ta Venezia[5] airfield in Malta. Another escort mission was flown on 26 June for five Cant Z.1007 bis sent to bomb Mikabba airfield. The Italian aircraft were attacked by RAF Spitfires and at the end of the fight the Italians claimed one British fighter destroyed and another probable. July began with a series of aerial clashes involving the fighters of the 2° *Gruppo Aut.* CT during the unit's bomber escort missions, generally involving battles with British Spitfires, some of which were claimed as shot down. In his autobiography, *capitano* Metellini described that period:

'*After the 'Battle of Mezzo Giugno'* [the Malta supply convoy, Operation Vigorous] *there was a period of relative tranquillity during which we conducted just a couple of escort missions for our Cant Z.1007 bis bombers. On these occasions we encountered the Spitfires based on the island and engaged them in combat, but without any noteworthy results. This phase of calm was apparently determined by the preparations for a new bomber offensive which commenced in early July, and which had as its objective the destruction of the British radar systems on the island and the airfields. As far as I was involved, the major part of our activities were directed at the airfield at Mikabba.*

'*On 2 July, my* Gruppo *managed to shoot down some six Spitfires, one of which was my work. As I used to say, in combat you must look in every direction, try not to be surprised and, if possible, to identify an adversary against which*

you can get into firing range. On that day, a Spitfire appeared in front of me in a dive, with its belly facing towards me. I opened fire with a short burst, without paying any attention to the aftermath. Again, on this occasion it was the other pilots of my Gruppo *who confirmed that they had watched the event and had seen the British aircraft go down. I do not know what happened to the pilot of this Spitfire, or to the Hurricane pilot shot down during the 'Battle of Mezzo Giugno'. I hope that they managed to bail out and were rescued from the waves. In fact, as far as I am concerned (and I think that I can speak on behalf of all the Italian pilots who fought over the island), in all of those battles, we hoped to hit just the aircraft, and never the pilot.*'[6]

Meanwhile, on 1 July 1942, the 22° *Gruppo* CT at Roma Ciampino, commanded by *capitano* Vittorio Minguzzi and formed of the 359ª, 362ª and 369ª *Squadriglia*, began to re-equip with the RE.2001CB, and in the following days commenced its training activities on the new fighter, transferring some of its pilots to Monserrato airfield in Sardegna.

In the same period, the 2° *Gruppo* CT continued its war in the skies over Malta, escorting bombers attacking British airfields and military infrastructure on the island, alternating successes with moments of discomfort. On 4 July, the pilots of the 2° *Gruppo* CT claimed three Spitfires as destroyed, but on the following day *sottotenente* Pagliani was lost. He had bailed out but died following a parachute malfunction.

On 12 July, sixteen Reggianes escorted some

---

[5] In Regia Aeronautica operational reports from the Second World War, the compilers used the name Ta Venezia to identify the Maltese airfield known as Ta Qali or Ta Kali, which was the first airfield to be built on Malta in the 1920s. The name was derived from the fact that the area was often flooded, and its inhabitants also used the same name.
[6] Taken from *Un pilota racconta* by Giacomo Metellini, self-published in 2007.

Like the C.202 Folgore, the similarly powered Reggiane RE.2001 received its baptism of fire over Malta. These aircraft first appeared over the island with 2° *Gruppo Aut.* CT during the early summer of 1942.

An overall dark green Reggiane RE.2001 of 369ª *Squadriglia* being serviced at San Pietro Caltagirone, Sicilia in September 1942. Note the scarecrow unit emblem has not yet been painted inside the white triangle on the fuselage side.

An RE.2001 at Reggio Emilia ready to be delivered to 2° Gruppo Aut. CT, late 1941.

The 369ª *Squadriglia* seen while operating from Pantelleria.

Promotional postcard produced by Reggiane.

Tenente colonnello Aldo Quarantotti, the well-respected commanding officer of 2° *Gruppo Aut.* CT. He was shot down together with *capitano* Seganti on 12 July 1942 while they were searching for a comrade who had been shot down over the sea.

German Ju 88s on a bombing raid to Ta Venezia. At the end of the mission, the Reggiane piloted by *tenente* Francesco Vichi was seen to crash into the sea, probably shot down by a British fighter. After refuelling, the commander of the 2° *Gruppo Aut. CT*, *tenente colonnello* Aldo Quarantotti, immediately took off with three wingmen in search of his comrade. Unfortunately Quarantotti and *tenente* Carlo Seganti never returned. Only years later, it was learned that the two pilots were shot down by the Canadian ace, George Frederick Beurling of the No.249 Squadron, RAF, who caught them flying together with his commander Flg. Off. Hetherington. The two RAF airmen were themselves engaged in the search for a pilot who had not returned from a previous mission. Beurling described the brief action,

'On 12 July I was ordered, together with another three colleagues, to intercept a raid by Ju 88 bombers escorted by a dozen Reggiane 2001s, targeting Ta Kali airfield. It was not the first time that we had encountered this type of aircraft in combat, and it was very good. The raid on Ta Kali was quick and had finished before we could get there. The Ju 88s returned to base undamaged, while the RE.2001s, exploiting their higher altitude, dived down onto us, hitting Jonesy's wing. We then began to follow them over the sea for around thirty-five miles in the direction of their base, and I eventually got the opportunity to attack from above the last of the RE.2001s. I dived down towards him around three hundred yards off his right-hand side. I fired a one-second burst, and with his aircraft hit, the pilot took to his

parachute; the episode was subsequently confirmed by a Spitfire pilot from another squadron present in the area, and who saw the event. I was then credited with an enemy aircraft "destroyed". Returning to base, I became aware that one of our pilots was missing over the sea. I had my aircraft refuelled and immediately left to search for him, together with Hether. After half an hour searching in the hope that we would spot his dinghy between the waves, we noticed a pair of RE.2001s flying low over the sea, below the banks of cloud, and heading towards Malta, these probably also searching for the pilot who had been shot down in the previous dogfight. We were much higher, and in a portion of sky which was much clearer, so Hether climbed up above the clouds to check that there were no other RE.2001s ready to bounce us. On my part, I headed towards the two Italians, who were proceeding one behind the other. I aimed at the second aircraft, hoping that the other pilot would not notice that I was overtaking them. The pilots were evidently intent on the search for their companion, lost at sea, as none of the two noticed me.

'When I was close to the tail of the second machine I fired a one-second burst. It immediately caught fire and crashed. I then aimed at the flight leader and fired another burst of one or two seconds, which made him fly into the sea, following his colleague. From the moment I fired my first burst until the moment in which both Reggianes ended up in the sea, no more than six or seven seconds passed. Everything happened in a rush during these kind of things.'[7]

Tenente colonnello Aldo Quarantotti and *tenente* Carlo Seganti were each awarded a posthumous *Medaglia d'Oro al Valor Militare*.

After that tragic day, and until early August 1942, activity by the 2° *Gruppo* CT was reduced in expectation of the arrival of its new commander designate, *maggiore* Pier Giuseppe Scarpetta. Operations were limited to a few escort missions and fighter sweeps.

The mission of the unlucky RE.2001GV

During August 1942, two pilots of the 22° *Gruppo Aut.* CT who at the time were still undergoing training prior to their operational debut, were protagonists in a mission which, despite its negative outcome, would prove to be particularly significant. This occurred on 12 August during the engagement known to the Italians as the 'aero-naval battle of mid-August'. Two RE.2001s piloted by *tenenti* Riccardo Vaccari and Guido Robone mounted a brave, but unfortunate attack against the British ships of the 'Pedestal' convoy, utilising for the first time a special armour-piercing bomb, fine-tuned by the two pilots at Furbara months before. The proposal to carry out such an attack had been advanced by *tenenti* Aldo Galimberti and Vaccari on 22 June 1941 and presented to *generale* Bernasconi, commander of *Centro Sperimentale* based at Guidonia. In their memorandum Vaccari

and Robone proposed using RE.2001s equipped with bombs to attack ships at anchor in ports or at sea, by commencing a dive from an altitude of around 4,000 m before pulling up into level flight at around 200 m to approach the target ship, then releasing the bomb at around 100 m from the target.

In other words, the attack was to exploit the high speed of modern aircraft in order to use the very tight trajectory that bombs took at such speed, so as to hit ships in their sides and escape enemy defence. This method had several advantages as it would not be impeded by torpedo nets that prohibited torpedo attacks on ships in port, and it allowed action in harbours and canals where shallow water would stop the torpedo, or where the limited area of water would prohibit launching. It would also be more economical than using torpedo-bombers, which required more flying personnel and more expensive equipment, and avoided the need for fighter escort as, after dropping its bomb, the RE.2001 could defend itself. Furthermore, the Pentaerythritol tetranitrate-loaded bomb was preferable to a torpedo because it was more powerful, easier to procure, maintain and load, and less expensive.

The idea was supported by senior commanders, and for the delivery aircraft the Reggiane RE.2001 was preferred over the AerMacchi C.202, as the large ventral radiator of the latter would not enable attachment of the bomb. A series of tests was conducted on the range at Furbara with an RE.2001 specially modified to drop 500-kg bombs. These trials yielded some generally good results, but some bombs were badly damaged. However, it was proved that it was possible to hit a target, but that a normal 500-kg bomb (as already previously reported to *generale* Bernasconi) was not sufficiently robust.

Thus it was decided to utilise a naval projectile weighing 381 kg, suitably modified to support a 120-kg explosive charge. The new bomb, the total weight of which increased to around 630 kg, was designated 630PD (*perforante-dirompente* – piercing and explosive) and was intended to penetrate the armour plating of a ship thanks to the kinetic energy from the launch exploding inside the vessel and a special time-delayed fuse. Further trials on the range, conducted by a Junkers Ju 87 Stuka in the presence of Mussolini, Göring and senior officers of the Regia Aeronautica, were crowned by success. Even those sceptical over the feasibility of the use of the weapon were convinced; during the various trials it cleanly pierced 7 centimetres without the slightest scratch.

In February 1942, *generale* Bernasconi authorised the preparation of the RE.2001, MM7226, which had, in the meantime been modified for the mission. At the end of March, having demonstrated the excellent capabilities of the aircraft thus equipped, two more aircraft were assigned, which was the minimum required to form a unit capable of carrying out such actions.

Tenente Vaccari was joined by pilots *tenente* Guido Robone and Giulio Reiner, the latter replacing *tenente* Aldo Galimberti, who, tragically, had died in an accident flying a CR.42.

---

[7] *Malta Spitfire The Diary of a Fighter Pilot*, George Beurling.

The fitting of a 630-kg bomb at Cagliari Elmas for the first and only attack operation. The mission carried out by two RE.2001GVs was a partial success as one bomb hit the carrier HMS Victorious but it did not explode.

The installation of the anti-ship bomb under the fighter's fuselage was supervised personally by Vaccari who carried out, together with Robone, the final practical deployment tests.

After waiting for the right moment to execute the operation, and in the light of the departure of *tenente* Reiner (who had left the *sezione* to return to his original unit), on the evening of 11 August 1942 an order arrived authorising the attack by two Reggianes on a convoy sailing from Gibraltar which was escorted by four aircraft carriers.

The pilots involved in the RE.2001GV attack on British warships. From left, *tenente* Vaccari, *capitano* Robone, *sottetenente* Petrucco.

An RE.2001CB and RE.2002, probably photographed on Furbara airfield, the home of a weapons testing range, during an official bombing demonstration.

A metal uniform badge of the 22° *Gruppo Aut.* CT, depicting the emblem of the unit, a scarecrow, or *Spauracchio*, which is smoking a pipe.

After deploying from Furbara to Cagliari Elmas airfield on the morning of 12 August, early that afternoon the two RE.2001GV departed, flown by *tenenti* Vaccari and Robone, each of them carrying a 630DP bomb with the objective of intercepting the British naval convoy. The two pilots skilfully manoeuvred into the best attack position for a strike against one of the carriers, HMS *Victorious*, splitting up in order that one aircraft could attack from the bow and the other from the stern. The two Italian aircraft succeeded in their efforts, releasing their bombs at a height of around 20 m at a range of 8 m from the ship.

Unfortunately, this audacious attack had no effect despite the bombs apparently striking the carrier. There are differing testimonies in this respect, but it does seem that the bombs did hit their target and they caused minor damage despite penetrating the armour of the ship. The failure of the bombs to explode was probably the result of a failure of the fuses fitted to the bombs, which were different to those proposed by Vaccari and Robone.

Justification for the selection of the Reggiane aircraft for this mission came soon after the attack on the carrier when the two fighters were intercepted by some Hurricanes flying a convoy protection sortie. Vaccari, having released his bomb, engaged in combat with two of them, managing to shoot down one and, through skilful manoeuvring, was able to avoid a fight with the other enemy fighters.

The 22° *Gruppo Aut.* CT commences operations

The 12 August 1942 also saw the first operation by the Reggianes of the 22° *Gruppo Aut.* CT, assigned alongside those of the 2° *Gruppo Aut.* CT to escort

Italian bombers and fighter-bombers attacking a convoy at La Galite. At the end of the engagement, three British aircraft had been downed against the loss of an Italian fighter flown by *sottotenente* Bizio of the 2° *Gruppo Aut.* CT, who did manage to bail out successfully but was captured by the British.

On 13 August the 150ª and 152ª *Squadriglia* of the 2° *Gruppo Aut.* CT were reunited at Trapani-Chinisia. But on 14 August the unit commander, *maggiore* Scarpetta, was shot down by British Spitfires together with *sottotenente* Disint and *tenente* Pocek during an escort mission for three German Heinkel He 111 torpedo-bombers returning from a mission to Malta. Of the three Italian pilots, the only one to survive was Pocek, who managed to bail out. This encounter brought the first operational cycle of the 2° *Gruppo Aut.* CT to an end.

Again, in his autobiography, *tenente* Metellini remembered the operations:

'*The period spent over Malta was, without doubt, the most demanding of my time as a*

fighter pilot during the Second World War because of the intensity of the combat, the difficulties and risks of conducting missions over the open sea and an enemy island, and for the number and bravura of the enemy fighters encountered.

'*The battle of Malta was for many years overshadowed by the more famous Battle of Britain, and only recently has the importance of the events been re-evaluated in terms of its length and the consequences for the outcome of the war in the Mediterranean and Africa. According to many British pilots who fought over Malta, the operational cycle in defence of the island was by far the most difficult and demanding in their defence of British territory, particularly because of the difficult conditions in which, objectively, they were forced to operate: food shortages, challenging environmental conditions, and the sustaining of numerous combat actions on the same day.*'[8]

In September, the 22° *Gruppo Aut.* CT also moved to Sicilia, taking over the operations of the 2° *Gruppo Aut.* CT which had been transferred to Lecce. During the month the two *Gruppi* had a daily average of twenty available RE.2001s. Besides undertaking fighter sweeps and shipping and bomber escorts, the pilots of the 22° *Gruppo Aut.* CT were also engaged in training activities related to the aircraft's use as a fighter-bomber, with bombs attached to a central fuselage hard point. The first fighter-bomber attack was conducted on 11 October 1942, targeting Ta Venezia airfield and radio location equipment at Salina.

[8] Taken from *Un pilota racconta* by Giacomo Metellini – self-published in 2007.

An RE.2001 of the 362ª *Squadriglia* of 22° *Gruppo Aut.* CT. This unit was active over the Mediterranean during the latter half of 1942, operating from bases in Sicily and Sardinia and also undertaking fighter-bomber missions.

An RE.2001 of 369ª *Squadriglia* with a white triangle painted on its fuselage, but without the 22° *Gruppo Aut.* CT unit emblem.

Left: The 369ª *Squadriglia* seen while operating from Pantelleria.

Seventeen aircraft were deployed, causing damage, but immediately after releasing their bombs, they were faced with British fighters which managed to shoot down a Reggiane.

On 17 October 1942, the 2° *Gruppo Aut.* CT was transferred to Castelvetrano and then, on the following day, to the island of Pantelleria, from where it was tasked with conducting free fighter sweeps. However, the serviceability situation with regard to the RE.2001 became increasingly precarious and with only one airworthy aircraft out of the 18 assigned in early November, the 2° *Gruppo Aut.* CT was withdrawn to Rome Ciampino airport to be re-equipped with new aircraft. In the same period, following the Allied landings in North Africa, the 22° *Gruppo Aut.* CT began to spread its *squadriglie* around several airfields, such as Castelvetrano in Sicilia, and Elmas and Monserrato in Sardegna, with some aircraft also based on Pantelleria. By early

November the unit had twenty-three RE.2001s on charge, and the pilots were still conducting the usual escorts for convoy, bombers and torpedo-bombers, defensive patrols, and searches for missing aircrew, with some attack missions against the bridgeheads at Bona and Bugia. During an attack on Bona, conducted on 6 December 1942 by five RE.2001s of the 362ª *Squadriglia* armed with 160-kg bombs, the Reggiane of *sottotenente* Pederzoli was shot down by British Spitfires.

In December, the 22° *Gruppo Aut.* CT completed its operational tour and at the end of the year returned to Capodichino, passing its remaining RE.2001s to the 24° *Gruppo* CT. At the end of 1942, the 2° *Gruppo Aut.* CT was renamed as the 2° *Gruppo Autonomo Intercettori* (Independent Interceptor Group) at Treviso, re-equipping with the RE.2001CN nightfighter variant. Despite this, by the end of 1942 when formations of American bombers penetrated the

skies of Italy in daylight, the Regia Aeronautica was forced to concentrate its interceptor operations to daylight hours. Thus, to increase the effectiveness of the response it was decided to bring in the RE.2001CNs as day fighters.

In the spring of 1943, furthermore, the *squadriglie* of the 2° *Gruppo Autonomo Intercettori* moved to the Liguria region, with the 152ª *Squadriglia* deployed to Sarzana and the 358ª to Albenga, this unit subsequently operating from Metato, near Pisa, paired with some former French Dewoitine D.520 'war prizes'.

The 160° *Gruppo Autonomo* CT at Olbia Venafiorita also received the RE.2001, some fifteen in total, of which around half were fitted with wing cannon, although these were unable to be used because of a lack of ammunition. Despite this, these aircraft conducted anti-submarine shipping escort flights, but on several occasions also faced American bomber formations and their

The front cover of an Italian promotional publication about the Regia Aeronautica published in 1941.

New RE.2001CBs lined up at Reggiane awaiting final completion prior to delivery to operational units.

RE.2001s of an unidentified unit.

An RE.2001 of 150ª *Squadriglia* with reduced dimension fuselage codes.

fighter escorts during which they managed to achieve some victories against P-38s. Despite further deliveries of aircraft from Reggiane, availability of RE.2001s remained precarious, to the point that in early July 1943, the 160° *Gruppo* CT had fewer than ten serviceable RE.2001s out of twenty-seven on charge.

At the beginning of June 1943, the 156ª *Squadriglia* also started operations flying Reggianes, but one month later it took over the disbanded 358ª *Squadriglia* at Albenga. Paired with the 152ª *Squadriglia* based at Sarzana-Luni, the two units were engaged in the protection of La Spezia and Genova, replacing the former *Sezioni Intercettori* which had been disbanded during the month of May.

In June the 152ª *Squadriglia* received four RE.2001CNs and before August, the pilots of the *Squadriglia* had managed to perform some fifteen night missions. Nevertheless, these missions were 'relegated' to the CR.42CN *Falco*, as at the time the RE.2001s were assigned exclusively to daylight interceptions. In early July 1943 the 2° *Gruppo Aut. Intercettori* was operating eighteen

CR.42s (of which at least eight were combat ready), only four serviceable RE.2001 *Falco* IIs and five Dewoitine D.520s.

Previously, the 150ª *Squadriglia* had moved to Capua, detaching itself from the 2° *Gruppo Aut. Intercettori* and being incorporated into the 22° *Gruppo Aut.* CT which, in turn, was controlled by the 42° *Stormo Intercettori*. Since May 1943 this *Stormo* had operated in the defence of Naples and central Italy with the 362ª *Squadriglia* deployed at Littoria, re-equipped with RE.2005s. The other two *Squadriglie*, 359ª and 369ª, operating from Naples Capodichino, flew the AerMacchi C.200 and C.202 as well as some D.520s. A few weeks prior to the armistice of 8 September, after the 22° *Gruppo Aut.* CT had resumed operations autonomously and reunited its *squadriglie* at Capodichino, the few RE.2001s available were used until exhaustion, to the point that at the end of August 1943 only four aircraft remained airworthy, but none were assessed as suitable for combat operations.

Between the end of 1942 and early 1943, other fighter units of the Regia Aeronautica began to

receive some RE.2001CN. Besides the 2° *Gruppo Intercettori* and 22° *Gruppo Aut.* CT, the RE.2001CNs began to fly with the 59° *Gruppo*, formed of the 232ª and 233ª *Squadriglie*, along with the 60° *Gruppo Autonomo Intercettori Notturni* with the 234ª and 235ª *Squadriglie*. But the number of available aircraft was always inadequate and there was little they could do to counter the overwhelming Allied air power.

Some RE.2001s were also assigned to the 1° N.A.I. (*Nucleo Addestramento Intercettori*), a unit tasked with the training of pilots posted to nightfighter duties with three *squadriglie* based at Treviso operating a mixture of aircraft including the FIAT CR.42, AerMacchi C.200, IMAM RO.41 and Caproni Ca.314. By early 1943 there were some thirty aircraft in total on charge. Furthermore, an undetermined number of Re.2001CNs, delivered in May (and strengthened in July by five aircraft ceded by the 59° *Gruppo*), were operated by the 160° *Gruppo Autonomo Caccia* and 167° *Gruppo Autonomo Intercettori* at Ciampino, formed by the 300ª and 303ª *Squadriglia*. In these moments of extreme

Reggiane RE.2001CN of 234ª *Squadriglia*, 60° *Gruppo*, 41° *Stormo Intercettori* at Lonate Pozzolo in December 1942. The aircraft is finished in the standard overall black nightfighter scheme, but is not fitted with underwing cannon pods. (G.Garello via F.Ballista)

Below: One of the few RE.2001s of the *Nucleo Addestramento Intercettori* operating from Treviso in mid-1943. (G.Garello via F.Ballista)

confusion, the Italian pilots were forced to perform real miracles, attempting to confront the Allied air forces with limited numbers of aircraft, and moving between various airfields to avoid Allied bombs.

It is estimated that in mid-July 1943 around seventy RE.2001s of various types were still on charge, spread throughout the fighter units of the Regia Aeronautica, of which around fifty were combat serviceable. From the minimal data available,[9] the Reggiane RE.2001s were distributed as follows:

- 2° *Gruppo Autonomo Intercettori*: four aircraft of which three were serviceable
- 60° *Gruppo Autonomo Intercettori* at Lonate Pozzolo with ten aircraft of which four were serviceable
- 167° *Gruppo Autonomo Intercettori* at Ciampino with eleven aircraft of which nine were serviceable
- 22° *Gruppo Aut.* CT at Capodichino with ten aircraft of which nine were serviceable.

- 59° *Gruppo Intercettori* at Metato with eleven aircraft, of which eight were serviceable
- 160° *Gruppo Autonomo* CT in Sardegna at Venafiorita airfield with twenty-two aircraft, of which ten were serviceable, and a section of the 160° *Gruppo* in Corsica with four serviceable aircraft.

The sad armistice situation along with the associated disintegration and disbanding of the units in a phase of extreme uncertainty, resulted in the majority of those RE.2001s still operational being destroyed on the ground by their personnel.

---

[9] It is essential to stress that a vast part of the data and information on the units of the Regia Aeronautica in 1943 was lost after the armistice.

A pair of RE.2001s of 359ª *Squadriglia* of the 22° *Gruppo Aut.* CT, probably taken in the autumn of 1942.

Aircraft of the 369ª *Squadriglia*. The 22° *Gruppo Aut.* CT emblem is visible on the fuselage of RE.2001 369-4 just aft of its cockpit.

After the Armistice

When the armistice was declared on 8 September 1943, around seventy aircraft were still on charge, although only half of them were considered to be in a combat-ready condition. Most of them were operated by the 160° *Gruppo* CT, with the bulk of its fleet, around thirty fighters, operating from Venafiorita airfield in Sardegna, while around ten were dispersed to the airfields at Littoria and Metato. Six Reggianes were still serving with the 2° *Gruppo Autonomo* CT, of which three were serviceable; the 41° *Stormo* had twenty aircraft of which half were operational, and at least fourteen

machines, seven of which were serviceable, were with the 167° *Gruppo* at Littoria. Of all these, little more than ten were able to relocate to Puglia after the armistice, while the twenty-three fighters operating from Venafiorita were immediately taken over and destroyed by German forces on 15 September.

During the weeks following the armistice, just over fifteen aircraft were recovered and returned to serviceability by the engineers of the Regia Aeronautica working in southern Italy, and these were assigned to the 51° *Stormo* CT. By mid-October 1943, the 21° *Gruppo* CT of the

51° *Stormo* CT had a fleet of seven RE.2001s, of which five were serviceable, while another six aircraft, all operational, were serving with the 155° *Gruppo* CT of the 51° *Stormo* CT, still operating from Sardegna.

The few RE.2001s serving alongside the Allies with the Regia Aeronautica were mainly engaged in training, although they were utilised sporadically over the Balkan territories in support of Italian troops, flying reconnaissance and air policing missions.

The *Diario Storico* (Operational Diary)[10] of Regia Aeronautica activities with the Allies

[10] Original text from the diary is presented in italics.

This page and opposite: An RE.2001 of 51° *Stormo* CT of the Regia Aeronautica Cobelligerante photographed during a training sortie in the spring of 1944. These fighters were the last aircraft type to be used operationally by the Regia Aeronautica, the last combat mission being performed on 24 June 1944. (ASF)

between 9 September and 31 December 1943 reports the following operations conducted by the RE.2001s:

5 October 1943

Two RE.2001 aircraft of the 21° Gruppo CT departed at 0900 hours to conduct a reconnaissance mission over Valona, Gianina, Paramythia and Corfù airfields. On Valona airfield 12 Ca.314 and some CR.42 aircraft were noted. The airfield at Paramythia was completely empty. At Corfù airfield, which was flooded, one Ju 52 and one Ju 87 were noted. The aircraft could not press on with their reconnaissance to Gianina due to prohibitive weather conditions. While returning, off the Otranto coast, three landing craft were seen, heading towards Brindisi. The aircraft returned safely at 10.30 hours.

12 November 1943

Between 09.40 and 11.15 nine MC.202s and five RE.2001s of the 21° Gruppo CT flew a mission from Lecce airfield, conducting a strafing action against Berat airfield. The aircraft arrived at their target at 10.45 hours. Three Me 110s lining up for departure were strafed on the ground. No fires were noted, despite the two subsequent attacks. Some trucks and anti-aircraft positions were also machine-gunned, and a large workshop wagon passing through the airfield. Heavy anti-aircraft reaction. Bad weather conditions along the entire route.

28 November 1943

Between 14.05 and 16.40 six MC.205s of the 4° Stormo CT departed Lecce to conduct an offensive patrol over Podgoritza as well as providing direct escort to the RE.2001 of the 21° Gruppo, airborne at the same time to air-deliver funds to the Divisione 'Venezia' at Pljieva airfield.[11] The RE.2001 arrived over Pljieva at 14.25 and dropped its cargo over the centre of the airfield. The MC.205s, which had orbited at 4,000 metres over Podgoritza between 15.25 and 15.35 returned safely to Lecce at 15.55, the RE.2001 returning at 16.40.

23 December 1943

Between 09.25 hours and 19.00 hours seven MC.202s and 10 RE.2001s conducted protective patrols over Elmas airfield.

On 1 January, the 21° *Gruppo* CT was disbanded, and its remaining RE.2001s, three operational out of a fleet of fourteen, were transferred to the 101° *Gruppo Tuffatori* of the 5° *Stormo* CT. The unit began to operate from Lecce under the new designation 101° *Gruppo Caccia* and undertook the RE.2001's final combat missions between May and June 1944.

These flights consisted almost exclusively of escort missions for bomber and transport aircraft. To carry out these missions, four fighters were transformed into the RE.2001S variant ('S'

[11] This was the aircraft flown by *Capitano* Paolo Spadaccini which had been fitted with a converted auxiliary fuel tank containing the sum of twelve-million *Lire* in banknotes for use by the *Divisione Venezia* of the Italian Army, encircled by the Germans in Yugoslavia.

Above: Reggiane RE.2001S was a variant equipped with auxiliary drop tanks, examples of which are seen here in a standard Dark Green camouflage. The darker areas on the rudder cover the white Savoia cross.

Above: The RE.2001 "82-8" of 82ª Squadriglia of 13° *Gruppo Autonomo* photographed at Cagliari Elmas airport in late October 1943.

Below: RE.2001CN of 101° *Gruppo*, 5° *Stormo 'Tuffatori'* on 24 December 1943 at Lecce airfield. It carried an unusual camouflage scheme consisting of Dark Olive Green squiggle patterns on Ocher Yellow (sand) base, applied over its previous overall Black night fighter scheme

RE.2001 of 51° *Stormo* CT returns to Lecce Galatina after an operational mission.

A silver-coloured RE.2001 used as an advanced training fighter by the Fighter School at Lecce for a short time after the war.

standing for *scorta* – escort) which was achieved through the installation of an external supplementary fuel tank recovered from those used by Ju 87s and Bf 109s.

Memorable among these missions was the operation of 9 May 1944 when three RE.2001s escorted some Cant Z.1007s to the Berane area, and also the mission of 13 May 1944 when two RE.2001s, paired with four C.202s, escorted some SM.82s engaged on an air-supply drop near Drenova in Montenegro. The final operational mission of an RE.2001 of the 101° *Gruppo Caccia* was planned for 24 June 1944, with some fighters, led by *maresciallo* Bernardi, tasked to escort some

Cant Z.1007s over Balkan territory. This mission, however, was not performed due to poor weather, and the aircraft safely returned to Lecce.

The total number of operational hours flown by the RE.2001s of the co-belligerent Regia Aeronautica amounted to 8 hours 49 minutes in 5° *Stormo* CT service and 24 hours and five minutes with the 51° *Stormo* CT, while in the same period the non-operational hours (mainly training flights) flown by the two units amounted to more than 342.

By the end of June 1944 at least nine surviving aircraft were employed by *Scuola Addestramento Caccia* at Leverano, while a pair of fighters was used by the *Squadriglia Autonoma di*

Collegamento (Independent Liaison Flight) of the *Comando Unità Aerea*, which used them for liaison flights as well as providing training for anti-aircraft artillery units.

In service with the
Aeronautica Nazionale Repubblicana (A.N.R.)

As previously mentioned, following the armistice of 8 September 1943, most of the aircraft relocated to northern Italy by the Germans were destroyed or sabotaged by Italian personnel to prevent them from being used. German forces managed, however, to take possession of some RE.2001s, which were subsequently used by the Luftwaffe as training aircraft. Some examples were also used for a brief period by the 2° *Gruppo Caccia* of the Aeronautica Nazionale Repubblicana on secondary duties, such as liaison and training.

The A.N.R. employed a few RE.2001 but not on an operational basis.

Post-war

In the post-war period some twenty RE.2001s which could be restored to flight had been found in Ferrara, as well as 35 airframes that could easily be completed. The newly-established Aeronautica Militare therefore requested Officine Reggiane to complete and rebuild these aircraft for training purposes. Unfortunately, mainly for political reasons, Reggiane's workforce opted to abandon the aeronautical sector and nothing came of this prospect.

At the end of the war, the Regia Aeronautica, having retired the nine remaining RE.2001s from training duties with the *Scuola di Volo* at Lecce, managed to return six of the aircraft to flying condition. With one aircraft set aside to serve as a source for spares for the others, three were assigned to the *Stazione Meteorologica* at Venezia-Lido airfield, and two to the *Sezione Autonoma Collegamenti* (Independent Communications Section) at Roma Centocelle.

In March 1947 some RE.2001s were assigned to Venezia Lido, finished in a silver colour scheme and wearing assigned codes U-31, U-32 and U-34. These fighters replaced the CR.42 biplanes used until that time for meteorological reconnaissance flights. To undertake this task the Reggianes were equipped with pods mounted below their left wings which contained a meteorograph, an apparatus for measuring atmospheric conditions at altitude and comprising a barograph, a

This rare sequence of photographs (and on the following page) shows the three RE.2001s used at Venice-Lido airport for meteorological observation for around two years after the end of the war.

thermograph, and a hygrograph, which recorded the pressure, temperature and humidity of the atmosphere, the data from which was used to create immediate weather forecasts.

Two of these RE.2001s were the target of sabotage attacks, probably by personnel from the nearby Officine Aeronavali (other acts of sabotage were perpetrated against the SM.95s and G.212s of the Italian-Egyptian company S.A.I.D.E.). Over the course of a few months, however, problems with the supply of spare parts and the age of the aircraft resulted in their retirement from service and their last flights were conducted in the autumn of 1947.

RE.2001 Factory Album

The photographs on this and the following pages bring together a series of rare photographs taken during the various stages of RE.2001 construction at the Reggio Emilia factory. In looking through the images, Reggiane's efficient methods can be appreciated, as well as the employment of female labour at various stages of construction.

One of the problems that Reggiane always had to face was the lack of skilled labour in an area with a predominantly agricultural economy. To remedy this, in the 1930s, an apprentice school was established with various specialities. The students were aged between 12-13 years or slightly older. Those who were promoted were hired in the main factory and could declare, with justifiable pride, that they were Reggiane employees.

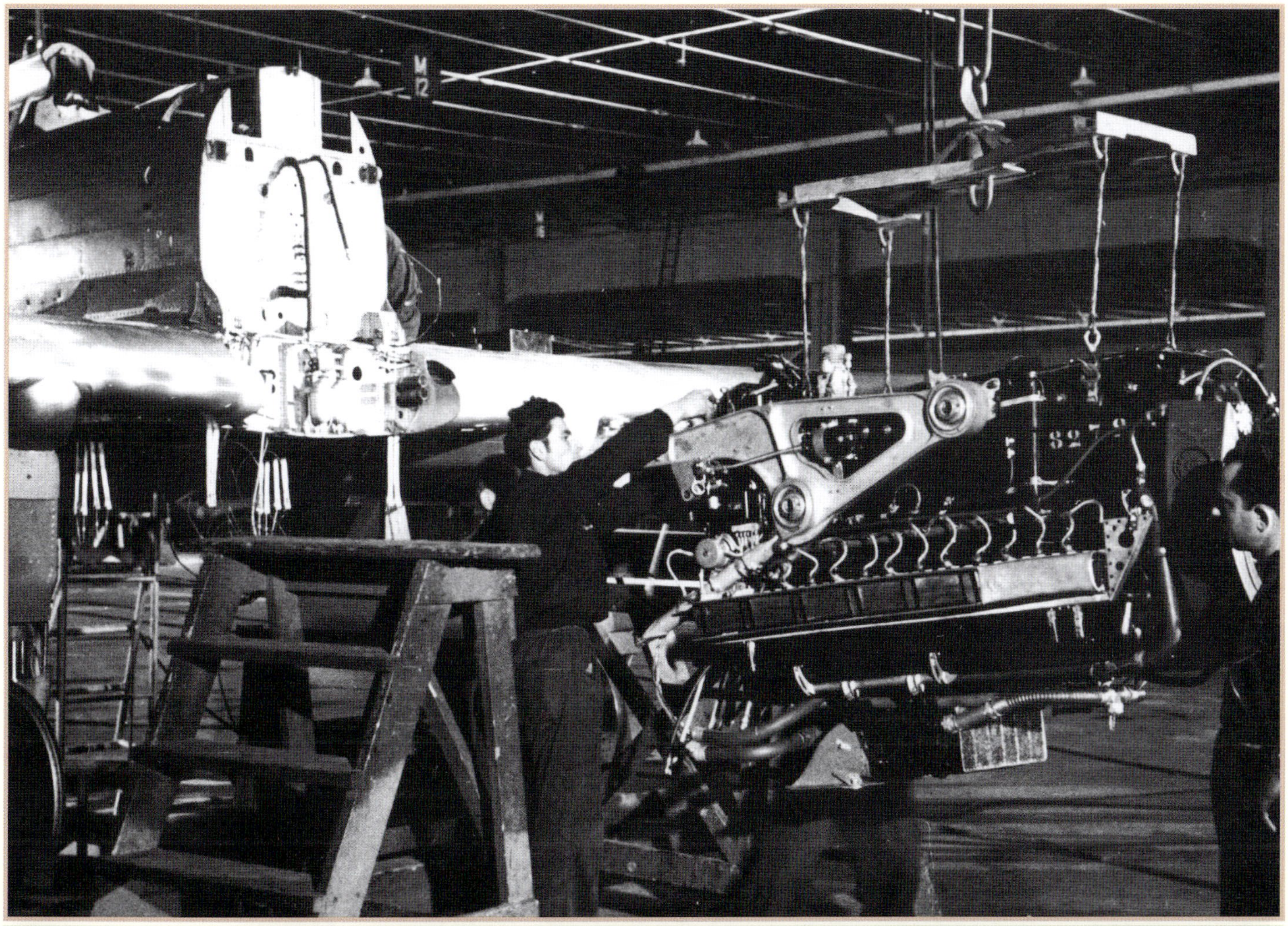

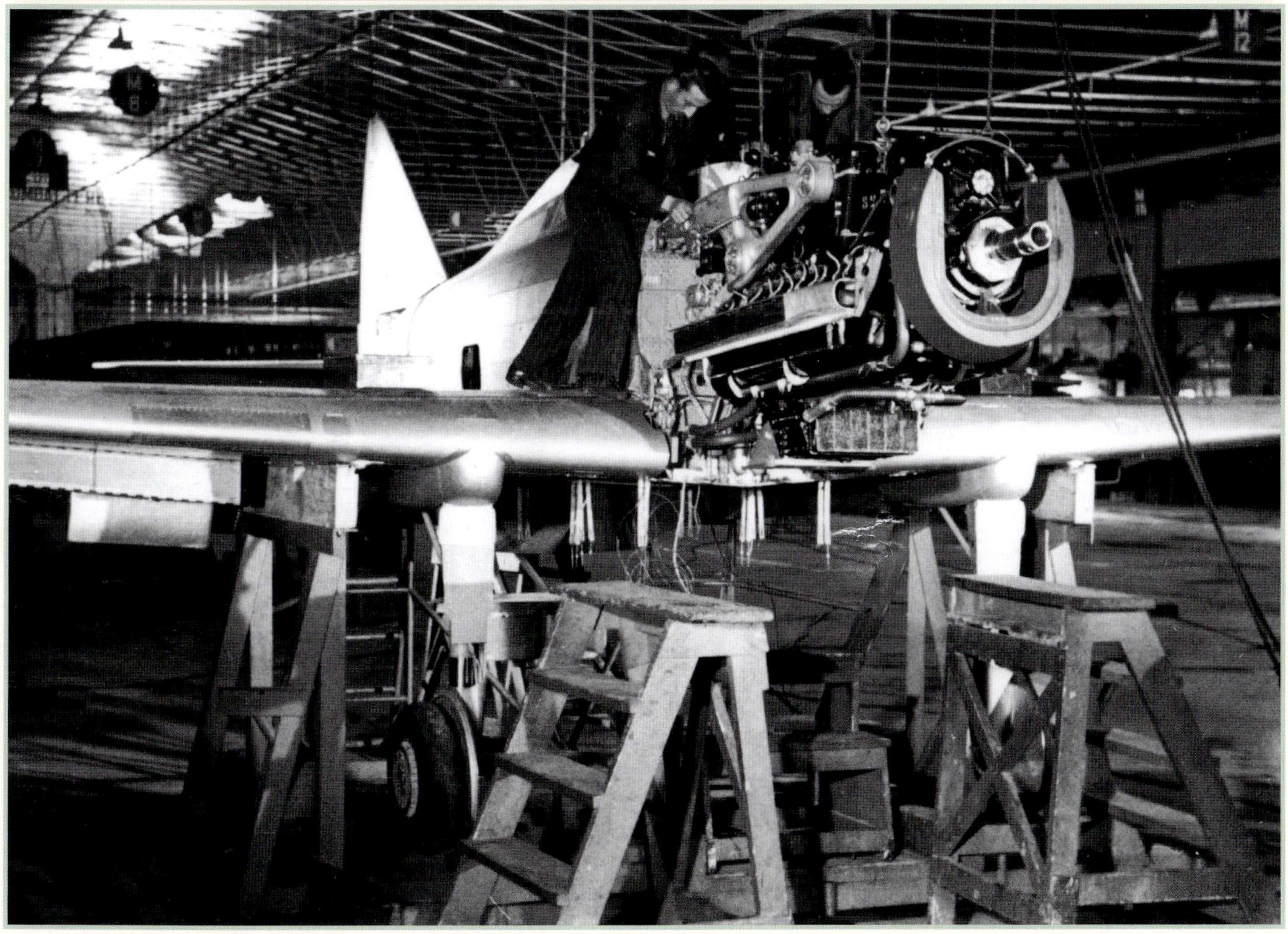

CHAPTER FOUR

RE.2002 *Ariete* II

Evolution and Production

THE RE.2002 *Ariete*[1] project was born from a study undertaken in the summer of 1940 by Reggiane for a fighter intended to be equipped with a domestically built radial engine to make up for the scarce availability of the water-cooled DB 601 engines built under licence by Alfa Romeo.

Initially it was planned to equip the first prototype, MM454, with the new FIAT 1,000-hp A76 RC40 radial engine, but problems with engine development led to its replacement by the Piaggio P.XIX R.C. 45 Turbine B., a 14-cylinder air-cooled radial with a power output of 1,180 hp, which was being fine-tuned at the time and promised particularly high performance. In practice, although resembling the RE.2000 from the outside, the RE.2002 was structurally similar to the RE.2001, differing only in the installation of the different engine. Indeed, on paper, the new aircraft had similar performance to the RE.2001, but the adoption of the radial engine, which was less vulnerable in combat than liquid-cooled engines, made the design of the new aircraft particularly interesting for use as a ground-attack aircraft, with the possibility of carrying 500 kg of external war load.

Postcard promoting the RE.2002.

The RE.2002 prototype, MM454, at Reggio Emilia. The aircraft was photographed on 19 April 1941 after it returned from evaluation flights at Guidonia.

[1] The aircraft was subsequently known as the *Ariete* II as the name of *Ariete* had been officially assigned to the RE.2001 which, in turn, had been identified by the name of *Falco* II.

As mentioned, although resembling the RE.2000 on the outside, the new RE.2002 had a very different front end since, in an attempt to have a more aerodynamic configuration, Reggiane lengthened the propeller shaft so that the cowling, already suitably reduced in diameter, would be more streamlined at the front.

The first flight of MM454 was performed by test pilot Tullio De Prato at Reggio Emilia in October 1940. However, its fine-tuning proved particularly laborious due to the unreliability of the Piaggio engine mounted in the aircraft, which had

not yet been fine-tuned. Flight-testing lasted for many months, partly due to a series of technical modifications needed to make the engine work. Before the final version of the aircraft was ready, several forms of fully or partially transparent canopies were trialled, as was the possibility of using a retractable tailwheel.

After tests were suspended in December due to serious engine failures that forced Piaggio's technicians to make numerous technical modifications to the propulsion system, in January 1941 the prototype, which in the meantime had

been subjected to a series of test flights by test pilot Mario De Bernardi, received a new power system and was sent to Guidonia in March 1941 for acceptance tests.

The flights at the *Centro Sperimentale* at Guidonia were marked by a contradictory trend. While the RE.2002 performed very well, especially in terms of speed, even equalling that of the RE.2001, there were still numerous technical problems caused by the unreliability of the engine. However, the new fighter had promising characteristics and it was hoped that the engine

This page and opposite: The RE.2002 prototype, MM454, at Reggio Emilia.

REGGIANE 2002 ARIETE II

issues could be resolved. On many occasions, test pilot Mario De Bernardi commented positively on the operational possibilities of the aircraft, reserving his only criticism for the engine. On 10 September 1941, the *Ministero della Regia Aeronautica* confirmed a first order for 200 aircraft with Reggiane, divided into two series of 100 aircraft to be assigned serials MM7309-MM7408 and MM8644-MM8743.

Following the trials, the RE.2002 was officially assigned to the attack and dive-bomber roles because of the failure of other Italian aircraft conceived for those roles, which had forced the Regia Aeronautica to acquire Ju 87s from Germany.

In August, work began on a second aircraft, in practice the first production machine, identified as MM7309. It had some substantial differences to the first prototype. Firstly, the rear pilot window was removed, with preference for a solid fairing and a side-opening canopy, similar to that of the RE.2001. The armament was modified with the installation of two additional 7.7 mm machine guns in the semi-wings and attachments for ordnance and tanks under the fuselage and wings. Additionally, a new propeller with a slightly larger diameter together with a new spinner and a fixed tailwheel were fitted. Later the two wing guns were removed to reduce weight for the benefit of the drop load, although the provision for their mounting was retained.

The most evident change, however, was related to engine installation as it was found that the extended propeller shaft solution caused vibrations and problems with the aircraft's centre of gravity, thus reducing its stability in flight. The Reggiane engineers adopted a new arrangement for the power plant without lengthening the propeller extension shaft, a solution that gave the aircraft a much squatter front profile, similar to that of the RE.2000.

Further delays in Piaggio's delivery of the final engine led to the completion of the new aircraft only in the spring of 1942, with the first flight made by Tullio De Prato on 18 May 1942. After a series of test flights the aircraft was sent back to Guidonia for further evaluation. In the meantime, in January 1943, the Ministry of Aeronautics had cancelled the RE.2003 two-seater project in favour of a new order for 198 more RE.2002s.

According to photographic evidence, compared to the previous aircraft built in the first production series of 100 aircraft, the RE.2002, MM7327, featured a lowering of the engine axis by 90 mm to the fuselage axis, as well as a series of bosses on the engine cowling to better accommodate the cylinder heads. A subsequent technical variation saw an air intake fairing for cooling the oil radiator positioned under the engine. It was a shortened type that extended only as far as the engine cowling flaps. This modification was made to significantly improve forward visibility for the pilot and could only be introduced from the 51st series aircraft as the production lines had not yet been completed for the series production of RE.2000s with lowered engine cases. After flight tests were carried out to

Continues on page 154

This page and opposite top: The first production RE.2002, MM7309, prior to camouflage paint being applied, photographed outside the Reggiane plant in May 1942. The aircraft had a redesigned engine cowling and spinner, modified cockpit canopy, and fixed tailwheel.

RE.2002
MM7309

RE.2002, MM7350, suffered a taxiing accident on 12 March 1945 due to a rupture of the right undercarriage following a ground loop.

Reggio Emilia airport. RE.2002s photographed in front of the test hangar, undergoing final operations before flight.

Interior of the Reggiane factory: several RE.2002 fuselages ready to move to final assembly.

The production line at the Caproni Taliedo plant. Some RE.2002s were built there.

An RE.2002 photographed on delivery to 208ª *Squadriglia*. The ventral bomb rack is clearly visible.

certify the modifications to the lowered engine, MM7327 returned to Reggiane to undergo another substantial modification in July 1943. This involved the replacement of the original wing with that of the RE.2005, without radiators and wing cannon, in order to verify possible improvements in performance as well as a possible production standardisation.

The aircraft was allocated the designation **RE.2002 bis**, but the experiment was abandoned even before the aircraft had flown. It was decided that the modification would not result in particularly satisfactory results, and that it could lead to a potential slow-down in the already initiated production of the RE.2002. Meanwhile, the aircraft was modified with the old wing and subsequently assigned to an operational unit.

During 1943, furthermore, there was an evaluation of a possible carrier-embarked version of the RE.2002, but the armistice on 8 September 1943 caused research to be abandoned.

In March 1943, Reggiane received a new order for 300 aircraft, with deliveries planned for the following August, but once again the armistice cancelled the order. By the time of the armistice some 140 aircraft had been built for the Regia Aeronautica, although not all of them had been delivered. After the armistice and the seizing of production facilities by the Germans, of the three

The prototype RE.2002 bis, MM7527, modified with an RE.2005 wing and with an outward-retracting main undercarriage, photographed at the *Reparto Sperimentale* on 12 July 1943. The experiment did not take place and the aircraft subsequently received its original wing.

Part of the eastern taxiway for the runway at Reggio Emilia airport – with some RE.2002s of the 239ᵃ *Squadriglia* – from where they and their pilots operated temporarily during transition to the new aircraft.

awaiting collection by the Regia Aeronautica at the time of the armistice. Following the destruction of the Reggiane facility, part of the surviving machine equipment was relocated to the Caproni works at Taliedo, which managed to resume production of the aircraft and handed over sixty examples before the end of the war. A few aircraft were also completed and flight-tested from Pavullo Frignano airfield (near Modena), where Caproni had established a small workshop following the destruction of the Reggio Emilia facilities.

A total of 191 RE.2002s should have been built (the exact number remains uncertain), by Reggiane to which must be added at least 25 aircraft produced of the 60 aircraft planned for production by Caproni. Because of the chronic unreliability of the Piaggio engine, as part of a resumption in production of the fighter it was also suggested to re-engine it with the German BMW 801 engine, but the course of the war caused this idea to be abandoned.

RE.2002 total production[2]

1 prototype	MM454
100 aircraft	MM7309-MM7408
90 aircraft	MM8644-8743
60 aircraft	MM97901-MM97960 (Caproni production – 25 aircraft delivered)

fighter types being manufactured at Reggio Emilia (RE.2001, RE.2002 and RE.2005), the occupiers showed interest only in the RE.2002, and after requisitioning the majority of the former Regia Aeronautica examples available, authorised production of new aircraft which continued until being permanently interrupted by the destruction of the factory as a result of Allied bombing raids on 7 and 8 January 1944.

By that time, Reggiane had managed to deliver to the Luftwaffe some fifteen new-build fighters and around ten of the aircraft which had been

Technical aspects

The Reggiane RE.2002 *Ariete* II was a low cantilever wing, single-engine, single-seat monoplane specialised for ground-attack. Technically, it was similar to the RE.2001, as was the case with its monocoque fuselage built in duralumin, being circular in section with ribs and stringers.

The cantilever wing, featuring an asymmetric, biconvex profile decreasing towards its extremities, and an elliptical planform (as used previously for the RE.2001), was formed around four longerons (three principal and a secondary). It was divided into two external elements with the attachments for the ailerons, a central section containing the fuel tanks and laterally arrayed housings for the main undercarriage, and two removable wingtip sections. The cladding was in duralumin. Each wing was fitted with metal split flaps divided into two sections, one on the outer wing and the other on the centre section.

The fuselage structure is clearly visible in this photograph of the RE.2002 under restoration and, at the time of writing, on display at the Museo Aeronautica Militare.

---

[2] This production data is the most reliable identified to date, and is taken from *FRECCE, SAETTE, FOLGORI E VELTRI* by *Ing.* Giulio Valdonio, published by Edizioni Rivista Aeronautica.

Drawing of the fuselage structure taken from the 'RE.2002 Catalogo Nomenclatore', 1943 edition.

Fig. 4. - Fusoliera.

Static fatigue tests being conducted on the wing of an RE.2002. The workers have used sandbags to lay on top of the test rig.

The wing underside, showing the structural build and wheel wells.

View of the underside of the central wing of the RE.2002.

This photograph is of particular interest since it shows the open engine access panels of a Dornier Do 17 at Guidonia, which was used by Reggiane to study possibilities for the engine door opening system for the RE.2002.

The Piaggio P XIX RC 45 in its mounting and fitted to the cockpit firewall.

The ailerons were fabric-covered metal structures, and the left-hand aileron was fitted with a trim tab that could be adjusted in flight.

The tailplanes were almost identical to those of the RE.2001, being entirely constructed of metal and compensated statically and dynamically, with the fin being offset at 5.8 cm to the right of the aircraft's axis to compensate for the torque generated by the propeller. The retractable undercarriage was also similar to that used on the RE.2000/2001, with the main undercarriage legs featuring shock absorbers that retracted rearwards, while the wheels were housed in a flat position and totally enclosed within the thickness of the wing. The tailwheel, also featuring a shock absorber, was steerable but not retractable.

The fuel was contained in three tanks: two in the wing centre with 270-litre and 200-litre capacities respectively, and another 130-litre tank positioned inside the fuselage behind the pilot's seat. The overall fuel capacity was around 600 litres, and all the tanks had internal SEMAPE cladding, which sealed holes created by projectiles of up to 12.7 mm.

A fourteen-cylinder, twin row, air-cooled Piaggio P.XIX R.C. 45 engine was fitted to production aircraft, with reduction gear and a compressor, producing 1,180 hp and power re-establishment at 4,500 metres. The engine drove a P2001M three-bladed metal constant speed Piaggio propeller, 3.10 metres in diameter, with variable pitch in flight by electro-mechanical control. The oil radiator was housed in the lower part of the engine cowling.

Communications were provided by an Allocchio Bacchini B.30 short-wave radio transceiver. Two 12 volt-18 ampere batteries fed the electrical system, the batteries being positioned in sequence in order to provide 24 volts.

The cockpit was enclosed by a canopy which opened to the right and which was fitted with sliding elements, held in place by a cable, and which could be completely detached in case of emergency. The windscreen was fitted with 50 mm armoured glass. Both the seat, adjustable vertically by mechanical controls, and the headrest, were protected by 8 mm of steel armour, and the seat incorporated a well to house the pilot's parachute. The instrument panel was equipped with the usual instruments for engine and flying control, and on the upper part a S. Giorgio type C 'a Tuffo' reflector gunsight was installed. The armament comprised two Breda SAFAT 12.7 mm calibre heavy machine guns mounted on the upper nose

An official graphic showing the instrument panel of the RE.2002.

The internal left side of the RE.2002 cockpit.

with the right-hand ammunition magazine containing 420 rounds and the left-hand 390. Two additional SAFAT 7.7 mm machine guns were installed in the wings, firing outside the propeller disc, and held a total of 640 rounds per gun. Frequently however, as a weight-saving measure, the two wing machine guns were not always installed. Rearming of the 12.7 mm gun was achieved mechanically, assisted by the pneumatic system, while rearming the wing guns was only possible on the ground through the use of an apposite cable.

The weapons that could be attached to the under-fuselage racks included a 450- or 500-kg bomb, which in the case of a dive-bombing attack, could be released by the actioning of a fork which distanced the weapon from the fuselage. There was also the ability to utilise two attachment points under the wings to support limited size munitions up to a total of 150 kg for each wing. As an alternative, a 240-litre supplementary fuel tank could be attached and eventually two other tanks of 100 litres each could be attached under the wings. Using external tanks led to the use of an extra oil tank of 25 litres. Stores release was either electrical or manual, and achieved through a dedicated switch positioned to the right of the pilot in the cockpit.

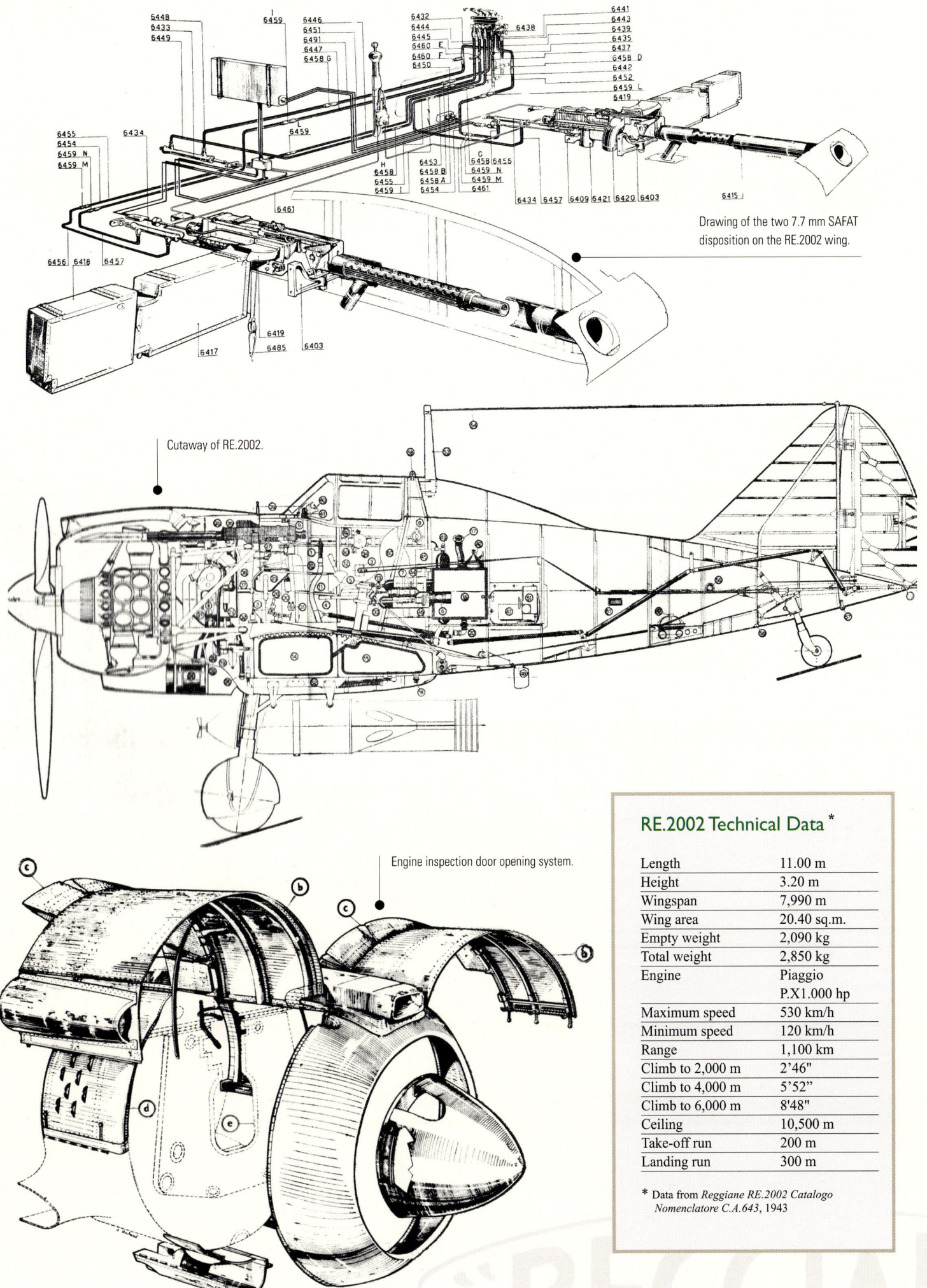

Drawing of the two 7.7 mm SAFAT disposition on the RE.2002 wing.

Cutaway of RE.2002.

Engine inspection door opening system.

RE.2002 Technical Data *

Length	11.00 m
Height	3.20 m
Wingspan	7,990 m
Wing area	20.40 sq.m.
Empty weight	2,090 kg
Total weight	2,850 kg
Engine	Piaggio P.X1.000 hp
Maximum speed	530 km/h
Minimum speed	120 km/h
Range	1,100 km
Climb to 2,000 m	2'46"
Climb to 4,000 m	5'52"
Climb to 6,000 m	8'48"
Ceiling	10,500 m
Take-off run	200 m
Landing run	300 m

* Data from *Reggiane RE.2002 Catalogo Nomenclatore C.A.643*, 1943

Operational service with the Regia Aeronautica

Trailed by dust, RE.2002s take off from Lonate Pozzolo in the late spring of 1943.

The first unit of the Regia Aeronautica to be equipped with the *Ariete* II was the 5° 'Stormo Tuffatori' (dive-bomber), formed by two *gruppi volo*, the 101° and 102° *Gruppo*, both previously flying the Ju 87 D. The first of the two *gruppi* to receive the new aircraft was the 102° *Gruppo*, which began to re-equip its two *squadriglie*, the 209ª and 239ª *Squadriglia*, on 27 January 1943 at Lonate Pozzolo airfield near Varese. The 101° *Gruppo*, comprising the 208ª and 238ª *Squadriglie*, commenced its transition onto the *Ariete* II on 6 February 1943.

The initial phase of the conversion process was particularly troubling due to technical problems and engine unreliability. It was found that, especially after a dive, engines had a tendency to lose power and to not function correctly when levelling out and pulling up. Nevertheless, training activities continued, albeit at a slow pace and not helped by the suspension of flying operations and a pair of fatal accidents. In the first of these, recorded on 31 March 1943, *sergente maggiore* Rastelli died in unknown circumstances while on a training flight, and it was a similar story with the second incident of 18 May 1943, which claimed the life of *sottotenente* Vaccari of the 238ª *Squadriglia*.

Following the delivery of *Ariete* IIs to the 102° *Gruppo* at the end of April 1943, and despite the difficulties encountered by the pilots who were still not adequately trained, on 19 June 1943 the unit, commanded by *maggiore* Giuseppe Cenni, was transferred to Tarquinia, near Viterbo.

Reggiane RE.2002 of 238ª *Squadriglia*, 101° *Gruppo*, 5° *Stormo* d'Assalto, Crotone, July 1943.

The 239ª *Squadriglia* was the first to arrive, and over the next few days the relocation of the entire 102° *Gruppo* was completed, leaving the 101° *Gruppo* at Lonate Pozzolo to finish its RE.2002 conversion training, the type having replaced the G.50s and RE.2001s operated up until then.

Some weeks later, as a result of the Allied landings in Sicilia, in the early hours of 10 July 1943, the 102° *Gruppo* was transferred urgently to Crotone airfield in Calabria to oppose the enemy forces. The same day, at their new base, the Reggianes were quickly prepared for their first

mission and led by *colonnello* Guido Nobili, the commander of the 5° *Stormo d'Assalto*[3] and *maggiore* Cenni, a formation of RE.2002s took off in the late afternoon to attack Allied naval units in Augusta harbour.

Divided into two flights of four and five aircraft respectively, the Italian pilots initiated a dive attack from 4,500 m and after withstanding a violent anti-aircraft reaction, managed to hit two cargo ships. However, shortly after pulling up, they were attacked by Spitfires from No. 229 Squadron RAF which, in a brief encounter, shot down three Italian fighter-bombers and badly damaged the

---

[3] The unit had officially assumed the designation 5° *Stormo d'Assalto* on 20 April 1943.

RE.2002s of 239ª *Squadriglia* at Tarquinia in June 1943, a few weeks before their transfer to Crotone to counter the Alled invasion of Sicilia.

Maggiore Giuseppe Cenni photographed sitting on the wheel spat of one of the Ju 87 Bs in which he flew with the 102° *Gruppo* until early 1943, when the unit received its first RE.2002s.

Reggiane RE.2002s of 239ª *Squadriglia*, 102° *Gruppo*, 5° *Stormo d'Assalto* at Reggio Emilia, June 1943.

Arriving in southern Italy only hours before the invasion of Sicily began in July 1943, the RE.2002s of 5° *Stormo Assalto* were in action from the first day but suffered heavy losses. These aircraft, seen amidst the dust of Tarquinia airfield, are from the *Stormo's* 239ª *Squadriglia*, 102° *Gruppo*. (P.Monti)

The emblem of the 102° *Gruppo Tuffatori*

The 102° *Gruppo* was established on 1 May 1942 at Lonate Pozzolo under the command of *maggiore* Giuseppe Cenni. The celebrated emblem, a cricket playing the guitar, was conceived in memory of the *Cucaracha* badge which decorated the CR.32s of the unit in which Cenni had fought in the Spanish Civil War. The badge of the *gruppo* was also associated with the radio callsign '*valzer*', derived from the war cry, '*Valzer, ragazzi!*' that Cenni had transmitted to his pilots since their first dive-bomber attack in the Stukas of the 239ª *Squadriglia Autonoma Tuffatori*. This radio callsign quickly became the motto used both in the air and on the ground by all personnel of the 102° *Gruppo*.

RE.2002s in the foreground, with an MC.202 and another RE.2001 beyond, photographed on a Sicilian airfield a few days before the Allied invasion.

aircraft of *sergente* Banfi, who was forced to make an emergency landing near Reggio Calabria.

Particularly significant and sad, was the loss of *colonnello* Nobili who crashed into the sea with his aircraft in flames, though some sources reported that his aircraft could have come down after a collision with the cables of the barrage balloons arrayed to protect the ships. The other two Italian pilots lost were *tenente* Beverina and *maresciallo* Perozzi.

Despite this tragic debut, on the following day, 11 July, nine RE.2002s were despatched to repeat the previous day's mission, dive-bombing the ships and strafing troops and landing craft. Although there was more heavy anti-aircraft fire, the Italian formation was not intercepted by the covering fighters, and the aircraft returned to Crotone.

In the afternoon of the same day, twelve aircraft of the 102° *Gruppo* again attacked Allied shipping, but were intercepted by British Spitfires which shot down three Reggianes piloted by *tenente* Lorenzi, *sottotenente* D'Arrigo and *maresciallo* Buffarini. At the end of the encounter, *sergente* Melotti claimed the destruction of a Spitfire.

In the meantime, that same day, the Reggianes of the 208ª *Squadriglia* of the 101° *Gruppo* arrived at Crotone, and in the morning of the 12th, a nine-aircraft mission was organised led by *maggiore* Rizzi, the commander of the 101° *Gruppo*. The outcome of the mission was positive, with four bombs released by the Italian fighter-bombers which damaged a large cargo vessel, while two others were hit. With no anti-aircraft fire, the Reggianes cruised around the area, performing several strafing attacks against naval units in the harbour.

In the afternoon twelve aircraft conducted a mission in support of German paratroops dropped onto the Catania plain to attack Allied armoured forces. However, the Italian pilots were forced to engage ever-present RAF Spitfires in defence of the slow and vulnerable Luftwaffe Ju 52 transports which carried the paratroops. One Reggiane was forced to return to base with engine problems and in the course of the dogfight, the Reggiane of *tenente* Noglia was damaged, and he was forced to make an emergency wheels-up belly-landing.

This initial period of the start of operations for 5° *Stormo* CT was particularly hard, since over the span of two days it had lost six pilots and ten aircraft either shot down or seriously damaged.

The last stragglers from the 101° *Gruppo* arrived at Crotone from Lonate Pozzolo on 13 July 1943, completing the establishment of the 5° *Stormo d'Assalto*. Attack operations continued throughout 13 July, and in the morning eleven Reggianes attacked British ships lying off the coast between Augusta and Siracusa, releasing 250-kg bombs after a dive from 4,500 m. Again, in this mission, the Italian fighters were attacked by Spitfires while pulling up from their dive, and two *Ariete* IIs of the 101° *Gruppo*, piloted by *sottotenenti* Vidulis and Bartolucci, were shot down, while a British Spitfire was claimed as destroyed and was seen to fall into the sea. According to reports from the Italian pilots, some ships were definitely hit, including the cruiser HMS *Nelson*, although this information has never been confirmed by the British.

The courageous, albeit limited activities of the Reggianes of the 5° *Stormo d'Assalto* had been of significant concern to Allied commanders. Having identified the location of Crotone airfield, on 13 July they sent several formations of B-24s to subject the Calabrian base to heavy bombing during one of which, the Italian aircraft were caught returning from a mission. The result of the bombing was devastating for the Regia Aeronautica, with the destruction on the ground of fourteen RE.2002s, ten Ro.37s of the 97° *Gruppo Osservazione Aerea*, fifteen G.50 bis of the 50° *Stormo Assalto* and some Bf 109 Gs of the 150° *Gruppo Caccia*. Crotone became too exposed to Allied air attacks, and on the following day, 14 July, those aircraft still in flying condition were transferred to the airstrip at Manduria, in the Puglia region, which became the new deployment base for the 5° *Stormo d'Assalto*. However, only the 101° *Gruppo* still possessed aircraft in flying condition, and the 102° *Gruppo* was forced to suspend flying operations temporarily to allow its personnel and assets to be reorganised. Despite this, on 16 July eight Reggianes were scrambled and together with other Italian and German fighters, contributed to the destruction of three B-24s.

Three photographs of RE.2002s of 208ª *Squadriglia*, 101° *Gruppo*, 5° *Stormo d'Assalto* at Crotone in mid-July 1943.

Reggiane RE.2002 of 209ª *Squadriglia*, 102° *Gruppo*, 5° *Stormo d'Assalto*.

Brand new RE.2002s of 209ª *Squadriglia* at Lonate Pozzolo shortly before being employed against the Allied invasion forces attacking Sicilia.

An RE.2002 from 208ª *Squadriglia* at Fano field, photographed on a stopover during the transfer flight to Crotone.

101° *Gruppo* departed to attack a naval force near Capo Santa Croce. On take-off, one of the fighters, piloted by *sergente* Bragè, had to return early with an engine problem. On reaching the target area, the Reggianes began a dive from 4,500 m, avoiding the anti-aircraft fire and releasing their nine 420-kg bombs, a type optimised for anti-ship attack. One Reggiane was quickly struck by machine gun fire from the ships and crashed into the sea, while the remaining aircraft, despite the escort cover provided by German and Italian units, were attacked by some Spitfire Mk Vs of No.152 Squadron RAF. At the end of the clash, six RE.2002s had been shot down and another two severely damaged. Amongst the pilots killed in the dogfight was *capitano* Gino Priolo, the commander of the 208ª *Squadriglia*, who for the valour demonstrated throughout his military service was decorated posthumously with the M.O.V.M. (*Medaglia d'Oro al Valor Militare*). At the end of the day, the remaining Reggianes of the 101° *Gruppo* returned to Manduria, where the unit spent several days reorganising and receiving new aircraft, while others had been made ready by the repair teams.

On 2 August, ten Reggianes of the 101° and 102° *Gruppo*, commanded by *maggiore* Cenni, who had been appointed as interim commander of the 5° *Stormo d'Assalto*, deployed again to the strip at Botricello. After being refuelled and rearmed, they engaged in a fruitless mission against Allied naval forces. Two days later, on 4 August, the fighters of the 5° *Stormo d'Assalto* were engaged in a series of attacks against the road network and railway bridge near Cefalù not far from Palermo city, hitting their targets and strafing Allied armoured vehicles and motor transport. Further operations directed at the advancing Allied forces were carried out with success over the following days. However, the situation for the Italian pilots was becoming increasingly difficult, and they were forced to operate with a small number of aircraft while confronting an enemy which was significantly stronger – factors that forced the unit to withdraw once again to its base at Manduria.

On 3 September 1943 the Allies landed in Calabria under *Operation Baytown* which saw the Eighth Army's XIII Corps, and the 1st Canadian Division, come ashore in Reggio Calabria. This allowed Allied forces to gain a bridgehead in the 'toe of the boot of Italy'. The *Ariete* II of the 5° *Stormo d'Assalto* were again tasked with attempting to stem the advance with a mission flown by ten Reggianes, all of which returned undamaged without having encountered the enemy.

On 4 September 1943, twelve RE.2002s took off from Manduria in order to relocate, to operate from Botricello strip to attack American landing craft on the stretch of sea between Villa San Giovanni and Reggio Calabria and against armoured units recently landed in Calabria. The Italian pilots were met by the usual intense anti-aircraft barrage, and *maggiore* Cenni, transmitting his final '*Valzer, ragazzi!*' war cry, dived towards the target. At the end of the attack at least four

This RE.2002 of 208ª *Squadriglia* crashed on landing at Manduria in July 1943.

An RE.2002 of 208ª *Squadriglia* which crashed on take-off from the airstrip at Botricello on 1 August 1943 while piloted by *sergente* Bragè. The pilot escaped without injuries.

Meanwhile, while the 102° *Gruppo* was reorganising, on 18 July the 101° *Gruppo* received an order to relocate again, this time back to Calabria to operate from the advanced field at

Botricello, some 15 km distance from the devastated Crotone. From this new base, in reality just a landing strip without any logistics infrastructure, on the 19th fifteen Reggianes of the

landing craft had been hit and sunk, and numerous vehicles had been strafed. While the escorting fighters from the 4° *Stormo* CT were engaged in ferocious combat with other Allied fighters, a group of Spitfires began to hunt down the Reggianes. The technical superiority of the enemy fighters did not permit an equal fight, and the Italian pilots dived down to extremely low altitude, flying between the rocks of the Aspromonte coastline to escape. However, there was to be no escape from the British Spitfires, and Cenni's aircraft was hit. His aircraft caught fire, preventing him from bailing out. Also shot down were the Reggianes flown by *tenente* Renato Moglia and *sergente* Walter Banfi, but only Banfi managed to escape by parachute.

A direct witness account of the loss of Cenni was provided in 1995 by two residents of S.Luca, who at the time were just ten-year-old boys:

'A little after midday and all hell broke out in the sky above the village. Around twenty aircraft were fighting each other, some trying to escape from danger, others following them. There was much firing of machine guns and cannon. I repeat, it was a real hell! One of the aircraft being followed tried to escape from the attackers. It crashed at the foot of the Pietra Castello mountain on the Bonamico river bed. One of the aircraft following it crashed into the mountain. Another tried to escape, heading west, following the Bonamico River at low level, but when it reached the Contrada Callisto, between S.Luca and Casignana, it came down. Explosions and flames followed. Another two aircraft managed to disengage from their adversaries, diving down to low level between the Aspromonte mountains, and disappeared. The fifth aircraft headed towards Bianco, and was followed and hit, crashing before it reached the village.' [4]

The loss of Cenni was a severe blow to the personnel of the 5° *Stormo d'Assalto* who, returning to Manduria, were caught by the events of the armistice announced on 8 September. The unit had 24 RE.2002s on charge, of which 22 were combat serviceable.

Maggiore Carlo Alberto Rizzi, who had been leading the 101° *Gruppo*, was appointed commander of the 5° *Stormo d'Assalto* as Cenni's interim replacement, and following a period of disorientation linked to the chaos in the aftermath of the armistice, in mid-September the personnel, by common accord, decided to prosecute their war against the Germans, offering their immediate availability to return to combat to the *Comando della 4ª Squadra Aerea*.

In the meantime, some weeks previously, the first RE.2002s were assigned to the newly reorganised 50° *Stormo d'Assalto*, commanded by *colonnello* Ferruccio Vosilla. The deliveries were made at a very slow rate and by 10 July 1943 only three aircraft had been received by the 159° *Gruppo* at Lonate Pozzolo airfield. Lacking aircraft, some of the unit's personnel, together with the 158° *Gruppo*, were deployed to Sicilia to

MAGGIORE GIUSEPPE CENNI

GIUSEPPE CENNI was born on 24 February 1915 at Casola Valsenio, a village in Romagna. Entering the Regia Aeronautica in June 1935, he was nominated as a 'pilota di aeroplano' on 19 August that year. In February 1936 he was posted to the 153ª *Squadriglia* of the 3° *Gruppo*, 6° *Stormo Caccia*. On 14 August 1936, Cenni adopted the false name of Victor Stella and arrived in Spain to participate in the operations of the Italian forces supporting the Nationalists. Cenni was forced to bail out on 29 January 1937 and was captured by the Republicans, in whose hands he remained for seven months prior to returning to Italy following a prisoner exchange. With the outbreak of war in Europe, Cenni was assigned to the 97° *Gruppo Bombardamento a Tuffo* and on 9 November was nominated as a *capitano* in the 239ª *Squadriglia*. After initial operational service over Malta and the Balkans, he was transferred with his unit to North Africa. Subsequently assigned as an instructor to the 1° *Nucleo Addestramento Tuffatori* at Lonate Pozzolo, in early March 1942 he was involved in the establishment of the 102° *Gruppo Tuffatori*, parenting the 209ª and 239ª *squadriglie*. Cenni, aware of the technical limitations of the Ju 87 Stuka, experimented in night-bombing tactics and with the new unit also participated in the principal air and naval engagements of 1942.

In the meantime, the intensity of the operations required the replacement of the outdated Stuka and the unit, still under Cenni's command, was again sent to Lonate Pozzolo to undergo conversion onto the Reggiane RE.2002. Cenni made his first flight in this aircraft on 3 February 1943 and the following June he led the transfer of the 102° *Gruppo* to Tarquinia, from 10 July fighting against the Allied landings in Sicilia. Following the death of *colonnello* Nobili, Giuseppe Cenni became interim commander of the 5° *Stormo Tuffatori* at the age of just 28, thus becoming the youngest *Stormo* commander in the Regia Aeronautica.

On 4 September 1943, after attacking enemy shipping at sea off Reggio Calabria, he was shot down by a Spitfire of 111 Squadron RAF while he was attempting to return to base at low altitude.

With 750 hours of combat flying out of a total of 1,460 flying hours, 200 combat missions, six *Medaglie d'Argento al Valor Militare*, promotions in the field, numerous other Italian and foreign decorations, for his service *maggiore* Giuseppe Cenni was decorated with a posthumous *Medaglia d'oro al Valore Militare* with the following citation:

'A highly able fighter and dive-bomber pilot, his brief youth was consumed for the greatness of the Nation. His particular spiritual and professional virtues shone through always and everywhere; always first to face risk, in the course of two hard-fought wars, he was awarded some six medaglie d'argento and two promotions for wartime merit. In the memorable days between 10 and 19 July, followed with absolute dedication by his wingmen, he confronted the advance of the invaders with tireless and aggressive determination, overcoming every human limit on bravery, and in bitter fights with enemy fighters managed, on three occasions, to disengage his wingmen from overwhelming attacks by superior numbers of enemy aircraft. During a dive-bombing action, in an inferno of fire and metal over a landing area in the straits of Messina, he disappeared, overwhelmed by numbers. An everlasting example of elite military virtues, sublime love of country, self-sacrifice and devotion to duty. In the skies of the Mediterranean, 10 July-4 September 1943.

confront the Allied landings, still flying the old and outdated FIAT G.50 equipped with under-wing bomb hooks.

At Lonate Pozzolo airfield, the announcement of the armistice caught most the personnel of the 50° *Stormo d'Assalto* by surprise and the few RE.2002s on charge at that time were requisitioned by the Germans.

[4] Extract from *Aeronautica* 9/2008 by *m.llo* D'Agostino.

In service with the Luftwaffe

Luigino Caliaro and Nick Beale

RE.2002, MM8685, in German markings after an accident caused by muddy terrain on 25 November 1943 following the end of a test flight. The pilot, who sustained injuries, was Silvio Casarotto.

An RE.2002 in the gun butts for calibration tests at the Caproni factory in Taliedo.

Following the armistice of 8 September 1943, the Luftwaffe requisitioned around ten RE.2002s from Lonate Pozzolo, then more awaiting collection after completion at the Reggiane factory. The first group had belonged to the Regia Aeronautica's 50° Stormo Assalto which was converting to the fighter-bomber. At the request of the Germans, around 50 RE.2002s were built, to which should be added 25 fighters manufactured by Caproni at Taliedo which had received an order for 60 (the remaining 35 aircraft were ordered to be scrapped). In total, it can be estimated that around 100 RE.2002s were received by the Luftwaffe, with around half of these newly constructed by Reggiane after the armistice.

The majority of these aircraft were operated by Fliegerzielgeschwader 2, towing targets for the Flak troops' firing exercises. The Luftwaffe's contingency plan for an Allied invasion in the West included using them as an 'operational fighter bomber Gruppe' in the Bandenbekämpfung role — combatting resistance groups. Under this plan the Stab, III. and IV./Fliegerzielgeschwader 2 became Geschwader Bongart, named after the commanding officer, Oberst Hermann-Josef Freiherr von dem Bongart. With its headquarters

at Bourges, it was equipped with a variety of aircraft types, having 18 RE.2002s on strength by the end of May 1944. These served with the Geschwader's III. Gruppe which consisted of the 7., 8. and 13. Staffeln. By 24 June, Bongart had 35 RE.2002s on strength, 22 of them serviceable. The 8. Staffel had lost RE.2002 W.Nr. 1282 at Mons-en-Chausée on 5 May, with Ofw. Walter Hartnack being killed; on the afternoon of the 24th, another 8. Staffel RE.2002 (W.Nr. 1260) suffered engine trouble taking off from Toul for a test flight. The pilot, Fw. Josef Knollmayer, suffered a fractured skull and a broken right knee, dying later that day. On the 26th, ferry pilot Fw. Richard Kircher was injured when W.Nr. 1221 overturned on landing at Mons-en-Chausée; the accident was attributed to pilot error and the aircraft was written off. On the eve of the Allied landings a 7. Staffel

RE.2002 (W.Nr. 1281) fell to friendly fire: Ofw. Walter Lorenz was reported shot down by an Fw 190 near Épernay and the Quartermaster General recorded the loss as non-operational and due to human error.

Once the invasion began, Maquis groups throughout central and southern France rose against the occupiers, provoking major German ground operations in response, with air support from Bongart. Facing no aerial opposition or anti-aircraft weapons heavier than light machine guns, most of Bongart's losses were to accidents or air raids. On 16 June however, after damage from ground fire, RE.2002, W.Nr.1256, DV+BI, Red 5, belly-landed near Amboiras, some 30 km from Limoges. By late July, the various elements of the Geschwader were located as follows: Stab, 9. and 10. Staffeln at Bourges; III.Gruppe with the 7. and

Left and above: RE.2002 Ariete, MM97919, W.Nr. 5219, completed for the Luftwaffe at Caproni's Taliedo factory following the armistice of 8 September 1943.

Above and below: Newly produced RE.2002, W.Nr. 5240, awaiting delivery to the Luftwaffe.

8.*Staffeln* at Bourges, 13.*Staffel* at Lissay-Lochy; IV.*Gruppe* with 11. and 12.*Staffeln* at Clermont-Ferrand. Operations reached their height that month: on the 21st, the RE.2002s were tasked with providing cover for 22 assault gliders which landed on the plateau of Vercors, south of Grenoble, delivering troops to fight against some 1,000 *Maquisards* who were building an airstrip and menacing German lines of communication. On that day, the Reggiane fighters (often mistaken for Focke-Wulf Fw 190s by those on the ground) conducted 44 sorties, dropping more than 7.5 tonnes of bombs. The total for 22 July was 68, with 63, 20, 32 and 18 on the succeeding days as the Resistance 'redoubt' on the Vercors was overwhelmed by German forces. The RE.2002s had been based at nearby Valence for this operation and some were lost to Allied bombing on 24 July; the wrecks of W.Nr. 1222, 1252 (DV+BE) and a third machine were found when the aerodrome was liberated.

Luftwaffe stocks of the RE.2002 over the spring and summer of 1944 were:

31 March	20 in "other units"
April–May	31 in "other units" + 1 in workshop or reserve
30 June	25 in "other units" + 2 in workshop or reserve
30 September	12 in "other units" + 2 in workshop or reserve

By early August, the *Geschwader* possessed around 32 fighter-bombers, but only fourteen were in flying condition. On the afternoon of the 6th, four RE.2002s led by *Oblt*. Higgelke were dispatched to attack Abondance, a guerilla-held village 10 km west of the Franco-Swiss frontier. Facing 8/10 cloud with its base at 1,500 m, rain showers, mist and 5 km visibility, the flight strayed 1.5 km over the border, bombing the Swiss village of Morgins, where 20 people were injured and many buildings damaged. Driven from its French airfields by the Allied advance, *Geschwader Bongart* was disbanded on 4 September 1944.

Below: Wrecked RE.2002s belonging to *Geschwader Bongart* after the war. The Luftwaffe's RE.2002s were grouped into a *Schlachtgruppe* based in France from where they operated as an 'anti-guerrilla' unit against the Maquis in the areas of Aisne, Vercors and Limoges. These photographs were probably taken at Lyon-Bron.

After the Armistice

At the time of the armistice, the fleet of RE.2002s still operating with the Regia Aeronautica amounted to little more than thirty aircraft.

In the chaos of the post-armistice period, the 5° *Stormo Tuffator i*,[5] operating on 8 September from the airfield at Manduria in Puglia, was incorporated into the ranks of the Regia Aeronautica del Sud[6] (that is to say, the Regia Aeronautica present in Allied-held territory), and placed under the control of the then 4ª *Squadra Aerea*. It possessed 24 RE.2002s, of which twelve were serviceable.

Despite pressure from Italian pilots and their commanders to be allowed to return immediately to action in support of the critical situation facing the Italian garrisons on the islands of Corfù and Kefalonia, the Allied Supreme Command hesitated for some days before authorising a resumption of operations. The airmen were restricted in their activities to the Balkans, in an effort to avoid fratricidal combat between those Italians adhering to the *Repubblica Sociale Italiana* as well as to prevent them bombing Italian soil.

---

[5] In documentation produced by the Regia Aeronautica in southern Italy, commonly identified post-war as the Co-belligerent Air Force, the unit is designated as 5° *Stormo Tuffatori*.

[6] On 15 October 1943, the *Comando Unità Aerea* was formally constituted. The unit controlled the operations, training, discipline, and functions of the *Raggruppamento Caccia* and *Raggruppamento Bombardamento e Trasporti*. The *Raggruppamento Caccia* parented the 5° *Stormo Tuffatori*, formed of the 101° and 102° *Gruppo Tuffatori* and equipped with the residual Reggiane RE.2002s.

After the armistice around forty RE.2002s join the Regia Aeronautica del Sud. This photograph shows a tail fin adorned with the name *Ariete* II.

Thanks to a document conserved in the *Ufficio Storico* of the Aeronautica Militare[7] detailing the combat operations of the *Comando Caccia*, it is possible to narrate chronologically missions conducted by the RE.2002s serving with the 5° *Stormo Tuffatori* during the turbulent months of 1943 while carrying their new tricolour roundels.

18 September 1943

Three RE.2002 of the 101° Gruppo Tuffatori departed at 12.20 to conduct a bombing attack against an enemy torpedo boat and landing craft reported in the port of Igoumenitsa. Returned at 13.10. Three RE.2002 of the 102° Gruppo Tuffatori departed at 13.30 to conduct a bombing attack against the same target. Two motor-barges loaded with troops were attacked, arriving from the east and heading for Corfù. One bomb fell on the prow of the first barge, which stopped; the second barge changed course. One aircraft failed to return from this action.[8] Two RE.2002 of the 101° Gruppo Tuffatori departed at 12.25 to conduct a patrol of the island of Corfù and a dive-bombing attack on the port of Butrinto. Four landing craft were attacked, one struck. Normal return at 14.35. Another two RE.2002S of the 102° Gruppo Tuffatori departed at 17.30 to repeat the same mission. One of the two aircraft attacked seven Ju 87s, breaking up the formation which was conducting a bombing attack on the port and machine-gunning the airfield at Corfù. Normal return at 19.30.

19 September 1943

Two RE.2002 of the 5° Stormo Tuffatori departed at 7.15 on a reconnaissance mission over Greece. They noted: a vast fire in the city of Corfù; a torpedo boat which opened fire, and seven landing craft in the Sagiada inlet; the airfield at Paramythia empty and full of holes; Argirocastro and the old airfield at Coritza empty. At 8.20 they bombed the airfield at Coritzu (Osenova), on which were noted five Ju 87s. At 8.40, in the port of Valona, they observed four merchant ships and other minor vessels, all at anchor: on the airfield there were many twin-engine aircraft. Safe return at 9.15.

Three RE.2002 of the 101° Gruppo Tuffatori departed at 10.55 with 100-kg bombs for a raid on the bay of Sagiada, west of Paramythia: attacked were a torpedo boat, a 300-tonne steamer and landing craft. Two landing craft were hit. One of our aircraft was shot down by anti-aircraft fire.[9] Return at 13.00.

Another three RE.2002 aircraft of the 101° Gruppo Tuffatori departed at 11.40 and repeated the same mission with 250-kg bombs. Two landing craft destroyed: the barracks and a villa from which significant anti-aircraft fire was coming were strafed. One of the landing craft hit by the previous mission was destroyed. Two torpedo boats and some steamers were spotted, coming from the Italian coast and heading towards Corfù. Safe return at 13.25.

20 September 1943

Three RE.2002 of the 101° Gruppo Tuffatori departed at 12.55 to bomb and strafe the barracks at Plathria. A large fire was started between the barracks and another northwest of the town; a motorboat was blown up. Routine return at 14.45.

Three RE.2002 of the 102° Gruppo Tuffatori departed at 12.55 to conduct a dive-bombing attack on landing craft in the bay of Plataria. Three motorised boats were destroyed and others damaged: notable anti-aircraft fire from machine guns on the hills to the west of the town. Routing west crossed over two torpedo boats and a tanker near the Italian coast. Safe return at 14.45.

21 September 1943

Three RE.2002 of the 5° Stormo Tuffatori, departing at 16.40, performed a dive-bombing and strafing attack on the crossroads north of Acrocoro Bliote. No anti-aircraft reaction observed, and neither were barracks or tents that would indicate the presence of enemy forces. A MAS (Motoscafo Armato Silurante – Armed Torpedo Boat) was seen, and also a similar unit, these proceeding at speed from the island of Leycas towards Kefalonia. Safe return at 18.55.

22 September 1943

Between 08.00 and 10.35, two RE.2002 of the 5° Stormo Tuffatori conducted an offensive reconnaissance over the Liscuri peninsula (Kefalonia). Some 28 12-kg incendiaries were dropped with the aim of identifying possible forces hidden in the heavily wooded parts of the Khaiadata area. Nothing to report. In the gulf of Argostoli, a 3,000-tonne steamer was noted, probably abandoned.

24 September 1943

Six RE.2002 of the 5° Stormo Tuffatori departed from Manduria at 07.25 and four MC.205Vs[10] of the 4° Stormo C.T. departed

[7] The *Diario Storico dell'attività operativa della Regia Aeronautica a fianco degli Alleati* (Historical Diary of Operations conducted by the Regia Aeronautica alongside the Allies between 9 September 1943 and 31 December 1943) (*Archivio Ufficio Storico* AM).

[8] The translation of the original text of the *Diario Storico dell'attività operativa della Regia Aeronautica a fianco degli Alleati* is presented in italics.

[9] The aircaft flown by *tenente* Vito Calenza was forced to make an emergency landing on Corfu.

[10] The original text of the Diario reported the AerMacchi fighters with the often-used prefix 'MC' (which stood for *Macchi Castoldi*) instead of the official technical prefix style, 'C.202' or 'C.205V'.

from Brindisi at 07.45 to conduct offensive operations against enemy naval vessels in the Corfù area. An RE.2002 crashed on departure due to unknown causes and was destroyed: the pilot was injured. At 08.20 near the south-west coast of Corfù, a corvette and three pontoons were located.[11]

Ten 100-kg bombs were dive-bombed onto the pontoons, one of which sank. The fighters and dive-bombers subsequently and effectively strafed an MAS which from Plataria was heading towards Corfù: of the four persons noted on board, three fell after being hit. Another MAS coming from Corfù and another coming from the bay at Plataria were machine-gunned. Observed and machine-gunned inside the bay of Plataria were two pontoons and four motorised fishing vessels close to the dockside. Embarkation operations were not noted, these probably having been suspended once the aircraft were sighted. An RE.2002 was hit by anti-aircraft fire. A large fire was noted on Corfù airfield. The RE.2002s landed at 09.25; the MC.205Vs returned at 09.20. Five RE.2002s of the 5° Stormo Tuffatori departed from Manduria at 10.45 and five MC.205Vs of the 4° Stormo C.T. departed from Brindisi at 11.05, tasked with undertaking offensive action against enemy landing craft in the Corfù channel and along the Greek coast. The RE.2002s reached their objective at 11.50 and dropped ten bombs on an isolated motorised barge close to the southern coast of Corfù. The fighters and dive-bombers subsequently machine-gunned the same barge which seemed to have been beached; anti-aircraft fire was observed. One dive-bomber, during the attack entry phase, spotted six Ju 87s. Detaching itself from the formation without performing the drop, it attacked the six Ju 87s, shooting one down, the aircraft crashing near the city of Corfù. Disengaging itself from three Ju 87s which had attacked it with the advantage of height, it followed them to Janina airfield and shot down a second Ju 87 in flames. During the return route a motorised fishing boat was attacked with two 100-kg bombs, the boat being seen to roll onto its side; the fishing vessel had been with many others in the bay of Lefkino (Corfù). An RE.2002 returned with damage caused by anti-aircraft fire. Another RE.2002 returned to Lecce airfield despite being hit during combat with two Ju 87s. The MC.205V, which pressed on as far as the Greek coast, spotted and machine-gunned an MAS which was heading west from the bay of Plataria. In the same bay they noted and strafed a motor fishing boat, and in the inlet north of the bay of Plataria strafed an anchored MAS and a motorised barge. During the machine-gunning of these vessels intense anti-aircraft fire was noted. The remaining RE.2002s returned at 12.55.

Manduria airfield, 22 October 1943. Two photos taken during the visit to 5° *Stormo Tuffatori* of the King of Italy Vittorio Emanuele III, accompanied by Italian *Ministro dell'Aeronautica generale* Sandalli and senior US officers. (E.Leproni)

25 September 1943

Six RE.2002 of the 5° Stormo Tuffatori *and four MC.205Vs of the 4° Stormo C.T. departed at 12.45 and 12.55 respectively to undertake a bomb and machine gun attack against enemy landing craft between the island of Corfù and the Greek coast. An RE.2002 returned with technical problems. The aircraft arrived over the target at 13.30: three motorised barges of around 350 tonnes were spotted, together with three MAS and two sailing ships that were at some distance, leaving the bay of Lefkino, and sailing on an easterly course. The 100-kg bombs were dropped on the three MASs and three motor-barges. The RE.2002s and MC.205Vs repeatedly strafed the enemy vessels. An RE.2002 returned with part of its left wing shot off by a cannon shell. Anti-aircraft*

response from the naval vessels was intense. The MC.205Vs landed at 14.20 and the RE.2002s at 14.40.

* * *

Meanwhile, on 13 October 1943, the Italian government in exile in southern Italy declared war on Germany, effectively sanctioning a state of affairs that had begun with the armistice. This decision was of extraordinary moral importance for the airmen, both because it justified their operations carried out immediately after the armistice, and the losses suffered were officially recognised within the context of the 'new' war. Also, it provided an immediate objective for the fighter pilots, namely, the liberation of national soil from Nazi/Fascist oppression. Finally, because it

---

[11] The aircraft of *tenente* Felice Fox was shot down by Flak from a German torpedo boat.

Above and below: Photographs of Reggiane RE.2002s operating with the Regia Aeronautica del Sud, also known after the war as the Aeronautica Cobelligerante, are extremely rare. These views show a 239ª *Squadriglia* aircraft in flight with its tailplane still adorned with the 102° *Gruppo 'Tuffatori'* emblem adopted by the unit prior to 8 September 1943.

Reggiane RE.2002 of 239 *Squadriglia*, 102° *Gruppo*, 5° *Stormo Tuffatori* armed with a ventral bomb, probably at Palata airport (Termoli) during late 1943-early 1944.

was a guarantee that the armed forces would be respected and that therefore they, and the political organs, would be able to redeem Italy's right to participate in the building of a new free world.

16 October 1943

Between 10.45 and 12.45, six MC.205V and six MC.202s of the 4° Stormo C.T. and six RE.2002s of the 5° Stormo Tuffatori *conducted a bombing action against the airfield at Scutari (Albania), dropping 160 12-kg bombs on the southern side of the airfield and hangars, around which were dispersed twenty Ju 88s and five Me 109s and Focke-Wulfs. Strafing of the airfield was also conducted. Three aircraft destroyed and many others damaged. Normal reaction from 88 mm cannon. All the aircraft returned safely to base.*

23 October 1943

Between 11.05 and 12.45 six RE.2002 of the 5° Stormo Tuffatori *and four MC.205V of the 4° Stormo Caccia conducted a dive-bombing attack and strafing in the Berane area. The dive was initiated from 4,000 metres, dropping 12-kg bombs. One RE.2002 was forced to return due to technical problems: subsequently another RE.2002 was also forced to return for similar reasons. The remaining four aircraft attacked troops in the Berane area, dropping six 100-kg bombs and fourteen 12-kg bombs. Strafing was conducted against troops moving at the sides of the road. In the same area it was observed that all farmhouses had been destroyed. During the return leg, along the valley that runs from Berane to Podgorica, an RE.2002 was hit by anti-aircraft fire and flew off, leaving a trail of smoke.*[12] *Intense anti-aircraft fire above Podgorica. In the same area two RE.2002s were*

attacked by two Bf 109 Gs, and in the resulting combat an Me.109G was shot down. During the same encounter an RE.2002 was also shot down.*[13] At 10.00, following the sudden seizure of its engine, another RE.2002 was forced to make an emergency landing at Ceglie Messapico. The surviving RE.2002 landed at 14.00 at Gioia del Colle. The MC.205Vs provided protective cover in the area at a height of 4,000 metres without spotting any enemy aircraft.*

11 November 1943

Between 12.45 and 14.30 four RE.2002 flew a reconnaissance mission along the Albanian coast between Durazzo and Valona. Nothing to report.*

12 November 1943

Between 14.30 and 15.30 three RE.2002 departed from Manduria and four MC.205V departing from Lecce attempted to perform a dive-bombing attack against enemy shipping moving between Valona and the Corfù channel. Prohibitive weather conditions forced the aircraft to return without bringing their mission to an end.*

18 November 1943

Between 14.00 and 16.20 eight RE.2002 of the 5° Stormo Tuffatori *and six MC.202 escort aircraft of the 21° Gruppo conducted a dive-bombing attack on motorised barges in the bay of Valona. The RE.2002 dropped 112 12-kg bombs. The attack was centred on the barges anchored in the inlets at Skelia and Valona. No anti-aircraft reaction; no enemy aircraft in flight.*

30 November 1943

Between 11.10 and 12.15, ten RE.2002 of the 5° Stormo Tuffatori, *six MC.202s of the 21° Gruppo in direct escort and six MC.205s of the 4° Stormo C.T. in indirect escort attempted a dive-bombing and machine gun attack on the airfield and roads around Scutari-Durazzo. The mission was not concluded due to bad weather conditions.*

15 December 1943

Between 12.00 and 13.50 six RE.2002 of the 5° Stormo Tuffatori *and six MC.205Vs of the 4° Stormo CT in direct escort departed Lecce to conduct a dive-bombing and machine gun attack on Podgorica airfield. No aircraft seen on Podgorica; during a close reconnaissance of the Cettigne-Podgorica road, a concentration of vehicles was noted near the bridge over the river that flows into the Scutari lake; 54 12-kg incendiaries were dropped on the target. During the return leg, four barges were observed in the inlet of the port of Antivari: the escorting fighters fired 500 12.7 mm calibre rounds against them. Anti-aircraft fire from 88 mm batteries coming from the south-east side of Podgorica airfield. No air opposition.*

16 December 1943

At 13.40 six RE.2002 of the 5° Stormo Tuffatori *and six MC.205Vs of the 4° Stormo CT departed Lecce and conducted a dive-bombing attack on aircraft dispersed around Podgorica airfield. Situation of aircraft on the ground as per previous reports. The RE.2002s dropped 77 12-kg incendiaries on these aircraft; no movement of vehicles or troops along the road that runs from Cettigne to Bar. No air opposition; some imprecise 88 mm salvos as anti-aircraft reaction. Return to Lecce at 15.20.*

18 December 1943

Between 14.00 and 15.50, five RE. 2002 of the 5° Stormo Tuffatori *and six MC.202 of the 21° Gruppo, operating from Lecce, conducted a dive-bombing and machine gun attack on German aircraft dispersed around Podgorica airfield. 70 12-kg incendiaries were dropped on the dispersals on the north-western side; the presence was noted of the aircraft already reported in preceding reconnaissance missions; it is assumed that these aircraft were made unserviceable by preceding operations; intense anti-aircraft fire from the 88 mm batteries located on the foothills of the mountains to the north-east of Podgorica; during the return leg, and as far as the Jugoslav/Albanian coast, the aircraft cruised at low altitude to avoid detection; having dropped their munitions and strafed their targets. On the return leg the aircraft were targeted by anti-aircraft fire from the port of Bar. All the aircraft returned safely to Lecce.*[14]

31 December 1943

At 14.10 six RE.2002 of the 5° Stormo Tuffatori, *escorted directly by six MC.202 aircraft of the*

[12] *Capitano* D'Ottaviano was declared Missing in Action.

[13] *Tenente* Ugo Bassi was declared Missing in Action.

[14] On 19 December 1943, *maresciallo* Sergio Rizzi was killed while on a training flight over Manduria airfield flying RE.2002 MM7404.

Wing Commander Shore, Air Force Sub-Commission Liaison Officer, *Raggruppamento Caccia*

By Frank McMeiken

D URING the negotiations prior to the armistice announced on 8 September 1943, the Allied commanders had issued instructions to the Italian representatives concerning the actions to be taken by Italian forces once the announcement had been made. This process was not simple, as there were disagreements and misunderstandings between the parties, mainly relating to the Italian request for immediate Allied action to capture Roma, which was not in the Allies' plans.

To add to the confusion, when the Italian commanders in the field opened their orders on the evening of 8 September, they found that they had to react to any aggressive action from whichever party it came. The plan for the Regia Aeronautica involved the relocation of as many of its assets as possible to Allied-controlled airfields in southern Italy and Sardegna.

The administration of Allied-occupied Italy was in the hands of the Allied Control Commission, and aviation matters were delegated to the Air Force Sub-Commission (AFSC), which was established at Bari alongside the Italian General Staff. Not unnaturally, the Allies had reservations about utilising their former opponents as partners in combat against the Germans, and there was much deliberation about the theatres in which they could operate and the roles they could fulfil. Nevertheless, those personnel of the Regia Aeronautica who had flown south quickly demonstrated their keenness to join the battle against the Germans and convinced the Allies to facilitate the resumption of operations, albeit under strict Allied supervision and in theatres which the Allies felt were less controversial. It was felt that Italians in the south should not come into conflict with their former comrades in the north, fighting alongside the Germans.

In this initial climate of suspicion, the AFSC installed liaison officers with the *Raggruppamenti*, who issued targets and attack orders to the Italian units. Wing Commander Shore was assigned to the *Raggruppamento Caccia*, and in order to monitor the performance of the Italian units, was elected to fly with them on some operational missions. Quickly convinced of the professionalism and courage of the Italian pilots, W/Cdr Shore soon reported to his seniors at the AFSC that the Italians needed no direct instructions on how to conduct operations, and that all they required were details of the target. The method of an attack would be determined by Italian commanders.

By the end of the war Allied senior commanders were full of praise for the efforts of the Italian pilots, flying either outdated former Regia Aeronautica aircraft or unfamiliar former Allied types. These would be retained in service and subject to the negotiations surrounding the post-war Peace Treaty.

21° Gruppo, departed from Lecce to attempt a dive-bombing attack against radio stations on Corfù. The aircraft reached their target at 14.45, but were unable to conduct their mission due to the total cloud cover. The aircraft subsequently diverted to the airfield at Valona where they dropped 100-kg bombs on the runway; they then moved on to Porto Valona where they released the remaining six 100-kg bombs onto some barges tied up on the quayside. No air opposition or anti-aircraft response. The aircraft returned safely at 15.55.

Despite the relatively limited number of missions conducted in little more than two months of operations, the RE.2002s began to suffer significant serviceability issues to the point that, on 31 December 1943, eighteen aircraft remained on charge, of which just twelve were combat serviceable.

Despite the initial activity in the months of January and February 1944 being significantly impeded by harsh weather, the Italian pilots managed to complete a certain number of important operations. In early January, moreover, the 101° *Gruppo* was re-equipped

with the C.202, passing its RE.2002s to the 102° *Gruppo Tuffatori*.

The early operations of the Reggiane fighters in 1944 are described in the '*Diario Storico dell'attività operativa della Regia Aeronautica a fianco degli Alleati*' as follows:

8 January 1944
Six RE.2002 of the 5° Stormo, escorted by four Mc.205 of the 4° Stormo CT departed Lecce at 11.30 to conduct a dive-bombing attack on aircraft reported as stationed on Berat Kukove airfield. On reaching their objective, the RE.2002s dropped six 350-kg bombs, targeting two aircraft. The circular taxiway to the south-west side of the airfield was hit; during the return leg, a motorboat was spotted leaving the port on the island of Sasenno and machine-gunned. The boat was immobilised by two successive passes by the fighters, which fired 100 20 mm rounds and 190 12.7 mm rounds. No enemy air opposition. Intense and precise anti-aircraft fire over the Berat Kukova airfield from 20 mm machine guns and 88 mm batteries. All the aircraft returned safely to Lecce at 12.35.

12 January 1944
At 11.30 four RE.2002 of the 5° Stormo, escorted by three Mc.205 of the 4° Stormo, departed Lecce to conduct a dive-bombing attack on the radio station that supported communications between Roma and Athens on the island of Corfù. The radio station was not identified; eight 100-kg bombs were dropped on the indicated location; moderate anti-aircraft reaction from 88 mm and 20 mm batteries. No air opposition. The aircraft returned to Lecce at 13.20.

24 January 1944
Between 08.20 and 10.00 eight RE.2002 of the 5° Stormo departed Lecce, escorted by four Mc.205s and four Mc.202s of the 51° Stormo, to attempt offensive action against Tirana airfield, where twenty enemy aircraft had been reported. The aircraft were forced to return without completing their mission due to total cloud cover over the target. No enemy shipping spotted between Durazzo and Valona; no air opposition or anti-aircraft fire.

Furthermore, from mid-January 1944, fourteen of the remaining RE.2002s of the 102° *Gruppo*

Tuffatori, drawn from the 209ᵃ and 239ᵃ *Squadriglia*, were relocated to the airfield at Palata (Foggia). The aim was to further reduce the distance to their potential targets, in view of the fact that flights across the Adriatic Sea towards Balkan territory were proving to be increasingly risky due to the state of airframes and worn-out engines.

31 January 1944

Four RE.2002s, escorted by a similar number of Mc.205Vs of the 51° Stormo, flying from Palata, conducted bombing attacks against enemy shipping near the bay of Civitavecchia. Two ships were hit and the Italian aircraft returned safely to their base.

2 February 1944

Between 12.30 and 13.50 five RE.2002 of the 5° Stormo Tuffatori, escorted by four Mc.202s of the 51° Stormo and indirectly by five Mc.205Vs of the 4° Stormo, flew a mission from Lecce to bomb the built-up area of Kelcyre. The aircraft arrived over the target at 13.00, staying overhead for five minutes and dropping ten 100-kg bombs. Developing fires were noted: the Mc.202 escorts conducted accurate machine gun attacks on vehicles on the roads south of Kelcyre; traffic movement noted between Kelcyre and Kugar and on the Kelcyre-Tepeleni road, around seventy vehicles in number. No air opposition or anti-aircraft reaction.
Between 13.50 and 19.30 six RE.2002 of the 5° Stormo Tuffatori, escorted by eight Mc.205Vs of the 4° Stormo, departing from Lecce, carried out a bombing attack on Kelcyre. The aircraft reached their target at 14.35 and dropped twelve 100-kg bombs on buildings. No air opposition or anti-aircraft reaction.

3 February 1944

Between 14.30 and 15.45, three RE.2002s of the 5° Stormo Tuffatori, escorted by four Mc.202s of the 51° Stormo operating from Lecce, effected a dive-bombing attack on the town of Kelcyre. The aircraft reached their target at 15.10 and dropped six 100-kg bombs. No air opposition or anti-aircraft reaction.

2 March 1944

Between 11.40 and 13.00 six RE.2002 of the 5° Stormo Tuffatori, escorted by five Mc.205Vs of the 4° Stormo, departing from Palata, conducted a dive-bombing action in the bay of Curzola and a strafing attack in the bay of Vela Luka. In the bay of Curzola a large tug-like vessel was bombed; the Mc.205Vs strafed the same target while at Vela Luka boats were effectively machine-gunned. Explosives dropped: ten 100-kg bombs; rounds fired: 530 20 mm calibre, 624 12.7 mm. Mediocre atmospheric conditions. No air opposition or anti-aircraft at Vela Luka. Anti-aircraft fire from light weapons from the port of Curzola.

11 March 1944

Eight RE.2002s, escorted by seven Mc.205Vs one of which was piloted by Wing Commander Shore [see text box]*, departing from Palata, conducted a bombing raid against two small merchant ships north of Dubrovnik. The steamer closest to the dockside was hit; the Mc.205Vs strafed a steamer and left the others smoking. A camouflaged landing craft was strafed and also damaged by the escort aircraft. Anti-aircraft reaction from medium calibre batteries on both sides of the canal. All the aircraft returned safely to their base at 15.30.*

13 March 1944

At 10.30 eight RE.2002 escorted by seven Mc.205Vs [of which one was piloted by W/Cdr Shore] departed from Palata to perform a dive-bombing attack against two ships reported in the port of Dubrovnik. Eight 250-kg bombs were dropped on the ships: light anti-aircraft reaction from the south-eastern zone of the port. The aircraft returned at 12.10, including two Mc.205Vs which had returned prior to conducting the mission due to technical faults, and escorted by another two aircraft of the same type.

Between 15.00 and 15.30, nine RE.2002 aircraft escorted by seven Mc.205Vs, flying from Palata, bombed the railway station at Metcovich. Nine 250-kg bombs were dropped in a dive-bombing attack from 1,500 metres. The target was hit. Three trains and a single locomotive standing in the station were hit. Anti-aircraft reaction from heavy, medium and light weapons. On their return, two RE.2002s crashed on landing due to crosswinds.

* * *

By now, however, aircraft were beginning to increasingly show their worn-out states following long months of service and war.

17 March 1944

From 14.00 until 15.50 nine RE.2002 of the 5° Stormo Tuffatori escorted by three Mc.205V [of which one was piloted by W/Cdr Shore] and by four Mc.202 of the 51° Stormo operating from Palata, conducted a dive-bombing attack on fuel tanks and a refinery near Dubrovnik. One RE.2002, presumably with a technical problem, departed the formation to attempt a return to base, but crashed into the sea 24 km from the Punta del Gargano.[15] The remaining aircraft dropped eight 250-kg bombs on the target from 400 metres. No air or anti-aircraft opposition. On the return, one Mc.205V made a forced landing near Manfredonia. Pilot uninjured. All the remaining aircraft returned safely.

29 March 1944

From 13.55 until 15.45 eight RE.2002 of the 5° Stormo Tuffatori and seven Mc. 205V from the 4° Stormo, departing from Palata, conducted a dive-bombing operation against fuel tanks and a petrol refinery near Dubrovnik. Eight 250-kg bombs were dropped; a medium-tonnage steamer was also hit. Anti-aircraft reaction from light weapons. While returning to base, one RE.2002 crashed due to unknown circumstances 12 km east of Gargano, the pilot taking to his parachute.[16]

Following the transfer of the 5° *Stormo Tuffatori* to Nuova, near Campomarino, between late April and early May 1944, the RE.2002s still serviceable were mainly used for training activities. During one of these flights, for unknown reasons, a Reggiane failed to pull up from a dive and crashed into the sea, resulting in the death of *maresciallo* Ferrari. His body was recovered on 3 June 1944.

Probably influenced by this incident, the *Comando Unità Aerea* realised that the operational viability of the aircraft had come to an end due to their worn-out engines and mechanical components, and with a lack of spares, decided to withdraw the aircraft from front-line operations.

The remaining aircraft of the 102° *Gruppo* of the 5° *Stormo Tuffatori* were consequently ordered to conduct a final operational attack mission on 2 June 1944. Four RE.2002s, escorted by four Mc.205Vs and two Spitfires, were sent to attack the bridge at Skadrin in Albania. Once again, during this mission, an RE.2002 suffered a mechanical failure, forcing its pilot, *maresciallo* Danieli, to make a forced landing near the runway on the island of Lissa, escorted by two Mc.205Vs.

Finally, the *Comando Unità Aerea* issued an order for all aircraft still in flying condition to be used strictly for training activities, and consequently, on 19 June 1944, all RE.2002s were passed to the *Scuola Addestramento Caccia* at Lecce Leverano, and the 5° *Stormo Tuffatori* replaced them with a fleet of C.202s. The unit was redesignated 5° *Stormo Caccia Terrestre* from 14 July 1944.

In reality, the appalling condition of the aircraft did not permit the conduct of any significant or safe flying activity and thus the last fifteen aircraft in flying condition were destroyed.

---

[15] The pilot, *tenente* Morichelli, was rescued, albeit suffering from some injuries.
[16] *Sergente* Banfi bailed out over the Adriatic, but was never located.

CHAPTER FIVE

RE.2003

Evolution, Production and Technical

A REQUIREMENT to replace the increasingly obsolete IMAM Ro. 37 reconnaissance biplane, together with the need to respond to a request from the Regia Marina for a two-seat catapult aircraft, resulted in 1941 in the development of a two-seat version of the RE.2000 optimised for the reconnaissance role.

In order to expedite the development process, Reggiane modified one of the RE.2000s originally assigned for export, fitting it with the Piaggio P.XI bis engine, slightly more reliable in comparison with the preceding P.XI, and assigning the aircraft as MM478. The fuselage was modified for the addition of a second crew position reserved for an observer. The inclusion of this position offered an increased cross section, enabling some limited forward vision, achieved by the particular configuration of the canopy that joined the observer's and pilot's positions, while lateral and lower windows provided the observer with good lateral and lower vision. A further technical characteristic was found in the 474-litre integral wet wing tanks.

The first flight trials commenced on 29 July 1941, conducted by *capitano* Francesco Agello,

A promotional postcard produced by Reggiane from 1941.

Left: Detail of the engine cowling opening/access on RE.2003, MM12415. The access design, similar to that adopted for the RE.2002, derived its inspiration from that of the German twin-engined Dornier Do 17.

Above: Reggio Emilia, 23 September 1942. A view of the cabin of RE.2003, MM12415. Note the difference between the front and rear canopies: the former is completely rigid, while the latter has a second hinge in the centre of the canopy.

Record A.V. 10-4-1933-XI
Maresc. F. Agello.

Ripn autor. Foto Vecchimoli
perenzani

FRANCESCO AGELLO poses in front of the Macchi Mc.72 after the speed record flight on 10 April 1933 of 682.078 km/h. Agello was born in 1902 and died in November 1942 following an in-flight collision in the skies over Milan-Bresso airport. He was at the controls of a Macchi M.C.202 he was testing. As fate would have it, he collided with an aircraft of the same type piloted by *colonnello* Guido Masiero, a former First World War ace, who became famous for having taken part in the Rome-Tokyo air expedition with Arturo Ferrarin in 1920.

Left, above, right: The prototype, MM478, built by converting an RE.2000 centre section with the addition of an observer's seat.

with the second crew-member simulated by ballast. From the seventh test flight a second crew-member was always carried, despite the fact that there was hardly any operational equipment installed for an observer, and no possibility of communication with the pilot since an intercom system was still lacking. The only specialised equipment was a rotating seat for the observer.

Following a further series of flights, the aircraft was further evaluated by test pilots from the 1° *Centro Sperimentale* at Guidonia Montecelio from where there were reported encouraging results.

Meanwhile, the Regia Aeronautica asked Reggiane to develop a new prototype, taking as the basis the airframe of an RE.2002. Compared to the preceding prototype, MM478, the observer's position had been improved, with new lower windows and the installation of a folding navigator's chart table, radio equipment and a second panel. It was also fitted with an intercom system, a radio transceiver and two cameras, one photo-planimetric and panoramic.

Meanwhile, on 16 December 1941, the Regia Aeronautica had submitted an intent order for 200 examples of the aircraft, identified by the designation RE.2003, with deliveries of the first machine expected in September 1942.

MM12415 incorporated some detail modifications to the engine cowling and a significant enhancement of the avionics equipment in the rear cockpit, as well as new engine exhausts fitted with flame dampers. This prototype, moreover, featured the ability to carry stores, with

Above and opposite page: The RE.2003, MM12415, the first and only production model. Note the difference in shape of the engine cover and the two 7.7 mm wing guns in addition to the 'standard' 12.7 mm SAFAT.

Caracciolo, wearing dark glasses, together with a group of workers from Reggiane's Sezione collaudo (Aircraft Testing Department).

ALFONSO CARACCIOLO

ALFONSO CARACCIOLO was another of Reggiane's test pilots. Born in Naples on 1 July 1914, after school in Gorizia he was assigned to the 4° *Stormo* CT and took part in the Spanish Civil War where he was shot down and taken prisoner. Returning to Italy, he was assigned to the 2° *Gruppo* CT with which he was deployed to North Africa. At the end of 1941, he joined Reggiane and over the next few years performed numerous test flights of aircraft built by Reggiane including the RE.2005 and S.79.

one central and two underwing hard points for a total munitions payload of 500 kg, or a supplementary fuel tank whilst retaining the two centrally mounted 12.7 mm machine guns and the two 7.77 mm guns as fitted to the RE.2002.

This second aircraft flew for the first time on 13 October 1942, with test pilot Alfonso Caracciolo at the controls. It was subsequently transferred to Guidonia for evaluation, piloted by Tullio De Prato, who had been charged by

RE.2003 Technical Data

Wingspan	11.00 m
Overall length **(MM478)**	7.99 m
Overall length **(MM12415)**	8.08 m
Height	3.20 m
Wing area	20.40 sq.m.
Wingspan	6.0 m
Empty weight **(MM478)**	2,280 kg
Empty weight **(MM12415)**	2,470 kg
Payload **(MM478)**	780 kg
Payload **(MM12415)**	850 kg
Total weight **(MM478)**	3,060 kg
Total weight **(MM12415)**	3,320 kg
Maximum speed at 4,900 m	475/510 km/h
Maximum speed at sea level	400 km/h
Cruising speed	340 km/h
Minimum speed	115 km/h
Climb to 4,000 m	4'20"
Climb to 6,000 m	7'00"
Range	720 km
Ceiling	10,500 m

'From the first flight, the RE.2003 proved a familiar aircraft to me. I took off solo, with no one and no ballast in the rear seat, and I consequently experienced the same sensation as I had when I flew the RE.2000. In fact, the two aircraft had the same structural characteristics: the same wing, the same engine, the same propeller and, more or less, the same wing loading.

'The RE.2003 proved to be manoeuvrable and completely free from the risk of autorotation, safe in all unexpected flight attitudes, stable and easy to manoeuvre, and within the handling capability range of any pilot. In the flights that followed to determine its characteristics, I always carried another person, to both verify the behaviour in flight with the relocated centre of gravity and to set up the intercom and connections of the radio system. I ended up taking a weight of 80 kg in the rear seat.

'Embarking a passenger and the radio systems, however, had no impact on the stability of the aircraft in flight. Even in this configuration, it was possible to perform all the aerobatic

manoeuvres without encountering any appreciable deterioration of its characteristics. In my opinion the RE.2003, utilised as an embarked, catapult-launched aircraft, primarily in the reconnaissance role and with a secondary role as a fighter, would, undoubtedly, have been a success.'

Aircraft characteristics

The RE.2003 was a low-wing, monocoque, single-engine, two-seat reconnaissance monoplane of all-metal construction. It was powered by a Piaggio P.XI bis twin-row, air-cooled engine fitted with a compressor and reducer developing 870 hp of power at sea level and around 1,000 hp at 4,000 m.

Armament comprised two Breda SAFAT 12.7 mm fuselage machine guns with a total of 400 rounds and, in MM12415 and the planned production series, two Breda SAFAT 7.7 mm machine guns were mounted in the wings with 600 rounds each.

A munitions payload of around 500 kg was attachable to three hard points, one under the fuselage and two under the wings.

The RE.2003 prototype, MM478. To accelerate the building of the aircraft, Reggiane decided to pick an RE.2000 fuselage from an aircraft assigned to an earlier order, maintaining the 'wet wing', but installing a P.XI engine and a second place for an observer, but without instrumentation.

Reggiane with following the development of this 'first of series' aircraft.

Despite the flight trials having confirmed the good handling characteristics of the aircraft, similar to those of the RE.2000, at the end of 1942 Italy's war situation had become precarious and the requirement to engage in the acquisition of a new two-seat reconnaissance was a luxury that the Regia Aeronautica could not afford to prioritise. Thus, the order for the 200 RE.2003s was limited to just the two prototypes and the rest of the order transformed to 198 RE.2001 fighters.

At the time of the armistice, the only RE.2003 on charge of the 1ª *Squadriglia* FF.NN of the Regia Marina Militare was the first prototype, MM478, operating from the base at Sarzana, near La Spezia.

Of the little information available, it seems that this aircraft was subsequently utilised by the Caproni company at Taliedo for training German pilots destined to fly in the RE.2002. Of the second prototype completed, MM12415, to date nothing has been discovered about its fate.

On his return to the 1° *Centro Sperimentale* at Guidonia in early April 1942 following his experieces with the RE.2000 *Catapultabile*, *tenente* Reiner had the opportunity to fly and demonstrate the first prototype of the RE.2003 (MM478) to a Hungarian Military Commission. He offered the following opinions about the aircraft:

A view of the rear seat that housed the observer.

Detail views of the Piaggio P.XI bis engine that powered the two RE.2003 prototypes.

CHAPTER SIX

RE.2005 *Sagittario*

Evolution and Production

THE Reggiane RE.2005 was the last and, undoubtedly, the best of the series of monoplane fighters produced by Caproni-Reggiane in the course of the Second World War.

On first sight, the RE.2005 can be viewed as an evolution of the RE.2001, but despite the relative similarities it was, from a technical perspective, a completely different aircraft, with a much more streamlined and aerodynamic fuselage, a new engine and armament, and a completely different undercarriage. Generally considered by many aviation enthusiasts as the most beautiful fighter of the '*Serie 5*' from an aesthetic aspect (incidentally, a view that the writer does not share), the *Sagittario*, as the RE.2005 became known officially, was certainly an excellent combat aircraft. Yet in the course of its brief operational life, it was characterised by structural problems encountered mainly during high-speed dives, problems that resulted in flutter of such violence that damage was caused to the tailplanes and deformation to the rear fuselage. Then the events of the armistice impeded any potential solution.

The design of the aircraft commenced in 1941, a period when it was difficult for Italy to compete

Promotional postcards produced by Reggiane in 1943.

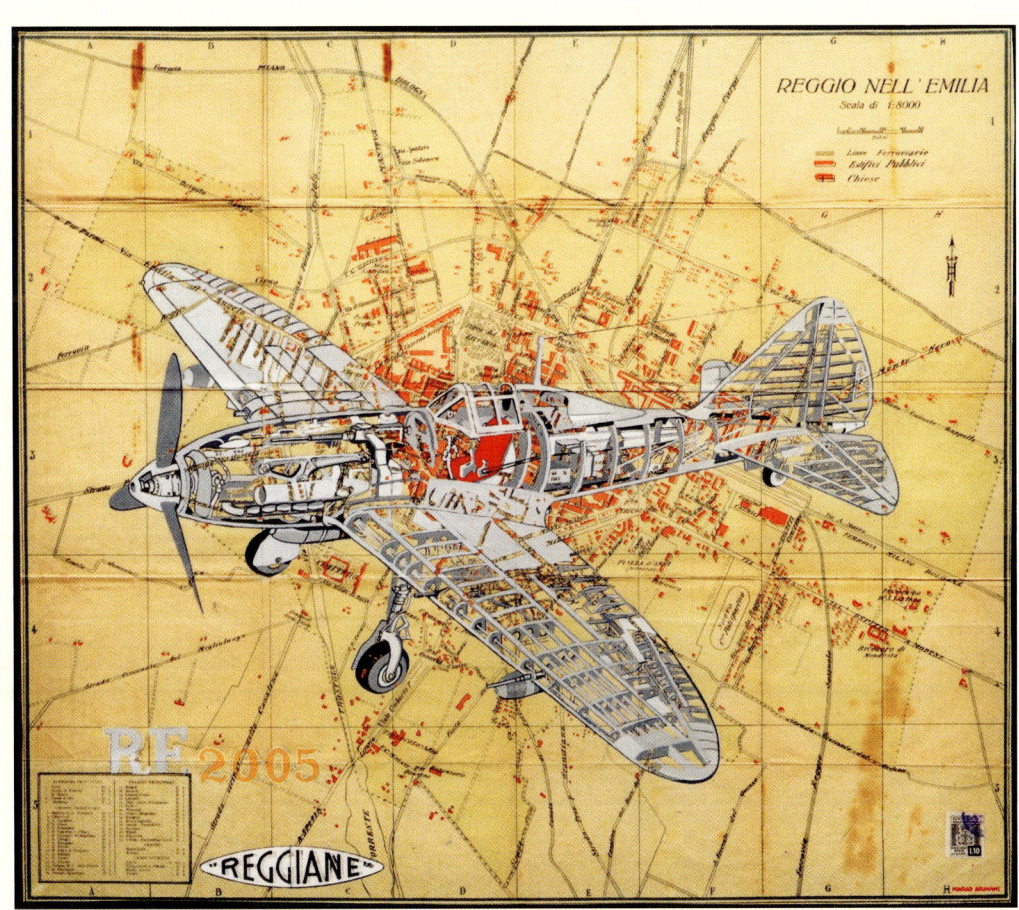

Left: A stylish poster produced by Reggiane to promote the RE.2005, published in 1943. It depicts a cutaway of the aircraft laid over a map of Reggio Emilia town (for a larger reproduction, see title page of this book). (P.Monti)

against the continual progress of Allied fighters and in particular, the inability of the otherwise excellent C.202 *Folgore*, armed with just two 12.7 mm machine guns, to counter Allied bombers which came at increasingly high altitudes. Consequently, in the summer of 1941, the Regia Aeronautica issued a requirement for a new fighter capable of operating at altitudes greater than 10,000 metres, developing a maximum speed of at least 620 km/h and, importantly, featuring armament comprising at least one 20 mm Mauser MG 151/20 cannon and four 12.7 mm machine guns.

In order to achieve the greater power necessary for this type of aircraft, after the failure to develop the FIAT A.38[1] engine which was intended to power the new FIAT G.55 fighter, *generale* Francesco Pricolo, the *Capo di Stato Maggiore* of the Regia Aeronautica, authorised adoption of the new German Daimler-Benz DB 605 engine, capable of producing 1,350 hp. This decision would later result in the celebrated generation of fighters known as the '*caccia della Serie 5*'[2] which was characterised by aircraft named after constellations and signs of the Zodiac: the FIAT G.55 '*Centauro*' (Centaur), AerMacchi C.205N '*Orione*' (Orion), and the fighter designed and manufactured by Reggiane, the RE.2005 '*Sagittario*' (Sagittarius).[3]

The design of the new fighter was entrusted to a team led by *ing*. Giuseppe Maraschini, and the result was excellent. The aircraft had little in

The '*Sagittario*' name painted on the tail fin. It seems it was applied in a single white colour and in similar style on both sides of the fin.

common with other Reggiane aircraft, from which it retained just the wing planform, albeit with slightly increased surface area, and the tailplane, while the fuselage, undercarriage, wing profile and armament were completely new and state-of-the-art. The aerodynamics were particularly refined, with the oil and water radiators, which were enclosed in an extensive fairing, centrally positioned under the fuselage, rather than under the wings as in the RE.2001.

At the start of 1942, while awaiting delivery of the first engine to complete the fitting out of the

first aircraft, Reggiane decided to construct a wooden mock-up to better study the installation of the new systems. The delivery of the first DB 605 was the subject of a strange affair, which led to a delay of several months in the preparation of the aircraft. Three engines were shipped from Daimler-Benz in Germany in December 1941, destined respectively for FIAT (the prime contractor for licensed construction engines), AerMacchi and Reggiane. However, once the engine sent to Reggio Emilia had crossed the Italian border, all trace of it was lost and it was

The wooden mock-up of the RE.2005 fighter during an early stage of construction. Note that guns have been installed, barrels protruding from the firewall. The photograph was taken on 10 January 1942.

---

[1] The FIAT A.38 R.C. 15-45 was a sixteen inverted-V cylinder liquid-cooled engine, a development of the design for the FIAT AS.8 and conceived by *ing*. Antonio Fessia. The intended technical specifications aspired to around 2,000 hp maximum power available between 500 and 4,500 metres, but the project was abandoned, as its long development timescale and complex difficulties were unsustainable, given the urgent need for combat equipment.

[2] See also this author's *Macchi Fighters* and *FIAT Aeritalia Fighters*, both Crecy Publishing.

[3] The AerMacchi C.205V, although often included as one of the three 'Series 5' fighters, did not actually belong to that class. Not surprisingly, it had a different name from the constellation/Zodiac signs – *Veltro*.

7 May 1942. A sequence depicting the prototype *Sagittario,* MM494 first outing. The aircraft had already undergone the necessary engine tests.

only found after a four-month search at a railway depot in Milan. The fact aroused considerable suspicion over alleged 'intentional sabotage' against the Reggio Emilia company.

Despite the delay to the delivery of the engine, the first prototype of the RE.2005, which had been assigned serial MM494, was prepared in rapid time, just twenty days after the prototypes of the G.55 and C.205V, benefitting from the fact that construction had been initiated simultaneously with that of the wooden mock-up, and had only been suspended because of the lack of an engine.

The prototype emerged from the assembly line of Reggiane's *Reparto Sperimentale* in early May 1942, and was entrusted to the skilful hands of test pilot Tullio De Prato, who performed some taxiing and take-off runs on the 7th. The first flight was performed on 9 May – a quick circuit of the airfield with the undercarriage down. The next morning

the prototype took off from Reggio Emilia for its first official flight, which ended in a minor landing accident. During a loop, the right-hand main undercarriage leg which, in the prototype, had still not been fitted with a mechanical block, broke its leverage system due to the acceleration, and extended swinging outside its bay. During the ensuing emergency landing, the left-hand undercarriage also failed, and the fighter ended its course on its belly on the grass runway. Fortunately, it had suffered only minor damage, as it returned to the air on 1 June, just twenty days later.

De Prato recorded his initial encounter and first flight in the new fighter:

'It was love at first sight; a lightning strike! A prototype aircraft usually generates a feeling of paternal benevolence in the test pilot.

I followed it lovingly from its first design and almost led it by hand into the air, from its "first steps" until it "came of age". Once it becomes an adult, safe, it can be entrusted to more rougher hands with the serenity of a parent who leaves his own child, who has reached maturity. Perhaps, to many people, the passion of a man for a machine is inconceivable. Yet the machine has shapes, and the strength to provoke the desire to possess it. The Sagittario *was, in my opinion, the most beautiful, the most elegant, and the most shocking fighter aircraft amongst similar fighters of the period.*

'I followed it with the passion of a lover, the load testing, the final assembly, and its final refinement on the ground. And I remember as though it was yesterday the faces and names of the many capable and modest men who

Continues on page 192

This page and opposite:
Additional photographs from
7 May 1942 depicting the
Sagittario's first outing.

Above and below: The prototype, MM494, ready for its first flight two days later on 9 May 1942. *Ing.* Alessio, Reggiane's general manager, leans on the wing, while Roberto Longhi (wearing sunglasses) and Maraschini are also present.

This photograph captures the first taxi on the field, without the wheels leaving the ground.

TULLIO DE PRATO

ULLIO DE PRATO was born at Pola (today Pula in Croatia) in 1908. On obtaining his *brevetto di pilota militare* in 1928 he entered service with the Regia Aeronautica with the rank of *sottotenente di complemento* (short service commission second lieutenant) and joined the 21° *Stormo da ricognizione* at Pisa which was equipped with the Ansaldo A.300. In 1930 he was admitted to the *Regia Accademia Aeronautica* at Caserta to train for a permanent commission and in 1934 was posted to the 4° *Stormo Caccia Terrestre* based at Gorizia. In 1936 he was assigned to the 12° *Stormo Bombardamento Veloce*, which was in the process of re-equipping at Guidonia with the S.79 *Sparviero* tri-motor bomber. He served in the Spanish Civil War, initially with the 12° *Stormo* and, after promotion to *capitano*, as commander of the 10ª *Squadriglia* of the 8° *Stormo Bombardamento Terrestre*. Returning to Italy, he assumed command of the 151ª *Squadriglia* of the 6° *Stormo Caccia Terrestre*, and with Italy's entry into the war he was transferred to the command of the 150ª *Squadriglia*, 2° *Gruppo Caccia Terrestre* at Grottaglie, equipped with the FIAT G.50. In December of the same year, the 2° *Gruppo* was transferred to North Africa, where De Prato was injured when his aircraft was shot down. After two months of convalescence, he returned to service and in September 1941 he made the first flight in a RE.2001 which was destined to re-equip the 2° *Gruppo* CT. In March 1942, he accepted an offer from Reggiane to become their company test pilot and to oversee the development of the new RE.2005 *Sagittario* fighter. After the armistice and the German occupation of the Reggiane factories, he temporarily abandoned the world of aviation, but later returned to the company, resuming his role as test pilot for the Gruppo Caproni. Post-war, he made the first flight in the Caproni Ca.193, while with Aerfer he performed the flight tests on around 100 Republic F-84G Thunderjet fighter-bombers delivered by ship from the United States. Subsequently rising to the honorary rank of *Generale di divisione aerea*, he died on 24 December 1981 at Coriano near Rimini. Amongst his honours are two *Medaglie d'Argento* and one *Bronzo al Valor Militare*.

Above and opposite page: The prototype's second flight on 10 May: test pilot De Prato performed a short acrobatic display which proved the excellent handling qualities of the RE.2005, but the flight ended with an emergency landing after the right landing gear broke loose in the air.

Further photographs of the recovery of the prototype following the flight on 10 May.

contributed to its realisation. Many times I sat in the pilot's seat to gain familiarity with the layout of the controls and instruments, the majority of which were new types. In the Sagittario, including its engine and some other details, everything was experimental and to be experimented with – from the propeller to the tailwheel. And at that time experimentation was conducted in flight, without the use of a simulator; pilot and aircraft had a common destiny.

'*The day finally arrived and everyone waited nervously for the maiden flight. I made an initial gentle taxi run to try out the brakes and rudder, and then, without any uncertainty, selected full power for a first taste. The aircraft, carrying no load, left the ground with unexpected ease following a straight and perfect take-off run that required no corrective inputs. I retracted the undercarriage, tailwheel and flaps, and the aircraft lifted into the air with the stability of a projectile.*

'*And it climbed very quickly! In the cockpit, with the doors all open, there was an unbearable heat, also because, to accelerate the execution of this first test, the firewall had been omitted, and the hot blast from the engine was burning my ankles. A rapid glance around the engine instruments showed water and oil temperatures just within limits: the rest were normal. Not so good was the Piaggio propeller which did not maintain a constant rpm and which, later, would compromise the manoeuvrability of the aircraft.*

'*Distracted by making my first, handwritten notes, I noticed that I had reached 1,000 metres height. I set the engine into a cruise regime, adjusted the incidence of the stabilisers until I felt no reactions through the stick, and then released the control column. The aircraft swung slightly to the right, but flew steady and safe, confirming the superlative qualities that its beauty had promised. The controls, well compensated, felt efficient and light. I quickly began a series of evolutions around the horizontal plane: it sped like a dolphin without any hint of the congenital defects of the fighter monoplanes of the period which, with the exception of the Reggiane, could result in dangerous autorotation. I no longer even felt my ankles burning, and one manoeuvre led to another, a roll in the turn, and then a series of three in straight line flight. It was like a cannon shot! I then pointed the nose towards the ground and pulled up, very gently, to fly the first loop.*

'*I was inverted and reducing power when a sudden jolt pulled me from my concentration. Something bad had happened; certainly, something had failed. I closed the throttle and closed out the loop, then set up a glide, reducing speed to the values close to the minimums planned which I had not yet had the*

time to explore. This reduced the stress; now it was necessary to return the aircraft to the ground, safe and sound, in order not to ruin the hoped-for success. I descended slowly, looking to try to locate the fault, but failed to achieve my plan. The controls were showing no anomalies, but I could feel that the aircraft was not flying well. There was no signal from the ground, there was no radio on board, and wishing to avoid further surprises, I decided to make an immediate landing.

'*I flew over S. Lazzaro, undercarriage and flaps lowered, and approached the airfield at low level. Once over the runway threshold, I closed the throttle and brought the manoeuvre to a perfect conclusion. I didn't even have enough time to breathe a sigh of relief after escaping from the danger because, as soon as I touched the ground, I noticed the lack of support on the right and the aileron that was unable to counteract the drop. Oh no! I realised in an instant that there was nothing I could do: the best thing would be to stay put and wait to see what my aircraft would do to bring its first adventure to a conclusion!*

'*The wingtip touched the ground, and the aircraft rotated around it. I slackened my harness, and waited for the inevitable violent flip-over, but the RE.2005 performed its first miracle: the left undercarriage leg, the good one, gave way under the stress of the rotation, and the beautiful aircraft wanted to end its run on its belly, sliding backwards through the high grass for around 200 metres.*

'*I spotted the small number of factory vehicles, the breathless, running technicians, and the ambulance, but I was unhurt. During the loop, the undercarriage, not connected by a locking mechanism and held only by hydraulic pressure, had unhinged the leverage system, leaving the right undercarriage leg hanging free in a neutral position. In a few days the fighter, which, apart from the undercarriage, propeller and radiators, had not suffered serious damage, was repaired, and I was able to resume the laborious task of performing the evolution trials.*' [4]

After repairs and subsequent test flights, which led to a brief grounding for some technical modifications, on 20 July 1942 the aircraft was flown to Guidonia for a series of comparative flight trials with the FIAT and AerMacchi fighters.

However, the *Sagittario* suffered greatly from a lack of fine-tuning. In the course of the first flights at Guidonia, other technical problems with the main undercarriage doors emerged during the dive trials and on 24 July, it was forced to return to Reggio Emilia to get them resolved. The aircraft was subjected to further modifications before being declared ready to return to Guidonia *Centro Sperimentale* two months later.

On 23 September 1942, officers from the *Commissione Ministeriale d'Esame* [5] (Ministerial

Examination Commission) arrived at the Reggiane factory tasked with performing a series of evaluation flights. Amongst them was *colonnello* Angelo Tondi, the commander of the *Centro Sperimentale*, *tenente colonnello* Giuseppe Baylon and *maggiori* Giovanni Borzoni and Mario Gasperi. The results of their flights were very positive, despite another accident being suffered by prototype MM494 when being flown by *colonnello* Tondi. At the conclusion of his flight and at a height of around 100 metres, while preparing to land, the aircraft's engine suddenly developed a mechanical problem. Lacking any space to manoeuvre and to avoid destroying the precious machine, Tondi performed a perfect wheels-up emergency landing. Luckily the RE.2005 prototype suffered only minor damage to its propeller and fuselage undersides.

Following the flight trials at Reggio Emilia, each member of the commission prepared his own report, but *Colonnello* Tondi submitted two: the first one dealt specifically with various flight characteristics while the second offered a comparison between the performance of the RE.2005 and the equivalent FIAT G.55:

'*The two aircraft, which seem to possess similar flying characteristics, have not revealed any*

Two views of RE.2005 MM494 in front of the hangars at the *Guidonia Centro Sperimentale*, where it arrived on 20 July 1942. The aircraft had received the official 'Continental' camouflage only a few days before.

[4] Taken from *Un pilota contadino. Storia di un asso della caccia italiana*, the autobiography of Tullio De Prato, MUCCHI Editore.
[5] The president of the *Commissione Ministeriale d'Esame* – constituted in May 1942 – was *generale* Renato Sandalli, *Capo dell'Ufficio Tecnico Militare*. The members were *generali* Guglielmo Cassinelli, *Direttore* of the CSA, and Aldo Guglielmetti of the DGCA, together with *colonnelli* Angelo Tondi, Nicolò Galante, Pierluigi Torre of the DGCA, *tenente colonnello* Giuseppe Baylon and *maggiore* Aldo Gaspari.

Rear view of the RE.2005 in front of the hangars at the *Guidonia Centro Sperimentale*.

Right: The main structural change requested by the Regia Aeronautica after the first trials at Guidonia was to shorten the cabin by 19 cm, as shown here in a first series machine which is still devoid of paint.

essential defects in their flying qualities, and it is therefore impossible to make comparative judgement. The RE.2005 seems to behave better in a tight turn and in manoeuvres, the controls appearing to have been perfected. Take-off and landing are similar in both aircraft. The G.55 is better in the very important diving condition, given a total absence of vibration, while on the RE.2005, vibration occurs at high speed and in the dive, which causes elastic movements to the fuselage and possibly the wing, which must be carefully observed.

'The G.55 gives the impression of being generally more robust. Once the reported drawbacks have been eliminated, it will be necessary to make a more thorough and prolonged examination of both aircraft, in order to achieve a more complete assessment, not only of their respective flying qualities, but also on their suitability for use.'

Similar conclusions were reached by *capitano* Mario Gasperi who also noted:

'On the RE.2005, the gyroscopic propeller torque is effectively corrected, and the tendency to swing to the left is clearly less. It is probable that the RE.2005's rate of climb will be superior to that of the G.55. The same can be said for horizontal speed. The rotation movement, and landings in particular, are easier in the G.55

than in the RE.2005 (although the latter is easy on the RE.2005). It was revealed that the G.55 rotates and lands in a smaller space than the RE.2005. Furthermore, the G.55 gives an impression of greater strength and robustness. A highly important factor in the comparison between these two aircraft is the layout of their weapons and their functioning, as well as their ease of inspection, as it is considered that, given the good qualities of both the prototypes, it would be preferable to select the one, irrespective of any slight differences, that is best able to utilise its weapons.'

On 1 October 1942 MM484 returned to Guidonia but some days later, in the course of a dive trial, it continued to experience problems with

the functioning of the undercarriage, similar to those that had occurred some months previously. During October, fitted with the central 20 mm cannon, the usual two 12.7 mm SAFAT machine guns in a central fuselage position and two 12.7mm SAFATs mounted in the wings, the aircraft moved to Furbara airfield where it carried out armament tests. These revealed some problems with the 20 mm cannon which had a tendency to jam due to a defect in the design and build of the ammunition belt. Further trials were conducted with the introduction of the second prototype, MM495, which had made its first flight at the end of October. The aircraft was eventually fitted with its definitive armament – two wing cannon replacing the two machine guns. Despite some other minor issues experienced during the flight

RE.2005, MM092352, the tenth of the first *'zero'* series was used to establish the series specification after changes proposed by the Guidonia and Furbara test centres. The aircraft was photographed at Reggio Emilia on 4 June 1943. Note the damaged port wingtip.

trials, the *Commissione Ministeriale d'Esame* expressed positive opinions about the aircraft, although a series of further structural modifications were also prescribed. In particular, it was suggested strengthening the fuselage which had demonstrated a level of weakness and vibration, particularly in the tail area, alongside other minor details related to engine functioning and the oil and fuel circuits.

The final evaluations of the three Series 5 fighters, which appeared in its report of the *Commissione Ministeriale d'Esame* issued on 28 December 1942, is controversial to say the least.

The report took into account not only performance, but also the respective industrial capacity of the companies and the ease of production of individual aircraft. It concluded a 'draw' between the three aircraft considered. However, there was a slight preference in favour of the AerMacchi C.205N *Orione*, even though the *Orione* had been evaluated on 'paper', using the data available from tests previously carried out with the C.205V *Veltro*. These had been integrated with the performance calculation forecasts for the C.205N submitted by AerMacchi.

This judgement seems to have overlooked the fact that the *Orione* was a very new aircraft – the result of a completely new design by AerMacchi's *ing.* Castoldi – which relied on results obtained previously with the company's *Saetta*, *Folgore* and *Veltro*!

The story of the *Orione* is well known.[6] The prototype was only available for evaluation at Guidonia at the end of January 1943, resulting in a delay of six months to the other two fighters, due to AerMacchi concentrating on getting the C.205V *Veltro* into production as soon as possible.

However, despite being some months later than the *Centauro* and *Sagittario* and the flight trials offering proof of the superior performance of AerMacchi's fighter, difficulties in preparing new assembly lines dedicated to the aircraft resulted in the cancellation of orders for the *Orione* in favour of the C.205V *Veltro* as well as the selection of the FIAT G.55 mainly for industrial (and 'political') reasons.

After evaluating the four Italian Series 5 fighters and comparing their performance to those of the Bf 109 G-4 and Fw 190 A-5, a German mission, led by *Oberst* Edgar Petersen, *Kommandeur der Erprobungsstellen* in Rechlin, issued a detailed report on 27 January.

The resulting evaluation saw none of the aircraft evaluated emerge as a favourite, with each having its own merits and defects. But the G.55 was favoured when it came to performance, and because the airframe would present problem-free installation of the new 1,750-hp Daimler-Benz DB 603 engine.[7]

There was no doubt that this further evaluation influenced the view that the G.55 was the best of the fighters, an outcome which, when added to 'political' and 'industrial' pressures, resulted in the FIAT fighter being favoured for production on a large scale. Yet even in this case, the rule of 'not disappointing anyone' prevailed, and so because of the excellent performance and potential demonstrated by the Reggiane fighter, and the somewhat 'contrasting' overall results of the flight tests, the *Ministero della Regia Aeronautica* decided to proceed with production of the *Sagittario*, ordering a first batch of sixteen aircraft on 16 November 1942. These were identified as the *Serie 0* and were assigned *Matricole Militari*

from 09234 to 092358.[8] This was followed by an additional, small order for eighteen aircraft as part of the same *Serie 0* (MM096100-086117).

Compared to the orders placed with FIAT and AerMacchi, these numbers were very small and it was not until 25 January 1943 that the Ministry issued a first purchase order for 100 RE.2005.

In February 1943 there was a meeting at Reggiane with a high-ranking member of the P.N.F. (*Partito Nazionale Fascista* – National Fascist Party) to explore the possibility of increasing production of the RE.2005. During this meeting, Reggiane workers did not fail to complain about the treatment of their aircraft when compared to that of FIAT. Their complaints, as well as the prospect of leaving several thousand workers idle, led to the decision to increase the order to 400 aircraft and in April 1943 to increase it further to 750 aircraft. Furthermore, there was the possibility of entrusting construction of the RE.2005 to other companies, including C.A.B. of Bergamo, part of the Caproni Group.

In the meantime, while production of the first series of aircraft had commenced, the second prototype, MM495, was subjected to some modifications, the most important of which was the installation of an original German DB 605 A-1 engine fitted with a German VDM propeller with MW-50 injection system, and replacing the two 12.7 mm machine guns with two 20 mm cannon. Commencing 10 June 1943, the tests produced performance better than the original version of the prototypes powered by Italian built DB 605. It seems that MM495 reached a speed of around 720 km/h (though a more credible figure is around 700 km/h). The aircraft was later passed to the Luftwaffe and sent to the *Erprobungsstelle* at

---

[6] See also this author's *Macchi Fighters* and *FIAT Aeritalia Fighters*, both Crecy Publishing.

[7] This possibility was realised the following year with the construction of two prototypes of the FIAT G.56. For further information see the author's *FIAT Aeritalia Fighters,* Crecy Publishing, 2024.

[8] In reality, eighteen aircraft in these series were produced, as MM092359 was also built.

Continues on page 202

Below and following two pages: The second prototype, MM495. This aircraft was slightly different to the first prototype, being fitted with a German engine and propeller, which involved the installation of a different and larger spinner, which looks to be from a Bf 109 F or G. Note the RE.2001 in the background.

M.M.495

Another photograph of RE.2005, MM092352, photographed at Reggio Emilia in 1943.

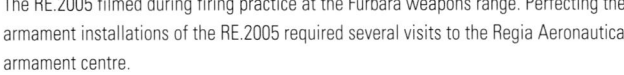

The RE.2005 filmed during firing practice at the Furbara weapons range. Perfecting the armament installations of the RE.2005 required several visits to the Regia Aeronautica armament centre.

The paddle-bladed VDM propeller and asymmetrically hung bomb identify this aircraft as MM495, photographed during tests at Guidonia.

Rechlin but after that, its tracks are lost. The tenth aircraft from *Serie 0*, (MM092352), which originally had been planned to feature the complete armament fit, comprising three cannon and two machine guns, was used for the final setting up of weapons at Furbara, while MM09108 was used to test ventral attachments for bombs or auxiliary tanks.

Production of the two *Serie 0* batches continued slowly, to the point that on 8 September, apart from the two prototypes, Reggiane had completed and delivered to Regia Aeronautica only thirty fighters from *Serie 0*, with the final five still incomplete at Reggio Emilia. With the German occupation of the factory, production of the *Sagittario* was suspended and of the eighteen aircraft of the second tranche of *Serie 0* still under construction, only thirteen were subsequently completed, with the last RE.2005, MM096112, flight-tested on 4 January 1944 by De Prato.

Mention should be made of Sweden's interest in the fighter, which put forward the intention to purchase around fifty aircraft without engines, since Swedish industry had the licence to build the propeller, but the negotiations did not materialise.

Production of the *Sagittario* can be summarised as follows:

- 2 prototypes MM494 / MM495
- 17 *Serie 0* aircraft assigned MM092343 to MM092359
- 13 *Serie 0* aircraft assigned MM096100 to MM096112*

* This production series included eighteen aircraft, but the remaining five RE.2005, which were assigned MM096113 to MM096117, were never completed.

Silvio Casarotto was another skilled Reggiane test pilot. After completing his engineering studies in 1935, he served as a pilot with the 7° *Stormo Bombardieri* and joined Reggiane in 1938 with dual flying and workshop duties. He took part in flight-testing all Reggiane types.

An engine failure, while being flown by *tenente colonnello* Angelo Tondi, on 23 September 1942 resulted in MM494 making its second emergency landing. MM494 is easily recognised because it was the only RE.2005 to carry the oval Reggiane logo on its fin. Roberto Longhi is present wearing jacket and sunglasses.

Technical aspects

The Reggiane RE.2005 was an all-metal, cantilever, single-seat, single engine monoplane.

The fuselage was of monocoque construction in duralumin, with a stressed skin covering its airframe which was formed of bulkheads and stringers.

The wing, constructed in one piece from duralumin, was elliptical in planform with a biconvex variable profile of decreasing thickness. It comprised three spars, sheet, stamped ribs with holes to lighten the structure, corrugated sheet metal and stringer reinforcement on the upper section, reinforcing stringers on the lower sections, and detachable wingtips attached by screws. Its construction of a single piece, with the exception of the two extremities, enabled the elimination of the junction between a central section and the outer wings, reducing weight and manufacturing time.

The two ailerons (the left-hand aileron had a trim tab adjustable on the ground) were of duralumin and were fabric clad: they were compensated statically and dynamically. The flaps were split flaps, and extended from one aileron to the other, passing under the fuselage.

The cantilever tailplanes had an elliptical form and were also of fabric-clad metal. The fin was slightly offset to compensate for the propeller torque.

Fuel was contained in four independent, self-sealing tanks positioned in the wings. The two forward tanks each had a capacity of 160 litres, while the aft tanks had a 108-litre capacity. Lubrication oil was contained in a wing tank with a capacity of 45 litres installed ahead of the first spar and partially housed in the leading edge of the wing. Between the two lateral fuel tanks, at the centre of the wing, was the position of the water and oil radiators, which were combined into a single block, but which functioned separately.

The position of the radiators beneath the fuselage enabled them to be invested directly by

Continues on page 214

A comparison of the fuselages of the RE.2005 (to rear) and RE.2001 (at front).

Before the production line was ready, both batches of 'Series 0' aircraft were built by the Reggiane *Reparto Sperimentale*.

Sagittario wings at different stages of assembly.

The RE.2005 split flap. Unlike those mounted on other Reggiane fighters, which comprised four pieces, on the *Sagittario* there were only two pieces, the wing formed of one piece.

Detail of the RE.2005 starboard aileron.

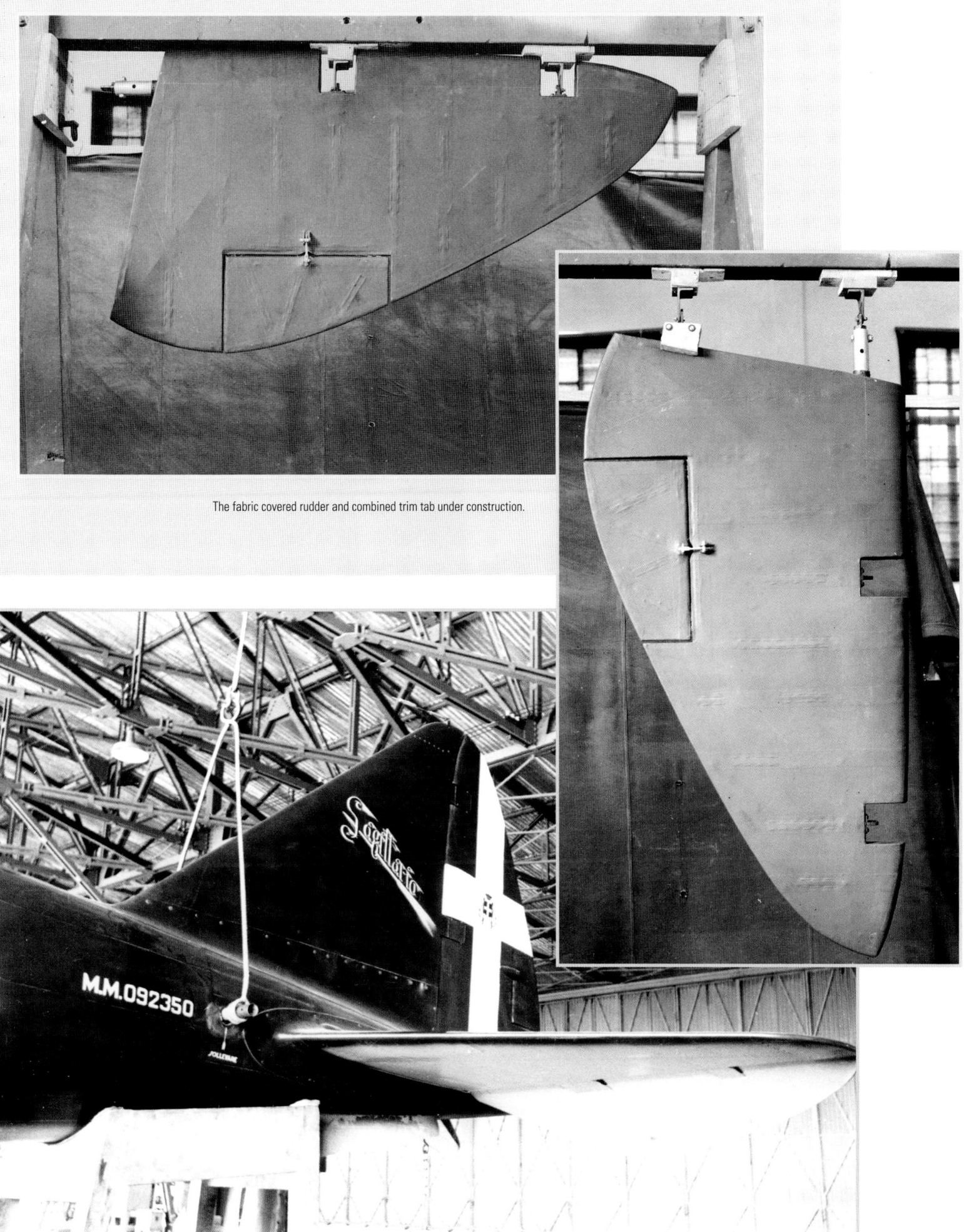

The fabric covered rudder and combined trim tab under construction.

Tail section of the Reggiane RE.2005. Note the lifting points, military serial number (MM092350) and the *Sagittario* inscription on the fin.

Frontal view of the fighter showing the coolant and oil radiator mounted under the fuselage in the ventral position.

Although apparently a single unit, the large ventral scoop actually held two radiators, each with its own exhaust flap. The larger radiator is for engine coolant, the other for oil. A number of slots are also visible.

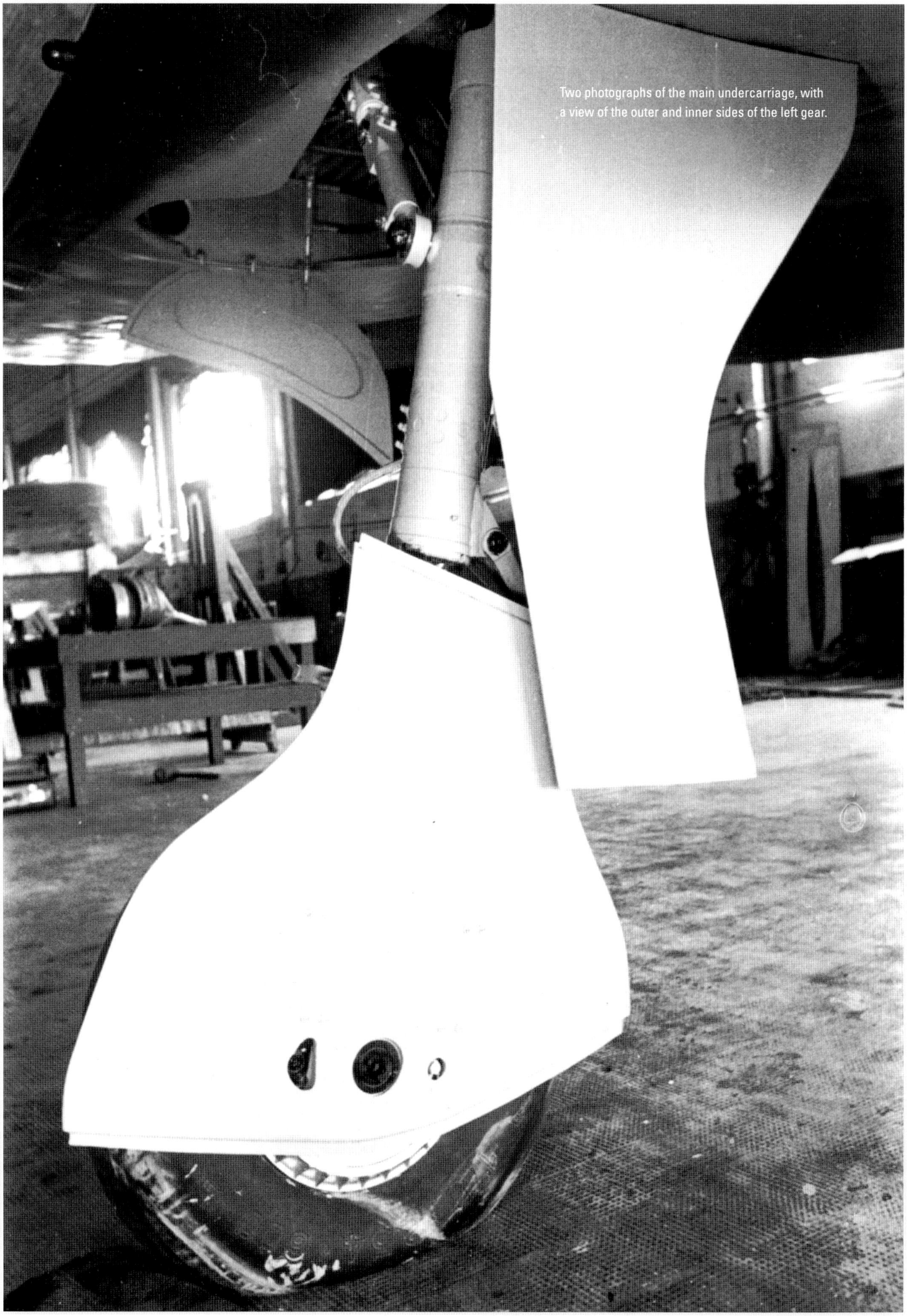

Two photographs of the main undercarriage, with a view of the outer and inner sides of the left gear.

A view of the inner sides of the starboard gear.

The retractable rear tailwheel of the *Sagittario*.

The arrangement of the RE.2005 landing gear differed completely from that of previous Reggiane fighters and offered a much simplified retraction movement. The complex geometry of the leg fairings and welded wheel fork are in evidence in this photograph of the RE.2005, MM09352, which served with R.S.I. in 1944.

Above, below and following page: Views of the 1,475-hp Fiat RA.1050 RC.58I *Tifone* engine. The *Tifone* was the German Daimler-Benz DB 605 engine built under licence. It equipped all the 'Series 5' fighters including the RE.2005 as, FIAT G.55 *Centauro*, AerMacchi M.205N *Orione* (which did not enter production), and also the C.205V *Veltro*.

Caption – See previous page.

the airflow generated by the propeller. The water-cooling tank was fixed to the forward part of the engine.

The undercarriage was a completely new design, departing from the usual undercarriages seen on previous Reggiane aircraft, with mechanical retraction and under-wing housings. Designed by *ingegner* Giovanardi, the RE.2005 undercarriage retracted completely into the wing, and was actioned hydraulically. It was formed by two independent main undercarriage legs retracting outwards in the direction of the wingtips and housed in a bay located between the first and second spars, entirely contained within the thickness of the wing. Once the wheels were retracted the ventral fuselage bay was closed by two doors actioned automatically by the return of the articulated support itself.

Above: Photograph taken on 23 September 1942, on the field at Reggio, of the first prototype of the *Sagittario*, MM494. The accident occurred during flight tests, but did not cause excessive damage to the aircraft, nor were there any consequences for the pilot *colonello* Angelo Tondi, a member of the Commission sent by the Ministry.

This new landing gear configuration allowed a significant reduction in aerodynamic drag on the wing, as well as an appreciable reduction in weight. The tailwheel was steerable, and its retraction was oleo-dynamically controlled, the wheel rotating backwards simultaneously with the retraction of the main undercarriage. It could also be blocked by the pilot if desired, and an automatic device, coupled to the undercarriage leg, remained locked at the moment of landing to avoid the potential danger of a yaw.

The powerplant, mounted in a milled duralumin frame, was a liquid-cooled Daimler-Benz DB 605 A-1 12-cylinder, inverted-V engine, providing 1,475-hp at take-off, constructed under licence by FIAT under the designation RA 1050 RC 58 'Tifone'. It drove a three-bladed metal Piaggio P.6001 propeller with variable pitch in flight.

Engine start was conducted through an electrical inertia starter mounted on the engine. Hand-starting was possible by actioning the starter through a handle inserted on the right-hand side of the engine. The propeller pitch control was located alongside the throttle, the latter being formed by a lever with a switch for the insertion of +100 boost.

The cockpit was particularly well designed and had the standard instrumentation for Italian fighters of the period, including a Patin telecompass and a San Giorgio reflector gunsight. It was enclosed by a three-part windscreen, together with a canopy with laterally sliding glazing and two panels above (three in the prototypes), opening laterally to the right and similar to those installed in the G.55 and MC.205V. The pilot was further protected by an anti-roll-over structure contained in classic fairing at the rear of the cockpit. The seat was armoured, made from standard 8 mm KEZ steel plate, and was height-adjustable.

Armament comprised two 12.7 mm Breda SAFAT machine guns installed in the fuselage over the engine and synchronised to fire through the propeller disc; a 20 mm Mauser MG 151/20 cannon mounted frontally and firing through the propeller boss; and two MG 151/20 cannon installed in the wing firing outside the propeller disc. The guns were fired by the pilot actioning a dedicated switch on the control column. Munitions supply comprised 350 rounds for the machine guns and 200 rounds for each cannon. Firing and rearming the machine guns was achieved by a flexible cable fitted with pneumatic servocontrols, while firing and rearming the cannons was completely electrical. The round counter was also electrical.

For combat, the pilot was provided with a San Giorgio type C free vision reflector gunsight.

Moreover, the aircraft possessed a ventral hard point installed in an asymmetric position capable of carrying up to 1,000 kg of stores and two wing points for bombs of a maximum weight of 160 kg or supplementary fuel tanks each containing 100 litres. The stores release control was electrical and actioned by the pilot by another switch mounted on the control column grip.

The radio installation comprised an Allocchio Bacchini B.30 transceiver powered by the on-board battery, the apparatus positioned in the fuselage behind the pilot. The electrical system was fed by a 24 V current provided by two Tudor batteries.

Continues on page 224

Above and below left: Engine covers for the RE.2005.

Above and opposite page: Two clear views of the *Sagittario* cockpit.

Above: Left side of the
M494 prototype cockpit
with the throttle system.

Right: The right side of the
RE.2005 cockpit with radio
and oxygen tube. Note also
the open canopy.

Seen here is the final canopy style, the 'Blenheim pattern' radio mast and the various inspection hatches around the cockpit area. The stencilling was seldom seen on operational machines.

In addition to showing the length of the nose, this view illustrates the troughs of the two 12.7 mm machine guns. The Regia Aeronautica asked that the air intake be fitted with a sand filter, but there is no photographic evidence that this was ever installed.

An overall view of the engine installation and the two Breda SAFAT 12.7 mm machine guns.

Detail of the gun barrel on the wing leading edge.

Left: The S.Giorgio *Tipo* B gunsight. The Reggiane RE.2005 was equipped both with *Tipo* B and *Tipo* C *tuffo* types.

The wing-mounted 20 mm Mauser MG 151/20 cannon.

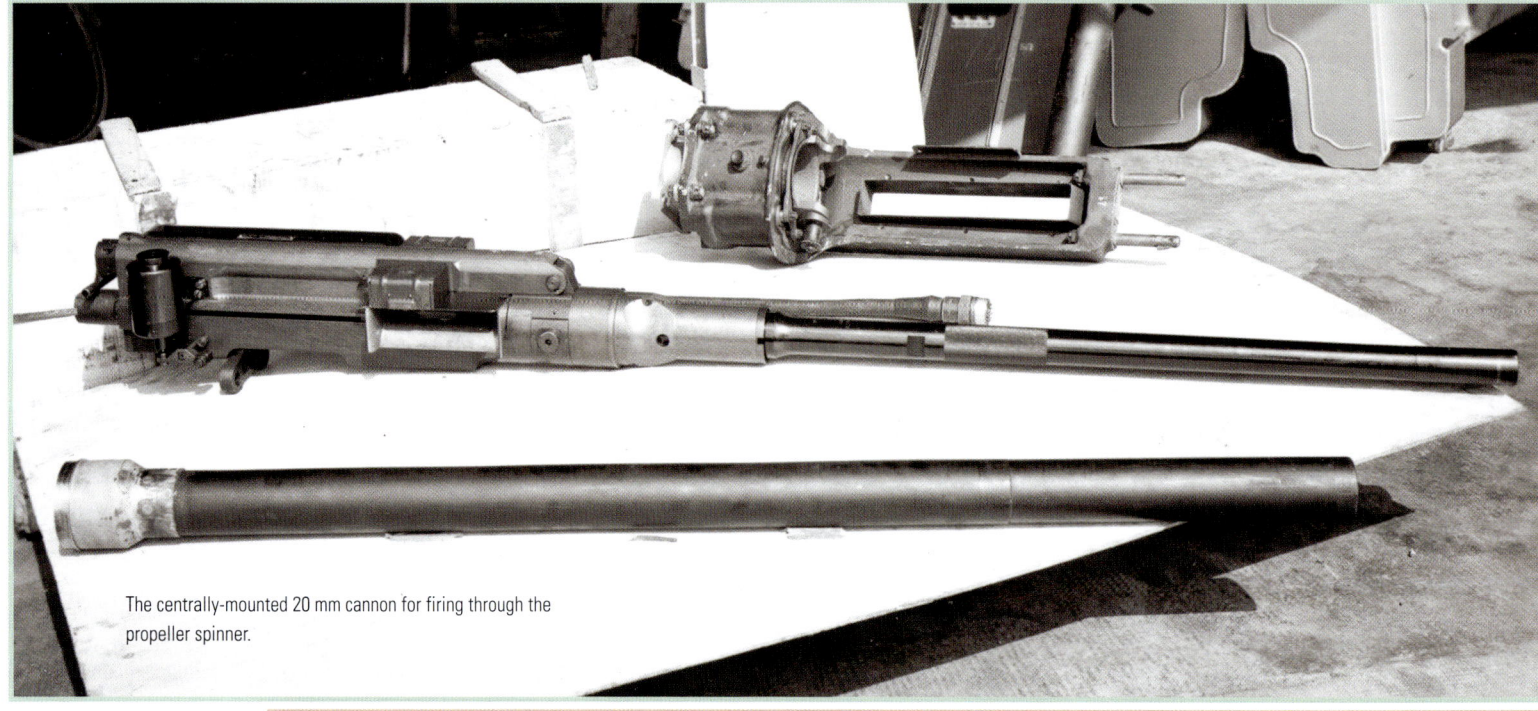

The centrally-mounted 20 mm cannon for firing through the propeller spinner.

Right: The Breda SAFAT 12.7 mm machine gun as used in the wing of the RE.2005. At left is a S. Giorgio Type C gunsight.

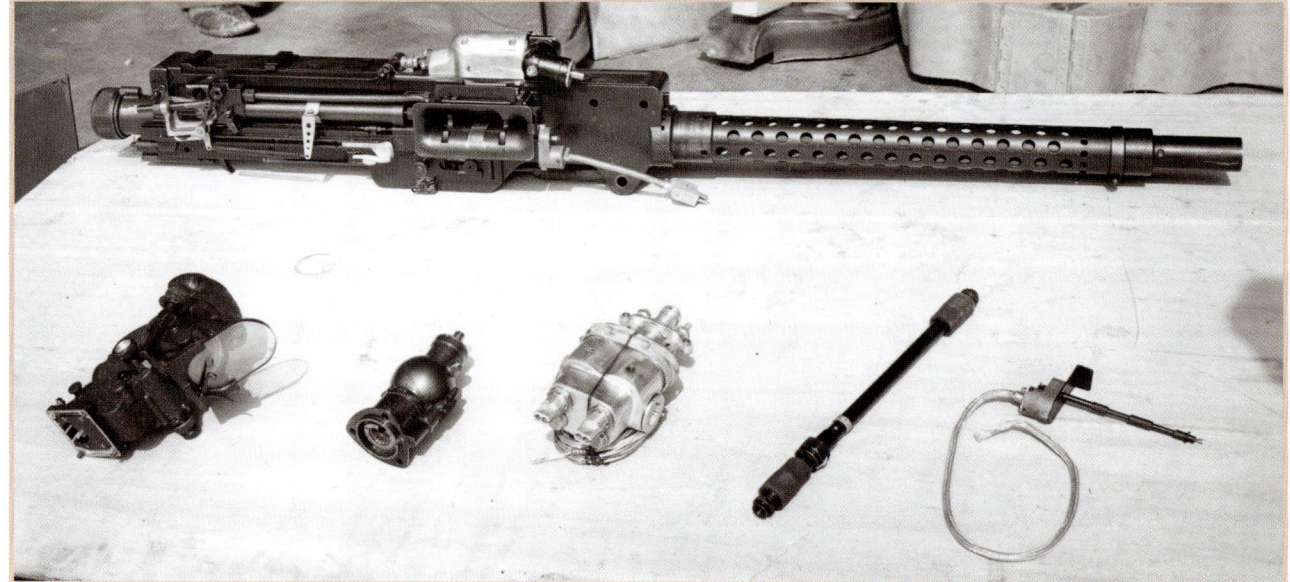

Above and below: A large bomb rack was mounted on the central joist of an RE.2005. The shift of the joist axis to the right, in relation to the fuselage axis, was due to the encumbrance of the water-oil radiator assembly.

RE.2005 Technical Data *

Length	8.91 m
Height	3.15 m
Wingspan	11.00 m
Wing area	20.25 sq.m.
Empty weight	2,600 kg
Total weight	3,600 kg
Engine	FIAT RA. 1050 RC58 *Tifone* 1,475 hp
Maximum speed	629 km/h at 7,000 m
Minimum speed	136 km/h
Range	1,250 km
Climb to 2,000 m	1'35"
Climb to 4,000 m	5'30"
Climb to 6,000 m	7'59"
Ceiling	12,000 m
Take-off run	200 m
Landing run	300 m
Weapons	2 x 12.7 mm SAFAT machine guns;
	3 x 20 mm MG 151/20 cannon;
	max. 1,160 kg of war payload

* Data from *Reggiane RE.2005 Catalogo Nomenclatore Iª Serie* – 1943

The ventral hard point installed in an asymmetric position was capable of carrying 1,000 kg of bombs or a drop tank.

In service with the Regia Aeronautica

The first RE.2005s to be delivered to the Regia Aeronautica were assigned to *maggiore* Vittorio Minguzzi's 22° *Gruppo Aut*. CT between April and May 1943, based at Napoli-Capodichino, Capua and Littoria airfields: the *gruppo* parented the 359ª, 362ª, 369ª and 150ª *Squadriglia*.

Maggiore Vittorio Minguzzi, commander of 22° *Gruppo*, when based at Naples Capodichino in 1943. He was an ace of the Regia Aeronautica, credited with three victories during the Spanish Civil War and another six confirmed during the Second World War of which three were B-24 bombers. He claimed other victories in Russia, but they could not be confirmed.

With the first aircraft received, the pilots of the 22° *Gruppo Aut*. CT were quickly engaged in the defence of Napoli, their baptism of fire being recorded on 2 April 1943 when *maggiore* Minguzzi took off in one of the first operational RE.2005s together with some twenty C.202s, tasked with intercepting American bombers. Flying faster than the *Folgores*, Minguzzi was the first to launch an attack on the bombers. On his return, he claimed the destruction of a B-24, although the USAAF reported no losses on that mission.

Some days later, on 28 April, twelve fighters from the 22° *Gruppo Aut*. CT, among which were at least three RE.2005s, scrambled to confront another bomber formation. *Maggiore* Minguzzi, flying in one of three *Sagittarios*, recalled the encounter, which saw him carry out an emergency landing after his aircraft was hit by fire from one of the bomber's gunners:

Personnel of 362ª *Squadriglia* proudly display a shield depicting their unit emblem damaged by machine gun fire. The emblem originated from the summer of 1941 when it was designed by *sottotenente* Giuseppe Biron before the transfer of the 22° *Gruppo* to Russia.

The prototype MM494 photographed at Napoli Capodichino. The fighter was assigned to 362ª *Squadriglia* of the 22° *Gruppo*.

Ground crew of 362ª *Squadriglia* working on a fighter coded 362-9 at Napoli Capodichino airport.

A machine of 362ª *Squadriglia* at Littoria in May 1943, coded 362-8, from where the type operated as an interceptor in the defence of Rome.

'*The alarm was timely and when we spotted the enemy formation, it was at an altitude of 7,000 metres. It consisted of two wedges in a line, each with three sections of five aircraft, still over the sea, far from the coast.*

'*Starting the approach for attack, I executed a dive and approached in a slight climb against the aircraft in the centre of the first formation. I felt it was going to be a good day – hard to say why; it was just a feeling.*

'*When the four-engine bomber was perfectly centred in my gunsight, I opened fire with all guns, firing from as far out as I could. A trail of tracers followed me along my escape route, and I saw the bomber flanking me to the left and then overtaking me, falling away below. A B-24 left the formation, drifting; there was not a wisp of smoke, but I noticed four parachutes as the aircraft continued its descent towards the sea. I regained altitude and repeated my attempts on the four-engine bombers. The RE.2005 manoeuvred well at all times and I had no trouble regaining contact with the enemy formation. The only difficulty was to remain calm, in order to be able to set up each new attack. It was virtually impossible to miss. I could see my volleys hitting the wings, disappearing into the engine cowlings, and shattering the cockpit. However, one has to get very close, too close to keep calm, and there was never enough time to fire effective bursts. Yet another lunge with ever-increasing speed when, suddenly, the RE.2005 begins to vibrate and the stick slips out of my hand due to the intensity of the vibrations.*

'*Moment of panic, a feverish look at the instruments and gauges. I realised that I had been hit in the engine by a burst that had knocked out the cooling system. The temperature quickly rose above the safety limit, and I immediately reduced the engine to avoid the danger of fire. I came out of the dive and the aircraft seemed to obey. I thought about bailing*

out, but the situation did not seem so critical. I therefore decided to glide back home, since I had sufficient altitude and the coast was close. The RE.2005 did not let me down, and I managed to get myself above the airfield, spiralling gently. I reached a suitable altitude for the final turn. I lowered the undercarriage and positioned myself for landing even though I realised that I was too fast! However, I had no margin for manoeuvre because without an engine, I could do nothing but rely on God's benevolence. I hit the ground and started braking desperately, trying to slow down the landing run of my Reggiane. I arrived at the end of the runway and to avoid crashing into the RUNA building positioned at the end of the field in the direction of my landing, I gave a sharp stamp to the pedal, diverting the fighter's course to the left.

The RE.2005 executed a perfect semi-circle and, bouncing slowly, reduced speed and came to a halt without any other problems. I could not believe the luck that had helped me, preventing the aircraft from being damaged badly. It was easily repairable at our SRAM, coming back on-line days later.

'*I got out of the cabin, my legs still shaking, and the specialists rushed to congratulate me on my*

narrow escape. I immediately went to the flight line to wait for our other aircraft engaged in the action. An eternity!

'*For the first time, I really realised what it was like waiting for "our" return. They returned in small numbers – two were missing. Two B-24s were claimed shot down (Donati and Minguzzi) and three others were declared probably shot down. The action was mentioned in the War Bulletin (of the following day), which confirmed the destruction of four four-engine bombers.*'[9]

At the end of May 1943, two weeks after the 22° *Gruppo* lost its *Autonomous* status as assigned to 42° *Stormo Intercettori*, at least nine RE.2005s were on strength, the majority of which were serviceable and to be used in the defence of the cities of Roma and Napoli.

Having received the first *Serie 0* RE.2005s, the unit had just time to become operational by early July before it was ordered to relocate the 362ª *Squadriglia*, commanded by *capitano* Germano La Ferla, and all the operational RE.2005s (around ten) to Catania Sigonella airfield, so as to reinforce the precarious situation facing the Italian fighter force given the imminent Allied landing in Sicily.

But within just a few days after its arrival in Sicilia, the 362ª *Squadriglia* was battered by the

[9] The combat account of *maggiore* Minguzzi is taken from the *Storia degli Aerei* Reggiane, published by GAE Editore in 1984 and with the generous permission of the editor, the late *sig.* Giorgio Apostolo.

OPERATION HUSKY

THE Allied landing in Sicilia, code name 'Husky' was a major development in Italy's war and the ultimate fate of the country. Since 10 June 1940, Italy had experienced appalling conditions: area bombing and destruction, black-outs, food rationing, hunger and curfews. Such factors directly affected the daily lives of those Italians not engaged on the battlefronts in Greece, Africa, and in the Balkans.

Sicily landings

The invasion of Italy was possible thanks to a series of events which occurred in the preceding months, including the Allied conquest of Tunisia in May 1943, the subsequent capture of the island of Pantelleria on 11 June 1943, and a series of heavy bomber raids on Sicilian cities and the island's military infrastructure that preceded

American troops wade ashore near Licata, Sicily, from a barge after being ferried from an outlying LST (Landing Ship, Tank) on 10 July 1943. (U.S. Signal Corps/National Archives, Washington, D.C.)

the landings. These took place between 10 and 13 July 1943, and saw 180,000 British, American and Canadian troops come ashore on the Sicilian coast between Licata and the Isola della Maddalena. This extraordinary military operation, involving vast numbers of air and naval assets, was exceeded only by the Allied landings in Normandy just under a year later, on 6 June 1944. In a span of around ten days, the Allied armies progressively conquered the island without having to face strong or organised resistance. The Italian Army melted away, although it had been supported by German forces, and over the coming weeks all the principal Sicilian cities were taken by the Allies, opening the way for the invasion of the Italian mainland and the European continent. A consequence of the Allied landing was the decision, taken on 25 July, by the Fascist *Gran Consiglio* to betray Mussolini, resulting in the fall of his government and leading to the armistice, which was signed at Cassibile near Siracusa on 3 September 1943 and announced on the following 8 September. It signalled the end of hostilities between Italy and the Anglo-Americans, and the beginning of the end of the Second World War.

bombing which preceded the Allied landings and which struck hard at the airfields situated on the Catania plain. The unit suffered the loss of at least four aircraft as a result of American bombs. Considering the destruction at Sigonella airfield, the six surviving RE.2005s of the

Squadriglia were moved on 9 July to Catania Fontanarossa, the only airfield that offered the possibility, albeit limited, for operations to continue.

On 11 July 1943, the *Sagittarios* of the 362ª *Squadriglia* had their baptism of fire in the skies over

Sicilia when, during the morning, some Reggianes clashed with Spitfires inbound from Malta, above Siracusa. At the end of the encounter, *tenente* Giulio Torresi claimed the destruction of an enemy fighter and another probable, shot down between Siracusa and Capo Passero. Unfortunately, during the action

The RE.2005, MM092344, damaged on landing at Capodichino on 13 June 1943. Pilot *maresciallo* Arduini was uninjured.

the unit's first loss was recorded with the death of *sottotenente* Traiano Dilissano in a flying accident, probably resulting from a malfunction in the oxygen supply system.

In the afternoon of the same day, five RE.2005s were involved, together with some *Veltros*, in another dogfight with RAF Spitfires from Nos.111 and 243 Squadrons near Siracusa. *Capitano* La Ferla, *maresciallo* Tullio Arduini and *tenente* Edoardo Vaghi each claimed the destruction of a Spitfire. Lost during the action, however, was the RE.2005 of *tenente* Luigi Nitolia, while the *Sagittario* of *tenente* Eugenio Salvi was badly damaged and Salvi was forced to make an emergency landing at Fontanarossa.

After the war Salvi described the bitter encounter:

'In the early hours of the afternoon of 11 July, a formation of five RE.2005s, led by capitano *La Ferla and split into two sections, was ordered to escort RE.2002 dive-bombers tasked to fly an attack operation in the ports of Augusta or Siracusa.*

'When we rendezvoused, we noted that the bombers and escorting G.50s were already heavily engaged with several Spitfire IXs. Capitano *La Ferla, followed by* tenente *Vaghi and* maresciallo *Arduini, threw himself into the fight. I, with my very young wingman,* tenente *Gigi Nitolia, who was on his first combat mission, followed them. However, looking around, I noticed flights of Spitfires which were higher than us and which were catching up with us. I broke off my dive and climbed up towards the Spitfires with the intention of blocking them from reaching the others, which were engaging aggressively with the RE.2002s and G.50s.*

'Before taking off, I had ordered Nitolia, aware of his inexperience and above all of his fiery enthusiasm, not to break away from me, and to view the flight like those which, in formation, we had performed at Rimini when I was his instructor. I was very aware just how dangerous and omnipresent the enemy fighters were.

'But tenente Nitolia, seeing that we had abandoned our other three colleagues, made a diving turn to the right, perhaps thinking that I wanted to withdraw from the dogfight, but I continued my dive to the left. I saw him pass below me and disappear into the distance, following a Spitfire, while below me two adversaries had suddenly appeared and were trying to get on my tail. For a moment I thought about running to help Gigi, but he was too far away, and then I found myself about to be surrounded by clusters of aircraft which were raining down on me, and I had to concentrate on defending myself. Looking for a final time at that small RE.2005, I said: "Ciao Gigi, we will not see each other again." And we never did see each other again. Nothing further was known about Nitolia. He had been betrayed by his keenness and his desire for combat.

Detail of an RE.2005 from 362ª *Squadriglia* at Naples Capodichino.

A factory-fresh Reggiane RE.2005 before delivery to the 362ª *Squadriglia* in a typical 'continental' scheme of dark green on upper surfaces with light grey under the wings.

'For me it was a fearful carousel. I saw and heard aircraft all around me. A huge fear of hitting someone or being hit came over me. I felt strangely safe from being hit because I was continually manoeuvring my RE.2005. No straight lines, but turns, climbs, dives, inversions, Derry Turns, continually and repeatedly. It was right then that the handling qualities of my aircraft proved to be marvellous and were an essential help to me.

'I did not want any of the numerous Spitfires to get me in their sights. During that eternal and tiring carousel, the speed of my RE.2005 varied between 240 and 100 km/h, but even at this low speed its controls responded promptly and faithfully. After – I've no idea how long, but a long time – I noticed that the fighting around me had gradually diminished, until eventually I could neither see nor hear anyone. Continually manoeuvring and turning, I looked to my rear, and there was an obstinate red spinner, just 20 metres away, and following me. I continued to turn tightly, and the Spitfire opened fire. I had never heard such a piercing, crackling sound. The noise of his machine guns was so

loud and rapid that it sounded like the noise produced when you tear a strong canvas. It was more rapid and louder than a perfect fart. His firing did not worry me. Our relative positions were such that as far as I was concerned his projectiles passed no less than two or three metres from my tail. But the Spitfire did not desist.

'In the turn I gained some degrees over him. But he was not interested in catching me, just not to lose me. But I wanted to break away because I was exhausted. Considering that the situation would not be resolved until one of us gave up, perhaps at the end of our endurance, and feeling that my weak physical condition would not permit me to sustain the fight for much longer, I decided to shorten the time by performing a manoeuvre that my adversary would not be able to follow, hopefully giving me the opportunity to disengage. While I was in a tight turn, I suddenly performed a violent roll, and stopped my aircraft on its side. The Spitfire pilot, surprised, was about to hit me. I saw his nose pointing at my cockpit at a distance of around four or five metres. I felt lost and

Above and right: Reggiane 2005, of 362ª *Squadriglia* of 22° *Gruppo*, 42° *Stormo Intercettori* at Littoria in June 1943, coded 362-9. This aircraft lacks unit insignia, and also has one-third of its propeller spinner painted white. The red and white codes across the fuselage band are standard. The national wing insignia are on clear roundels in four positions, and the standard *'Sagittario'* inscription is visible on the fin.

One of the few operational Sagittario of the 362ª *Squadriglia* of 22° *Gruppo* at Littoria (today known as Latina). The aircraft, coded 362-5, with military serial MM092347, has the famous *'Spauracchio'* (scarecrow) emblem painted on the white band fuselage.

instinctively twitched, waiting for the inevitable collision. But the Spitfire departed in a spin. That was what I wanted. I thought that his unintended manoeuvre would not be stopped quickly, thus allowing me to make my escape. I was mistaken. I was dealing with a pilot who had absolute mastery over his aircraft. He replicated my manoeuvre and stopped his aircraft in the same position in which he had

been earlier. We were turning again, and he was behind me.

I felt demoralised and exhausted. I felt that I would not be capable of continuing to pilot my aircraft. It was 18.00 hrs, and a splendid sun was at thirty degrees on the horizon, so I headed for it and slumped over the controls.

'My adversary immediately profited from my wavering and began to hit me. I heard his guns firing and saw that my starboard wing was seriously hit. I heard a loud explosion to my rear. My situation was so bad that I wanted any rapid solution to it, even of the worst kind. But that game of cat and mouse ended very early. After the violent strike on my tail, I heard no more firing. I waited a few seconds and then

A poor quality image of the few operational RE.2005s on the strength of 362ª *Squadriglia* at Littoria.

decided to look around. My friend was still there; I even had the impression that his red spinner was no more than five metres from my tail. I headed towards the sun. More time passed, and behind me there was absolute silence. My strength, in part, had returned.

'*I looked behind me. The Spitfire was not there! How come? Where had it gone? Why had it gone away, abandoning me when it had me in its grasp? I did not know how to respond. I waited for a few seconds and then began to glide back towards the airfield. I manoeuvred gently and at a low speed, as I did not know the state of the spar on the starboard wing, which had been hit repeatedly.*

'*I checked the damage to my aircraft with the mechanics. The wing damage was not severe, while the hits on the tail had produced holes in the skin and had broken some stringers, the repair to which would require time and equipment.*'[10]

On 12 July, *capitano* Torresi and *tenenti* Vaghi and Salvi were called into action, intercepting two Spitfires of No. 40 Squadron SAAF between Lentini and Pozzallo. Torresi shot down the Spitfire Mk V of Lt K. Robinson, who bailed out and was taken prisoner, while the other South African fighter, despite suffering damage, was able to recover to Malta.

On 13 July, some strafing missions were flown by the RE.2005s to attack advancing Allied troops.

During one of the final air engagements, near Catania Fontanarossa airfield, *capitano* Torresi was again involved in a victorious combat, managing to get on the tail of Spitfire Mk V, ES282, of No. 93 Squadron RAF, which was manoeuvring to attack the *Sagittario* of *tenente* Vaghi while he was approaching to land. Torresi shot it down and it crashed near the airfield, but the pilot managed to bail out and was taken prisoner. On 14 July, realising that it would be impossible to continue flying operations, *capitano* La Ferla ordered the ground personnel to return to the Italian mainland. The two surviving RE.2005s still in flying condition, piloted by *maresciallo* Arduini and *sergente maggiore* Lucio Biagini,

were transferred to Reggio Calabria airfield and reassigned to the 371ª *Squadriglia*, but were destroyed some days later following Allied bombing of the Calabrian airfield.[11]

On their arrival at Catania Fontanarossa, Allied forces discovered all that remained of at least five RE.2005s, three of which were identified as 362-4 MM494 (which was the first prototype built by Reggiane), 362-3 MM092346 and 362-7 MM092354.

After two weeks and clashes with British fighters, the *Squadriglia* returned to Napoli with its few remaining serviceable aircraft and was reunited with the 22° *Gruppo*.

One of the few *Sagittarios* still operating was destroyed in a flying accident on 20 July 1943 when, following a propeller fault, *maggiore* Minguzzi was forced to execute a disastrous emergency landing in which he was injured and his aircraft destroyed. He was replaced as commander of the 22° *Gruppo* by *capitano* Enzo Sant'Andrea.

At the end of July 1943, the 22° *Gruppo* possessed six or seven RE.2005s, of which at least four were combat ready. However, in August, the availability of Reggiane fighters fell sharply, aggravated by the temporary suspension of operational flights due to a series of structural problems found in the airframe, located in the tail and caused by abrupt manoeuvring.

Despite this, even with just a few aircraft in flying condition, the pilots of the 22° *Gruppo* courageously continued their operations with the Reggiane, and on 25 August 1943 a pair of *Sagittarios*, piloted by *tenenti* Salvi and Signorini, took off from Capodichino to confront an American formation flying over the gulf of Salerno. At the end of a brief fight, the aircraft flown by Signorini failed to return. After the pilot was recovered having bailed out of his aircraft, he revealed that his fighter had become uncontrollable following its well-known structural problems. Following this incident, some aircraft were sent to Reggiane to be modified to try to remedy this serious problem but a few days later, on the day of the armistice of 8 September 1943, the personnel of the 22° *Gruppo* destroyed the last seven aircraft of the unit, undeservedly ending the history of this beautiful but unfortunate fighter in the ranks of the Regia Aeronautica.

Photograph taken by the Allies after the occupation of Catania Sigonella airfield. Visible in the background is the wreckage of RE.2005, MM092346, 362-3.

---

[10] Combat testimony of *tenente* Salvi taken from *Storia degli Aerei Reggiane*, published by GAE in 1984, with the generous permission of the editor, the late sig. Giorgio Apostolo.

[11] Other Italian sources report that the two RE.2005s were taken safely to Capodichino.

The wreckage of the RE.2005, MM494 (the second prototype), after being assigned to 362ª *Squadriglia*. It made an emergency landing on 20 July 1943 due to a propeller problem, with *maggiore* Vittorio Minguzzi at the controls. The pilot was injured but survived the incident.

To conclude, an interesting opinion was given by *capitano* Giovanni Cervellin, a pilot in the 22° *Gruppo*:

'*The RE.2005 was a very good aeroplane, indeed, a "great" aeroplane. Its basic feature was the elliptically-shaped wing, thanks to which the aircraft behaved phenomenally well even at high altitude. It could go over 6,000 metres and fly, while the Macchi C.202 was a jewel of an aircraft, but its wing was too thin and too narrow, and therefore showed its best* characteristics at lower altitudes, while at higher elevations it presented some "inconveniences". The RE.2005 was also an excellent war machine for us. Although with the usual pair of 12.7 mm machine guns and three cannon, shooting was quite difficult for us, because when firing at the same time with all weapons, there was considerable kick-back. Initially, its speed astounded us; like the occasion when one of us flew from Reggio Emilia to a base near Milan, but was not able to see the city, despite his low altitude, clear sky and ... the unmistakable stretch of Milan! The fact is that his speed was so much higher than expected, that he had already passed the city by some distance, without realizing it, and only knew so when he was in sight of Lake Maggiore! And on the subject of speed, the pilot of an RE.2005 had to pay careful attention when diving, as there were several cases of torsion damage to the rear part of the fuselage, just before the tail, and this was one of the reasons why the availability of efficient aircraft with the Gruppo was never very high.'

In service with the A.N.R.

Following the armistice and the consequent state of confusion and uncertainty, the Germans requisitioned at least twelve *Sagittario* still under completion at the Reggiane factory, among which were the two prototypes. They instructed the Italian company to introduce some substantial modifications, including a reversal of the throttle control function. It seems that at least eight[12] of these aircraft were modified

and at least one, MM096105, was taken to Germany, where all traces of it were lost. These aircraft were used for some months by the *Luftdienst Kommando Italien* at Maniago (later redesignated as *Fliegerzielstaffel* 20). Of the little information available, it is known that at least three aircraft were lost or severely damaged in an Allied raid on 18 March 1944 (MM096100, 096106 and 096110), while three others were involved in

flying accidents which required repair at the factory. In the course of 1944, some RE.2005s were also delivered to the A.N.R. where they were little utilised because of the policy of standardising the fleets of the operational units. Those aircraft that were received were relegated to training and liaison activities under the auspices of the '*Reparto Aereo Collegamento*' at Bresso (Milano).

RE.2005, MM96109, of *Luftdienst Kommando Italien* based at Maniago in February 1944.

One of the few RE.2005s operated by the R.S.I. The handful of aircraft were not used operationally and served for a few months for advanced fighter training and liaison. This aircraft belonged to the *Reparto Aereo Collegamento* (RAC) based at Bresso (Milano) in March 1944.

---

[12] According to the diaries of the company's *Reparto Sperimentale*, the following appear to have been modified: MM096100, 096102, 096105, 096106, 096107, 096108, 096109 and 096110.

Additional photographs of the few RE.2005s operated by the R.S.I. The handful of aircraft were not used operationally and served for a few months for advanced fighter training and liaison. This aircraft belonged to the *Reparto Aereo Collegamento* (RAC) based at Bresso (Milano) in March 1944.

CHAPTER SEVEN

Projects unrealised

I N the wake of the RE.2005, Reggiane conducted studies of versions or variants of the aircraft using new engines or using the fighter's basic configuration for new projects.

In mid-1942, following difficulties with the supply of the DB 605 engine, the Regia Aeronautica approached the design office of Reggiane regarding a design for a new aircraft, identified by the designation **RE.2004,** powered by the 1,250-hp Isotta-Fraschini *Zeta* RC.25/60 engine. This engine was a 24 X-configuration motor built by the joining of two Isotta Fraschini Gamma engines, and was air-cooled. In early June 1942 Reggiane received an order from the Regia Aeronautica for the preparation of two prototypes (MM505 and MM506) and the production of an initial batch of twelve aircraft. Despite this, problems with the availability and functioning of the engine created delays and a re-evaluation, to the point that by the end of the year the order and the design had been abandoned. The possibility of re-engining the

design with the RE.103 engine, built by Reggiane, had also been explored, but again it came to nothing.

An interesting, if somewhat unrealistic design, was that of the **RE.2005 R,** a hybrid concept, not conceived by Reggiane itself, but by *maggiore* Antonio Ferri of the Genio Aeronautico. The bizarre design, developed on the basis of the *Sagittario*, saw the installation of an auxiliary FIAT 370-hp A.20 12-cylinder engine installed in a central position just aft of the cockpit. Coupled to the engines were two centrifugal compressors, the first to stabilise the pressure of the two engines (DB 605 and A.20) at altitude, and the second to provide supplementary thrust to the aircraft, transforming the engines into a kind of 'turbo-compound' thanks to the thrust produced. The overall power was estimated at 2,030 hp and the maximum speed, according to the calculations, would oscillate between 710 and 760 km/h at altitude, but the downside would be a reduction in

The design of the RE.2005 R project as a 'hybrid' aircraft was undertaken not by Reggiane, but by *maggiore* Antonio Ferri of the Aeronautical Engineers. The ingenious design of this aircraft, developed on the basis of the *Sagittario*, involved the installation of a 370 hp,12-cylinder FIAT A.20 auxiliary engine. However, the concept remained only on paper.

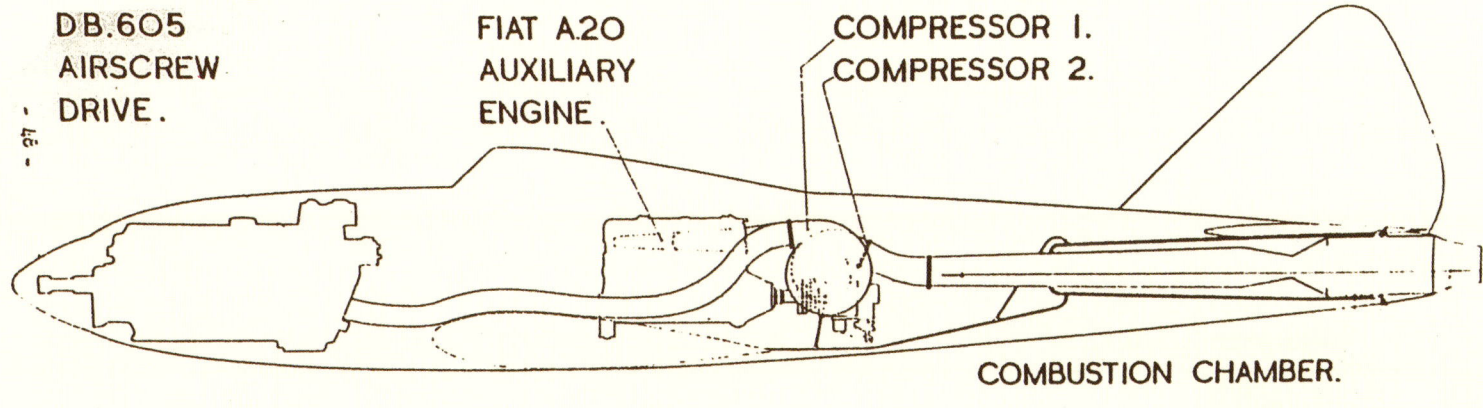

DB.605
AIRSCREW
DRIVE.

FIAT A.20
AUXILIARY
ENGINE.

COMPRESSOR I.
COMPRESSOR 2.

COMBUSTION CHAMBER.
IGNITERS.
EXHAUST.NOZZLE.

RE 2005 R. (PROJECT)

P.I. No. 1715.   14/8/4n

endurance together with a significant increase in the weight of the aircraft.

The selection of the RE.2005 airframe as the basis for the project originated from a series of technical reasons, amongst which was the fact that the Reggiane aircraft was considered the most easily modifiable in the light of the inevitable variation in the centre of gravity created by the supplementary engine.

Besides doubts about its feasibility and technical shortcomings, the design generated not a little perplexity at Reggiane, since to introduce the required modifications would have resulted in the need to redesign the fuselage. It is enough just to consider the challenge of installing a second engine and the compressors in the fuselage, let alone to modify the rear fuselage to house the exhaust pipe, without considering the fact that it would become essential to relocate the cockpit forward to introduce a minimum of stability to the aircraft. Fortunately, in some ways, the armistice of September 1943 brought an end to any further development of this unrealisable design.

Amongst the other projects which never came to fruition was a potential version of the RE.2005 built entirely of wood production with a twin-fuselage (**RE.2005 bifusoliera**). This aircraft, conceived as a heavy fighter similar to the SIAI Marchetti SM.92 and Caproni CA.380, was none other than two RE.2005 fuselages united by a central wing section with the cockpit positioned in the left-hand fuselage. The project, which was overseen by *ingegner* Giuseppe Maraschini, was to be powered by two standard 1,475-hp DB 605 engines, while the intended armament would be particularly heavy, comprising four 20 mm cannon together with two 12.7 mm machine guns and the ability to carry around 500 kg of stores. Despite being a tangible design, with a maximum speed of 680 km/h at 7,000 metres, it was not possible to develop the aircraft after the armistice.

Very different and far more achievable was the **RE.2006** design developed by the Reggiane Technical Office on the basis of the RE.2005 and which saw the utilisation of the more powerful 1,750-hp Daimler-Benz DB 603A engine, similar to that adopted by FIAT in the G.56 design.

The incorporation of the new German engine would have further improved the performance of the fighter and even though, externally, it appeared almost identical to the RE.2005, numerous and substantial modifications would have had to be introduced. The design, in fact, incorporated substantial modification to the wing, the introduction of integral fuel tanks similar to those of the RE.2000, but also the adoption of entirely water-filled radiators, similar to those trialled on the RE.2001 bis. Other detail modifications, besides those necessitated by the adoption of the new engine, involved the tailplane and the aircraft's mobile surfaces.

In the spring of 1943, the *Ministero* of the Regia Aeronautica approved the design and ordered the preparation of two prototypes, to which the serials MM540 and MM541 were

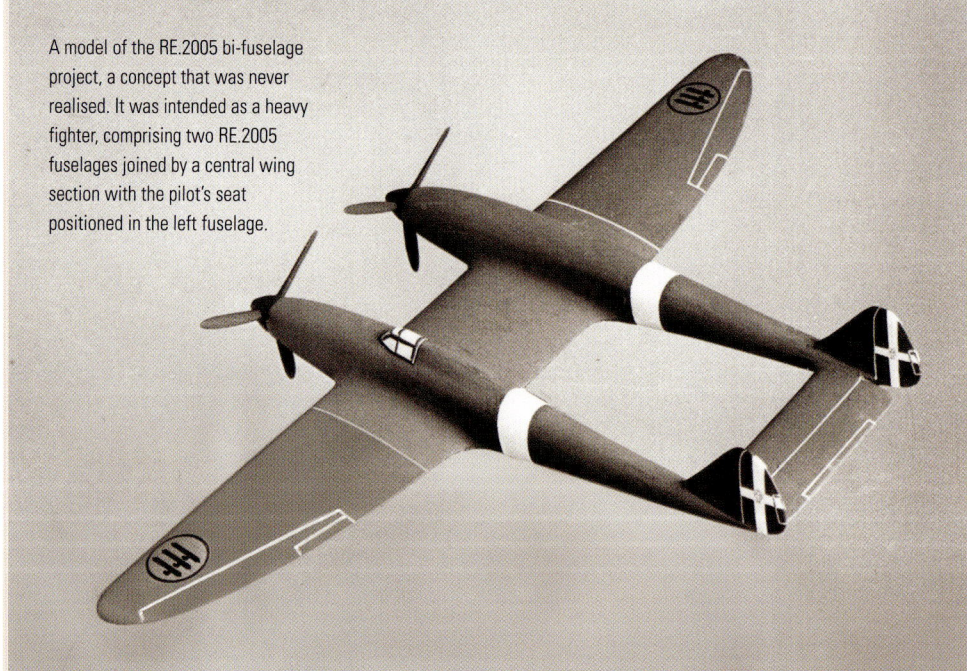

A model of the RE.2005 bi-fuselage project, a concept that was never realised. It was intended as a heavy fighter, comprising two RE.2005 fuselages joined by a central wing section with the pilot's seat positioned in the left fuselage.

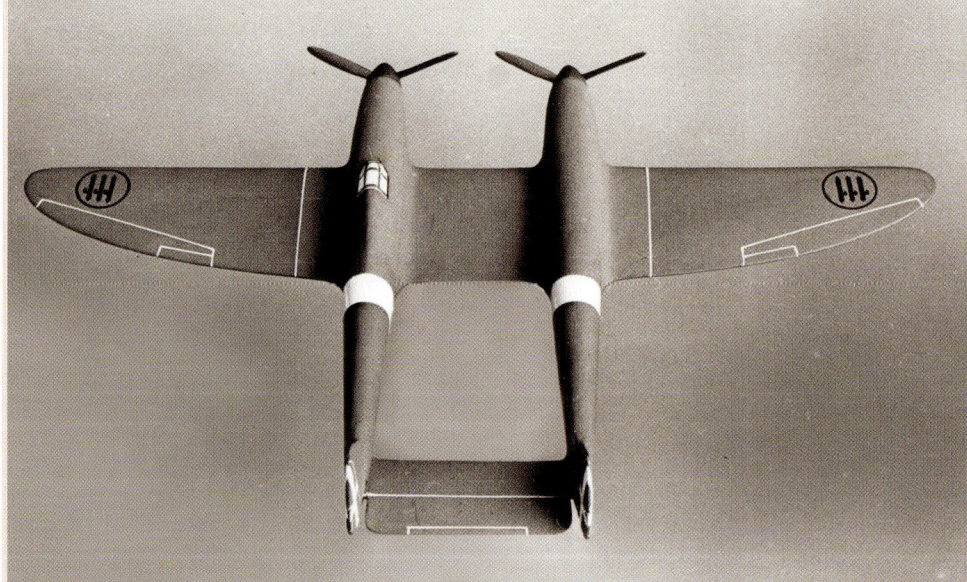

allocated. After the armistice of 8 September, and the assuming of control of Reggiane's activities on the part of the Germans, work on the construction of the prototype continued with the preparation of the wing, albeit provisionally combined with the fuselage of an RE.2005, which saw the completion of MM540 in February 1944. However, the progress of the war

resulted in a subsequent halt to the project and, eventually, it was abandoned. The RE.2006 prototype, which had never actually flown and which, by sheer chance, had ended up away from Reggiane, escaping the destruction caused by the bombing of the factory, was transferred to the Caproni facility at Taliedo at the end of 1944, where it remained at the end of the war.

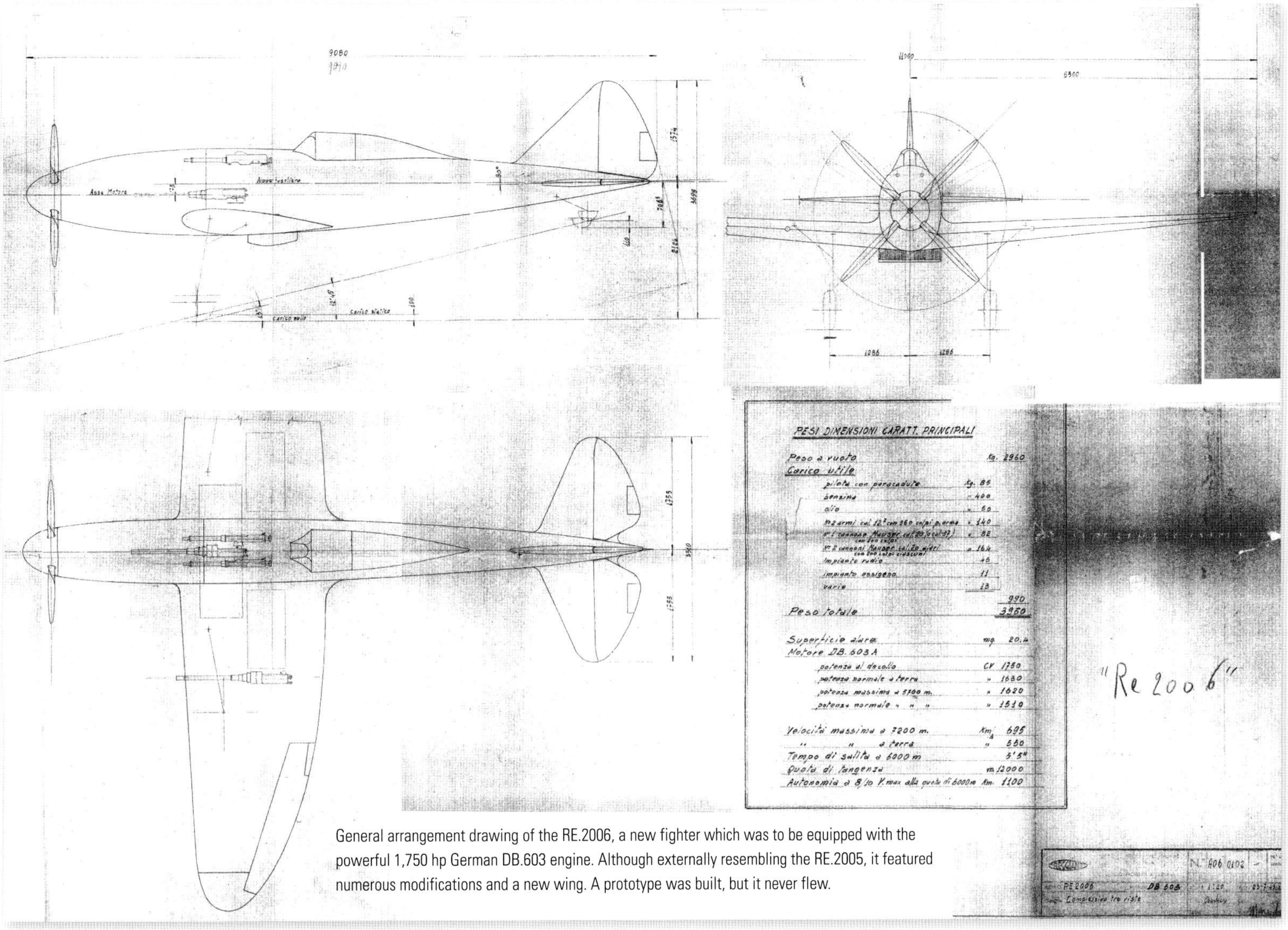

General arrangement drawing of the RE.2006, a new fighter which was to be equipped with the powerful 1,750 hp German DB.603 engine. Although externally resembling the RE.2005, it featured numerous modifications and a new wing. A prototype was built, but it never flew.

Left: The wooden model of the RE.2006PP, a post-war project for a single-engine aircraft for passenger and mail transport. However, the idea was not advanced further due to the cessation of all aeronautical work at Reggiane as required by the company's new management after the war.

see practical realisation, apart from as wooden models, because of the complete cessation of aviation activity by Reggiane post-war. This was a change brought about by the new company management board established in 1945 after the end of the war.

One first such design was the **RE.2006P** (*postale*), in practice an RE.2006 with an American 1,500-hp radial engine capable of carrying a payload of 1,100 kg. Another potential design was the **RE.2006C**, a 'racing' version intended for participation post-war on the American speed-racing circuit. The **RE.2006PP** (passengers and post), was developed for passenger transport with a fuselage modified to carry six passengers and two crew together with 100 kg of postal mail. The planned engine would be the same as that fitted to the RE.2006P.

Subsequently, part of the aircraft was passed to the *Istituto di Aeronautica* of the Politecnico di Milano in May 1945 for practical training. It was dismantled over the course of the coming years.

In connection with the RE.2006, it is also worth noting designs which were in their early stages at the end of the war, and which would never advance beyond drawing stage, or never

Two photographs of the wooden model of the RE.2006 *'corsa'*, an aircraft that was intended for speed races in the USA after the war.

Right: This sketch, actually prepared after the war, has given rise to much speculation regarding the RE.2007 project for an alleged jet fighter designed by Reggiane. In reality, it was only speculation and nothing concrete.

Remaining in the field of diversification into the civilian arena, just prior to the end of the war the Reggiane Technical Office initiated studies for a large passenger transport, all-metal flying boat. Once again this design, which was designated the **Caproni CA.8000**, would never see any practical realisation following the end of the war.

To conclude, mention should be made of the more than controversial story of the **RE.2007**, a hypothetical jet aircraft, various rumours and information about which circulated in the immediate post-war period. Designs and sketches have also appeared, showing an aircraft with a swept-wing design and with a profile similar to that of the American and Soviet fighters from the end of the 1940s. To date, nothing concrete has been discovered about this project, and it remains solely the subject of rumours and drawings of dubious provenance.

A wooden model of the CA.8000, a project for a large seaplane for transatlantic flights, which also remained at early design stage.

CHAPTER EIGHT

Camouflage and Markings

By Paolo Waldis

Colours and Camouflage Schemes

Reggiane RE.2000

The prototype RE.2000 left the factory in 1939 with all surfaces left in natural metal and no paintwork, except for three green-white-red rudder stripes, which extended to the horizontal tailplanes. At a later stage the national insignia were completed by the addition of the wing fasces in four positions and a polychrome *'fascio'* on the engine cowling. **1.** Subsequently, the prototype was sent to Guidonia for evaluation tests, where it received a three-colour camouflage, as prescribed by the 1937 painting regulations, consisting of a soft-edged, green and brown mottled scheme on a sand yellow background. **2.** The wing roundels had black fasces on a white background on the wing upper surface and white fasces on black below. All production aircraft also received the same three-tone scheme, with *Verde Mimetico* (camouflage green) and *Marrone Mimetico* (camouflage brown) blotches on the *Giallo Mimetico* (camouflage yellow) background, while the lower surfaces were painted *Grigio Mimetico* (camouflage grey) overall. Besides the aircraft produced for the *Regia Aeronautica*, any machines exported to Sweden and Hungary eventually received the same three-tone factory scheme, obviously differing only in their respective national insignia. The only RE.2000s receiving different camouflage colours were the *'Catapultabili'*, for which the prototype displayed an experimental colour invariably described by all sources as overall light blue (of an undefined light shade, apparently different from any officially prescribed colour) on the side and upper surfaces, with the undersides seemingly painted *Grigio Azzurro Chiaro* (light blue-grey). **3.** This particular variant carried out two distinct cycles of tests respectively in 1941 and 1942, always maintaining the same colour scheme. All other production C*atapultabili* received, instead, the officially prescribed fighter scheme: overall *Verde Oliva Scuro* (dark olive green) on the sides and upper surfaces and *Grigio Azzurro Chiaro*

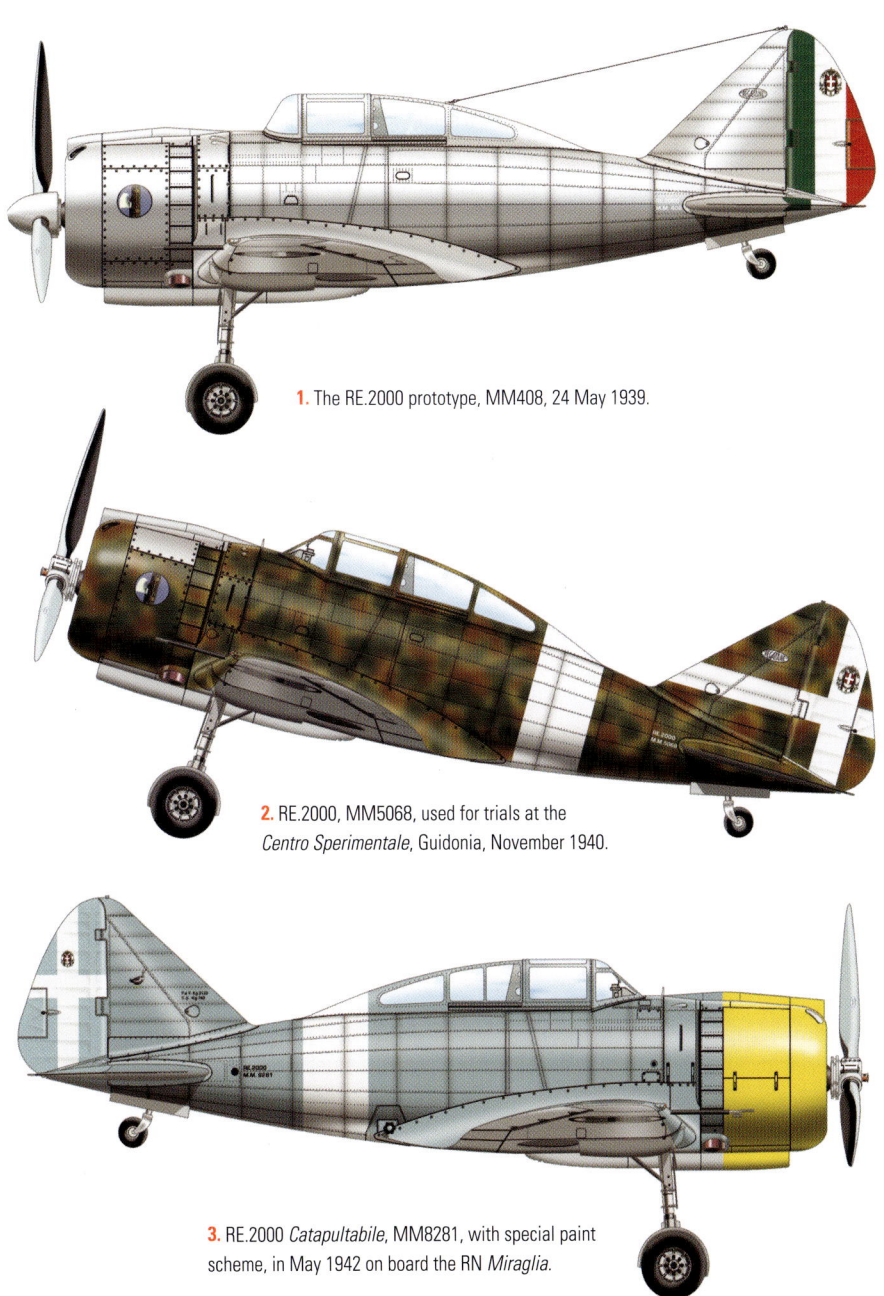

1. The RE.2000 prototype, MM408, 24 May 1939.

2. RE.2000, MM5068, used for trials at the *Centro Sperimentale*, Guidonia, November 1940.

3. RE.2000 *Catapultabile*, MM8281, with special paint scheme, in May 1942 on board the RN *Miraglia*.

on the lower surfaces. **4.** Once both testing cycles were completed, the same dark olive green scheme was also, probably, applied to the prototype, as it entered service beside the production machines. The type designator, production batch and military serial were all painted in white on the fuselages of the mottled aircraft and light blue on those finished in dark green, next to the tail. Even the RE.2000 *Heja* II, licence-built by Mavag in Hungary, originally received a three-tone colour scheme on the production line, very similar to the style displayed by Italian-built aircraft, possibly using colours of Italian origin. But, unlike the Italian aircraft, the separation line between the upper and lower surface colours ran along the centre line of the wing leading edge, instead of continuing under the centre line as traditionally done on most Italian aircraft. Eventually, in 1944, some *Heja* IIs were repainted in an overall dark green scheme with light grey undersides.

Reggiane RE.2001

The two RE.2001 prototypes, manufactured in 1940, were the only machines to receive the same three-tone camouflage scheme previously seen on all RE.2000s, with soft-edged blotches of *Verde Mimetico* and *Marrone Mimetico* on a *Giallo Mimetico* background, and the lower surfaces in *Grigio Mimetico*. **5.** At a later stage, all production aircraft, having been delivered after the camouflage reforms of July 1941, received, instead, the standard 'Schema Metropolitano' (home scheme) of *Verde Oliva Scuro* upper surfaces, with *Grigio Azzurro Chiaro* lower sides. **6.** The only exception were aircraft produced as nightfighters, these leaving the factory in an overall black scheme covering all upper and lower surfaces. After the Italian armistice of September 1943, a few aircraft based in Sardinia which later entered service with the so-called Co-belligerent Air Force, were overhauled and repainted, receiving a scheme quite similar to that used on the Macchi fighters. Curiously, these aircraft were the only ones to carry an 'A.S.' type scheme (for *Africa Settentrionale* – North Africa) consisting of a *Nocciola Chiaro* (light hazelnut brown) background with irregular *Verde Oliva Scuro* blotches. **7.** This type of camouflage was never applied at the factory to any Reggiane fighters, since they were never intended for service overseas. Wing insignia (fasces), as prescribed at the time, were black on a clear background, except for the camouflaged prototypes which, in typical Reggiane practice, were painted black on a white background above the wings and white on black below. Furthermore, the typical Reggiane trademark was painted white on the fin of all RE.2001s, comprising the name *Reggiane* inscribed within an elongated oval, best known as the 'Reggiane Cigar'. The type designator and military serial number were painted light blue on the fuselage, next to the tailplane. Finally, a few RE.2001s still in use after the war and used for liaison duties and for the weather service, were finished in an overall aluminium livery on all their surfaces. **8.**

4. RE.2000 *Catapultabile* of 1° *Gruppo* FF.NN on board the RN Roma, August 1943.

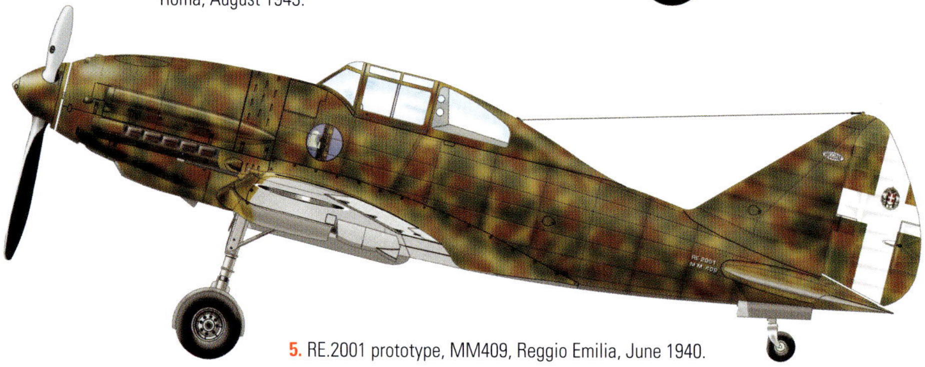

5. RE.2001 prototype, MM409, Reggio Emilia, June 1940.

6. RE.2001, MM7209, the personal aircraft of *tenente* Remo Cazzolli, 152ª *Squadriglia*, 2° *Gruppo Autonomo* CT, Santo Pietro di Caltagirone, May 1942.

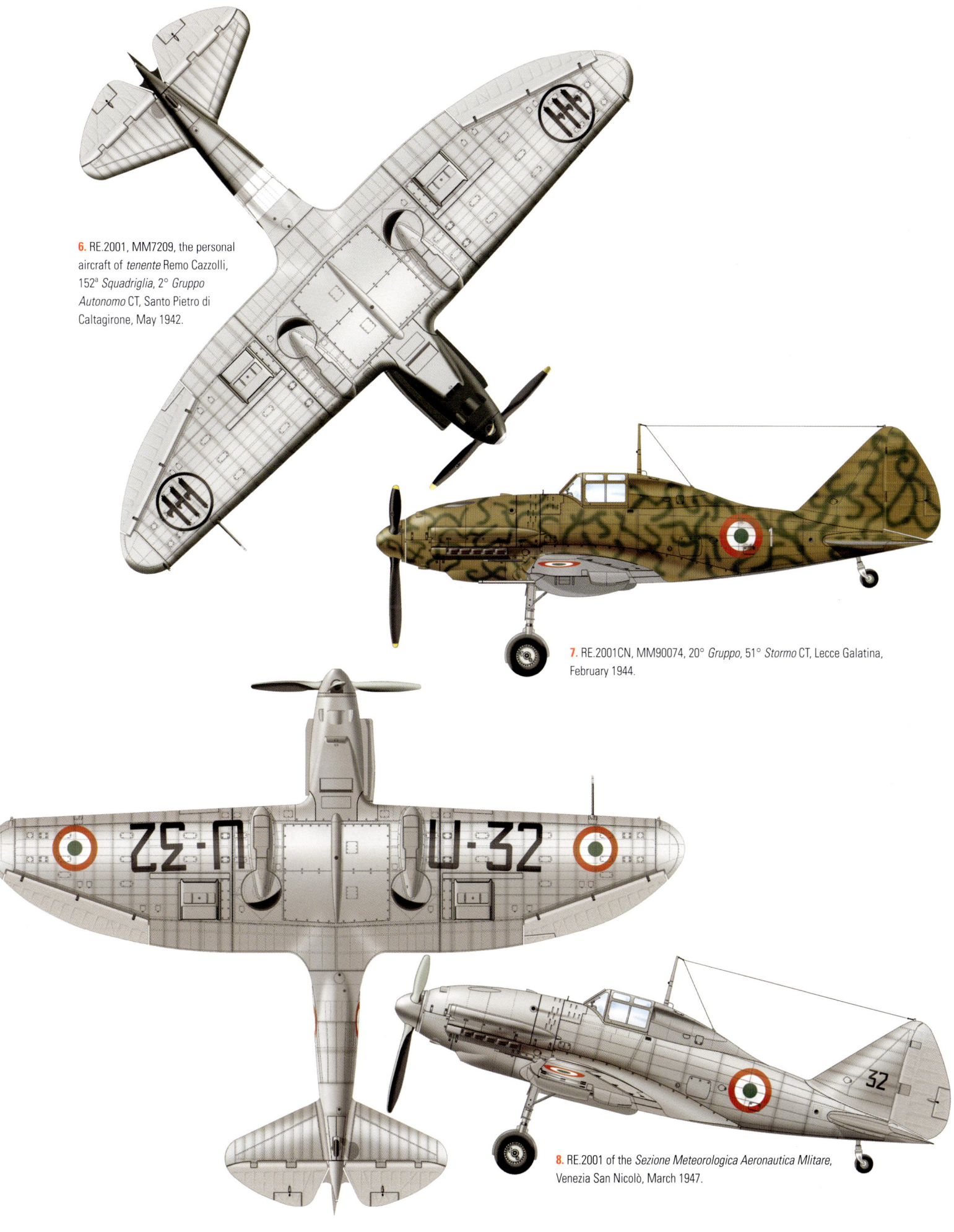

6. RE.2001, MM7209, the personal aircraft of *tenente* Remo Cazzolli, 152ª *Squadriglia*, 2° *Gruppo Autonomo* CT, Santo Pietro di Caltagirone, May 1942.

7. RE.2001CN, MM90074, 20° *Gruppo*, 51° *Stormo* CT, Lecce Galatina, February 1944.

8. RE.2001 of the *Sezione Meteorologica Aeronautica Militare*, Venezia San Nicolò, March 1947.

Reggiane RE.2002

The RE.2002 prototype, first flown in 1940, was the only one of this type to receive the standard three-tone scheme of the 'Mimetico' series colours. **9.** In fact, as development of the new type became extended, all production machines received the overall *Verde Oliva Scuro* 'Metropolitan' scheme with *Grigio Azzurro Chiaro* ventral surfaces, as prescribed by the new paint regulations issued in July 1941. Since all aircraft produced, and which entered squadron service from January 1943, were flown in Italy in the fighter-bomber role, none of them ever received tropical or nightfighter schemes. National insignia were the standard types of the period, with black fasces on a clear background in four wing positions. Early production aircraft, being those delivered to the *239ª Squadriglia*, had the word *'Ariete'* painted in white on the fin, after the official name assigned to the new aircraft. **10.** Later production machines, instead, carried only the cigar-shaped Reggiane trademark on their fins. Also, RE.2002s had their type designator and military serials painted light blue in front of tailplanes. Of note is the very last production batch – twenty-five aircraft built by Caproni at their Taliedo factory in 1944 to fulfil a German order. These received a German 'splinter' camouflage of two shades of green (RLM 70 *Schwarzgrün* and RLM 71 *Dunkelgrün*), with the lower surfaces most probably RLM 76 *Lichtblau*. **11.** Furthermore, some of the aircraft that survived the Allied bombings of 7/8 January 1944 which completely destroyed the factory at Reggio Emilia, were finally assembled and flight-tested at Pavullo (in the mountains near Modena) where, in accordance with German specifications, they received the three-tone grey scheme prescribed for Luftwaffe fighters: a two-colour 'splinter' of RLM 74 *Dunkelgrau* and RLM 75 *Grau* on wings, with RLM 76 *Lichtblau* fuselage sides over-sprayed by a soft-edged layer of RLM 74 and RLM 75. **12.** Of course any aircraft produced for the Luftwaffe carried standard German national markings (*Balkenkreuze* – black crosses) in six positions on wings and fuselage, and with *Hakenkreuze* (Swastikas) on their tails.

9. RE.2002 prototype, MM454, Reggio Emilia, October 1940.

10. RE.2002, 239ª *Squadriglia*, 102° *Gruppo*, 5° *Stormo Tuffatori*, Reggio Emilia, February 1943.

11. RE.2002, W.Nr. 5240 of the Luftwaffe, Milano Taliedo, March 1944.

12. RE.2002 of the Luftwaffe, probably at Pavullo nel Frignano, April 1944.

Reggiane RE.2005

After the first test flights flown in bare metal finish with just a *Verde Oliva Scuro* painted rudder, **13.** the RE.2005 prototype received the usual *Verde Oliva Scuro* and *Grigio Azzurro Chiaro* 'Metropolitan Scheme', like any other aircraft subsequently produced, all leaving the factory at Reggio Emilia around the Italian armistice of September 1943. **14.** They also carried a white, stylish *'Sagittario'* tail logo, after the name officially assigned to the type.

Of note is that in spite of the very limited quantity produced, the type wore the colours of three different air forces. Indeed, besides the Regia Aeronautica, which was unable to equip more than a single operational squadron before the armistice, a

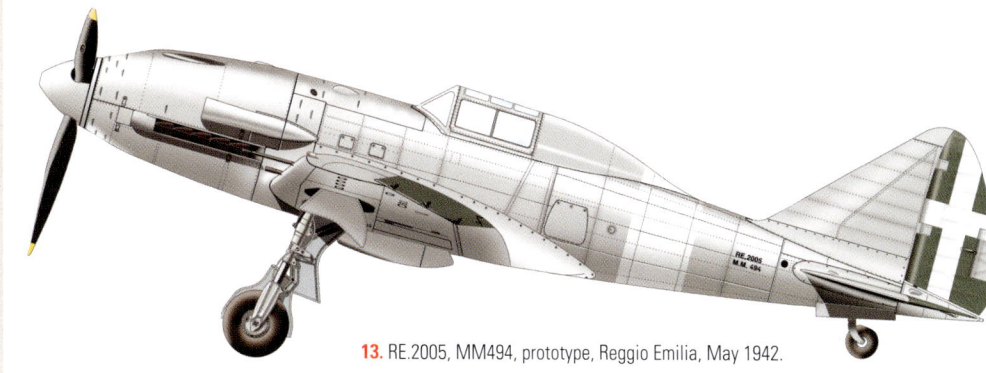

13. RE.2005, MM494, prototype, Reggio Emilia, May 1942.

14. RE.2005, MM092347, 362ᵃ *Squadriglia, 22° Gruppo, 42° Stormo Intercettori*, Littoria, June 1943.

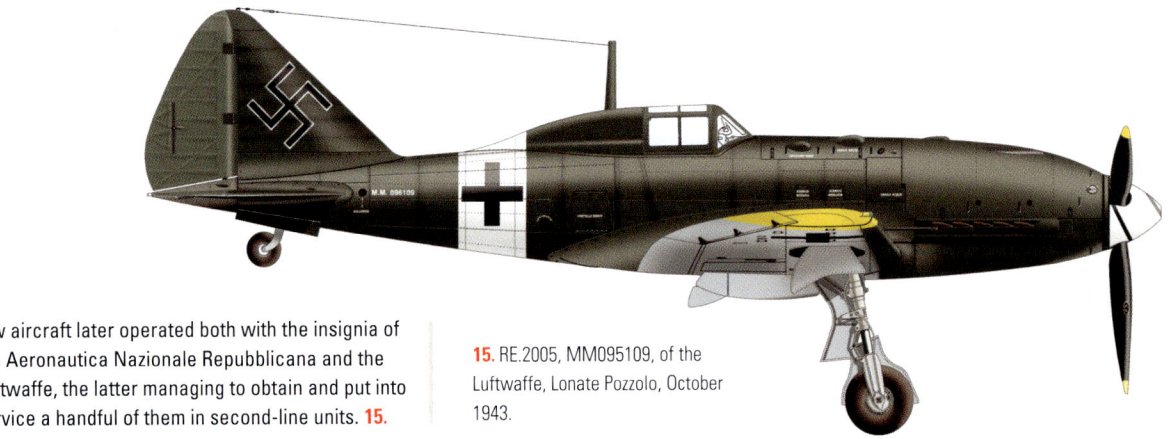

15. RE.2005, MM095109, of the Luftwaffe, Lonate Pozzolo, October 1943.

few aircraft later operated both with the insignia of the Aeronautica Nazionale Repubblicana and the Luftwaffe, the latter managing to obtain and put into service a handful of them in second-line units. **15.**

Markings and Insignia

Regia Aeronautica

The first five RE.2000s entered service with the *Sezione Sperimentale* of the 74ª *Squadriglia* in the spring of 1941 wearing the standard three-tone camouflage scheme. They carried standard national markings consisting of a white fuselage band and a white 'Savoy' cross on the rudder, completed by the usual wing fasces above and below the wings. The national wing insignia carried in four positions consisted, in fact, of three parallel black fasces, with the blade always facing outwards and painted inside a roundel which, unlike the prototype, now had a clear background.

As usual, on the vertical arm of the white cross, just above the intersection with the horizontal arm, the official emblem of Italy was applied (usually as a decal) consisting of the symbols of the Royal House of Savoy, completed by two small fasces, symbols of the regime. The absence of the colour fasces prescribed as the national fuselage insignia since 1927 was unusual. To complete the national markings, the engine cowling was painted yellow, often including the gills and propeller spinner, as prescribed for any operational aircraft in the spring and summer of 1941. **16.** Unit codes consisted of the squadron number painted in black on the fuselage. The very same national markings were also applied to the RE.2000 *Catapultabile* prototype, during the catapult test cycle on board the battleship *Vittorio Veneto* in July 1941, including a yellow nose (removed before the second test cycle in 1942). Also, a small emblem depicting a black duck appeared for the first time on the fin of this aircraft, and would later be applied to all other RE.2000 *Catapultabili*. In August 1941 the Experimental Section was then re-formed as the 377ª *Squadriglia*, eventually receiving all the RE.2000 *Grande Autonomia* produced for the Regia Aeronautica. They operated with two sections which, in the autumn, when the yellow noses were discontinued, began to paint their engine cowlings black on the first section machines and red on those of the second section. Sometime in 1942, a unit

16. An RE.2000 formerly of the *Sezione Sperimentale*, reassigned to the 74ª *Squadriglia* of 23° *Gruppo* Aut. CT. at Comiso, spring 1941.

17. RE.2001, MM08074, 150ª *Squadriglia*, 2° *Gruppo Autonomo* CT, Ravenna, October 1941.

emblem was also added to the fuselage of some squadron machines, next to the white band. It depicted an owl armed with a blunderbuss, seated on a crescent moon. Unit codes were formed simply of red individual numbers on a white band, with no indication of the squadron number, similar to the naval RE.2000s which also carried simple red individual numbers. However, unlike the land-based machines, these aircraft had the prescribed fuselage fasces painted in colour on both sides of the engine cowling.

The RE.2001s assigned to 2° *Gruppo* did not carry, at first, any unit badge and could be distinguished only by their light blue squadron codes

followed by red individual codes on the white band (for the 152ª Sq.) or behind it (150ª Sq.). **17.** A brand new *Gruppo* badge was later painted on the tail, depicting a chick armed with a machine gun. Similarly, the machines of the 22° *Gruppo* had red (362ª and 369ª Sq.), white (358ª) or black (359ª) squadron codes, with contrasting individual codes astride of the white band. Even the *Gruppo* insignia, representing a pipe-smoking scarecrow with five red stars, was later painted on the fuselage sides, next to the cockpit. **18.** This famous unit badge was the same used by this group during its tour of duty in Russia. Even the RE.2002s, all finished in the same overall *Verde Oliva Scuro* scheme of the RE.2001, displayed

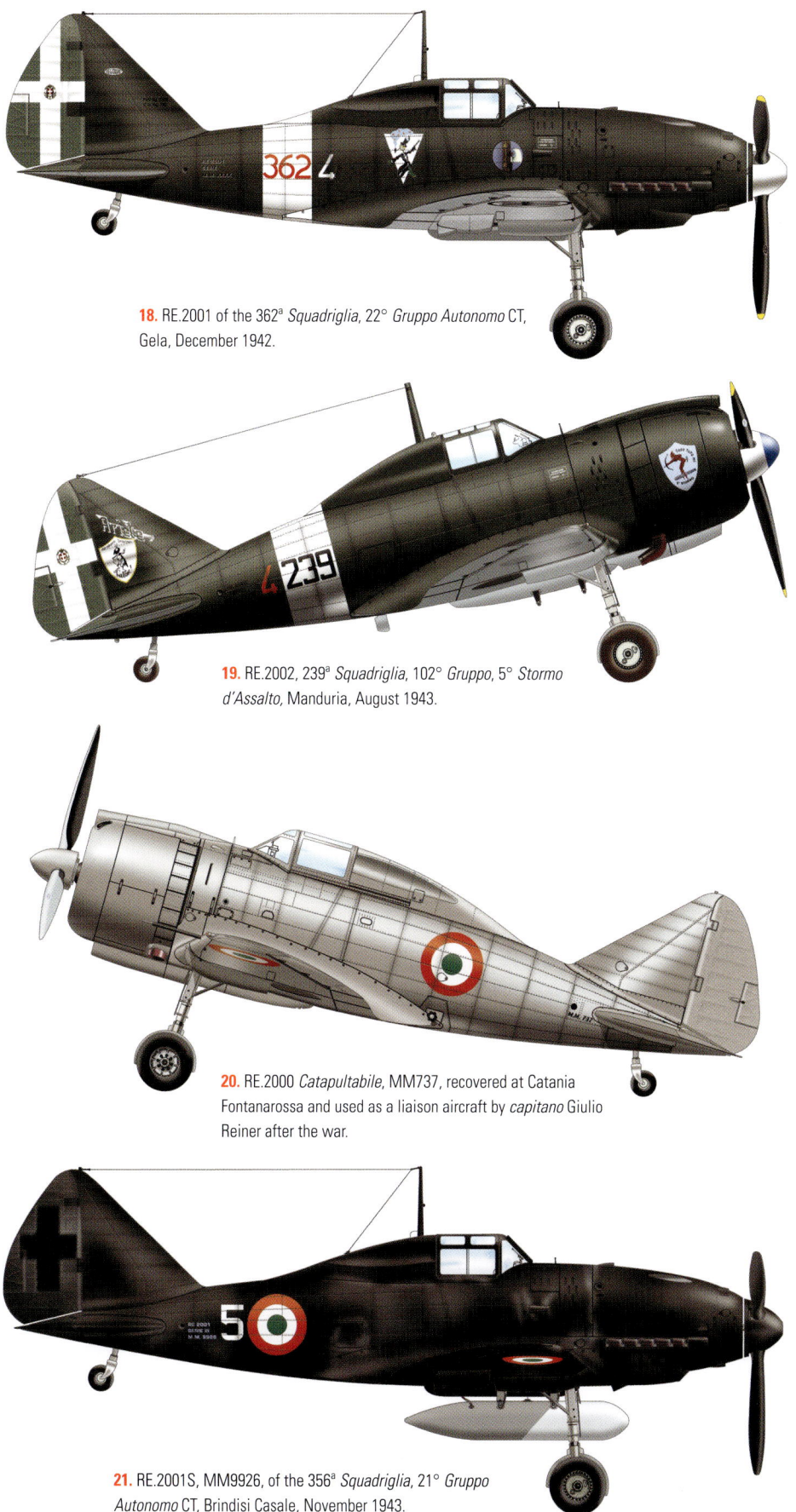

18. RE.2001 of the 362ᵃ *Squadriglia,* 22° *Gruppo Autonomo* CT, Gela, December 1942.

19. RE.2002, 239ᵃ *Squadriglia,* 102° *Gruppo,* 5° *Stormo d'Assalto,* Manduria, August 1943.

20. RE.2000 *Catapultabile,* MM737, recovered at Catania Fontanarossa and used as a liaison aircraft by *capitano* Giulio Reiner after the war.

21. RE.2001S, MM9926, of the 356ᵃ *Squadriglia,* 21° *Gruppo Autonomo* CT, Brindisi Casale, November 1943.

similar unit codes, generally with the squadron number in black and the individual number in red. Within 102° *Gruppo* only the 239ᵃ *Squadriglia* had the unit emblem painted on fins, in the form of a guitar-playing cricket on a white shield with the word *'Valzer!'* (Waltz!), after the unit's battle cry. **19.** The same went for the RE.2005s assigned to 362ᵃ *Squadriglia* in the summer of 1943 which, in addition to red squadron codes and white individual codes across the white band, carried the traditional 'Scarecrow' emblem on the fuselage band.

The Co-belligerent Regia Aeronautica

The single RE.2000 used after the armistice, recovered in Catania after the war, bore only six green-white-red tricolour roundels – the new Italian national markings used since 21 September 1943, from when they were applied to wings and fuselage with the green in the centre and the red on the outer ring. **20.** The same insignia was also carried on the few RE.2001s and RE.2002s surviving the armistice and used by the Regia Aeronautica until the summer of 1944. **21.** No unit insignia was carried except for those used before the armistice and still carried by some 239ᵃ *Squadriglia* aircraft, depicting the guitar-playing cricket of 102° *Gruppo* complete with the unit's famous *'Valzer!'* war cry.

A.N.R.

No RE.2000, 2001 or 2002 ever entered service with the Aeronautica Nazionale Repubblicana. The few aircraft captured by the Germans on Italian airfields after the armistice were distributed only to second-line Luftwaffe units, such as the handful of RE.2005s delivered to the Luftwaffe after the armistice and operational with German markings. At least one RE.2005, recovered at Castiglione del Lago, eventually entered service with the A.N.R. in 1944. All such machines at this time were painted in the factory-applied *Verde Oliva Scuro* and *Grigio Azzurro Chiaro* 'Metropolitan' scheme. The German aircraft had the usual black Luftwaffe crosses in six positions with Swastikas on their tails, while the A.N.R. national insignia consisted of two opposing black fasces, inscribed in a black-trimmed white square, carried in the usual four wing positions. In addition, the Italian tricolour flag – green-white-red (nose to tail) – was painted on both fuselage sides, repeated in smaller size on the tail fin. Note that the green element always faced forward and the flags themselves were fringed with small yellow triangles and a yellow post on the forward side, representing a flagpole. A red individual number was displayed on the fuselage, forward of the tricolour flag, while the military serial was painted white next to the horizontal tailplane.

Reggiane RE.2000

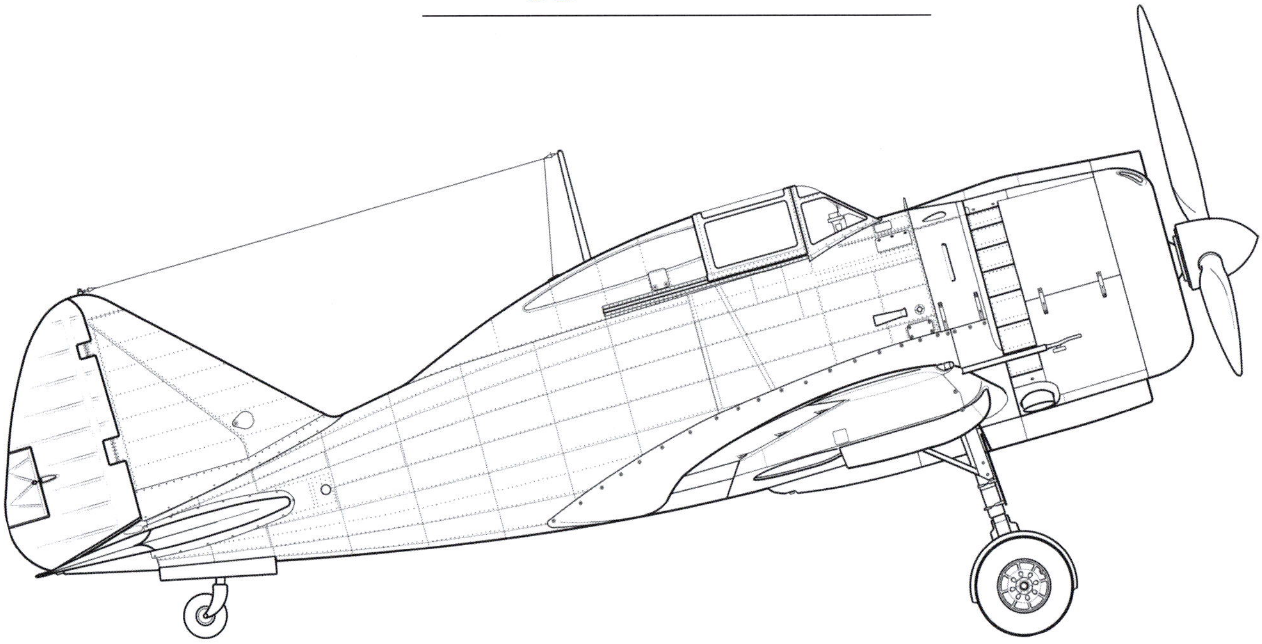

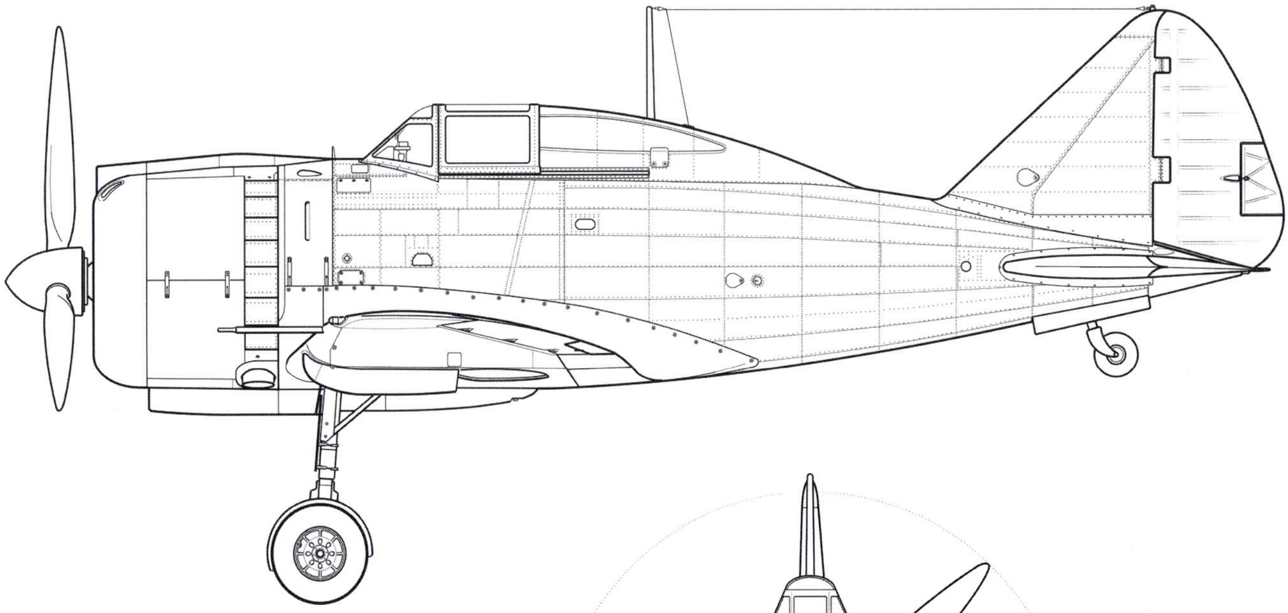

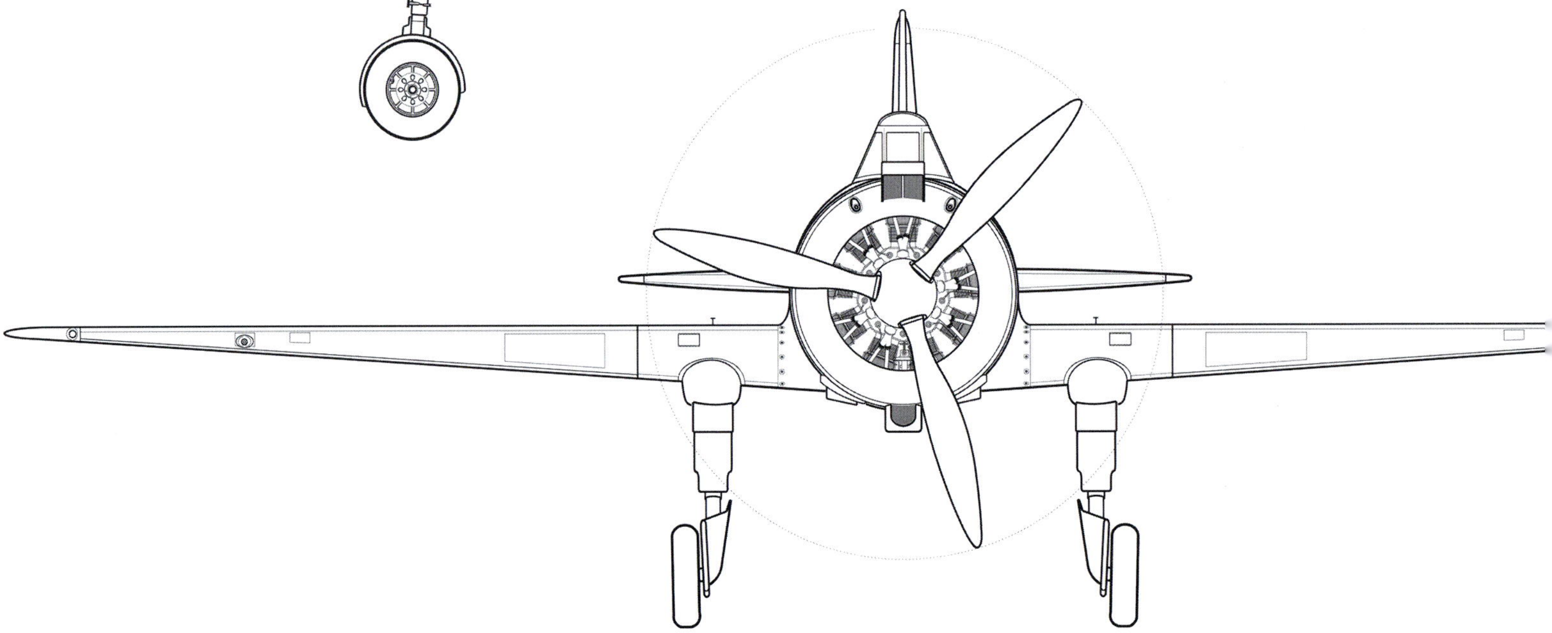

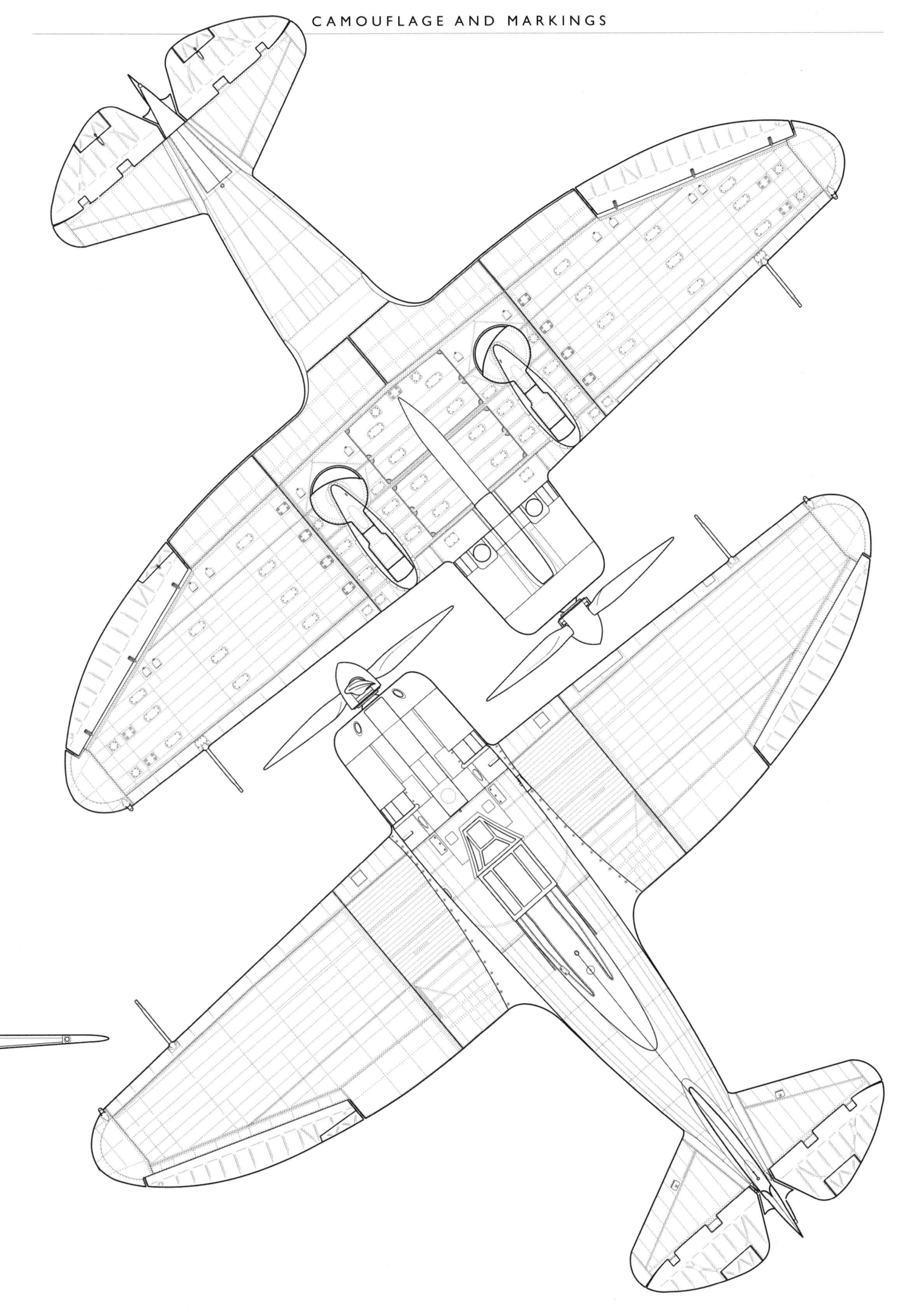

RE.2000GA, MM5072, of the 377ª *Squadriglia Autonoma* CT,
Trapani Milo, October 1941.

RE.2000GA of the 377ª *Squadriglia Autonoma* CT operating from Pantelleria, January 1942. The black
cowling replaced the yellow colour from autumn 1941 and indicates aircraft of the 1ª *Sezione.*

RE.2000GA of the 377ª *Squadriglia Autonoma* CT, Palermo Boccadifalco, May 1942.
The red cowling indicates aircraft of the 2ª *Sezione.*

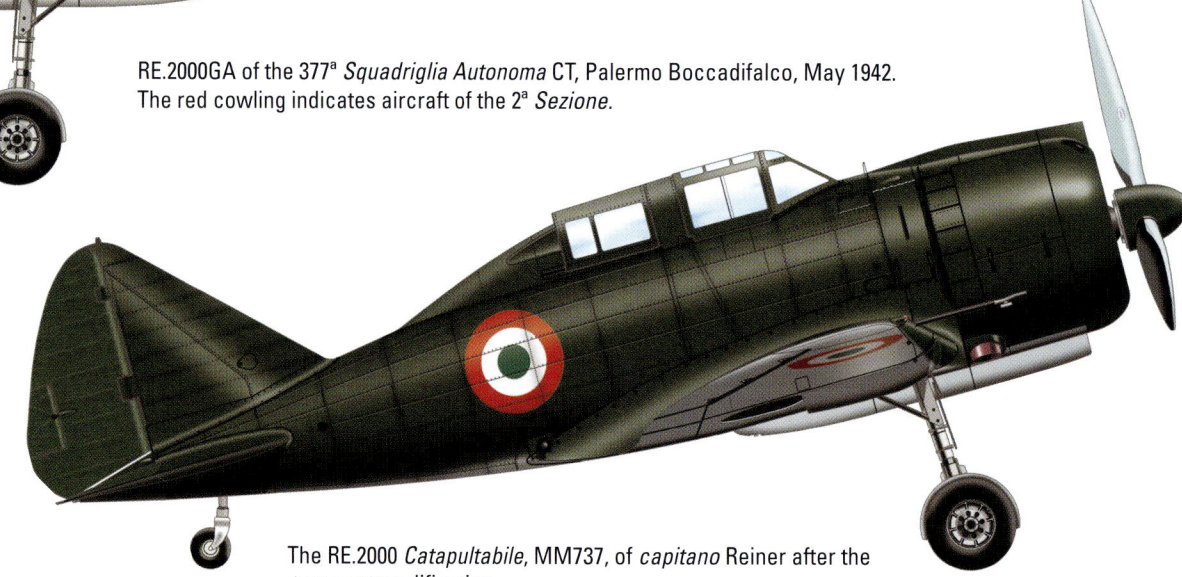

The RE.2000 *Catapultabile*, MM737, of *capitano* Reiner after the
two-seat modification.

Reggiane RE.2001

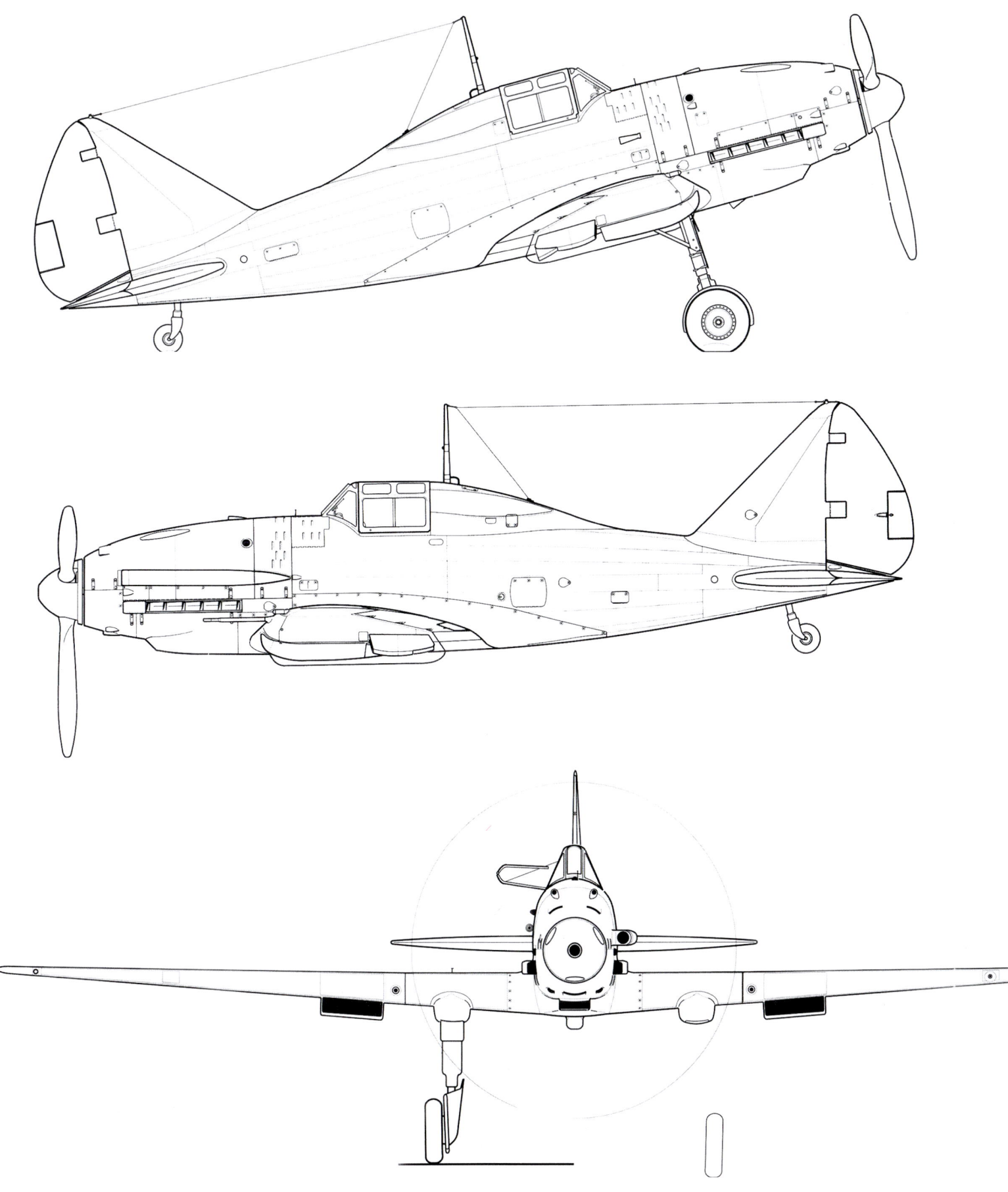

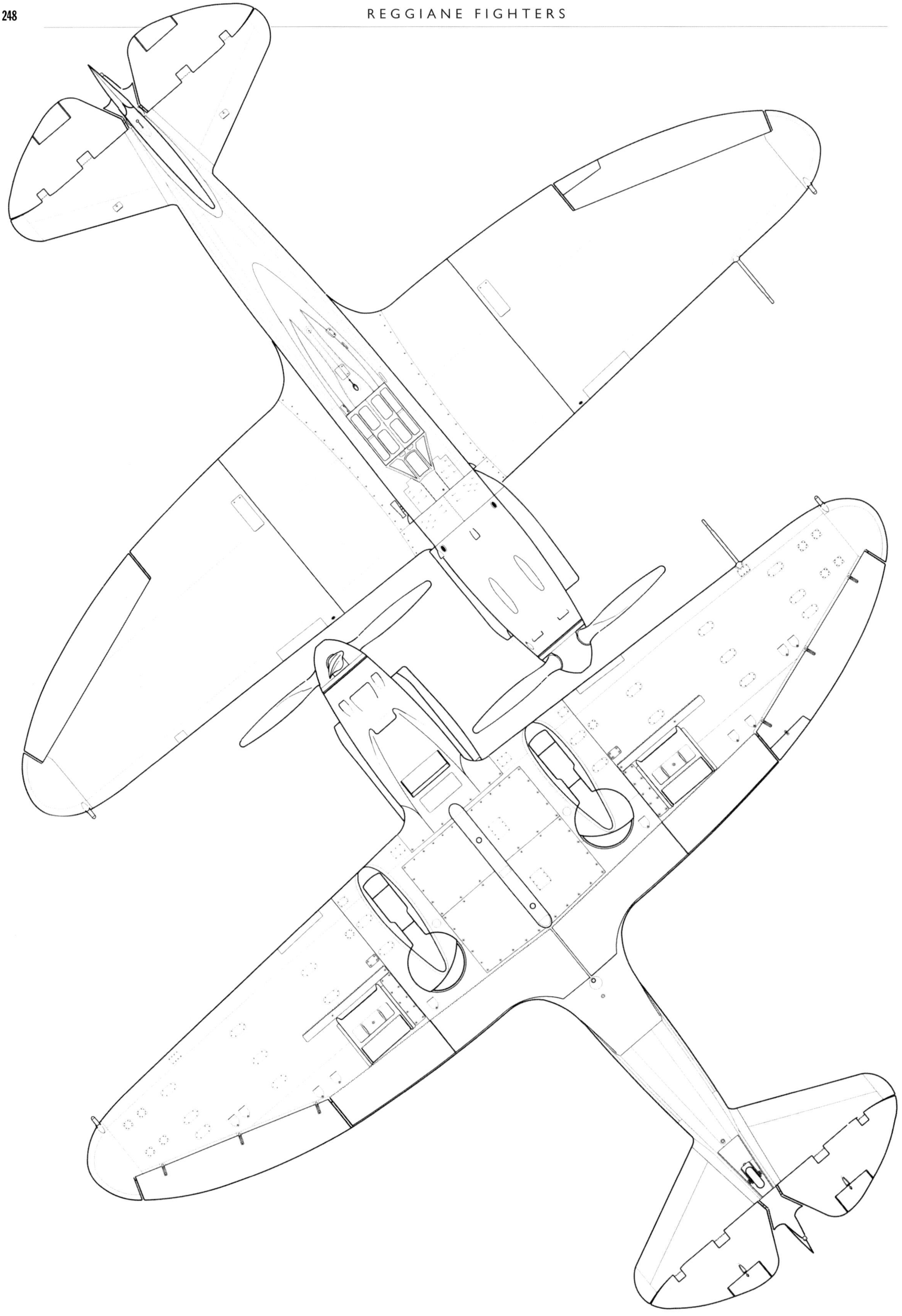

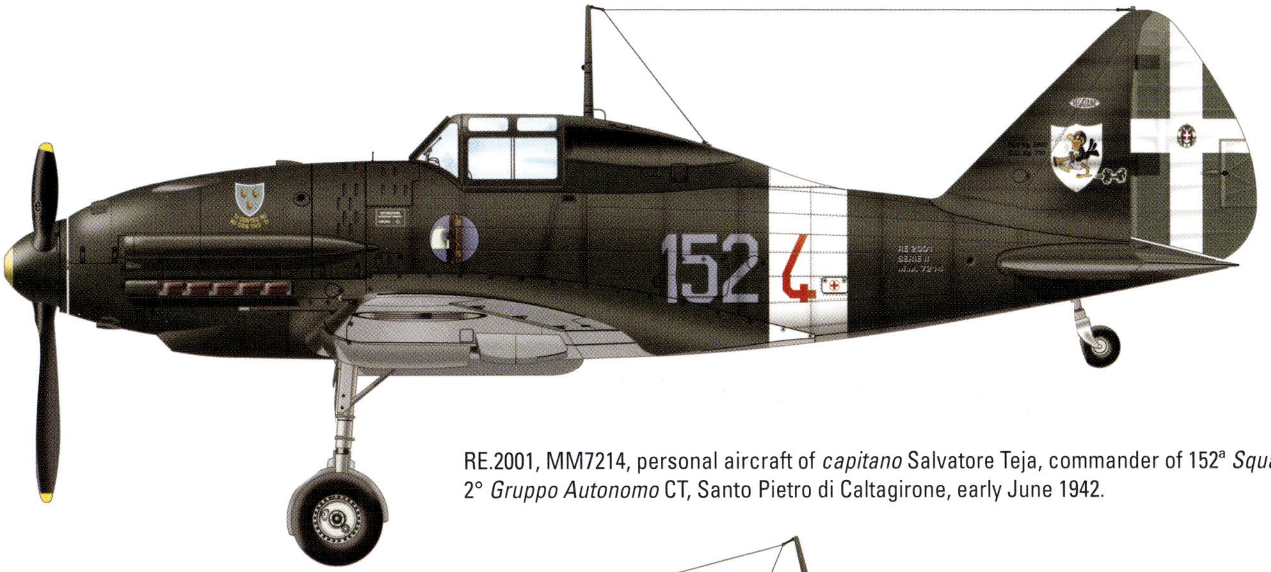

RE.2001, MM7214, personal aircraft of *capitano* Salvatore Teja, commander of 152ª *Squadriglia*, 2° *Gruppo Autonomo* CT, Santo Pietro di Caltagirone, early June 1942.

RE.2001, 358ª *Squadriglia*, 2° *Gruppo Autonomo* CT, Santo Pietro di Caltagirone, June 1942.

RE.2001, 369ª *Squadriglia*, 22° *Gruppo Autonomo* CT, Santo Pietro di Caltagirone, September 1942.

RE.2001, 359ª *Squadriglia*, 22° *Gruppo Autonomo* CT, Pantelleria, late 1942.

RE.2001CN, 234ª *Squadriglia*, 59° *Gruppo*, 41° *Stormo Intercettori*, Rimini, May 1943.

RE.2001, 1ª *Squadriglia*, 1° *Nucleo Addestramento Intercettori*,
Treviso, June 1943.

RE.2001G.V., MM7226, 362ª *Squadriglia*, 22° *Gruppo Autonomo*
CT, Cagliari Elmas, 12 August 1942.

RE.2001OR, MM7260, 394ª *Squadriglia*, 160° *Gruppo Autonomo*
CT, Perugia S. Egidiio, February 1943.

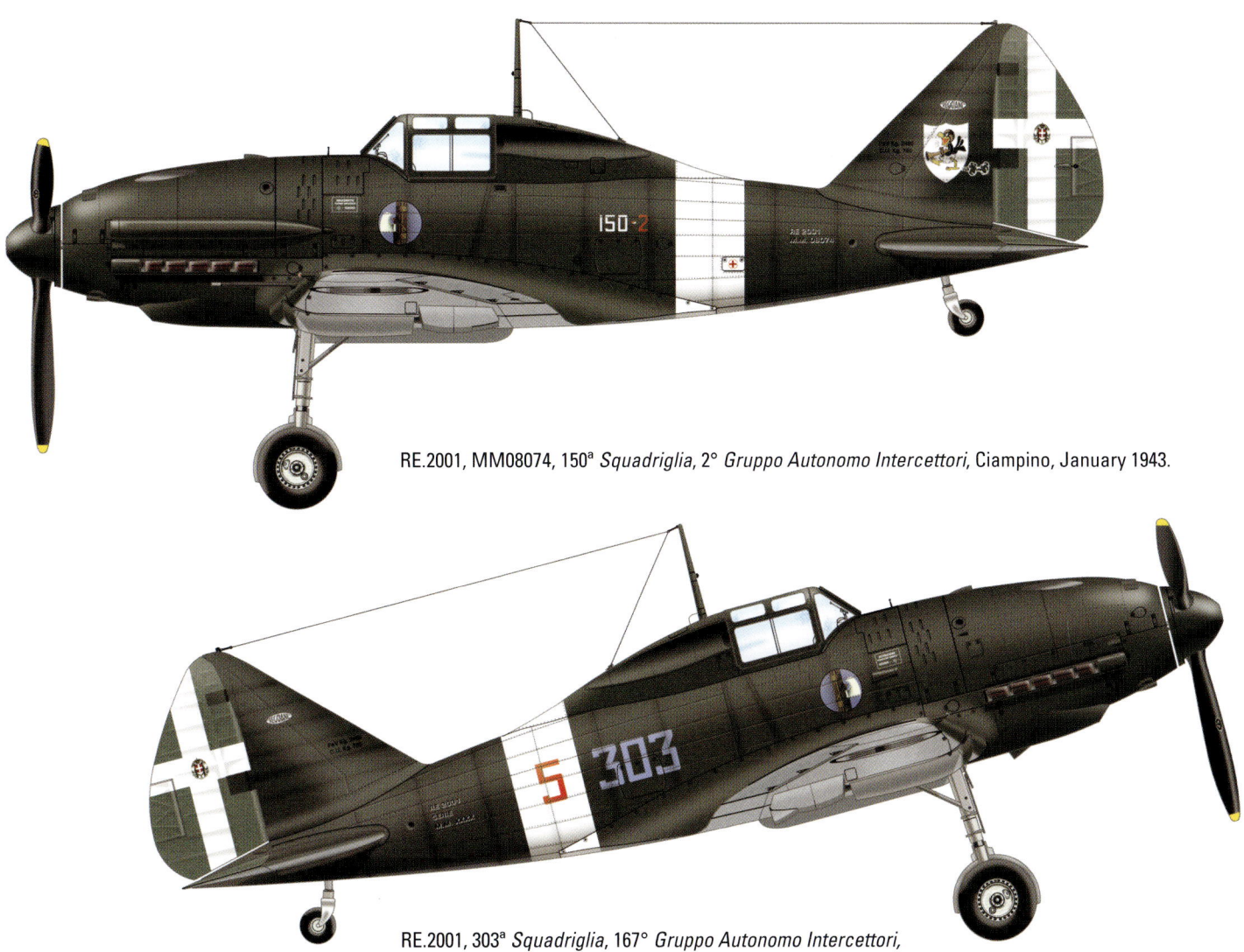

RE.2001, MM08074, 150ª *Squadriglia*, 2° *Gruppo Autonomo Intercettori*, Ciampino, January 1943.

RE.2001, 303ª *Squadriglia*, 167° *Gruppo Autonomo Intercettori*, Ciampino, February 1942.

Reggiane RE.2002

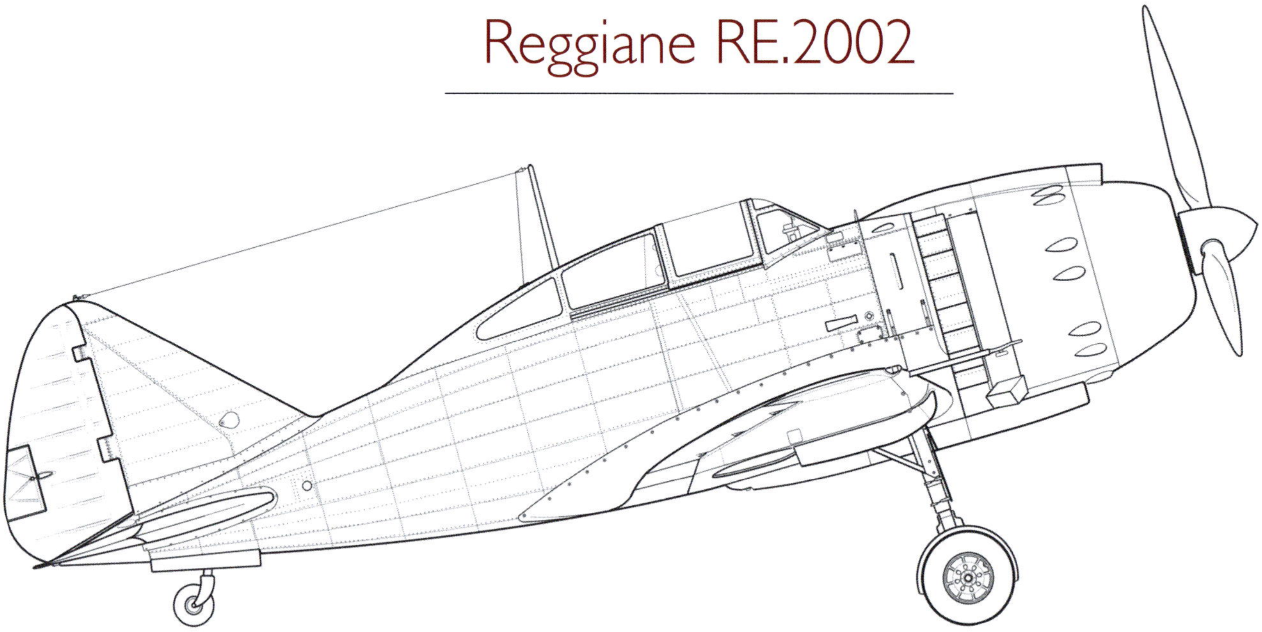

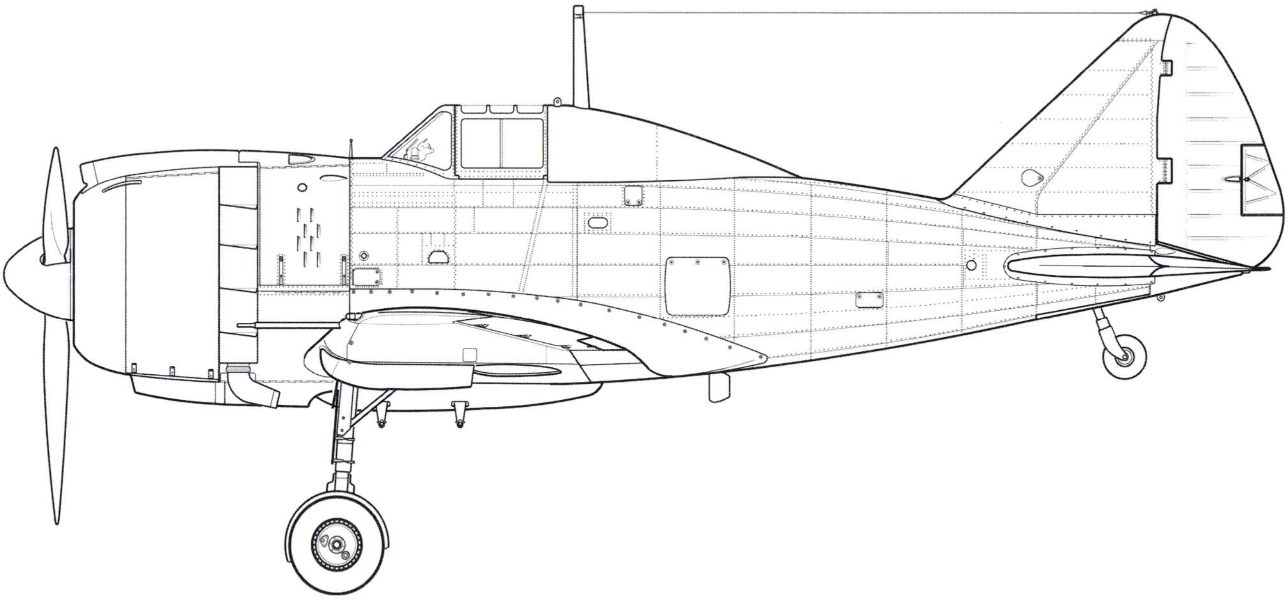

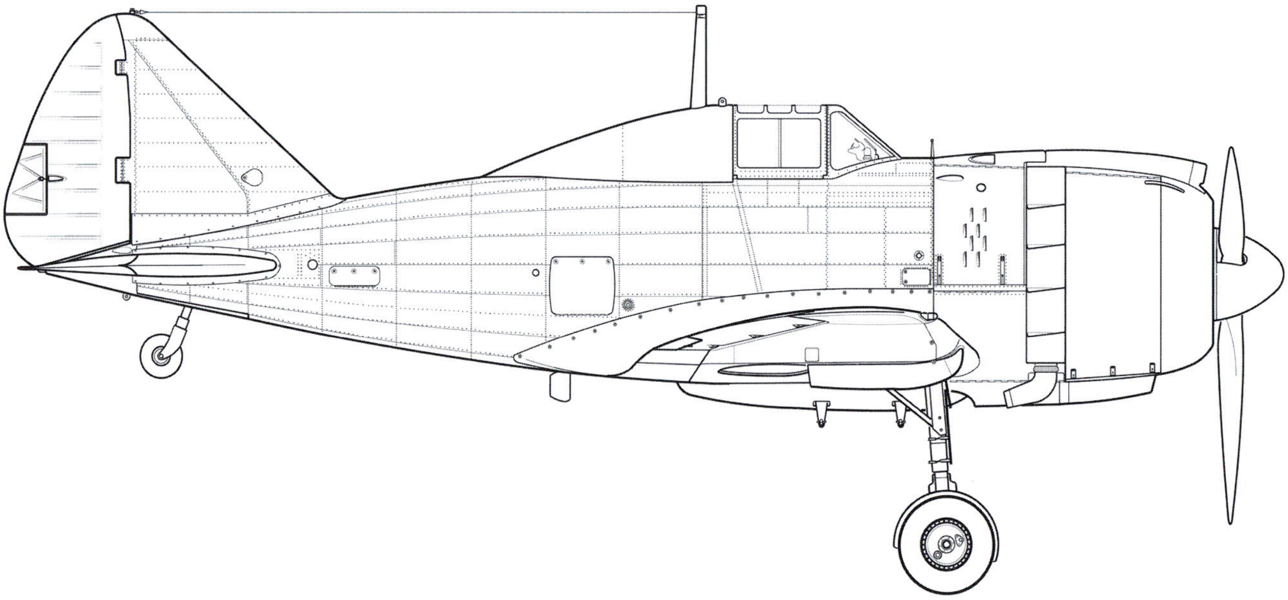

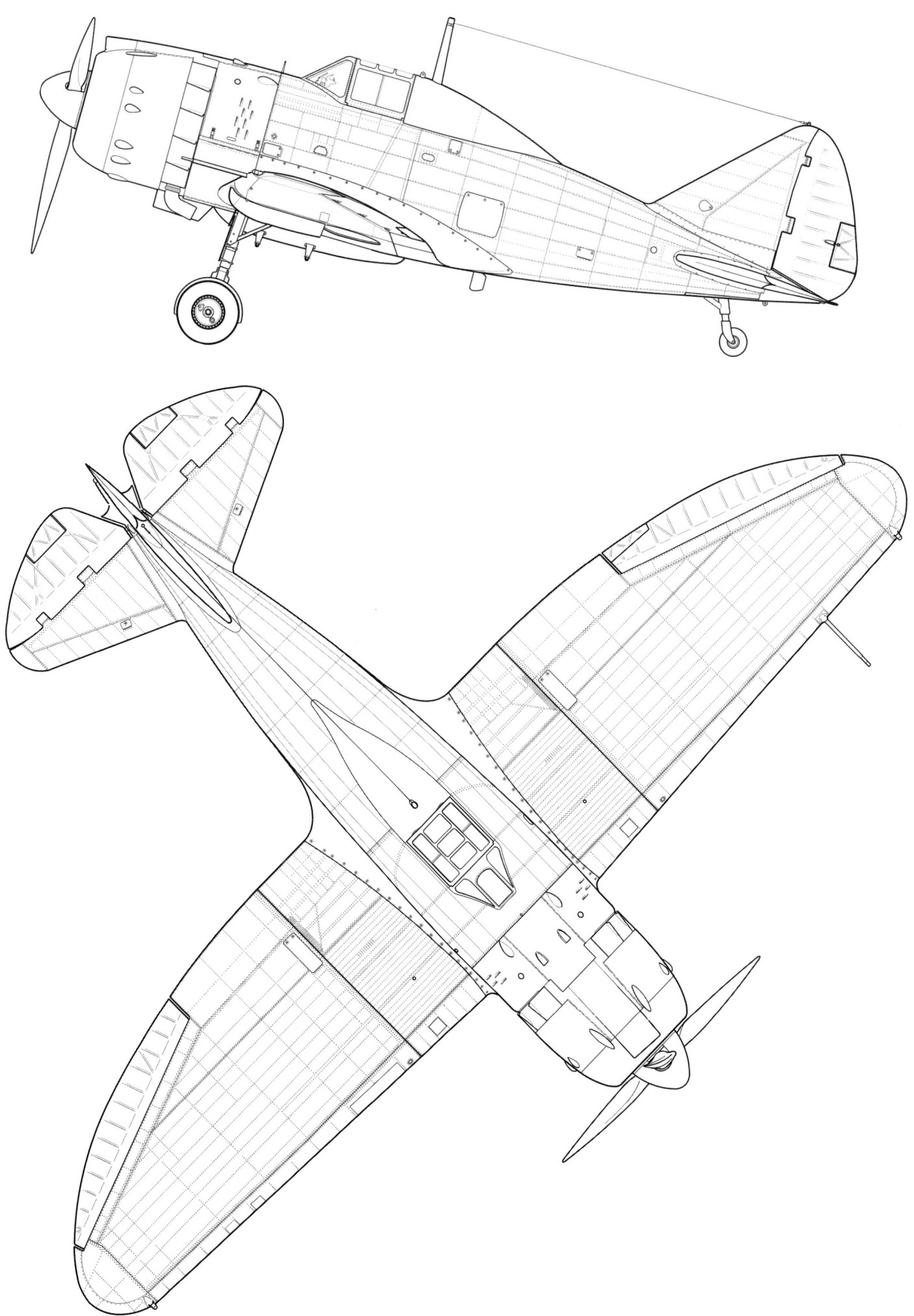

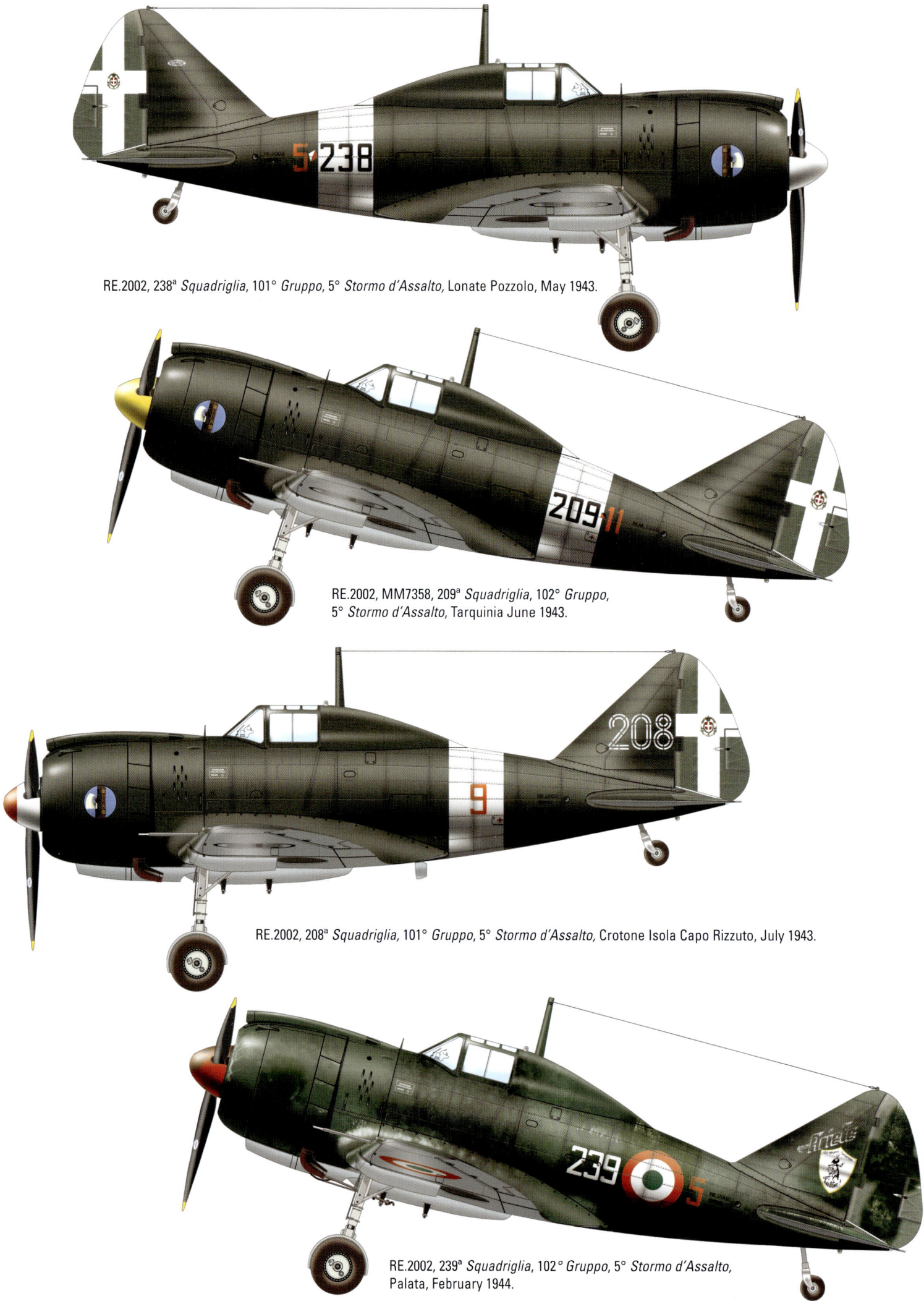

RE.2002, 238ª *Squadriglia*, 101° *Gruppo*, 5° *Stormo d'Assalto*, Lonate Pozzolo, May 1943.

RE.2002, MM7358, 209ª *Squadriglia*, 102° *Gruppo*,
5° *Stormo d'Assalto*, Tarquinia June 1943.

RE.2002, 208ª *Squadriglia*, 101° *Gruppo*, 5° *Stormo d'Assalto*, Crotone Isola Capo Rizzuto, July 1943.

RE.2002, 239ª *Squadriglia*, 102° *Gruppo*, 5° *Stormo d'Assalto*,
Palata, February 1944.

Reggiane RE.2005

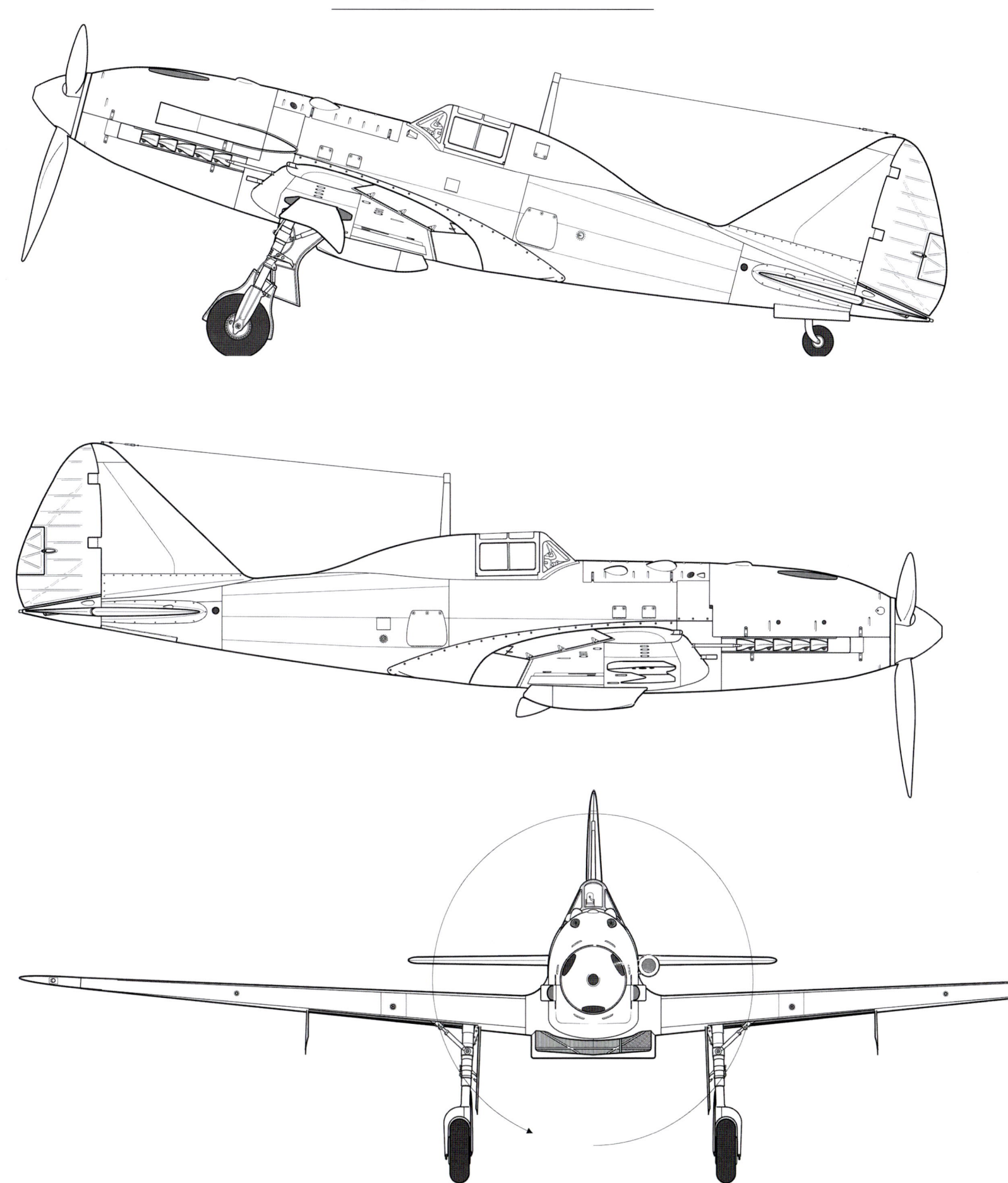

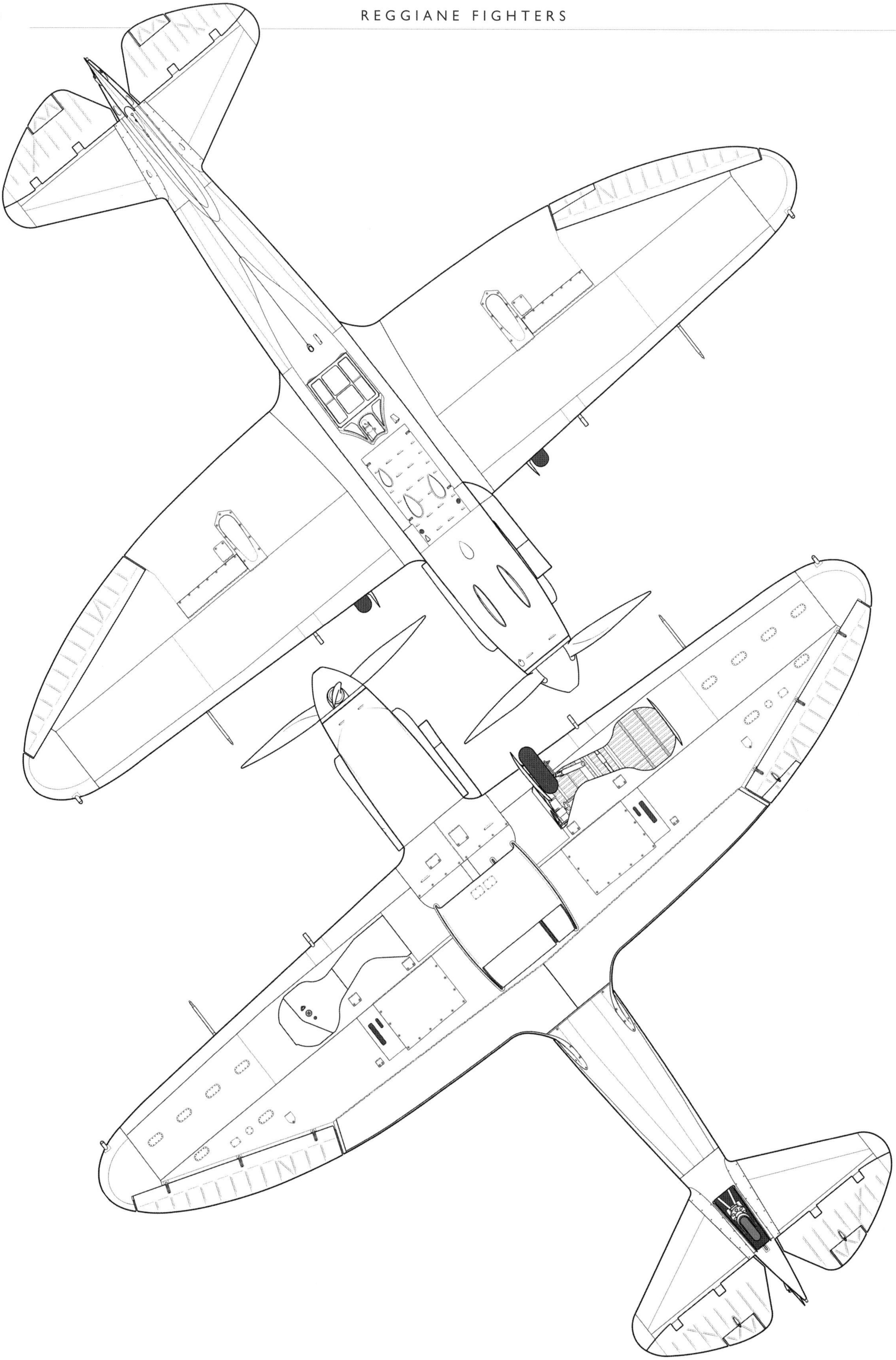

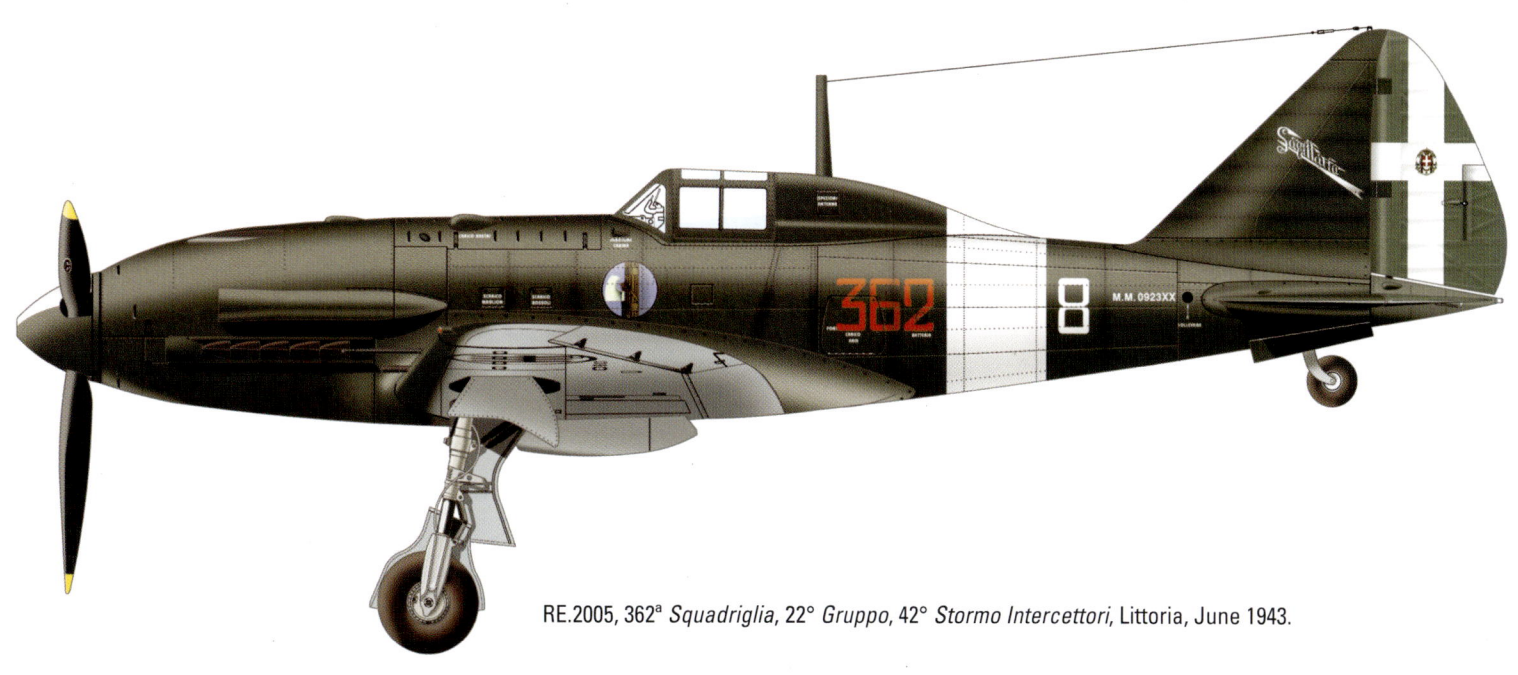

RE.2005, 362ª *Squadriglia*, 22° *Gruppo*, 42° *Stormo Intercettori*, Littoria, June 1943.

RE.2005, *Luftdienstkommando Italien*, Maniago, February 1944.

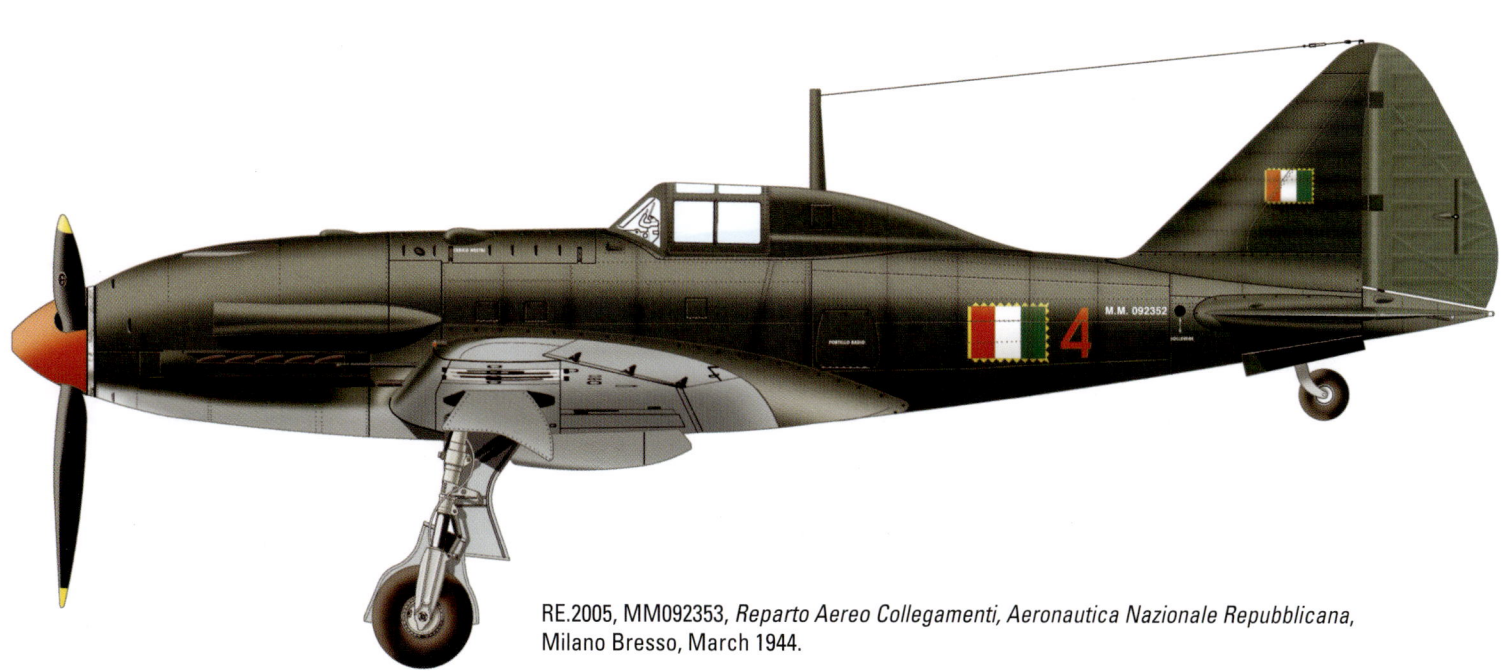

RE.2005, MM092353, *Reparto Aereo Collegamenti, Aeronautica Nazionale Repubblicana*,
Milano Bresso, March 1944.

CHAPTER NINE

The Survivors

As a result of the relatively small number of aircraft built, few Reggiane fighters are preserved in museums today.

Reggiane RE.2000

Flygvapenmuseum

THE only RE.2000 that has survived complete to this day is conserved in Sweden in the Flygvapenmuseum at Linköping. This is J 20 Nc 405 (MM.2340), which made its first flight on 3 March 1942 with test pilot Caracciolo at the controls. It was delivered to F 10 at Bulltofta with the identification number '40' in mid-August 1942.

After three years of active service, the aircraft was retired in August 1945 and used as a training airframe for technicians, with the removal of some panels and their replacement with transparencies to facilitate instruction via the display of the internal structure.

At the end of the 1960s, it was transferred to the Flygvapenmuseum collection.

Museo Caproni, Trento

WITHIN the store of the Museo Caproni at Trento, unfortunately not accessible to the public, is the fuselage of RE.2000 'catapultabile', MM8287, which was recovered in 1944 and utilised by capitano Giulio Reiner as his personal aircraft while he was commander of the Presidio Regionale di Sicilia. This aircraft, which had also been converted into two-seat configuration, was operational until 1947 at Palermo Boccadifalco airfield. It was entrusted to the Museo Caproni by the Aeronautica Militare, and for numerous years was stored in expectation of a restoration.

The J 20, c/n 405, (MM2340), preserved at Linköping Flygvapenmuseum. It is exhibited with the left side fuselage panels (above) removed to display the aircraft's internal structure.

The fuselage of RE.2000 *Catapultabile*, MM8287, preserved at the Caproni Museum in Trento. The photograph was taken in 1972 and since that time the aircraft has remained in storage. (G.Apostolo)

Försvars-
industrin
och
neutraliteten

The wreckage of RE.2000 *Catapultabile*, MM8281, of the 1ª *Squadriglia Forze Navali* lost in the Tyrrhenian Sea while returning from a reconnaissance mission on 16 April 1943. The aircraft was recovered and is exhibited 'as is' at the Italian Air Force Museum in Vigna di Valle (Rome).

Museo Aeronautica Militare

Currently preserved with the Museo dell'Aeronautica Militare at Vigna di Valle is the wreckage of RE.2000 '*catapultabile*', MM8281, of the 1ª *Squadriglia Forze Navali* based at Luni Sarzana airfield. It was lost in an accident while returning from a reconnaissance mission on 16 April 1943. Found in April 2012 by a Marina Militare minesweeper off Porto Venere, it was in poor condition because of its position and years of immersion in a saline environment. The wreckage was recovered in 2013 and, following conservation work, has been on display in a central position in the Badoni hangar, which houses aircraft from the Second World War, since 2023.

Reggiane RE.2001

Museo Aeronautica Militare

ALL that remains of the sole surviving RE.2001 is conserved, but stored away from the public, by the Museo dell'Aeronautica Militare at Vigna di Valle.

The aircraft, MM8071, was flight-tested at Reggio Emilia in May 1941 and subsequently assigned to the 2° *Gruppo* CT, but following a wheels-up landing was returned to Officine Reggiane to undergo repair. Returning to the unit on 16 November, in the early months of 1943 it was reported at Guidonia and then at Roma-Centocelle with the *Reparto Sperimentale di Volo*, where it was painted overall yellow and fitted with cine cameras to participate in the film *Primo volo* made by the *Istituto Luce*. On completion of this task, it was repainted in camouflage colours and allocated to the 24° *Gruppo Caccia* in Sardegna. The transfer flight was assigned to *sergente* Giulio Zangheri, but on 11 April 1943, during the delivery flight, technical issues caused Zangheri to make an emergency ditching near Capo Ferrato, from where the pilot was rescued thanks to the intervention of a fishing boat.

In November 1991 the wreckage was discovered on the sea floor by a diver at little more than a depth of a few tens of metres. The GAVS (*Gruppo Amici Velivoli Storici*) in conjunction with the *Carabinieri Subacquei* at Cagliari, were engaged to undertake its recovery. The wreckage was subsequently passed to the Aeronautica Militare. Having for decades been covered by layers of sand, the aircraft was almost intact and was subjected to an initial restoration by the GAVS Torino section, while the Museo personnel undertook the restoration of the undercarriage, engine, and tailplane. Despite the importance of the aircraft, the wreck, albeit only partially restored, is not currently displayed.

The only remains of an RE.2001 are stored away from public view at the Italian Air Force Museum in Vigna di Valle (Rome). The aircraft ditched on 11 April 1943 near Capo Ferrato and was recovered in 1991 thanks to the effort of GAVS (Gruppo Amici Velivoli Storici).

Reggiane RE.2002, a former Luftwaffe aircraft, W.Nr. 1256, is preserved at the Musée de la Résistance in Limoges. This aircraft was probably shot down on 16 June 1944 near Limoges by a group of *Maquis* or made a forced landing on its belly following a technical fault. (Musée de la Résistance)

Reggiane RE.2002

Two examples of the RE.2002 survive today.

Musée de la Résistance

THE first example, an RE.2002 with the Luftwaffe code 'BI+DV', 'Red 5', is preserved in France at the Musée de la Résistance in Limoges. The fighter belonged to the *Geschwader Bongart* and its pilot, who remains unidentified, was forced to make an emergency landing near Jumeau-le-Grand on 16 June 1944 following a fault in machine gun synchronisation which resulted in damage to the propeller, forcing the flight to be abandoned.

The aircraft was the target of looters, but after some of its lost parts were recovered, it was placed on display in the garden of the Bishop's Palace in Limoges between 1947 and 1976. Its condition having deteriorated, in 2004 it was restored by personnel from *Base Aérienne 274 de Limoges-Romanet* in order to be displayed as a memorial to the French *Maquis* in a museum dedicated to the Resistance.

Museo Aeronautica Militare

THE RE.2002 preserved at Vigna di Valle is the result of a lengthy and complicated restoration, often interrupted, and in some respects, still incomplete and unsatisfactory. The fuselage, which in all probability is that of MM8669 (n.c. 126), which performed its first test flight on 30 July 1943, was recovered in the immediate post-war period at Reggio Emilia airfield and sent to the Università di Bologna for use as an instructional airframe until the end of the 1970s.

On the fuselage were traces of former Luftwaffe insignia, and technical stencilling in German. The wings come from several examples of the RE.2002, the left side having been almost completely repanelled, while the moving surfaces of the tailplane belong to an RE.2001. The aircraft features the insignia of the 239ª *Squadriglia*, 102° *Gruppo*, 5° *Stormo Assalto*, representing an example in service with the Co-belligerent Regia Aeronautica at Palata airstrip (Campobasso) in February 1944. The aircraft has been restored with a blue propeller spinner colour although, more accurately, it should be red.

The Reggiane RE.2002 exhibited after restoration in 2021 at the Badoni hangar of the Italian Air Force Museum in Vigna di Valle. It is painted in the colours of an RE.2002 as flown by the Regia Aeronautica del Sud.

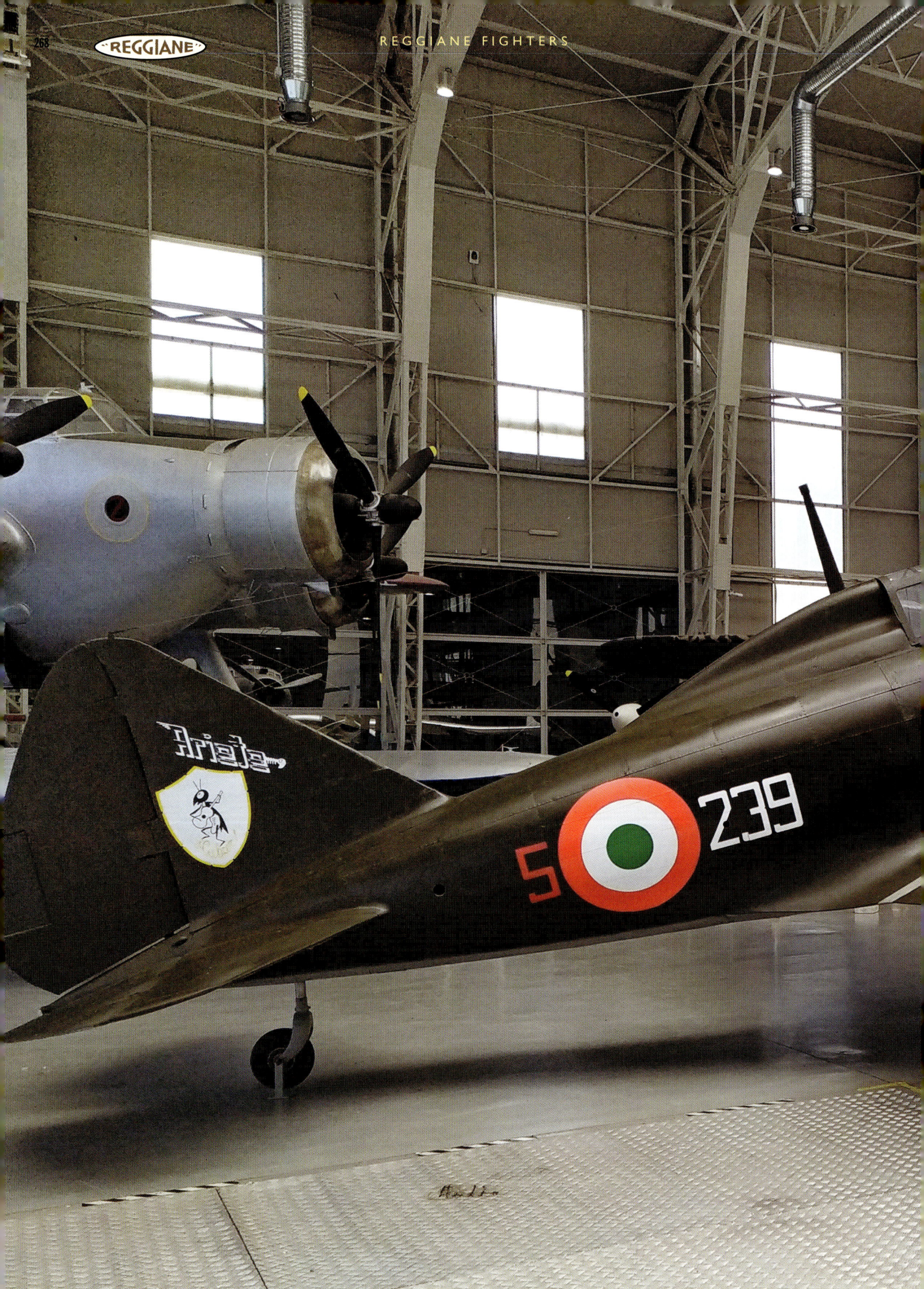

Reggiane RE.2005

Museo Caproni, Trento

OF the sinuous lines of the RE.2005, unfortunately only the rear section of the fuselage of MM 92351 survives today. This was the ninth of the sixteen examples, which wore the code '2' of the 362ª *Squadriglia*, 22° *Gruppo*, 52° *Stormo* CT in August 1943. All that remained of the aircraft was recovered from Capodichino (NA) airfield and assigned to the engineering faculty of the Università di Napoli. In the 1970s, having lost any educational value, it was passed to the Museo Caproni. Since 1995, following the completion of a delicate restoration and evaluation by the GAVS (*Gruppo Amici Velivoli Storici*), it has been displayed at Trento complete with the codes and insignia of its original unit.

The Caproni Museum houses the tail section of RE.2005, MM 092351, in the colours of 362ª *Squadriglia* of the 22° *Gruppo Aut.* CT.

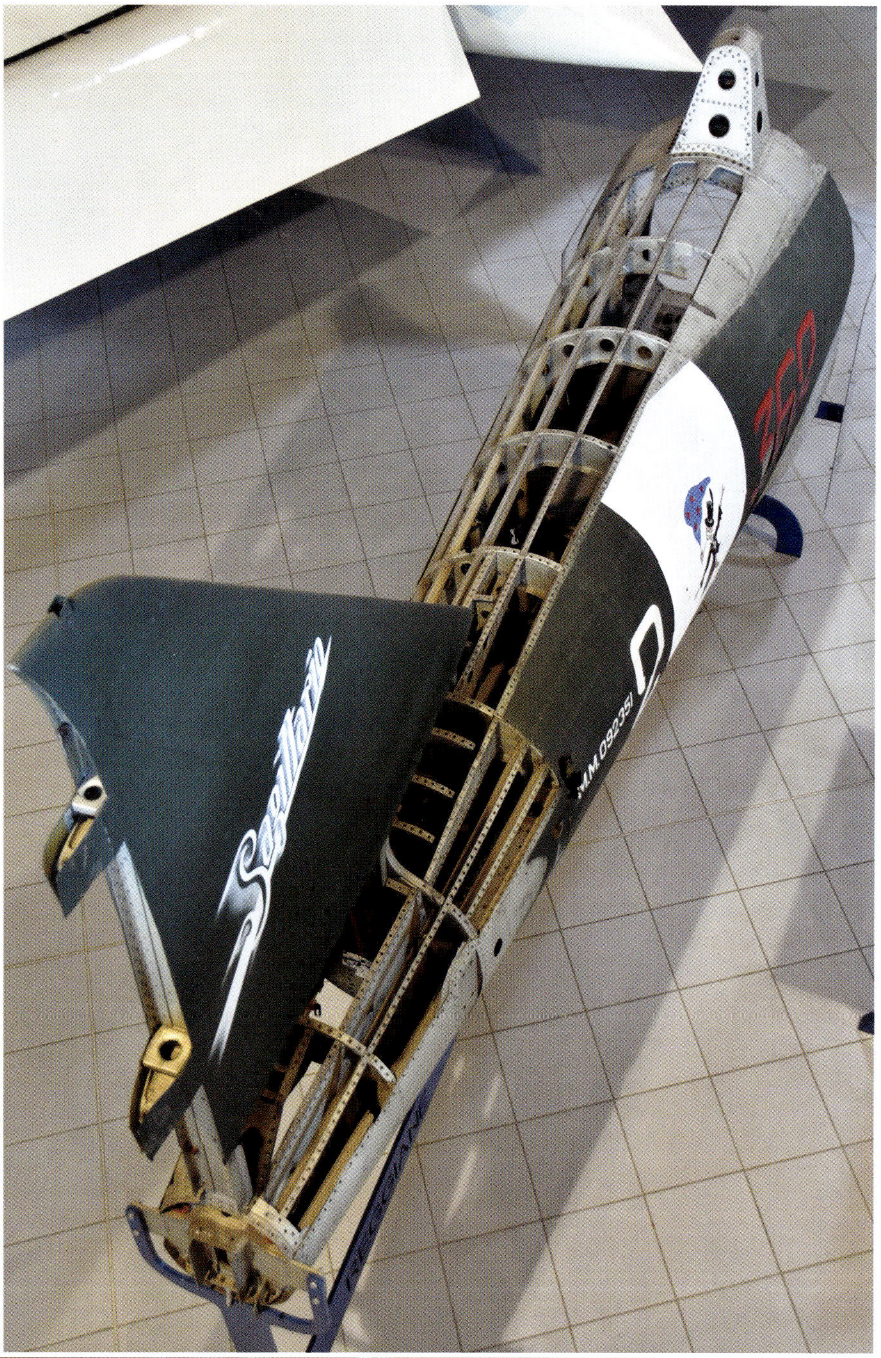

SOURCES AND BIBLIOGRAPHY

Archives
Ufficio Storico Aeronautica Militare, Rome
Archivio Centrale di Stato, Rome
G.A.E. archive

Historic aviation magazines and newspapers
Rivista Aeronautica
L'Ala D'Italia
Le Vie Dell'Aria
Aerofan
Storia Militare
JP4
Ali Antiche

Published books
A.Emiliani, G.Ghergo, A.Vigna, *REGIA AERONAUTICA: Mediterranean, East, African and Italian front*, Intergest
Achille Vigna, *AERONAUTICA ITALIANA: dieci anni di storia 1943-1952*, Storia Militare, 1999
Adriano and Paolo Riatti, *Il caccia RE 2000*, Edizioni Bertani &C. 2017
Angelo Lodi, *L'Aeronautica Italiana nella guerra di liberazione 1943-1945*, Brigati Glauco, 2008
Brian Cull, *Spitfires over Malta*, Grub Street 2005
Brian Cull, *Hurricanes over Malta*, Grub Street
C.Shores, G. Massimello, *A History of the Mediterranea War vol 1-5*, Grub Street
E.Brotzu, M.Caso, G.Cosolo, *DIMENSIONE CIELO caccia ASSALTO VOL 1/2/3*, Edizioni Bizzarri
Enrico Leproni, Carlo Lucchini, *Dai biplani agli aviogetti*, Gino Rossato Editore, 1990
Eugenio Tarantola, *Il 150°, 151° e 153° Gruppo Caccia*, Ufficio Storico AM, 1987
F. D'Amico, N. Beale, G.Valentini, *Air War Italy 1944-45 – The Axis Air Forces from the Liberation of Rome to the Surrender*, Airlife, 1996
Fabio Galbiati, *La Caccia della Regia Aeronautica 1936-1943*, Storia Militare, 2023
Ferdinando D'Amico, Gabriele Valentini, *Camouflage and Markings of the Aeronautica Nazionale Repubblicana 1943-1945*, Classic Publications, 2005
George Beurling, *Malta Spitfire*, Grenhill Books, 2002
Giacomo Metellini, *Un pilota Racconta*, self printed 2007

Giancarlo Garello, *BATAILLE AERIENNE: La Guerre sur le Desert nr.55/58/60/62*, Lela Presse, 2011/2012
Giancarlo Garello, *Centauri su Torino*, La Bancarella Aeronautica, 2010
Giancarlo Garello, *L'Aeronautica Nazionale Repubblicana - Part 1/2*, Storia Militare, 2015
Giovanni Massimello, Giorgio Apostolo, Italian Aces of World War 2, Osprey Publishing, 2000
Giovanni Massimello, *Gli Assi Italiani della Regia Aeronautica*, Edizioni Rivista Aeronautica, 2023
Giorgio Apostolo, *Reggiane RE.2001*, La Bancarella Aeronautica 1996
Giulio Cesare Valdonio, *Frecce, Saette, Folgori e Veltro*, Edizioni Rivista Aeronautica, 2019
Giuseppe Pesce, *L'8° Gruppo Caccia in due conflitti mondiali*, Ufficio Storico AM, 1975
Giuseppe Santoro, *L'Aeronatuica Italiana nella Seconda Guerra Mondiale vol 1-2*, Edizioni Esse 1966
Gregory Alegi, *I velivoli*, Ufficio Storico AM, 2013
Gregory Alegi, Baldassare Catalanotto, *Coccarde Tricolori*, Ufficio Storico AM, 2010
Gregory Alegi, *Reggiane RE.2005*, La Bancarella Aeronautica 2001
Michele Bellelli, *Reggiane, cronache di ua grande fabbrica Italiana*, Aliberti Compagnia Editoriale 2016
Nicola Malizia, *Quelli del Gatto Nero*, 1998
Nicola Malizia, *Il 23° Gruppo Caccia*, Edizioni Bizzarri, 1974
Nicola Malizia, *il Reggiane 2000*, Edizioni dell'Ateneo e Bizzarri 1978
Nino Arena, *La Regia Aeronautica dall'Armistizio alla Cobelligeranza - Part 1/2*, Mucchi Editore, 1978
Paolo Pesaresi, *Cuore, Patria, Volo*, Gli Archivi Ritrovati, 2020
Paolo Waldis, Marino De Bortoli, *AERONAUTICA ITALIANA: caccia e assalto- Part 1/2/3*, La Bancarella Aeronautica
Sebastiano Licheri, *Il Raggruppamento Caccia nella guerra di liberazione*, Ufficio Storico AM, 1978
Sebastiano Licheri, Mario Piovan, *il 22° Gruppo Caccia. 65 anni di storia*, Ufficio Storico AM, 1987
Sergio Govi, *I caccia Reggiane vol.1-5*, Giorgio Apostolo Editore 1986
Tullio De Prato, *Un pilota contadino*, Mucchi Editori 1985

INDEX